MIZORAM

LAND AND PEOPLE

MIZORAM

LAND AND PEOPLE

Edited by

Dr. Raj Kumar

Dr. S. Ram

Mizoram - Land and People

First Published, 2020

ISBN 978-93-87436-54-1

Published by :
NATION PRESS
4831/24, Govind Lane,
Ansari Road, Darya Ganj,
New Delhi - 110002
Phones : 23272541, 23242541
e-mail: nationpress1970@gmail.com

Typesetting by :
Simran Computers
Delhi

Printed at :
Divine Digital Press
Delhi

Preface

Mizoram is an exotic state located in northeast india. It became the 23rd state on 20th february, 1987. Aizawl is capital city of Mizoram and language spoken in this state is Mizo. The state is home of many tribes.

Material collected for this volume is varied and different. It is mainly district wise. However there are some special charastics of this state like its unique social and cultural history, women and politics, the domestic products and the new industrial policy. These topics therefore are covered in separate chapters.

This state of india is unique in many ways. Not much work has been on this state. This book therefore will serve well to scholars, policy makers and even general readers.

Contents

1 Introduction

Area : 21,081 sq km

Population : 6,89,756

Capital : Aizawl

Principal Languages : Mizo and English

History and Geography

Mizoram is a mountainous region which became the 23rd state of the Indian Union in February 1987. It was one of the districts of Assam till 1972 when it became a Union Territory. After being annexed by the British in 1891, for the first few years, Lushai Hills in the north remained under Assam while the southern half remained under Bengal. Both these parts were amalgamated in 1898 into one district called Lushai Hills District under the Chief Commissioner of Assam. With the implementation of the North-Eastern Reorganisation Act in 1972, Mizoram became a Union Territory and as a sequel to the signing of the historic memorandum of settlement between the Government of India and the Mizo National Front in 1986, it was granted statehood on 20 February 1987. Sandwitched between Myanmar in the east and the south and Bangladesh in the west, Mizoram occupies an area of great strategic importance in the northeastern corner of India. Hills in Mizoram run from north to south with a tendency to be higher in the east and tapering in the north and south. The average height of hills is about 900 metre, the highest peak being Blue Mountain (Phawngpui), rising to 2,210 metres.

Mizoram has great natural beauty and an endless variety of landscape. It is rich in fauna and flora.

The origin of the word 'Mizo' is not known. The Mizos came under the influence of the British Missioneries in the 19th century and now most of the Mizos are Christians. One of the beneficial results of missionary activities was the spread of education. Mizo language has no script of its own. The missionaries introduced the Roman script for Mizo language and formal education.

Agriculture

About 60 per cent of the people of Mizoram are engaged in agricultural pursuits. The main pattern of agriculture followed is *jhum* or shifting cultivation. Out of the estimated potential available area of 4.4 lakh hectares for horticulture, the area put under plantation is around 25,000 hectares only. The main horticulture crops are oranges, lemon, *kagzi* lime, passion fruits, *hatkora, jamir,* pineapple and papaya. Other crops are sugarcane, tapioca and cotton. With the processing unit coming up such as the Ginger Dehydration plant at Sairang and fruit juice concentration plants, people have started extensive cultivation of ginger and fruit crops. The Agriculture Department has introduced a new system of contour farming with contour trenches and hedging with the intention of switching over to permanent cultivation on the hill slopes. The Department had completed 55 minor irrigation projects covering an area of 2,245 hectares.

Irrigation

The ultimate surface irrigation potential is estimated at 70,000 hectares of which 45,000 hectares is under flow and 25,000 hectares for river lift irrigation. The irrigated area has now gone up to 7,260 hectares by constructing and completing 30 *pucca* minor irrigation projects for raising double and triple crops in a year.

Industry

The entire Mizoram is a Notified Backward Area and is categorised under 'No Industry District'. However, concerted efforts were made in the last decade to accelerate the growth of industries in Mizoram. For the development of industries in the State, the Mizoram government framed the industrial policy of Mizoram in 1989. In the policy resolution priority industries have been identified. These are : agro and forest-based industries, followed by handloom and handicrafts, electronics, consumer industries. Sericulture is operating at Aizawl with two full-fledged wings, *viz.*, handloom and handicrafts wing and geology and mining wing.

The completed projects of Ginger Oil and Oleoresin Plant and Ginger Dehydration Plant at Sairang and Fruit Preservation Factory at Vairengte and the projects under implementation namely Mizo Processing Unit (renamed Mizo Milling Plant) at Khawzawl and Fruit Juice Concentrate Plant at Chhingchhip were transferred to the incorporated Mizoram Food and Allied Industries Corporation (MIFCO) for commercial operation. Maize Milling Plant also has been completed and commissioned by MIFCO.

Development of tea industry/gardens and raising of Tooklai approved varieties of ten seedlings has been taken up by the government around Biate areas.

Power

The Serchhip-Marpara 132 kv transmission line has been completed up to Thenhlum. The Lunglei 132 kv sub-station, Saitual and Khawzawl (66 kv substations) have also been completed. The Central government has given clearance for Tuirual Hydro project capable of giving 60 MW. The Government has commissioned a 5 MW Diesel generation set at Zuangtui and another set of 15 MW at Champhai. The State is generating 14.07 million units of power.

Transport

Total road length in the State is 4,787 km. National Highway No. 54 links Tuipang the southern most district of Mizoram to Silchar town in Assam on the border of Mizoram. Rail link in the State had been established at Bairabi. Aizawl, the capital town of the State is air-linked. Mizoram State transport besides running passenger services in 33 routes including two inter-state services to Silchar in Assam and Shillong, also provides goods carriages on hire and also functions as Railway Out Agency for Silchar railway station in Cachar district of Assam. The Public Works Department completed metalling and black topping of 87.52 km and 146.53 km respectively. A full-fledged Air-Field at Lunglei has started functioning from December 1998.

Festivals

Mizos are basically agriculturists. All their activities centre round *jhum* cultivation and their festivals are linked with such agricultural operations. *Kut* is the Mizo word for festivals. Mizos have three major festivals called *Chapchar Kut, Mini Kut* and *Pawl Kut.*

Tourist Centres

The hilly city Aizawl located at nearly 4,000 feet above sea-level, is a religious and cultural centre of Mizoram where indigenous handicrafts are also available. Champhai is a beautiful resort on the Myanmar border. Tamdil a natural lake with *virgin forest* is 60 km from Aizawl and 10 km from tourist resort of Saitual. Vantawng falls, five km from hill station Thenzawl, are the highest and most beautiful waterfalls in Mizoram. The Department of Tourism has opened Tourist Lodge at Aizawl, Lunglei, Champhai and wayside restaurant at Thingdawl, Hnahthial, recreational centre at Beraw Tlang and Alpine picnic hut at District Park near Zobawk.

Government

Governor : A. Padmanaban

Chief Secretary : H.V. Lalringa

Chief Minister : Zoramthanga

Jurisdiction of High Court : Falls under the jurisdiction

Speaker : R. Lalawia

Area, Population and Headquarters of Districts

S.No.	*District*	*Area (sq. km.)*	*Population*	*Headquarters*
1.	Aizawl	12,581	4,78,465	Aizawl
2.	Lunglei	4,536	1,11,415	Lunglei
3.	Chhimtuipui	3,957	99,886	Saiha
4.	Lawngtlai	—	—	Lawngtlai
5.	Champhai	—	—	Champhai
6.	Kolasib	—	—	Kolasib
7.	Mamit	—	—	Mamit
8.	Serchhip	—	—	Serchhip

2 Land and People

Mizoram occupies an area of great strategic importance in the north-eastern India. It is bounded by Tripura state and Bangladesh to its west, and the Chin Hills of Myanmar (formerly Burma) to its east and south. To its north, are the state of Manipur and Cachar district of Assam are its neighbours. The state is divided into three districts :

(i) Aizawl

(ii) Lunglei

(iii) Chhimtuipui

Physical Features

Mizoram is a mountainous region. It has great natural beauty and an endless variety of landscape. It is rich in fauna and flora. The climate in Mizoram is pleasant to cool in the upper reaches and humid in the plains but still tolerable. The winter temperature varies from 11 degrees Celsius to 24 degrees and in the summer the range is 18 to 29 degrees which makes the state fairly comfortable throughout the year. Naturally, the higher you go, the cooler and even colder it becomes, and the Mizos like to have their houses, and, therefore, the villages, along the hills. People everywhere in India value hill tops and mountains for locating major shrines as we know.

The average rainfall is 254 centimetres every year but in the southern part of the state it rains more. Thus, in the capital town of Aizawl the average rainfall is 208 centimetres, but in Lunglei town, which is to the south, the rains are heavier and the average precipitation is 350 cm. With such heavy rainfall the state is endowed with rich vegetation and dense forests. Mizoram has an abundance of trees, bushes, plants, shrubs and grasses. Bamboos grow in large numbers everywhere. New plants have also been introduced and the picturesque character of the state is being built up. Whereas earlier the farmers returned to the same plot after a gap of 10 years the gap has been reduced in recent years to just four years. This naturally results in decreased output of foodgrains and other crops because, if the forest is burnt without allowing proper growth, the production would automatically become less.

Mizoram has hill ranges running from north to south. They are higher in the middle and taper off at both ends. The average height of the hills is 900 metres (about 3,000 feet) but the highest peak, the Blue Mountain, also called the Phawngpui, goes up to 2,165 metres and is located in the southern part of the territory. The hills are steep and are separated by rivers which flow either northwards or to the south, and create deep gorges between the hill ranges. There are many rivers in the state but mention may be made of the Tlawng, also known as the Dhaleswari, in the north, the Tuirail (Sonai) and the Tuiwal which start from the middle of Mizoram and then flow into the Barak river in the Cachar district of Assam. In the south the Karnafuli flows in a northerly direction and then enters Bangladesh where a major hydroelectric project has been built over it. The river Koladyne enters Mizoram from Myanmar and flowing southward it again goes back into that country. The state, which has small stretches of plain surface, has a few lakes of which the biggest is the Palak Lake in the southern part of the state. The south-west monsoon arrives early in the region sometime in May, and brings copious rains to Mizoram.

Tlawng (Daleswari) and Taivai are the two main rivers of the Aizawl district. In addition, there are a few lakes and springs, some of which are Tamdil and Rungdil.

Aizawl district is mostly hilly; hills ranging in the south-north directions very sharp at places with average height of 3,000 ft intercepted by deep ravines and *nullahs.* The types of forests in the district are of the following categories :

(i) Tropical wet evergreen forest

(ii) Tropical semi-evergreen forest

(iii) Montane sub-tropical forest.

The terrain of the Chhimtuipui district is mostly hilly in character ranging from the south to the north direction, the ranges being very sharp at places. The average height is 3,000 ft intercepted by deep valleys. The types of forest found in the district of Chhimtuipui are the tropical wet evergreen, semi evergreen and montane sub-tropical.

Conservation of forests and other development activities like construction of buildings at various places, constitution of reserve forests including wildlife sanctuary at Ngengpuitlang were also undertaken. The main river of the district is Chhimtuipui (Kolodyme). Palak Lake is situated at a distance of 25 kms south-west of Tulpang.

The types of forests found in the Lunglei district are tropical, semi-evergreen forests and montane sub-tropical forests. In the earlier period, the forests were thick and valuable, but due to the traditional practice of jhuming from time immemorial, large areas of forests in the district are being gradually converted into barren lands. The forest department, however, has taken necessary steps to regenerate the forest areas. Riangte Lui is one of the very important streams in the district.

History

Mizoram became the 23rd state of the Indian Union in February 1987. The Mizos are a Mongoloid race who originally came from the Chin Hills of neighbouring Myanmar (formerly Burma). Mizo is a generic term and means a man from the hills, and denotes that Mizoram is essentially a mountainous area. Like the rest of India, the British captured Mizoram and they finally established their rule in the region in 1898, not before some violent incidents, as the independent-minded Mizos were not easily amenable to foreign subjugation.

Afterwards the Mizo area became a district of Assam and the position continued for some time after India became independent. In 1952, a Mizo district council was created under the Indian Constitution. This was done to give the region a separate identity from the rest of Assam, as the Mizos then had a strong feeling of being different. This, however, did not succeed and did not satisfy the Mizos, or the vocal elements among them.

There was a big famine in the Mizo region in 1959. The government organised relief in a big way but the people were more impressed by the relief work under the auspices of the Mizo National Famine Front and other voluntary bodies. Laldenga, a retired subaltern of the Indian army, was the key figure in the Mizo National Famine Front, and because of his oratory and organising skill he soon won the hearts of the people. The Mizo National Famine Front was converted into the Mizo National Front and Laldenga emerged as a rebel leader.

In 1966 Laldenga led a rebellion, and unrest began to spread in the Mizo Hills. The area was now separated from the state of Assam and created into a separate union. The Mizo region was also given a separate assembly. But Laldenga was carrying on a fight against the union forces and was now getting full support from neighbouring Pakistan which was then still in the eastern region as East Pakistan. Pakistan also provided him with arms and training for his men. There was also the support of some Christian groups abroad although the Church often pulled its weight in the direction of amity and reconciliation. The situation eased somewhat with the creation of Bangladesh in December 1971 but the killing of Sheikh Mujibur Rahman, the father of Bangladesh, by some of its army officers in August 1975, removed the main plank of friendship for India and Laldenga's men got back their sanctuary and their support. They had, of course, their sanctuaries in neighbouring Myanmar where a kind of anarchical situation prevailed in the border region. Laldenga himself shifted to Surrey in Britain and he was controlling his armed rebels from a remote control point. Now began the negotiations phase and Laldenga also began to realise that the goal of an independent Mizo land was impossible for attainment. By 1980, first a "peace accord" was reached between Laldenga and the Indian government, The accord did not hold and rebel activity continued for some more time.

But things had begun to look up and Laldenga was even permitted to visit the Mizo Hills area. He was now openly saying that he was an Indian and the Prime Minister Mrs. Indira Gandhi declared in 1984 when she visited Aizawl that the path of negotiations was open within the framework of the Indian Constitution.

Finally an accord which was to hold was reached on June 30, 1986 between Laldenga, the Home Secretary of the Indian government and the Chief Secretary of the Mizoram government. The rebellion came to an end and the problem of Mizoram was more or less finally settled within the Constitution. The Mizoram National Front (MNF), under Laldenga, had accepted to give up the path of violence and work within the four corners of the Constitution. The rebels came out of their hideouts and laid down their arms Laldenga became the Chief Minister of Mizoram with the Congress leader, Lalthanhawla, joining his cabinet as a minister along with some other Congress ministers.

Very soon, on February 2, 1987, Mizoram became a full-fledged state of India, and in the first elections to the state assembly the MNF got a good majority but lost it subsequently.

Irrigation and Agriculture

Mizos are basically agriculturists. About 60 per cent of them are engaged in agricultural pursuits. State farms and integrated agricultural and veterinary farms have been established to encourage the modern methods of farming, and teach the people the new practices. Maize, rice and other crops are grown while pigs and fowls are reared by many farmers. Exotic varieties and breeds of pigs and fowls have been introduced and have become popular among the villagers. The area of jhum cultivated land is being reduced, and the area under ordinary cultivation is being fully exploited so that the target of self-sufficiency in rice production is achieved by 1997-98. Rice is the staple diet of the Mizo people as in all the north-eastern states, with locally available meat. High-yielding varieties of paddy are being distributed to the farmers and they are encouraged to grow such varieties as would fetch a good return to them and fill the state's granary.

The state has considerable cultivation of fruits. Some 25,000 hectares of land are set apart for horticulture. The main horticultural crops are oranges, lemon, *kagzi* lime, passion fruits, *hatkora, jamir,* pineapple and papaya. Other crops are sugarcane, tapioca and cotton. With processing unit coming up such as the Ginger Dehydration Plant at Sairang and fruit juice concentration plants, people have started extensive cultivation of ginger and fruit crops.

About 85 per cent of workers in rural areas are engaged in agricultural activities. The main aim of the agricultural department is to achieve self-sufficiency in food production. With this aim in view, it was envisaged to bring the maximum area under crop production by way of land acclamation, construction of link roads, providing irrigational facilities and adoption of high yielding variety of grains.

In order to encourage and bring about permanent cultivation in Aizawl, the biggest district of Mizoram, a time-bound programme on horticulture known as Garden Colony was taken up. The administrative areas of Aizawl district were divided into two agricultural districts called Aizawl (East) and Aizawl (West). Agricultural seed farms have also been established in each of these districts for multiplication of recommended varieties of seeds.

The highest Peak in Mizoram is Blue Mountain (Phawngpui) situated in the district of Chhimtuipui with a height of 2,165 metres. The slopes of the mountain are covered with dense forests. The lower slopes of the mountain are being cleared for potato and maize cultivation which thrive very well. In this district, more than 80 per cent of the workers in the district are engaged in agricultural activities.

Land being the common property of the village, individual villagers normally have no separate holdings for the purpose of shifting cultivation. Some lands were, however, allotted to individuals for the purpose of terracing, plantation and wet rice cultivation in the district.

The cultivators are beginning to realise the wasteful character of jhuming and this being so, all the flat lands available in the district are proposed to be reclaimed for permanent cultivation. Special attention was therefore given to the flat lands of Chamdur and Palak areas. Every available facility is given to the cultivators to enable them to establish permanent farms and start cultivation.

Minor irrigation projects are being completed in different parts of the state. The surface irrigation potential of Mizoram is estimated at 7,0000 hectares of which 2,5000 hectares can be irrigated by the lift irrigation method and the balance by canals and other methods. The potential created so far is not large but that has induced the farmers to go in for double and triple cropping already. Thirty minor irrigation works have been completed and another 14 projects are under implementation.

One veterinary dispensary was established at Saiha during 1972-73 with one Veterinary Assistant Surgeon looking after the health of the livestock population scattered in the district. Under the subsidy scheme some poultry birds and pigs were distributed to progressive and needy villagers in the Chhimtuipui.

Till the end of the Fourth Plan period, the animal husbandry and veterinary department was only one wing of the agriculture department. With the launching of the Fifth Plan they started to function as an independent department.

Animal husbandry has also received considerable attention in the state where, in the old days, only the *mithuns* were known as an all purpose animal which could even be offered in lieu of cash. Now the consuming of milk has been spreading and cows and buffaloes are being reared to cater to the growing demand. Exotic varieties of pigs and fowls have also found much acceptability and have helped in improving the local breeds.

Presently, the price of milk, meat and eggs in local markets acrose the country is beyond the reach of the common man. Stepping up of production coupled with systematic marketing facilities alone could bring the required protective foods within reach of the common man.

In the sectors of goats, sheep and wool development, it was proposed to distribute to selected farmers on subsidised rates imported exotic sheep and goats for intensive development within the district. In order to achieve all the programmes, adequate health centres such as veterinary dispensaries, mobile dispensaries and rural animal husbandry centres were established so that even the remotest villages in the district are brought under proper coverage. Livestock and poultry were treated for various diseases and other ailments.

In the dairy development sector, the Central Dairy and Town Milk Supply Scheme for Aizawl has been expanded.

The Mizoram Khadi and Village Industries Board has done its bit to set up cottage industries and units in the area of silk spinning and weaving, cotton spinning and weaving, soap making, oil extraction, carpentry, cane and bamboo works. The has been set up by the Mizoram government in collaboration with the Industrial Development Bank of India (IDBI). On the whole, there is much scope for industries in the state.

Various schemes of agricultural development were being operated in the district of Lunglei during the decade, such as irrigation, land reclamation, green manuring, subsidised supply of tools and implements, distribution of seeds, plant protection schemes, etc.

With the attainment of union territory status by Mizoram the subdivisional veterinary office at Lunglei was upgraded to that of district office with sufficient staff to run the office and to work for the development of the livestock in the district. Besides, two rural animal health centres were also established at Hnahthial and Tlabung with district poultry farm at Lunglei. From that time onwards, the department was making further progress and development in the district.

Trade and Commerce

The development in the field of industry is still in an

infantile stage in Aizawl. It has not been possible to achieve much development in the field of industry due to lack of technical knowhow, shortage of skilled labour and raw materials, etc.

The government, as a matter of industrial policy laid much stress and importance on the development of cottage and small scale industries. Development in these sectors were envisaged as part of an overall programme of social and economic growth. To enable small scale industrialists to create preliminary facilities like factory buildings as well as plant and machinery required for starting their industries, the department has been extending loans to deserving entrepreneurs in Aizawl.

Mizoram Small Industries Development Corporation has also been set up at Aizawl with an authorised share capital of Rs. 60 lakhs. This corporation has been declared a refinancing institution by the IDBI. The corporation is going to introduce this scheme shortly on completion of some formalities.

The channel of trade and commerce is mainly through the district of Cachar in Assam by road communication. Other means of communication are negligible. The existing communication infrastructure hardly permits smooth trade and commerce on account of the fact that the roads are full of strains and hazards. Aizawl has to get from outside most of the consumer goods including the staple food, rice. But it produces marketable surplus like oranges, pineapples, bananas and other fruits, chillies, ginger and cotton. The district lacks the facilities of marketing, storage, processing, etc.

The entire district of Chhimtuipui can be termed as an extremely backward area in the field of industry. In view of the most difficult hilly terrain of the district, it has not been possible to achieve much development in industry. The industrial development of the district is practically confined to the “Village Small” types only, *e.g.*, handicraft, knitting, tailoring, etc. Village and small industries are the main industries producing almost all the domestic goods and materials. The department, therefore, has to play a vital role in the field of extending industrial loans and disbursing the same in cash as well as on hire purchase basis.

Besides the schemes of financial aid, the department started one craft centre at Saiha in 1974 which imparts training to 15 girls in a year. In 1979 another handicrafts centre was also established at Saiha.

There are other wings like sericulture, weaving and bee-keeping under the department of industries. But these wings could not function effectively due to the absence of skilled and efficient staff. No proper survey could be done for the development of industries in the district due to lack of communication. There is no major industry located in Chhimtuipui.

In the pre-independence days, Chhimtuipui used to enter into trade with the then undivided Bengal. The latter would get rubber, cane, bamboo, timber, cotton and tobacco from Chhimtuiput district. After partition, the only channel of trade and commerce was through the Cachar district in Assam. The district has to obtain much of the consumer goods, including rice, from outside. In view of the fact that the district has no marketable surpluses like orange, pineapple, bananas and others, the present deficit economy of the district can be coped up if more horticultural and crash crops are grown and produced in the district and the facilities of transport, marketing and storage for trade and commerce are provided.

After Lunglei subdivision became a district, industries office was started at Lunglei, there being only one at Aizawl prior to the birth of Union Territory in Mizoram. However, the types of industries are mainly of village and small Industries like handloom, handicraft, knitting and tailoring, etc., these being the industries in the district. Again in September 1979, district industries centre was established at Lunglei.

Population

With an area of 20,987 sq km Mizoram has a population of 891,058 people according to the 2001 Census. Of these 459,783 are males and 431,275 are females. The total population of each district are given below.

District	*Area sq km*	*Population (2001)*	*Headquarters*
Aizawl	12,588	339,812	Aizawl
Champhai	3,185.85	101,389	Champhai
Kolasib	1,282.51	60,977	Kolasib
Lawngtlai	2,557.10	73,050	Lawngtlai
Lunglei	4,538.00	137,155	Lunglei
Mamit	3,025.75	62,313	Mamit
Chhimtuipui	3,957	60,823	Chhimtuipui
Serchhip	1,421.60	55,539	Serchhip

Literacy and Education

Mizoram is one of the highly educated states of India with high literacy levels and what is more a level of literacy among the women which hardly obtains anywhere in India. The main languages spoken in the district are Mizo and English. According to the 2001 census, the percentage of literacy in Mizoram is 88.49. It was already high in the previous decadal census when the literacy in the state was 81.23 per cent. About 90.69 per cent of males are literate and 86.13 per cent of women can read and write.

This extremely high level has been attained over years during which the Christian missions, who were allowed in by the British played a notable role in the spread of education. They not only converted the people to Christianity, with 95 per cent of the Mizos now being Christian, but set up schools in every village. Now there is a church and a school in every village in Mizoram, and the people lay great deal of stress on education without which no real progress of any kind is possible. Now there are not only schools at all levels, primary, secondary and higher secondary, but also colleges, to satisfy the urge of the Mizos to educate their children.

Communication

As soon as Mizoram became union territory on 21 January 1972, the transport wing was converted into a directorate called "Directorate of Supply and Transport, Government of Mizoram" (S&T). The main function of General Transport wing was to operate trucks and jeeps for carrying essential commodities from Silchar to Aizawl and thence to various places within the district as well as Lunglei and Chhimtuipui district. Mizoram, being not self-sufficient in regard to foodstuffs especially in rice, transport wing was working as Task Force carrying essential commodities from outside the territory and distributing the same to the needy places.

Under the Director of Supply and Transport, the state transport was created in 1972. The main function of state transport is to run passenger, bus services to various places in and outside the district. Apart from passenger services, state transport buses are also carrying postal mails/bags to all places along the main road. Buses are also made available on hire to various parties like religious, wedding, picnic parties at the rates fixed by the government.

The bus station at Silchar in Cachar district of Assam is functioning on hire basis. Buses are plying on different routes from Aizawl within and outside the district. The bus service routes are on the increase. The operations of bus services are increasing, year by year with the construction of new roads, and there are fair weather bus service routes also which are operated mostly in winter.

The railway out-agency also started functioning since 1975 at Aizawl. This agency affords facilities to traders and government department to book their goods from various stations of Indian railways at cheaper rates.

In Chhimtuipui district besides roads, all other means of transport like railways, air services and ropeways are out of question. The only available means of transport in the district, which is road transport is also in an infant stage. The existing roads are being constructed, maintained and improved by the PWD of Mizoram. The Border Road Development Board took up the construction of some crossroads. The Saiha link road 27 km long, was taken up and completed in 1979, Lunglei to Luipang road 162 km long, which was taken up in 1968 was completed in 1978. As a matter of fact there was no transport system worth the name in the district. The Government of Mizoram has since started bus services on these roads to facilitate the travelling public.

A new project of Lawngtlai to Chawngte road has also been taken up by the Border Development Board. As road communication develops and other developmental activities take place, it is essential that more emphasis is laid on better road transport system so as to ensure greater mobility of available goods and services in the district and to give priority to this aspect of development. A good road transport system plays a vital role in bringing the people of all districts together giving them opportunities to exchange their respective views and also in the matter of stabilising the prices of goods and services uniformly in the district.

The inland water transport has not been developed as it should be. Otherwise this mode of transport could play an important part in the economy of the state.

Religion and Culture

Not only are the people getting the best possible

education but also the process of modernisation has enveloped all aspects of life in Mizo society. But it still has its traditional dances and festivals which are preserved. The dances are common to the Mizos, the Lakhers and Pawis, the main tribes in the state, along with the Chakmas who are believed to have migrated there from the neighbouring Chittagong hills of Bangladesh much before independence. Many more Chakmas, who are Buddhists, came as refugees after independence because of religious persecution by the Muslims in the Chittagong Hills and because their lands have been taken away by the land-hungry people from the plains of Bangladesh. The Government of India has been very keen to send them back from Tripura and Arunachal Pradesh where they have been living. But the Chakmas are not convinced that they would be safe from religious persecution and their lands seized by the Bangladeshis would be returned to them. They refuse to go back. These Chakmas are ethnically and culturally the same as the Chakmas in Mizoram but the latter are permanently settled although their nomadic habits and their Buddhist religion would not be given up by them.

Of the Mizo dances the most popular and attractive even to the others is the Cheraw or bamboo dance. In this, six girls sit on the ground holding bamboo sticks which are rhythmically moved and struck against one another while six other girls move rhythmically between the bamboo sticks. Khal Lam is another popular dance of Mizos in which a group of boys wearing specially made shawls dance to the beat of drums and gongs. In another dance, called Solakia, men and women dance in a big circle to the accompaniment of drum beats. This was originally a Lakher dance which the Mizos have also adopted.

Every village in Mizoram earlier had a bachelors' dormitory called Zawlbuk. It was a notable Mizo institution which has now died following the impact of modernity. The bachelors of the village would reside there and learn wrestling, other martial arts and the Mizo way of life. The dormitory would also provide shelter to the itinerant hawker and other visitors, and would act as the guest house of the entire village. Women had to keep away from it. Mizoram has a high percentage of urbanisation and there are 22 towns in the state. Men now wear trousers and shirts even in the villages, and women sport blouses and frocks.

Mizos are well advanced and have taken up occupations and services in neighbouring states and at the Centre. They can thus be seen in sufficient numbers in places far and near their state. Wearing of hats is common and these are made of bamboo and cane. The villagers carry an artistically designed and handwoven shoulder bag in which they carry their tobacco pipe and other equipment. Both men and women smoke although the pipes for the two are different. *Zu* is an alcoholic drink brewed indigenously from rice. There were several occasions when the entire village would indulge in an orgy of drinking and *Zu* would flow like water. Now the spread of Christianity, the modern ways of living and the impact of education have all helped in curbing drinking among the people although it cannot be said to have been eliminated.

Marriages are generally arranged by parents among the Mizos. Among them there is yet another interesting custom of inheritance. The youngest son inherits all the movable and immovable property of the father. The elder sons are supposed to move out of the parental home after marriage. The youngest son has the responsibility of looking after the parents in their old age. There was no system of making a will in the Mizo society but an Inheritance Act was passed by the Mizo District Council in 1956 under which a will could be made by any property holder.

Kut is the Mizo word for festivals. Mizos have three

major festivals called Chapchar Kut, Mim Kut and Pawl Kut. The Mizos belong to a Mongolian race. Mizo means man of the hills or highlander. On the western border of the Aizawl, there are very few Chakma immigrants from Chittagong Hill Tracts in Bangladesh. An absolute majority of the population in the district are Christians. Most of the Christians are Protestants in denomination and a few are Roman Catholics. There are several denominations, the main ones being Presbyterian, United Penticostal, Salvation Army, Roman Catholic, Seventh Day Adventist and Isua Krista Kohhran. The Mizos are a distinct unit linguistically, culturally and ethnologically. Mizos are dedicated people bent on preserving and consolidating their identity and religion.

There are some very good principles of self-help and cooperation in the Mizo social customs. The Mizos are expected to contribute labour for the welfare of the community. Services are rendered to the people in distress as a social obligation.

There being three major different cultures in the district of Chhimtuipui such as Pawi, Lakher and Chakma, the three district councils had been created so that each community will be in a position to safeguard its own culture and tradition in the best manner and thus be free from the exploitation of larger communities.

The Sangau Pawi call themselves as 'Lai' which is a tribe commonly known as Chins in the Chin Hills District of Myanmar. Therefore, some Pawi speak the Lai dialect at home and amongst themselves. But they have accepted Lusei or Duhlian (Mizo) as their language in schools and for use with outsiders. But most of the Pawi speak the Lusei or Duhlian (Mizo) language and have similar customs and ways of life with the Mizo. There are several Pawi in the Mizo community, Pawi being one of the several clans in the Mizo society.

The Lakher, however, have a distinct pattern of

customs and traditions. They call themselves 'Mara' and speak Mara language which is altogether different from the Lushei or Duhlian (Mizo) language. The Pawi, and the Lakher are mostly Christians like their Mizo brothers and sisters. They have the traditional dances in common. The most popular of these dances is the 'Solakia'.

The Chakma are culturally entirely different from the Pawi and the Lakher. They are comparatively backward and a majority of them are Buddhists. They speak their own dialect (language) and use Bengali script. They worship Buddha and also some of the Hindu gods and goddesses. Like their religious rites, the social customs of the Chakma are also a mixture of Buddhist, Hindu and old tribal customs. The Chakma are semi-nomadic. They prefer to have their villages by the riverside. The most popular entertainment is the open air theatrical performance by the village drama party.

The main culture in the Lunglei district is the Mizo culture. The people of this district are fast giving up their old customs and adopting the western mode of life. Among the Mizos, the present customs are mixtures of the old traditions and the western pattern of life. The Chakmas who are living in the western part of the district, are culturally different from the Mizos.

Tourism

Aizawl, located at nearly 4,000 feet above sea level, is a religious and cultural centre of Mizoram. Champhai is a beautiful resort on the Myanmar border. Tamdil, a natural lake with virgin forest, is 60 km from Aizawl and 10 km from the tourist resort of Saitual. Vantawng Falls, five km from the hill station Thenzawl, are the highest and most beautiful waterfalls in Mizoram. The department of tourism has opened tourist lodges at Aizawl, Lunglei, Champhai and wayside restaurants at Thingdawl; Hnahthial, a recreational centre at beraw Tlang and an Alpine picnic hut at District Park near Zobawk.

·A brief account of important places of interest in Mizoram are given below.

Thasiama Seno Neihna : This is a steep, craggy hill rising some 6,000 ft above sea level near the village of Chawngtui, a few miles from the Myanmar border.

Twin graves of Tualvungi and Zawlpala : At phulpui village.

Lamsial Puk : This is a wide, deep cave on a steep hillside between the villages of Samthang and Farkawn. This cave is one of the biggest caves in Mizoram, and is about 75 feet wide.

Chhingpuii : A memorial has been erected at the place where Chhingpuii was killed, which can be seen at the Aizawl-Lunglei Road between the Baktawng and Chhingchhip villages.

Kungawrhi Puk : This is a cave lying between the villages of Farkawn and Vaphai.

Sibuta Lung (Lung-stone, rock or monument) : Sibuta Lung is a tall stone monument erected by Sibuta, a chief who dominated over a large area in and around Tachhip village. This monument can be seen near Tachhip, about 20 kms from Aizawl

Flara Tui (Tui-water or spring) : The villagers of Lamsial learned of the spring which came to be known as Fiara Tui or Fiara's Spring.

Tamdil : At approximate distance to the east of Aizawl, between Saitual and Tualbung villages, there exists a lake which known as Tamdil.

Rungdil : The name means the 'lake of partidges'.

Phawngpui : Phawngpui, known to the outside world as Blue Mountain, is the highest peak in Mizoram which rises to a height of 2,165 metres above sea level. It is claimed that on a bright day, even the Bay of Bengal is visible from this peak.

Palak Lake : This lake is situated in Chhimtuipui

district at a site 25 kms south-west of Tuipang. It is oval in shape with a maximum radius of 660 yards.

Chawngvungi : Mizo folklore is incomplete without the story of Chäwngvungi. Today, locations associated with this tragic tale can be visited in Pangzawl village.

Thanghlianga : Thanghlianga of the Pawi Tribe was chief of the Halkha clan and of Halkha village (now in Myanmar). The death of Thanghlianga signified the end of Pawi dominance over early Mizoram.

Khawnglung Run : During the years of AD 1856 and 1859 there was a great conflict between the north and south of Mizoram. Historically, it is remembered as Khawnglung Run 'Khawnglung' means the name of the village and 'Run' means 'raid'.

The Khawnglung village raid was one of the most famous and the greatest massacre in Mizo history.

Administration

The state is divided into three districts: Aizawl, Chhimtuipui and Lunglei. Aizawl district at present comprises 12 rural development blocks, i.e., Zawlnuam, West Phaileng, Reiek, Tlangnuam, North Thingdawl, Darlawn, Aibawk, Serchhip, Thingsulthliah, Ngopa, Khawzawl, and East Lungdar. Aizawl district alone has 21 assembly segments, *i.e.*, N. Vanlaiphai; Khawbung; Champhai; Khawhai; Saitual; Ngopa; Suangpuilawn; Ratu; Kawnpui; Kolasib; Kawrthah; Sairang; Phuldungsei; Sateek; Serchhip; Lungpho; Tlungvel; Aizawal North; Aizawl East; Aizawl West and Aizawl South.

Aizawl has 18 towns and 391 villages (342 inhabited villages and 49 uninhabited villages). This district is bounded on the north by Cachar district of Assam and Manipur state, on the east by Myanmar, on the west by Bangladesh and Tripura state and on the south by Lunglei district of Mizoram. Total area of Aizawl is 12,588 sq kms. The district headquarters is at Aizawl. It is not only the district headquarters but also the state capital of Mizoram.

The village administration is headed by the village council. The village council is also elected on the basis of adult suffrage.

Chhimtuipui district is situated in the southernmost part of the territory, flanked in the east by Myanmar and Bangladesh in the west. The district is named after a rather big river called Chhimtuipui flowing through the district.

Chhimtuipui district at present comprises of four rural development blocks, *i.e.*, Chawngte, Lawngtlai, Sangau and Tuipang. It has one town and 214 villages (198 inhabited villages and 16 uninhabited villages). There is four assembly segments, *i.e.*. Tuipand, Sangau, Saiha, Chawngte.

Lunglei district is situated in the middle of the territory, being sandwiched in the north by Aizawl district and by Chhimtuipui district in the south. It is bordered in the east by Myanmar (Chin Hills) and by Bangladesh in to the west. The total area of the district is 4,536 sq kms. The district headquarters is located at Lunglei.

The district at present comprises four rural development blocks, *i.e.*, West Bunghmun, Lungsen, Lunglei and Hnahthial. It has three towns and 178 villages. The village councils are also elected on the basis of adult suffrage. The elected members would then elect the President from amongst themselves. Thus the village council administration is headed by the President. There is five Assembly Segments in this district, *i.e.*, Demagiri, Buarpui, Lunglei, Tawipul, and Hnahthial.

MIZORAM

Introduction

Mizoram occupies the north east corner of India. In shape

it is rather like a narrow and inverted triangle. It is bounded on the north by the district of Cachar (Assam) and the state of Manipur, on the east and south by Chin Hills and Arakan (Myanmar) on the west by the Chittagong Hill Tracts of Bangladesh and the state of Tripura. Mizoram borders three states of India—Assam, Manipur and Tripura.

In the local language, the term 'Mizoram' means the land of Mizos. Mizo itself means highlander. The state has the most variegated hilly terrain in the eastern part of India. The hills are steep and are separated by rivers which flow either to the north or south creating deep gorges between the hill ranges. The average height of the hills is about 900 m. The highest peak in Mizoram is Phawngpui (Blue Mountain) with a height of 2210 m.

History

The origin of the Mizos, like those of many other tribes in the North Eastern India is shrouded in mystery. Historians believe that the Mizos are a part of the great wave of the Mongolian race spilling over into the eastern and southern India centuries ago.

The Mizos, so goes the legend, emerged from under a large covering rock known as Chhinlung. Two people of the Ralte clan, known for their loquaciousness, started talking noisily while coming out of the region. They made a great noise which leg God, called Pathian by the Mizos, to throw up his hands in disgust and say enough is enough. He felt, too many people had already been allowed to step out and so closed the door with the rock.

History often varies from legends. But the story of the Mizos getting out into open from the nether world through a rock opening is now part of the Mizo fable. Chhinlung however, is taken by some as the Chinese city of Sinlung or Chinlingsang situated close on the sino-Burmese border. The Mizos have songs and stories about the glory of the ancient Chhinlung civilization handed down from one generation to another powerful people.

It is hard to tell how far the story is true. It is nevertheless possible that the Mizos came from Sinlung or Chinlungsan located on the banks of the river Yalung in China. According to K.S. Latourette, there were political upheavals in China in 210 B.C. when the dynastic rule was abolished and the whole empire was brought under one administrative system. Rebellions broke out and chaos reigned throughout the Chinese State. That the Mizos left China as part of one of those waves of migration. Whatever the case may have been, it seems probable that the Mizos moved from China to Burma and then to India under forces of circumstances. They first settled in the Shan State after having overcome the resistance put up by the indigenous people. Then they changed settlements several times, moving from the Shan State to Kabaw Valley to Khampat to Chin Hills in Burma. They finally began to move across the river Tiau to India in the Middle of the 16th Century.

The Shans had already been firmly settled in their State when Mizos came there from Chhinlung around 5th Century. The Shans did not welcome the new arrivals, but failed to throw the Mizos out. The Mizos had lived happily in the Shan state for about 300 years before they moved on the Kabaw Valley around the 8th Century.

It was in the Kabaw Valley that Mizos got the opportunity to have an unhindered interaction with the local Burmese. The two cultures met and the two tribes influenced each other in the spheres of clothing, customs, music and sports. According to some, the Mizos learnt the art of cultivation from the Burmese at Kabaw. Many of their agricultural implements bore the prefix Kawl which was the name given by the Mizos to the Burmese.

Khampat (now in Myanmar) is known to have been the next Mizo settlement. The area claimed by the Mizos as their earliest town, was encircled by an earthen rampart and divided into several parts. The residence of the ruler stood at the central block call Nan Yar (Palace Site). The construction of the town indicates the Mizos had already acquired considerable architecture skills. They are said to have planted a banyan tree at Nan Yar before they left Khampat as a sign that town was made by them.

The Mizos, in the early 14th century, came to settle at Chin Hills on the Indo-Burmese border. They built villages and called them by their clan names such as Seipui, Saihmun and Bochung. The hill and difficult terrain of Chin Hills stood in the way of the building of another central township like Khampat. The villages were scattered so unsystematically that it was not always possible for the various Mizo clans to keep in touch with one another.

The earliest Mizos who migrated to India were known as Kukis, the second batch of immigrants were called New Kukis. The Lushais were the last of the Mizo tribes migrated to India. The Mizo history in the 18th and 19th Century is marked by many instances of tribal raids and retaliatory expeditions of security. Mizo Hills were formally declared as part of the British-India by a proclamation in 1895. North and south hills were united into Lushai Hills district in 1898 with Aizawl as its headquarters.

The process of the consolidated of the British administration in tribal dominated area in Assam stated in 1919 when Lushai Hills along with some other hill districts was declared a Backward Tract under government of India Act. The tribal districts of Assam including Lushai Hills were declared Excluded Area in 1935.

After independence of India, Mizoram continued to be part of Assam. In 1966 the Mizos resorted to the use of armed struggle to put forth their demands to set up a homeland.

Under British rule the state was named as Lushai Hills. In 1954 by an Act of Parliament, the name was changed to Mizo Hills district. In 1972, when it was made into a union territory, it was named Mizoram. Mizoram became the 23rd state of the Indian union on February 20, 1987.

It was during the British regime that a political awakening among the Mizos in Lushai Hills started taking shape the first political party, the Mizo Common People's Union was formed on 9th April 1946. The Party was later renamed as Mizo Union. As the day of Independence drew nearer, the Constituent Assembly of India set up and Advisory Committee to deal with matters relating to the minorities and the tribals.

A sub-Committee, under the chairmanship of Gopinath Bordoloi was formed to advise the Constituent Assembly on the tribal affairs in the North East. The Mizo Union submitted a resolution of this Sub-committee demanding inclusion of all Mizo inhabited areas adjacent to Lushai Hills. However, a new party called the United Mizo Freedom (UMFO) came up to demand that Lushai Hills join Burma after Independence.

Following the Bordoloi Sub-Committee's suggestion, a certain amount of autonomy was accepted by the Government and enshrined in the Six Schedule of the constitution. The Lushai Hills Autonomous District Council came into being in 1952 followed by the formation of these bodies led to the abolition of chieftanship in the Mizo society.

The autonomy however met the aspirations of the Mizos only partially. Representatives of the District Council and the Mizo Union pleaded with the States Reorganisation Commission (SRC) in 1954 for integrating the Mizo-dominated areas of Tripura and Manipur with their District Council in Assam.

The tribal leaders in the North East were laboriously unhappy with the SRC Recommendations. They met in

Aizawl in 1955 and formed a new political party, Eastern India Union (EITU) and raised demand for a separate state comprising of all the hill districts of Assam. The Mizo Union split and the breakaway faction joined the EITU. By this time, the UMFO also joined the EITU and then understanding of the Hill problems by the Chaliha Ministry, the demand for a separate Hill state by EITU was kept in abeyance.

Inter-tribal wars were reputed to have forced various tribal settlements to move to the densely forested Lushai hills from the Chin hills in what is now called Myanmar over 500 years ago. These tribes fiercely opposed British rule but were dominated by the gun in 1892. In 1894 Rev. F.W. Savidge and J.H. Lorrain learned the Lushai language, opened a school and wrote out the Lushai/ Mizo alphabet that is still in use today.

By 1924 the British allowed missionaries to enter the Lushai Hills. Over time the local tribes converted to Christianity and today Mizoram is almost completely Christian. As much as 81.23 per cent of the population is literate, with 62 registered newspapers and 30 magazines being published regularly. The state suffered traumatic violence for decades but has remained peaceful for over two decades ever since those fighting for Mizo liberation became the democratically elected government in the state.

One of the beneficial result of Missionary activities was the spread of education. The Missionaries introduced the Roman script for the Mizo language and formal education. The cumulative result is high percentage 95% which is considered to be highest in India. The Mizos area distinct community and the social unit was the village. Around it revolved the life of a Mizo.

Mizo Village is usually set on the top of a hill with the chief's house at the centre and the bachelor's dormitory called Zawlbuk, prominently. In a way the focal point in the village was the Zawlbuk where all young bachelors of the village slept. Zawlbuk was the training ground, and indeed, the cradle wherein the Mizo youth was shaped into a responsible adult member of the society.

The fabric of social life in the Mizo society has undergone tremendous changes over the years. Before the British moved into the hills, for all practical purposes the village and the clan formed units of Mizo society. The Mizo code of ethics or Dharma moved around 'Tlawmngaihna", an untranslatable term meaning on the part of everyone to be hospitable, kind, unselfish and helpful to others.

Tlawmngaihna to Mizo stands for the compelling moral force which finds expression in self-sacrifice for the service of the others. The old belief, Pathian is still use in term God till today. The Mizos have been enchanted to their new-found faith of Christianity with so much dedication and submission that their entire social life and thought-process been transformed and guided by the Christian Church Organisation and their sense of values has also undergone drastic change.

The Mizos are a close-knit society with no class distinction and no discrimination on grounds of sex. Ninety percent of them are cultivators and the village exists like a big family. Birth of a child, marriage in the village and death of a person in the village or a community feast arranged by a member of the village are important occasions in which the whole village is involved.

Places of Historic Importance

Blue Mountain

The Highest peak in Mizoram, the Blue Mountain (Phawngpui) is situated in Chhimtuipui district overlooking the bend of the river Koldyne (Chhimtuipui) close on the state's border with Myanmar. The peak 2,157 m in height and encircled by bamboo groves at the top where there is a level ground of about 200 hectares, offers a grand view of the height hills and the meandering undulated valleys. The woods around are home to various species of beautiful and rare flora and fauna.

Sibuta Lung

This is a memorial stone found at Tachhip village, 20 km from Aizawl town. It was erected by a Palian chief about 300 years ago. A young orphan, Sibuta, was adopted by the chief. He killed his adoptive father and became the chief of over 2,000 houses. But he failed in his love life and was jilted by a girl. For having his revenge he put a young and beautiful girl, Darlai, in a big pit on which he wanted to erect a memorial for himself. The huge rock was dragged with great pains from the bed of the Tlawng river, 10 km away. The stone was bathed with the blood of three human beings who were sacrificed. The stone was erected putting Darlai alive on the pit below the stone.

Phulpui Grave

There are two graves at Phulpui village in Aizawl district. Zawlpala, Chief of Phulpui village, married the legendary beauty, Talvungi of Thenzawl. She was subsequently married to the chief of Rothai, Punthia. But she could not forget Zawlpala. After many years when Zawlpala died, grief stricken Talvungi came to Phulpui, dug a pit by the side of Zawlpala's grave and induced an old woman to kill her and bury her in the grave. The love story, the graves and other associated places at Phulpui are attractions to visitors.

Memorial of Chhingpui

There is a memorial stone for a beautiful young woman called Chhingpui in a place between Baktawng and Chhingchhip village on the Aizawl-Lunglei road. Chhingpui came from a noble family and was extraordinarily beautiful. From among the many young men wanting to marry her, She chose Kaptuanga and married him. They were very happy. But bad days came upon them when war broke out between the rival chiefs. Chhingpui was kidnapped and killed. For days all the villagers mourned her death. Kaptuanga could not bear the loss and killed himself. Chhingpui's memorial has kept the love story alive among the people.

Pangzawl

Pangzawl village of Lunglei district is associated with the tragic folklore of Chawngungi. She was a very beautiful girl sought for, by all young men. But her mother demanded a very bride price which could not be afforded by anyone. Ultimately, the Chief's son, Sawngkhara, won her by using a magic drug. However, she died soon after the marriage. Sawngkhara lived the rest of his life mourning the death of his beautiful, young wife.

Mangkahia Lung

At Champhai in Aizawl district, near the Burma border, there is a very large memorial stone called Mangkahia Lung (Mangkhaia's stone). It is 5 in high with heads of mithun engraved on it. This was erected around 1700 AD in memory of Mangkhaia who was a very prominent chief of the Ralte tribe.

Tomb of Vanhimailian

Vanhimailian Sailo was a great chief who ruled over Champhai. A tomb was erected in his memory overlooking the vast Champhai plain.

Tualchang

Near Tualchang village in the eastern part of Aizawl district, there is a row of stone slabs. The largest of the rocks is 3m wide 1m thick and 4.5m high. It is the biggest monolith in the state.

Lungvandawt

Lungvandawt means a stone reaching heaven. A very

tall beautiful chiselled pillar made of stone about 75 cm in diameter and 3 m in height is found between Biate and Lungdar in the eastern part of Aizawl district. The story goes that in ancient times this stone pillar was very tall, almost touching heaven and hence nothing could go in between. Once a peacock squeezed into it and got crumbled into pieces. It appears that this probably was a very tall memorial stone of a chief of the Biate tribe who was resident of the area before the Lushais came and defeated the Biates who mostly went down to the plains of Cachar to settle there.

Buddha's Image in Mualchang Village

An engraved image of Lord Buddha has been found about 8 km away from Mualchang village and 50 km from Lunglei town. On either side of the Lord's image there are images of dancing girls. On another slab of stone there are engravings of foot marks and various articles like spear head and dao. It appears that these engravings were done by metal chisels as there are marks in nearby stones which indicate the sharpening of metal implements.

Thangliana Lung

At Demagiri there is a memorial stone erected in memory of captain T.H. Lewin who was the first Britisher to enter Mizoram. He was very friendly with all the tribesmen and they honoured him by giving him the Mizo name of Thangliana which means 'greatly famous'. His memorial stone at Demagiri shows how the Mizos held him in great esteem.

Suangpuilawn Inscriptions

At Suangpuilawn village in Aizawl district there is a stone with inscriptions which have not been deciphered as yet. The stone slab of the size of 1 m length and 1 m width is placed by the side of the stream.

Thansiama Sena Neihna

This literally means, a place where a man called

Thansiama saw the calf of a mithun. There is a barren hill top, about 2000 m high, near Chawnglui village in Aizawl district, near Burma border. The top of the hill has a beautiful flat land but it is almost inaccessible because of the steep hill. A folklore says that Thansiama, who lived very long and became a very old man, was once searching for his missing mithun. He saw a calf at this hill top. The missing mithun had climbed up the hill, an impossible task and given birth to the calf at this place. This is a story of hallucinations of old and lonely men.

Caves

Milu Puk : Milu Puk means cave of skulls. There is a big cave situated near the village Mamte in Lunglei district, about 130 km from Lunglei town. In this cave a big heap of human skeletons were found. The skeletons appeared to be of people who were taller than the Mizos and might have belonged to some other race inhabiting the area before the Mizos came. The Legend is that these people belonged to a tribe called 'Tlau".

Pukzing Cave : Pukzing cave, which goes 25 m inside is the biggest cave in Mizoram. It is situated at Pukzing village near Marpara in the western hills within Aizawl district. The legend goes that the cave was carved out of the hills by a very strong man called Mualzavata, the name meaning a person who could clear hundred ranges of forest in one day.

Lamsial Puk : The cave *Lamsial Puk* is situated near the village Farkawn in the south-east side of Aizawl district. This cave carries gruesome evidence of a fight between two neighbouring villages in which many warriors were killed. The bodies of the warriors of the Lamsial village were kept in this cave. The village is no longer there. But there are many skeletons in the Lamsial puk which recall this gory incident.

Kungawrhi Puk : It is a big cave situated on a hill

between Farkawn and Vaphai villages in the South-east part of Aizawl district. The folktale associated with this cave speaks of a beautiful young girl named Kungawrhi, after whom this cave was named. She got married to a brave young man, named Pnathira. When the couple was going to Pnathira's village after the marriage, some spirits, bewitched by her beauty, abducted her. The spirits brought her to this cave and kept her confined in it. She was later rescued from the cave by her brave husband.

The People

The total population of Mizoram as of March 2001 stood at 891,058 as per the provisional results of the Census of India 2001. The State has density as low as 42 persons per sq. km. of area.

The inhabitants of Mizoram are known by the generic name of Mizo, which literally means people (mi) of the hills (zo). There are a number of separate tribes under the general ethnic broad group of Mizo. Mizos included the following tribes—Ralte, Paite, Dulien, Poi, Sukte, Pankhup, Jahao, Fanai (Molienpui), Molbem, Taute, Lakher, Dalang, Mar, Khuangli, Falam (Tashous), Leillul and Tangur. The main sub groups are Lushais, Pawis and Lakhers.

Lnshai

The meaning of 'Lushai' is persons with long heads, pertaining to the fact that Lushais bind their hair in knots at the back of their head. In the north Lushai Hills, the predominant tribes were the Lushais, Raltes and Pawis, the Raltes belonged to the Kuki tribe and were brought under subjugation by the Lushais, who migrated from the Chin Hills. They had distinct social customs and marked differences in dialects. They used to live in a separate-portion of the village assigned to them.

The Lushais were described as short, sturdy and heavy people of Mongolian type. Generally the height of men were between 162 cm to 170 cm and the women's height varied from 140 cm to 160 cm. The complexion varied from dark brown to light yellow.

In the Lushai clans both the sexes are slight in build. The colour of their skin varied from dark yellow, brown, dark olive, copper and yellow olive. Beards and whiskers were almost unknown and a Lushai, when he could grow a moustache, would pull out all the hairs except at two ends. The hair was worn by both sexes in a knot over the nape of the neck, and carefully parted in the middle. The children's hair were left to grow freely till it was long enough to be tied in a knot. The young men dressed their hair with much care using pig's fat. But changes have been taken place in modern clays.

An average woman bore five to ten children. However, infant morality being high, only two to three children in a family would survive to become adults. Both men and women could walk long distances and they were able to swim. They also climbed hills with ease which was natural in the hilly terrain of the Lushai hills. Some mental abnormalities were found in the people of Lushai Hills. There were common cases of transvestites, when some men would dress and live like women. They were accepted as such in the society. One would also come across cases of lunacy rather frequently. Suicide, particularly amongst old people, was also quite common. The difference between the clans was mostly evident in the different methods of performing the Sakhua sacrifice to the guardian spirit of the household. Some of the clans were not yet absorbed by the Lushais but they were much influenced by the Lushais. These tribes were the Fanai, the Ralte, the Paite and the Rangte.

Pawi

In the south Lushai Hills one found the Fanais inhabiting the land between the rivers Tuichawng and the Kolodyne on the west and the Tao and the Kolodyne on the east. Their southern boundary was the ridge running from the Darjaw Range towards the Blue Mountain. Further south the Pawi tribes inhabited the territory on both the Indian and the Burma sides. The term 'Pawi' was not strictly speaking, the name of a clan, but it was the term used by the Lushais for all the people living near the Kolodyne. Further south, were the people belonging to the Lakher tribe.

Several tribes called themselves as Lai, which literally-meant middle. They got this name probably because they were inhabiting the central area of the Chin Hills. One of the sub-tribes of the Lais had a chief named Tlang Hang who used to frequently raid villages in the Arakan and Chittagong. These tribes along with sub-tribes were known as Shendus. The Lushais used the name Pawi for the Lai tribes. The Pawis were settled in Lunglei sub division. They had their own distinct language and wore their hair in a knot on top of their head. Their distinctive cultural features were in songs which were broadly categorised into two groups-funeral songs and songs for other occasions. The Lakhers lived in the villages immediately in the south of the Pawi villages.

There were inter-marriages between the Lais, the Tlang and the Lakhers. In the Lushai hills most of these people were living in the north and the east of the Blue Mountain. They were collectively called Shendus by the tribes in the western hills and the plains which dreaded their frequent raids. The Shendus were also referred to as Lakher-Pawis or Lakhers.

Lakhers

The Lakhers call themselves Mara, but the Lushais call them Lakhers. The term appears to have originated from the practise of plucking cotton. The Lushais used to pluck cotton from the fruit with their hands whereas the Lakhers did it with a stick. The name Lakher came from this method of plucking cotton with stick, la meaning 'cotton' and kher meaning 'to pluck or remove with stick'.

There are various conjectures as to the origin of the name Mara. Probably it came from 'Mirang', a name of one of the hordes of the tribes presently inhabiting the Arakan Hills. The Mirangs who migrated from central and eastern Burma were also called Rakhong or Kalasa or Mara.

The Lakhers are physically well built and strong. The average height of the men is about 5 feet and 6 inches. They are taller than the Lushais and their physical fitness compares very favorably with that of their neighbours. The women are taller than Lushai women and are of very good physique. The Lakhers have brown complexion but are darker than the Lushais. They have broad noses, high cheek bones and mongoloid eyes.

Chakmas

The Chakmas are the latest migrants to the Mizo hills. Their present name is widely believed to have been derived from the word 'Chak' as they were called by the Burmese. They first came and settled in Arakan. Later, they came to settle in the Chittagong Hill Tracts. The Chakmas moved further into the interior and started a semi-nomadic life. They came up to Demagiri and settled extensively in areas now bordering Mizoram, Tripura and the Chittagong Hill Tracts.

In appearance, the Chakmas look like Mongolians of the Tibeto-Burman group. They have a round face, snubbed nose and high cheek bones. Their chests are broad and arms and legs are well built. They are fair and brown complexioned. Facial hair is sparse amongst the men and women generally do not have long hair. The skulls of the Chakmas are smaller but broader compared to those of other tribes in the north-east.

The Chakmas were believed to have been Hindus during their early period of settlement in Arakan. Brahmanism was the religion in Arakan from about the fifth century to the eleventh century. The Chamkas later became Buddhists.

The Chakmas have their own language and script. The Chakma script has similarity with Burmese and Sanskrit scripts. The Chakma language sounds almost like a dialect of Bengali. Agar Tara is their old scripture which appears to be a version of Buddhist scripture, Tripitak in broken Pali. The Tara is used extensively on ceremonial occasions like marriages, funerals, etc. The Chakmas also recount their history in ballads called Genkhuli.

Languages

Although several languages were spoken in the Lushai Hills, the main language was Lushai. Other languages of the Kuki-Chin groups spoken by the different tribes were Zahao, Lakher, Hmar, Paite, Lai and Ralte. Many of the smaller tribes used their own language amongst themselves but used Lushai for conversation with persons of other tribes or with outsiders. Lushai language was a spoken language and did not have any written literature.

Occupation

The State has good potential for economic growth in the areas of agriculture, horticulture, tourism, handicraft, etc. The agricultural scenario in Mizoram is very bright with population per sq. km. The farmers of the state have gradually been motivated to accept the latest technologies available. Mizoram Government has taken action to distribute tractors and power tillers to the farmers on subsidy to boost up the production of food grains to become self sufficient and to export. The main agricultural products are rice and maize.

Handloom and Handicrafts, which is a traditional industry in Mizoram, will continue to receive prime attention from the government. Modernisation of this sector by induction of improved design and technology to make it an export oriented sector will he encouraged and promoted. Export oriented textiles and readymade garments industries will receive special attention of the government. Induction of power-looms will be encouraged selectively while safeguarding the interests of traditional weavers of Mizoram.

Culture

In Mizoram people are getting the best possible education and the process of modernisation has enveloped all aspects of life in Mizo society. But it still has its traditional dances and festivals which are preserved. The dances are common to the Mizos, the Lakhers and Pawis, the main tribes in the state, along with the Chakmas who are believed to have migrated there from the neighbouring Chittagong hills of Bangladesh much before independence. Many more Chakmas, who are Buddhists, came as refugees after independence because of religious persecution by the Muslims in the Chittagong Hills and because their lands have been taken away by the land-hungry people from the plains of Bangladesh.

Mizos are well advanced and have taken up occupations and services in neighbouring states and at the centre. They can thus be seen in sufficient numbers in places far and near their state. Wearing of hats is common and these are made of bamboo and cane. The villagers carry an artistically designed and handwoven shoulder bag in which they carry their tobacco pipe and other equipment. Both men and women smoke although the pipes for the two are different. *Zu* is an alcoholic drink brewed indigenously from rice. There were several occasions when the entire village would indulge in an orgy of drinking and *Zu* would flow like water. Now the spread of Christianity, the modern ways of living and the impact of education have all helped in curbing drinking among the people although it cannot be said to have been eliminated.

Marriages are generally arranged by parents among the Mizos. Among them there is yet another interesting custom of inheritance. The youngest son inherits all the movable and immovable property of the father. The elder sons are supposed to move out of the parental home after marriage. The youngest son has the responsibility of looking after the parents in their old age. There was no system of making a will in the Mizo society but an Inheritance Act was passed by the Mizo District Council in 1956 under which a will could be made by any property holder.

There are some very good principles of self-help and cooperation in the Mizo social customs. The Mizos are expected to contribute labour for the welfare of the community. Services are rendered to the people in distress as a social obligation.

Religion

Majority population of the state is under the religious fold of Christianity. According to the 1991 Census report, about 85.73 per cent of the total population is Christians. Christianity in the hill tracts of north-eastern region spread as a result of the British religious policy in the area. At present almost all of the hill tribal population is Christian.

The greatest contribution of Christianity has been the spread of education. The Lushai and other tribal languages. The priests are mostly from South India. The churches are spread throughout the hills in villagers. Most of these churches have schools attached to them. The tribal Christians celebrate Christmas with full enthusiasm.

There are scattered populations of Buddhists in different parts of the state. Buddhists form the 7.83 per cent of the total population. The process of Buddhist festivals sees a variety in religious rites. Festivals and fairs form an integral part of their life.

The Hinduism in Mizoram seems to have been adopted after the period of animism. The geographical isolation of Mizoram seems to be the major factor to resist the immediate religious transformation from animism to any sect of Hinduism, Shaivism and Vaishnavism.

In ancient period there was a Hindu Majority in Mizoram. After the arrival of Westerners conversion took place in a massive rate and majority of the tribals converted as Christians. Current there is only 5.04 per cent of Hindus are in the State.

The Hinduism of Mizoram has a peculiar character showing the indigenous character. The ritualistic performances are carried out by youngsters especially women. Hindus show warmth of humanity in their hearts. There are no social or religious restrictions to accept any one visiting their homes. Most of them have deep knowledge of the Guru, Mahabharata, Ramayana and the Puranas. They will show their temple, deities and other things without hesitation and queries. If there is some festivals in the temple, they will invite others to witness the festival.

Islam entered through the Muslim migrants from East Bengal, but Muslim population in the valley is very little (0.66 per cent). They are a section of people who are Mohammedans. All Mizo Muslims read Koran. The holy book is translated in Mizo languages. The days solemn business of daily routine of Musalman's starts with the Lord's prayer. The Mizo Muslims observe two festivals in a year. They are Ramjan or Roza Id and Bakrid. Haj pilgrimage is performed by several Muslims in Mizoram.

Customs and Traditions

The most permeating factor in the Mizo society was the rule of the chiefs. Mizo chief was the guardian of the society. A son of a chief, after marriage would get from his father a new rite to set up his own village and some families would be allotted by his father to go to the new village under the new chief. Thereafter, he ruled as an independent chief. The youngest son inherited his father's village.

The chief was a despot, but he had to rule according to custom; otherwise the subjects would leave the arbitrary chief and move over to other chief. The society was egalitarian and the chief was one amongst his fellow villagers. The presents given to the chief were often treated as common property and all villagers could take some share out of it. But at the same time the chief was the owner of the village and the surrounding land. He could ask his people to furnish him with everything that he required.

Every man was bound to labour for the chief three days in a year. Each house in the village contributed its share of any expense incurred in feeding or entertaining the chief's guests. The villagers would voluntarily offer their services to build the house of the chief. They would also help in his cultivation. The power of the chief would have to be so exercised as to keep intact the village without attrition. Anyone finding the rule of the chief oppressive, despite the risk of having his paddy confiscated could migrate to a rival chief who would very much welcome such additions to his strength.

The chiefs were assisted, aided and advised by a group of elders (Upas). They would discuss all matters concerning the villages and adjudicate all disputes. Three or four upas would sit with the chief to hear and decide cases. In all such cases, customary procedures would be strictly followed. Punishments were also according to age old customs. As remuneration for their efforts in trying cases the upas received fees, called Salam. Usually, the party who lost the case would pay the Salam.

Before money, economy was introduced most of the punishment was in terms of fine paid in kind like giving a mithun, a pig or a fowl. Gradually, with money flowing into Mizo economy, cash alternative came into being.

The ceiling of fine was put at forty rupees which was a very considerable sum during those days. The rate of Salam was fine rupees. The fine would be paid as compensation to the aggrieved party. The Salam would be spent by the chief and his upas on feast. The offenders would pay fine within the period fixed by the chief. In case of default, proportionate property of the person would be confiscated to meet the demand. In case of habitual defaulters, the chief would turn him out of the village.

There were traditional village officials apart from the upas as part of the chief's administration. They were appointed by the chief's for specific functions. Every village had a village crier, called tlanger, who would go round the village in the evening and proclaim the chief's orders. As remuneration for his work, the tlamgau would get basket of paddy from each household.

Each village had a blacksmith, called thirdeng, who make agricultural implements and weapons for the villagers. He would get one basket of paddy from each of the families. In addition, he would get a fixed share consisting of the spine and three ribs of every animal shot or trapped by any villager. To perform village ceremonials there would be a village priest, the puithiam. He conducted all sacrifices to propitiate the spirits.

For his services he would get paddy from the villagers. Then there were the ramhuals who advised the chief where Jhum for the year should be done. As remuneration, the ramhuals, would get, after the chief, the first choice of their jhum plot in the site selected. For their preference in selecting their own plots they paid higher tax (fathang) to the chief. There were other appointed persons to help the chief in his personal matters. The Zalen would assist the chief when the Chief's household ran short of paddy and help him in other similar difficulties.

For his services to the chief he was exempted from

payment of fathang. There were two other officials to assist the chief in his own personal matters. The sadwat was the private priest of the chief to conduct his sacrifices and ceremonials. He would be assisted by the tlahpawi, who was usually a friend of the chief.

Like the institution of chieftainship, most of the tribes have a system of bachelor's dormitory where the young men learn the customs of the tribes and get indoctrinated into the norms of social behaviour. The Lushais had in every village a bachelor's dormitory, called Zawlbuk. The Zawlbuk would be situated at prime place in the village, generally opposite the chief's house. The hall of the Zawlbuk would be big enough to accommodate all the young men of the village. The hearth in the centre of the hall would always have a smouldering fire. Every evening, after the days work, the young men would gather in the Zawlbuk and would have common pastimes like wrestling, singing songs, telling stories, etc. Later in the evening, the young men would go round the village in nula rim, to court the young girls. Late in the night they would return to the Zawlbuk which had raised sleeping platforms. Usually travellers halting at a village for the night would stay at the Zawlbuk. The chief also used the hall of the Zawlbuk to hold meetings of the villages as this would be the only common hall and the biggest hall available in the village.

All the young men of the village would be available in the Zawlbuk for emergencies and common work for the village. Along with the spirit of co-operation, completion would be encouraged. The most industrious young men and the best hunter among then would be rewarded with special cups of zutaima zuns given to the former and huai zuno to the latter.

Boys, naupangs, till they attained puberty would live with their parents, but they were required to do odd jobs for the young men of the Zawlbuk like collecting fire wood and helping in the digging of graves by carrying bamboos and stones. Once they attained puberty they would be admitted to the full membership of Zawlbuk. The naupangs were commanded by a captain called hotu. There would be a number of hotus in the village—one for each veng or part of a village. They would ensure complete control by the Zawlbuk over all the boys in the village. Every morning there would be roll calls to ensure attendance of all boys and young men in the Zawlbuk. The leader of the young men of the Zawlbuk, called tlangval upa, would distribute work among the inmates of the Zawlbuk and enforce discipline amongst them. A review would be done to see that the boys had done their work as allotted to them. The defaulters would be allotted extra work to compensate.

Zawlbuk had a strict system of discipline. There was an interesting system of punishment for the recalcitrant. If the father of a boy would admonish or assault a hotu for ill-treatment of his son, all the tlangvals would gather at the house of the offending man and vigorously shake the house to make it nearly tumble down. This treatment would be sufficiently deterrent for others not to interfere in enforcement of discipline by the hotus. Only the chief of the village had some control over the Zawlbuk. He could throw a stone on the roof of the Zawlbuk signaling the young men to quiet down if they made too much noise at night. Theft of any article from the Zawlbuk would attract fine of forty rupees, irrespective of the value of the article.

Zawlbuk was mostly prevalent in Lushai and Pawi villages. The Raltes did not have this system but adopted it after coming under influence of the Lushais. The Paites did not have Zawlbuk as such, but young men would sleep in the verandah or front porch of the houses of influential men of the village who would provide adequate sleeping platform for the purpose. They would help their host in construction and repairs of his house and also in his cultivation, who in return would occasionally give them a feast.

The Lakhers did not have Zawlbuk. The young men, however, did not sleep in their parents house. They would sleep in the house of the maidens whom they were courting.

Tlawmngaihna

There was an excellent custom called Tlawmugaihna by which one was duty bound to help others. Under this custom everyone was required to be courteous and considerate and to help others always and every time, irrespective of one's inconvenience. Every one would try to surpass others in unselfishness and cooperation. This was an excellent custom in the daily life of a Lushai.

With the advent of Christianity the institution of Zawlbuk and the custom of tlawmngaihna gradually died. The Christian in a village would not join a Zawlbuk and hence when the majority in a village become Christians, the Zawlbuk in the village languished and ultimately become extinct. Similar was the fate of tlawmngaihna. When the people were turning away from their old beliefs, the customary network of duties and obligations was also snapped. New structures and institutions like village churches, schools, medical centres and administrative centres, etc., were coming up. The people started depending, individually and collectively, more on the church and the Government for guidance and help.

Bawi

In the hills social system permitted was partly a type of slavery and partly a system of social security. Amongst the Lushais this was the system of the bawi. Under this system a chief would have a number of dependants (bawis) who would remain with the chief, work for him and help him in all respects and in turn would get food and shelter from the chief. He could free himself from the obligation to the chief only under certain conditions, usually on giving a mithun or payment of certain amount.

Apart from the bawis, there was another class of dependants consisting of the persons captured during raids. They were called sals. The victors in a raid would kill the adult warriors and old women of the defeated side. The marriageable women and children would be taken captives. They would be treated well in the captor's family.

Sei

Lakher counterpart of the Lushai bawi was Sei. Unlike the Lushais among whom only the chiefs could have bawis, the Lakhen custom allowed anyone to keep one's captive as a Sei. A Sei was sometimes allowed to set up his own house hold. But the obligation was hereditary. A Sei could acquire property of his own, but his master could always take a share of the crops or animals of the Sei.

With the British administration prohibiting raids by the chiefs, the custom of tuklut bawi, sal and sei ceased to have new entrants. The custom was of mutual assistance, help and obligation and not of slavery. The bawi was after treated as a part of the family and could be adopted in the family by the saphun (adoption) ceremony.

The bawi custom gradually died. The administration liberally allowed freedom of the bawis on usual cash payment. A bawi was allowed to leave at will and the chief only had the remedy to sue for the compensation.

Customary Dues

There were many types of taxes and dues traditionally payable by the villagers to their chief. There were dues payable to the village officials and companions in hunt. The payments were in kind, mostly in paddy in case of cultivation and a portion of the animal in case of a hunt. Some of the important due are described below.

Fathang : It was in the nature of land revenue for

cultivated land. A chief had jurisdiction over a certain tract of land (ram). When a villager would cultivate a land in the ram of a chief he would pay a predetermined measure of paddy to the chief. The earlier measure of heaps was replaced by that of empty Kerosene caus or tins. Normally fathang was fixed at six tins (twenty litre kerosene tins) of unhusked paddy. In lieu, two rupees in cash could also be paid.

Sachhiah : It was the share of the animal hunted or trapped by a villager, which he gave to the chief of his village. The consisted of the animals left foreleg. If sachhiah was not paid, the defaulter was fined forty rupees and salam as compensation to the chief.

Sabawp : These were the dues payable to companions in hunting. When an animal was wounded by one but caught in chase by another, the latter was entitled to a hind leg. One who touched the animal first had the first claim. If an animal was shot by a hunter with a borrowed gun, the lender of the gun would get the right foreleg. The thian or friend of the man shooting the animal would get the ears and a piece of flesh. Thus the flesh of a hunt would be shared by the hunter with the chief, the companion in hunting and many others making hunting a collective effort and a collective gain.

Khuaichhiah : Honey collection from the forest was an important source of food for the Mizos. The chief was entitled to a share of the honey collected by his subjects. This due was called Khuaichhiah. This included honey and wax.

Chi-Khur-Chhiah : This was the share of salt given to a chief. Salt was a prized commodity in the hills. One of the commodities for which a Mizo would walk a number of days to go to a market in the plains was salt. But sometimes mineral salt would be available in the rocks. Anyone collecting such salt would pay a share to the chief from whose ram the salt was collected.

Hnathlang : Villagers had certain obligations to do common work for the village and the chief. This was in the form of voluntary labour called hnathlang. Everyone in the village would contribute voluntary labour to build the Zawlbuk, clear all jungles in and around the village, clear and fence the source of water supply. A chief could call upon his villagers to contribute for his private work also.

The Lakher villager performed certain common duties which was similar to Lushai hnathlang and was called tlaraihria in lakher. Anyone refusing or failing to do tlaraihria would be fined (leu) to pay rice, fowl, axe or dao or one rupee in cash. If paid in cash or by rice, the chief and the elders would use it to have some beer.

Customs of Lakher

In Lakher villages, there were regular system for contribution by villagers for common entertainment, general feast and other general purposes. By the custom of Sathi a villager was required to kill a pig for a common feast or for entertaining a visiting chief of for some other similar entertainment. By a custom called vohel, a piglet, immediately after its birth would be collected for any purpose chosen by the villagers. Sakhei was a system of subscription of paddy for village entertainment to a distinguished visitor or for a similar other purposes. The Lakhers followed the tradition of hospitality. By duty of tlongang every Lakher was required to be hospitable.

Birth

The Lakhers would perform sakia ceremony to beget children. The pregnant woman and her husband would have to follow certain restrictions—like not participating in some sacrifices, crossing a river or touching *a* corpse. While delivering, the expectant mother kneeled down by the side of a bed and female relations helped her in the delivery. After birth, the baby would be given a bath in cold water to wake it up and the mother would bathe in warm water. The baby would not be taken out the house for three days. On the fourth day the baby would be taken out in the village street and its earlobes would be pierced for wearing earrings. On the ninth or tenth day, the former for a girl and the latter for a boy, a fowl would be sacrificed at the spot of the birth. After this ceremony, called radeide, the child was taken to pupa's house and pupa would give some meat or fowl and rice. On this day the baby's hair would be cut and it would be kept short till the child was eight or nine years old; thereafter the hair would be kept uncut and tied in a knot for a boy or a bun for a girl. Two or three months after the birth, a ceremony called nawhri was performed to propitiate the child's shri or disease germ to keep it free from illness. A child would be given two or three names to help God remember at least one of the names. Generally a boy would get a name same as the grandfather's and the girl, grandmother's.

Inheritance

The Lakher system of inheritance was patrilineal. The eldest son would inherit the property of the father. Generally, he would share the property with his youngest brother. The sons in the middle or the daughter or the widow would not get any share. In the absence of sons, the property would go to the brothers-eldest and the youngest brothers. If a person died leaving behind a widow and minor children, the widow would take care of the property and the children. In case of the widow remarrying anyone except the brother of the deceased, the property and the care of the children would vest in the brother of the deceased.

A Lakher did not have any right to make any will regarding the disposal of his property after his death. The line of inheritance was determined by custom and it could not be changed. Nor was it left to one to refuse an inheritance. Along with inheritance went the obligation to discharge the debts and obligations of the person from whom inheritance flowed.

Death

The Lakhers believed that one would die when the God or the spirits would be angry with one and hence would snatch away one's soul from the body. When one is very sick, he would be placed on the floor near the bed and would be surrounded by friends and relatives. When death would be imminent one would be raised up to a sitting position and would die in the arms of the relations. A gun would be fired, if there was a gun in the house, to inform villagers about the death. After death, the soul would go to the abode in the other world where the status and condition of the soul would be similar to those in this world. Those who attained virtues by killing certain number and categories of wild animals like tiger, elephant or bear would go to paradise called peira, which was a place of bliss.

After death the body would be washed in warm water and it would be dressed in best clothes. Then it would be placed on a mat in a reclining position. Above the head a shelf would be made where rice, meat and egg would be placed. Friends and relatives would gather in the house, they would bring with them rice beer. Mithun, pigs and fowls would be sacrificed and feasts would be held for three days. Some food would be placed in the mouth of the dead. There would be dancing with beatings of drums and gongs. Thus the dead would happily go to athikhi.

The young men of the village would dig a grave in front of the house. The body would then be taken out one evening after three days of the death. The pupa of the deceased would perform some rituals and sacrifices and then the body would be laid to rest. On the grave some wooden posts would be put on which the heads of the animals killed in the funeral ceremony and some fruits would be placed. After some days a memorial stone would be erected on the grave.

Marriage

The custom relating to courtship amongst the Lakhers was similar to that of the Lushais. The boy and the girl after they started courting would share work in the field and would be together during the day. At night the suitor would sleep in the girl's house, gradually, with consent of the girl, advancing further. Anyone accusing young unmarried persons of having intimate relationship was fined an earthen beer pot, racha, or ten rupees and also a portion of meat, vopia.

Unlike under the Lushai custom, the fine was payable irrespective of whether the charge was true or not. The Lakhers generally had their brides selected by their parents. Marriage was generally outside one's own family. Marriage amongst very close relatives was rare. Maternal uncle's daughter was considered a favourable match.

The marriage negotiation started with the boy's father sending an emissary (leuchapa) to the girl's parents with the proposal and a present of a dao. If the latter had a lucky dream—dreams of fish, clear water, necklace, gun or dao, that night the proposal would be accepted. If the dream was unlucky—dreams of animals shot or killed by tiger, dead snakes, anyone stealing pig or fowl were considered unlucky and the proposal would be rejected.

Once the proposal was accepted, bride price would be negotiated over rice beer in the house of the girl's father. With the settlement of the price, the marriage date would be fixed. On the marriage day, certain number of pigs would be killed by both the sides. After drinking sahma, the bridegroom's marriage procession would start from his house. There would be exchange of several gifts like dao, axe, cotton thread, etc., before the bride and her party would enter the groom's house.

The groom and the bride would sit around a beer pot where the marriage ceremony would take place.

Some ceremonial beer drinking would take place when the groom and the bride would drink beer together, a fowl would be sacrificed and songs would be chanted. Then the bride would return to her parents' house. Next day, the father of the bride along with friends would go to the groom's house with a pot of beer and would get the bride price, in full or in part.

The day would be spent in feast and drinks. In the evening, the bride would again return to her parents place. The third day was the day of gifts. The groom would present pork, fowl and cash to the relations and friends of the bride. On the fourth day, the bride would finally move over to her husband's place which would be thoroughly cleaned for the occasion and a fowl would be sacrificed for casting out all evils and ensuring good jhum and crops for the couple.

Unlike the Lushais, the Lakhers did not consummate the marriage on the nuptial night. For some, months, the young husband would sleep in some other house and continue courting his wife. After an interval considered decent enough by custom, the husband would consummate the marriage and remain permanently in his house.

The marriage price of each clan differed higher the clan, higher was the price. The marriage price of a Lakher girl consisted of a main price called, 'angkia' and various subsidiary prices and dues. The rates were fixed in number of different types of animals or house hold goods or in their cash equivalents. The rate of angkia varied from ten rupees to seventy rupees. Angkia is given to the father of the bride and if he was dead, to the eldest brother. But generally angkia would be shared by the father and all the brothers. Angkia was composed of many different prices like mithun, brass and earthen pots, etc. payable to father, brothers, father's brothers, father's friend etc. For getting a major portion of angkia, the claimant had to kill a certain number of pigs, usually three.

The subsidiary prices and dues were many—these rates were related to the rates of angkia puma was the price payable to the bride's maternal uncle, pupa. This amount, equivalent to angkia, was payable at different times from the day of marriage and when the couple settled down. The pupa must kill a pig before he claimed puma and after puma was paid he would give the bride an embroidered skirt and a white cloth or ten rupees.

Nongcheu was the price payable to the bride's mother if she was divorced and if not, to the mother's sister and in the absence of both to the brother. Here also pig, was to be claimed by the claimant and in return the groom was to kill a pig and the cooked or uncooked meat and beer would be sent by one to the other party. Nongcheu, aunts' price, was payable to the bride's eldest paternal aunt. Here also formalities of killing pigs and sharing the meat is followed. Apart from these main dues, there were minor dues, known as ahlas, which would be given to the chief, an elder, the cooks, beer makers and meat carriers, etc.

Festivals

In Mizoram, there are three main festivals in a year. Festivals are called Kut in Mizo language. The three Kuts are Chapchar Kut, Mim Kut and Pawl Kut. All the three festivals are connected with agricultural activities. The festivals are celebrated with feasts and dances.

Chapchar Kut

Chapchar Kut was celebrated after completion of the cutting of jhums. It was a thanksgiving festival. The villagers faced many dangers and difficulties in cutting down dense forests with their simple Daos and axes. They would organise a big feast in the month of March to celebrate the success in jhum cutting. The festival continued for seven days and even beyond if the villagers would afford it.

Mim Kut

The Mim Kut was a festival celebrated before the hard work in the jhum was over. It would take place in September. The festival lasting for one or two days would be in memory of someone who had died during the previous year. Fresh vegetables, maize bread, necklaces and cloth would be placed on the memorials of the dead as offerings to them. It was believed that their spirits would revisit their house during the Mim Kut. Zu would be taken in houses in which someone had died during the year. On the second day everybody would have a meal of bread.

Pawl Kut

Pawl Kut was the harvest festival which was celebrated after the village had gathered its harvest. Lasting for one to two days, the villagers would feast and dance in thanksgiving for the harvest. There is a legend regarding the origin of this festival. In the olden days when the Mizos were living to the east of the Tiau river in the Chin hills, which is now in Burma, there was famine for three consecutive years. In the fourth year the people had a bumper crop. The people believed that this was a blessing of the supreme god and as a thanksgiving they celebrated Pawl Kut.

It was customary for everyone to eat meat and eggs during Pawl Kut. A few days before the day is fixed for the feast, the men would go out hunting wild animals, trapping birds or fishing. One would get as much meat as one's means would permit. Even the poorest would kill at least a fowl for the household feast. As in Chapchar Kut, mothers and children would gather together at the Lungdawh bringing with them plates of rice, boiled eggs and meat and feed one another performing Chhawnghnawt. The youngmen and girls would also attend the Chhawnghnawt. The men would gather in the houses of well-to-do persons and Zu would be drunk. The festivities were followed by Eipuar Awm Ni or the day of rest. As Christianity spreads in Mizoram these festivals gradually faded out.

Ceremonies Connected with Cultivation

After sowing, the main work is periodic weeding. A well burnt jhum would remain comparatively clear of weeds, otherwise growth of weeds would be prolific and labourious weeding would have to be carried out intensively. After the last weeding in September, the cultivators celebrate the end of the hard season by having songs, dances and feasts. The vegetables in the jhum are harvested in June and July, maize in August, and the early paddy in September. The harvest of the principal paddy starts in the middle of October and ends by the middle of December.

The men and women cut the ripened paddy ears and they are brought to the jhum hut where the grains are separated from the chaff by trampling on them. The first such operation is celebrated by friends and relatives over feasts and sing—songs. Also sometimes threshing and winnowing are done from a platform about 3 m high with a sieve. After the harvest has been collected in the jhum hut, the paddy is shifted to the home in the village. Thus, almost the whole year is spent in the full operation of one jhum.

Paddy is commonly measured in terms of a full-load of kerosene tin which contain about 8 Kg. of paddy. Three tins of paddy measure a load called phur. A Mizo considers 15 phurs of paddy as the annual food requirement per person. This comes to about a Kg. of paddy per day. There are different traditional measures of the conical heap of paddy when the collected paddy is put together before threshing. Mipa Zawn means the heap unto a man's height and Hmeichhe-zawn, up to a woman's height. Kak zawn is a heap going up to the fork of thumb and index finger when the hand is vertically raised above the head. Silai zawn is up to the end of a gun held vertically above the head of a man.

Apart from the main jhum field, every household has a small field generally near the house or at the bottom end of the jhum, where vegetables and maize are grown. This is like a kitchen garden. It is called Leipui and is very convenient and useful for every family.

There were ceremonies and sacrifices connected with each phase of jhumming. *Rialongchhi* ceremony was performed by the whole village when the jhum was half cut. The villagers would gather in the middle of the village with a particular type of fruit and make a bonfire. After the jhum were fully cut the villagers would perform a dance called Pakhupila and a feast Khutla, would be held. Everyone in the village would participate in the festival for good crops.

The rich men of the village would liberally provide beer and others would also contribute. Pigs and fowls would be killed for the feast. For two to three days men and women would dance, going from one house to another. Accompanied by drums and gongs the men alternating with women would form a ring and with arms over shoulders the dance would go on in slow rhythm over long periods. After this festival, the jhums were burnt and paddy was sown in the field. This festival was to make everyone happy and fit to start the hard work in the jhum for good crops.

The next ceremony was *Leuhrangna* which performed jointly by the ones whose jhums were adjacent. They would sacrifice a sow and a red cock or a boar of same size and a hen to propitiate the spirit of the slope on which their jhums were situated. Another sacrifice performed was Sachipachhua when a black fowl would be sacrificed and some seeds of rice and other crops which had been sown would be anointed with the blood.

Before the second weeding a sacrifice called Chithla was performed. This was to please the spirit of the field who would protect the crops from animals and ensure a good harvest. Posts were erected in front of each jhum house and fowls, pigs, dogs, etc., would be sacrificed and certain ceremonies of cooking in a jhum house with the use of salt were performed. After the paddy plants had been pulled up and before the grain had been gathered, a sacrifice called Leuhmathawna was performed in front of each jhum house.

With chanting for bountiful crops a red hen would be sacrificed and seeds would be anointed with blood. After the sacrifice, the people would go to the field and collect the paddy. During the harvest strangers were prohibited from entering into a jhum house. There was also prohibition for eating certain types of meat like bird and rat. After threshing, the grains would be collected in a granary in the jhum house.

On storage of all the paddy, a sacrifice called Sikisa would be performed in which a white fowl or a dog would be sacrificed and the family would come to the village to eat a meal with meat. While returning to the village, the people would blow a bamboo whistle to call back their spirits from the jhum to the village.

After the harvest a ceremony called *Pazusata* would sometimes be performed. This was the feast for the children of the entire village. The chiefs and all others would contribute meat, particularly of barking deer and porcupine. The whole village would have saved some such meat and preserved it as dried meat for this purpose. Barking deer was treated as the weeder of the jhums and porcupine by turning soil would make it fertile. On this occasion there would be the sacrifice of a fowl at the Tleulia ground and families would bring cooked rice. The chief and the men would drink beer at the tleulia ground from a common pot through reeds.

The boys would have a bonfire in front of the chief's house and would dance round it. They would collect contributions from each house and would have feasts which would continue for two or three days. During these feasts the boys would recount aloud the scandals and gossip of the village regarding philandering and other escapades. This had a good effect on morals in the village as it would keep in check bad or frivolous adventures.

There was another ceremony which was ancestor worship for good crops. This was called *Laliachhia* and was performed around October every year. A broad road would be made in the village for this purpose and the villagers would march on this road accompanied by beatings of drums and gongs. A rich man of the village would be selected to perform the sacrifice. He provided sahma to everyone who came to his house. A red hen would be sacrificed. The villagers would visit the graves of the people who had died during the previous three years and offer them food.

When the grain had been stored in the granary, a pig or a red hen would be sacrificed in the granary invoking the paddy to increase and last from the present winter to the next so that the family would have sufficient rice to eat. This ceremony was called *Sawa Awhthi.* After husking the paddy, the rice for daily use would be stored in a pot in the house. For the rice to last a sacrifice called Bei Pariawthi would be performed in which a fowl would be killed and blood of the fowl would be sprinkled over the rice.

There were ceremonies to invoke the rain god for sufficient rain necessary for good crops. In the ceremony to call rain, *Khitiawna,* a selected person of the village would plant a cardamom stalk in the village street. By rubbing the plant, sounds resembling thunder would be made and some water symbolising rain would be poured on the man. In another ceremony a stone with a hole in it which would contain water would be taken near the river and a sacrifice of a fowl would be made after emptying the water.

The spirit of the stone, it was hoped, would get the rain-deity to pour rain and fill up the empty hole in the stone. As against these magical ceremonies there was a direct devotional method by which a white fowl would be sacrificed with prayers to the rain god to come down to the earth.

Arts

Dance and Music

The dances of the Lushais, Pawis and Lakhers are mostly common. Most popular of the Mizo dances now is the cheraw or the bamboo dance. Six girls wearing colourful, ceremonial dresses and flower crowns as head gears squat on the ground holding bamboo poles which are rhythmically shifted and struck against one another. Six other girls dance, moving between the shifting bamboos. The dance has a fast rythm and symbolises the pulsating youth. Bamboo dance, exactly in this forms, is found in some south-east Asian countries, notably in the Phillipines.

Khal Lam

Khal Lam is another popular dance of Mizos in which a group of boys wearing specially made shawls dance to the beat of drums and gongs. The dancers wear one type of striped loin cloth (puan) and a uniform striped shawl (puandum). While one beats a gong, the dancers in a row more gradually forward, with small forward-backward steps, keeping with the time. The arms would be flayed, along with the steps.

On occasions of Chapchar Kut festival the boys and girls would dance chai the whole night. The boys would sit with their backs to the wall. Each boy would have a girl sitting in front of him, in between his knees, with her back towards him. Individual dancers would perform in the clearing in the middle, all the others joining in the music.

The young folk would perform another type of dance in the open courtyard. They would make a circle with a girl in between two boys with their arms over the shoulders of the girls. In the midst of the circle, one would beat a drum or gong and all in the circle would move forward and backward and would also progress slowly along the circle. The person in the middle would chant a song and the refrain would be taken up by all. All the time the dancers would get rounds of Zu and the dance would last as long as the supply of Zu could be kept up.

Sawlakin

Another popular dance is *Sawlakin.* This was originally a Lakher dance, but now it has been adopted by all the Mizas. Sawlakia means spirit of the slain. The dance was led by the warrior who had hunted a big game or killed a man. He would wear his best clothes and a plume of red feather. He would wield a gun or dao and a shield.

He would be followed by other dancers in a row, who would also carry weapons, or cymbals or gongs. Some boys would stand in a group beating drums or blowing bugles. The dancers would move forward and slowly go round the head. While dancing weapons and shields would be wielded keeping time with drum or gong beats. All the time dancers would be plied with Zu by the women. This dance is a popular dance now. The modifications now are that there is no head in the circle and no Zu.

Chhilam

Chailam is a popular dance performed on the occasion of 'Chapchar Kut' one of the most important festivals of the Mizos. In this dance, men and women stand alternatively in circles, with the women holding on to the waist of the man, and the man on the women's shoulder. In the middle of the circle are the musicians who play the drums and the mithun's horn.

The musician playing the drum choreographs the entire nuances of the dance while the one with the mithun's horn chants the lyrics of the 'chai' song. For the dance to start, the drummer beats on the drum, and upon the fourth stroke of the drum the chai song is sung with the rhythmic swaying of the dancers to the left and right, in accordance with beats of the drum.

Depending on the nuances followed, the chailam' has four versions, viz 'Chai Lamthai I', 'Chai Lamthai II', Chai Lamthai III and 'Chai Lamthai IV'. Legend has it that once a king and his men went out for hunting. Unfortunately, they failed miserably and had to be contended without a kill.

The king, then seeing the utter disappointment of his men, rose to the occasion and consoles them by inviting them for a drink of rice beer at his palace. On being intoxicated by the drinks, the party then culminated by singing and dancing followed by a sumptuous feast.

Since then, every year, the community continues to enliven the memory of this occasion be celebrating it with various entertainment programs, thus giving rise to one of the most important festivals of the Mizos, the 'Chapchar Kut'. In this dance, musical instrument like drum and horns of mithun are used for making beats. The festivals continues for a week or more. In olden days, the 'Chai' dancers used to drink rice beer continuously during singing and dancing.

Chawnglaizawn

This is a popular folk dance of one of the Mizo communities known as Pawi. It is performed by a husband to mourn the death of his wife. The husband would be continuously performing this dance till he gets tired. Friends and relatives would relieve him and dance on his behalf. This signifies that they mourn with the bereaved. Chawnglaizawn is also performed on festivals and also to celebrate trophies brought home by successful hunters. On such occasions, it is performed in groups of large numbers. Boys and girls standing in rows dance to the beat of drums. Shawls are used to help the movement of the arms, which also adds color to the dance. Only drums are used in this dance.

Chheihlam

'Chheihlam' originated after the year 1900 on the lines of the songs known as 'Puma Zai' and the dance known as Tlanglam'. It is a dance that embodies the spirit of joy and exhilaration. It is performed to the accompaniment of a song called 'Chheih hla'. People squat around in a circle on the floor, sing to the beat of a drum or bamboo tube while a pair of dancers stand in the middle, recite the song and dance along with the music. It was a dance performed over a round of rice beer in the cool of the evening.

The lyrics are impromptu and spontaneous on the spot, compositions recounting their heroic deeds and escapades and they also praise the honored guests present in their midst. While singing the song accompanied by sound produced by beating of the drum or clapping of hands, an expert dancer performs his dance chanting verses with various movements of the body, with limbs close to the body and crouching low to the ground.

As the tempo rose and the excitement increases, people squatting on the floor leave their seats and join him. Guests present are also invited to join the dance. Today 'Chheihlam' is performed on any occasion with colorful costumes, normally in the evening when the day's work is over.

Tlanglam

Tlanglam is performed throughout the length and breadth of the State. Using music of Puma Zai, there have been several variations of the dance. This dance is one of the most popular dances these days by our cultural troupes in various places. Both sexes take part in this dance.

Zangtalam

Zangtalam is a popular Paihte dance performed by men and women. While dancing, the dancers sing responsive song. A drummer is a leader and director of the dance. The duration of the dance depends on the drummer.

Mizo traditional songs and dances were the common amusements of the people. A Zu party would always be an occasion for songs and dances. The songs were slow and generally sounded mournful. Songs would be accompanied by beat of drums or gongs. The theme would mostly be narration of some events or praise of some hero or former villages, description of some hunt or simply of love. In a gathering of Zu party or on the occasion of marriage or after a successful hunt, one would start the music by reciting a verse and it would be followed by singing of the verse by all others and this would continue in the same sequence for a long time sometimes even throughout the night.

The young Mizos have, in the recent past, taken up western music and dances with great aplomb. In all the villages, groups of young men and women gather in the evening and sing and dance, sometimes the whole night. The only musical instrument used is the Spanish guitar, called ting tang by the Mizo. The young Mizos, both boys and girls, have a very lilting musical voice and they have a natural flair for music. A very recent development is pop music with a composite band which is popular in towns and big villages.

Crafts

The original garment of the Mizos is known as *puan.* They were used by men and women more or less in the same fashion. One has to see them to believe the intricate traditional designs woven by the Mizo women, born weavers who produce what can only be described as art on their looms. The Mizo have held on to certain patterns and mottos that have come down through the ages. These design have become deep rooted in their tribal consciousness and has become a part of the Mizo heritage. The unique value of *Mizo PUAN* comes from the personal involvement of the weaver, who with great labour weaves her dreams into each work and weft until every design has a story to tell. These traditional hand woven apparels are of different shades and designs without exquisite play of colour combination and intricate weaving patterns has been evolved.

3 Social and Cultural History of the Mizos

The Mizos are Tibeto-Burma people who in course of time, arrived in the Chin Hills of Burma from Southern China along with other ethnic tribes as a result of population movements. They lived there for centuries and formed themselves into a homogenous group of varying clans, thus settling down at various places. They developed their culture into different dimensions. Chieftainship was instituted as a single source of authority in the society. They also developed their economic life by inventing a new method of cultivation known as “slash and burn” the oldest system of cultivation in the world. In the same way, their religious life was also immensely improved by adding new chants and incantations to the existing ones. In short, the social and cultural life of the people in Burma had attained a certain degree of maturity in one form or the other.

The various systems thus developed in Burma were brought down by the people themselves to their present habitat for their continuous use. The purpose of this paper is, therefore, to throw some light on the structure of the pre-British social and cultural history of the Mizos in the erstwhile Lushai Hills. With this end in view, our discussion is condensed as follows :

The Family Structure

The family is perhaps the oldest institution in human society. In early Mizo society, family life centred round the father who exercised a prerogative power in the family with responsibility to procure food for the family through the "slash and burn" system also known as *jhuming.* Children gained inheritance through the paternal descent and lineage was traced through the male descendant. This is still true even today. Marriage was "by purchase" and the price was determined in terms of *sial* (*mithun*) which was of three kinds namely (1) *sepui ngalkal* (2) *tlai sial* and (3) *puisawm sial.* In fact, the girl's price was solely settled on mutual agreement of the two parties. The father could accept anything as equivalent to *sial.*[1]

As a general rule, exogamy was the system but the tendency among the Sailo clan was endogamy for they wanted to consolidate their position as a strong ruling family through marriage bonds. Although there were eases of polygamy,[2] the custom among the Mizos was monogamy.[3] Some Chiefs however, kept concubines in addition.

Social Institutions

Social institutions are the major components of human culture. In dealing with the social institutions of the Mizos we will discuss here only the major explicit cultures of the people namely *Zawlbuk, Bawi, Sal* and *Tlawmngaihna.*

Zawlbuk, the "bachelor's dormitory", fostered and nurtured a pure and uncorrupted life in the society. Hence, it was the most powerful agency in enforcing law and order in the village.

Its origin was probably connected with the inter-tribal feuds which were at times common among them. Therefore, all young men of the village would sleep together in one common place in case of emergency.[4] It may also be traced back to China where "Long Houses" and "Communal Houses" were found.[5] From there, the Tibeto-Burman peoples brought it down to different places in South-East Asia.[6] The Commander of the

Zawlbuk was known as *Valupa* and he was obeyed and respected in the society. A junior group known as *thingnawifawm.* However, supplied firewood and water to the *Zawlbuk* by turn.

Another important institution was *bawiship.* A person who surrendered himself for protection to the Chief for any reason was a *bawi* and lost the right of his freedom of action.[7] There were three kinds of *bawis* namely *inpuichhung bawi, chemsen bawi* and *tukluh bawi.*

The *inpuichhung bawi* was one who was driven by want of food and shelter because of extreme poverty and took refuge in the Chief's house. He was treated as member of the royal household. He was permitted to have and acquire a private property and freedom by paying one *mithun* or its equivalent in goods.[8]

The *Chemsen bawi* was a criminal who took refuge for his safety at the Chief's house. If a person had a chance to touch the Chief's *sutpui* (centre pillar of a house) he was saved. He, however, remained *bawi* during his life time.

The third category of *bawi* known as *tukluh bawi* was one who deserted his side and joined the victor in times of wars or feuds and promised to be *bawi* of his captor.[9] He lived in a separate house and could buy his freedom on payment of one *mithun* to the Chief.[10]

Lewin thus aptly remarked that the condition of these *bawis* was very little different from that of the free people.[11] According to Shakespeare, the custom was very suited to the society and it would be unwise to make attempt to alter it.[12] Parry was also of the view-that the system was appropriate to the Mizo society.[13] In spite of these positive views, yet many had a wrong notion on the custom of *bawi.* Dr. Peter Fraser was one such a man.

Very similar to the custom of *bawi* was *sal* (slavery). A person who was captured in times of wars or feuds and possessed by his captor was called *sal.*[14] Every household was entitled to keep as many *sal* as it could collect. Like *bawi*, he could buy his freedom by paying a big ransom. Webster said that unlike the neighbouring states there were a few number of *sals* among the Mizos.[15]

Tlawmngaihna, the unwritten moral code, was valued among the Mizos. A person who possessed it was honoured at a special function where he was presented a *Tlawmngai No,* the highest award ever presented to a meritorious person in the village.

Tlawmngaihna was also assessed among the unmarried girls. It was known as *hmeichhe tlawmngaihna* and was judged on the basis of how she received and welcomed her *inleng* (suitors). Honours were not, however, facilitated to them as they were to men.

The Village Life

In early Mizo society, village life was very simple. They lived a nomadic life which required selection of new sites for settlements at regular intervals. They took utmost care that the site should have a good source of water supply, and that it was an inaccessible and an impregnable place.[16] A team slept overnight at the proposed site with a cock but if the cock failed to crow at dawn, it would be taken as unhealthy for human settlement. Having selected the new village, it was arranged in such a way that the Chief's house and the *Zawlbuk* would be located first, followed by others. Houses were arranged in rows with one row facing another. No house was allowed to be built above the Chief's house.[17] Houses normally did not have windows.

Every village had a number of officials assisting the village Chief in discharging his daily duties. The officials were : the *upas,* the *tlangau,* the *thirdeng,* the *puithiam,* the *ramhual,* the *zalen* and the *khawchhiar.*[18] The last official was a British creation.

Every citizen, except the *Zalen* (free men or men of

possessions), were tax payers. *Fathang,* the main due paid to the Chief by every household was a fixed rate but paid according to the demand of the Chief. The other taxes were, *sachhiah, chikhurchhiah,* and *khuaichhiah, Thirdengchhiah,* a due payable to a village blacksmith was also paid. The Chief's house was built and repaired on voluntary basis in which every household was obliged to give labour for this purpose. The service thus rendered was also counted as part of the tax known as *thachhiah.*

Village handicrafts formed a very important part of the social and cultural life of the early Mizos. Besides their clothing, the distinctive crafts were also obviously observed in other articles like musical instruments, basketry, tools, utensils, weapons and traps. The role of the blacksmith in a village was considerably important because he made and repaired the tools of the village people. Therefore, each village paid tribute to its blacksmith.

Warfare and inter-tribal feuds were the dreadful activities which badly endangered the peaceful life of the people. Besides there were two kinds wars in which the whole community of the two parties were involved. They were the *leilawn mal zawha indo* and the *vawklu vuak thlaka indo.*[19] The latter was the custom mainly practised among the Lusei clan.

Before cotton was invented for use, men and women of the Mizos wore *hnawkhal* and *siapsuap* respectively. They were made of a coarse material from the bark of trees.[20] Later on, women used *hmaram pawnfen,* a petticoat coloured with various designs. *Kawkpui zikzial* and *lenbuangthuam* are the two beautiful designs which are still popular among Mizo women today. Both men and women wore earrings made of ivory. *Saingho, thihna, thimkual* and *dawhkilh* were common ornaments of women. A head-dress known as *vakiria* was worn only on important occasions.

Dances also marked the social and cultural life of

ancient Mizos. They were performed only on certain occasions like *khuangchawi*. *Chheihlam,* otherwise known as *zuhmunlam* was performed generally whenever *zu* drinking was held. The popular dances which are still preserved as traditional are *khuallam, cheraw, solakia, chheihlam, sarlamkai, sakeilulam etc.*

Dances are always accompanied by music. The early musical instruments of the people were *darkhuang, darmang, khuang, Mizo tingtang, phenglawng, rawchhem, benghung, lemlawi* and *tuiumdar*. These indigenous musical instruments are still significantly relevant even today. Indigenous games and sports were equally important in shaping the Mizos society *Inbuan* (wrestling) and *ritchawi* weightlifting) were the popular and common games. *Inbuan* was regularly held at the *zawlbuk* every evening. *Ritchawi* was done only on certain occassions. The stone used as *chawilung* was about 20-25 Kgs. weight. *Inzawnchuh,* an inter-village group fight over the carriage of a sick or dead person was another event in which even grown-up male of both the villages would be involved. It was always a fair-fight which the Chiefs of the two opposing parties witnessed. Another favourite game among the boys was *inhnawk,* and girls also played *inbah* (games played with *kawi*) *bahte, bahpui* and *insalman* were the different kinds of *inbah.*[22] Like other children of the world, Mizo boys and girls played *inbihruksiak* (hide and seek) fondly.

The Economic Life

Although the economy of early Mizos was simple, it was the mainstay of the people. Before paddy was cultivated Mizos used maize, millet, gums, arum-bulbs, sweet-potatoes etc. as their staple food.[23] We do not know when rice substituted these items but tradition says that rice was first cultivated only when they came to the Chin Hills of Burma.

Domestic animals like pigs, chicken, goats, *mithuns,*

dogs etc. played a very important part in the economic life of the Mizos. In addition to being important sources of food and protein, they were also used extensively, as sacrifices in rituals relatings to marriage, birth, death sickness, festivals and healing ceremonies.

Hunting also formed a part of the early Mizo economy. Elephants were hunted for their tusks and meat for food. Other animals and birds were also killed for their meat. Meat was the favourite food of the Mizos.[24] From time immemorial, fish is a delicious food of the people. They catch fish by trapping known as *ngawi.* They also catch them by stupefying the fish with poisonous materials locally known as *ru.*

Raids and wars sometimes brought wealth to the family. The booties were brought home, and the captives were employed by their captors at home. In this way, the slaves brought wealth to the owners in the form of increased labour power.[25]

Sial also played a significant role in the economic life of the people. It was the Chief measure of wealth and a wealthy man was one who possessed a good number of *sials.* Similarly, the girl's price was fixed in terms of *sial.* When a baby girl was born she was blessed as se *man tur* meaning "the she would-cost *mithun*". Its economic implication was that the girl would bring wealth to the family.

Salt, like today, was one of the economic items of the people. But being extremely difficult to procure for family consumption it was valued very much. It was consumed by the family only on certain occassions.

Cotton was also grown as an indigenous crop which they later developed for garments. They dyed their cloth from indigo grown in the locality.

Hnatlang, community work, was another aspect of the economic life of the Mizos. Since paid labour was not known, economically weaker sections of the people were supported and uplifted by this system. An inter-village path, a village spring, *jhum* path etc. were kept clean by the local people through this basis.

Zu drinking, being a part of social life, adversely affected the life of the people economically. They consumed a large quantity of rice for making it.

Tobacco, like cotton, was grown unlike today for local consumption and cultivated along with other agricultural crops.

Before money was circulated, the people bartered their agricultural items with other crops. In fact, they did not require many articles for their daily life. Their economic life was however, soon disrupted by the coming of currency and the subsequent establishment of trade centres at various places in Mizoram.

The Religious Beliefs

Although the origin of primitive religion is lost in oblivion, the possible theory is that there was a time when men thought that they could control the forces of nature. At the same time, there were many times when they failed to govern the spells with their own limited devices.[26] The moment they realised and accepted their failures and limitations, they turned and created supernatural beings, whose presence around them they mysteriously felt, to do what they could not do.

The primitive Mizo religion perhaps similarly originated. Tradition says that there was a time when they were in a state of bewilderment and confusion. In such precarious situations, the people probably began to feel that they greatly needed divine providence. But the were totally at a loss and full of apprehension about their future. Then they mooted that their forefathers should have a certain religion with a definite pattern of worship. On the strength of this belief they began their religion with a simple chant, saying *"pi biakin lo chhang ang che, pu biakin lo chhang ang che* meaning *"answer me whom our forefathers worshipped".*

Primitive religion had three fundamental characteristics : animism, ancestor worship or worship of the dead and worship of a supernatural being. A close examination of the Mizo religion shows that it had the same characteristics and was animistic in nature. Believing that the spirits lived in them, they, therefore, worshipped rocks and mountains etc.[27] Like other primitive people of the world the Mizos also worshipped their ancestors in *mithirawplam.* They also believed in the existence of a living Reality whom they believed to be the creator of the universe and the source of everything.[28]

Religion, like other aspects of culture, is subject to stages of development. The inclusion of *Lurh* and *Tan* ranges clearly indicate that the religion was undergoing changes in one form or the other. Consequently, slight differences in incantations emerged from clan to clan and village to village.

It appears that the Mizo religion was not a religion of community worship but performable by each individual household separately provided it had the means.[29]

They also believed in the existence of other subordinate good and evil spirits. They therefore performed sacrifices by offering animals with intent to satisfy the evil spirit, who caused sickness and misfortunes to men.[30]

The people also believed in the existence of life after death. They believed that there were two places of abode known as *mithikhua* and *pialral.*

Kut

Kut, a Mizo word for "festival" or "feast" is said to have originated from *Thlanrawkpa,* a Mizo legendary originator of the feast. Though the origin was not known, it is said that *kuts* had been observed while the Mizos lived in Burma.[31] There were three kinds of *kuts* namely *Mim Kut, Pawl Kut* and *Chapchar Kut.*

Mim Kut, otherwise known as *tahna kut* was linked with death. It was a *kut* in which offerings were made to the dead. It is said that the *kut* had its origin from *Ngama* and *Tlingi.* It was held for 3 days.

Pawl Kut got its name from the *Pawl* (straw). Held soon after the harvest was over, *Pawl Kut* was meant for children. *Chhawnghnawt* was the main event and lasted for a day.

Another colourful festival celebrated with pomp for four days was *Chapchar Kut.* Held soon after the cutting of a *jhum* was over, the origin of the *kut* was, however, lost in oblivion. The main important events of the feast were the *Chhawnghnawt* and the *Chai.* No squabbles were permitted nor should the couples quarrel during the feast.

Head-Hunting Custom

Head-hunting, a tribal way of life, was said to be found all over the world in one form or the other. According to Hutton, headhunting was practised and carried out for the following reasons :

First, it was done as an act of cannibalism with an intention to consume the body in order to transfer to the eater the soul matter of the eaten. Finally, it was connected with agriculture so that the soul could be imbued with the productivity.[32]

Formerly, the Mizos were known to outsiders as *milula hnam* meaning "head-hunters". The person who was most admired in the society was *mithat sa kap* which meant "slayer of both men and animals"'. Therefore, head-hunting among the people had three main purposes. In the first place, they needed heads for use at the ceremonies performed at the funeral of their Chiefs. A search for human heads thus usually happened quite soon after the death of a Chief.[33] Secondly, the Mizos desired heads to supply themselves with servitors in another world. For this purpose, any head even that of an embryo would serve the purpose. Lastly, he killed man and carried his head to prove that he was a warrior, and a slayer of man. The heads would be displayed as trophies at *sahlam* and at the *zawlbuk*.[34]

Earlier, killing women and carrying away their heads were avoided, but in course of time, it became an approved act for it was a great advantage for the enemy to kill a pregnant woman as this was taken as killing two persons at a time.[35]

When the heads of the enemies were brought home even children were asked to hit them with a *dao* because the action was considered as tantamount to killing enemies. As a recognition and appreciation of what he did, the family should hold a feast. Therefore, head-hunting had been undisputedly a fact of Mizo life until the advent of the British in the erstwhile Lushai Hills.

SOCIAL LIFE OF THE MIZOS : SOME ASPECTS

Society, by the most simple term, is a group of people living together with the purpose of helping one another. The Mizo society, like most tribal societies, is segmentary. There are obviously certain fields or forms in which the social life of the Mizos finds expression. In this study, an attempt is made to delineate what makes the social life of the Mizos possible. The period of study covers mainly the pre-British society. Further, it is proposed here to deal only with the explicit culture of the Mizo society.

The study is made under the following heads :

Jhumming Cultivation

Jhumming system of the Mizos depicts the kind of agro-social life of the Mizos was, and is, all about. The staple food of the Mizos is rice. People in the past earned their livelihood by practising shifting cultivation. The system was a part of tribal life since the age-old pre-historic times.[36] *Jhumming* is the method and technique of food production by the Mizos and many other tribes of North-east India.

The Mizo Village

The practise of shifting cultivation forced the Mizos to shift from one place to another. The whole village had to move in search of more productive lands. But they were very particular in making a new village. The selection of the new site was not that easy. They chose the steepest and most inaccessible hills to build their villages.[37] The hill top was the first favourite, secondly, an impregnable stronghold combined with a good water supply which would not dry up in the hot season. These two factors accounted mainly for the selection of the new village.[38] The final selection was made only after the superstitions obligations were performed. To do this, the elders would sleep at night at the proposed site along with a cock. If the cock did not crow before dawn, it would be taken as a bad omen. Then they had to abandon it and had to go for a suitable site.

Having found a suitable site for settlement, the village was planned with a sense of orderly designs. As far as practicable, they arranged the houses in two lines facing each other with a wide space or street in between. It was a practice that the Chief's house be built at the centre of the village. Then *Zawlbuk* was built just near the Chief's house. The houses of his *Upas* (advisers) were clustered together nearby the Chief's. No person was allowed to build a house above the Chief's.

When they moved to a new site they would not carry the hearths of the old village. Instead, the old hearth was dumped with water so that none of the misfortunes and disabilities of the abandoned village should venture further at they new site.

Type of the house

Since the Mizos were a migratory tribe, they did not build very strong houses. The houses were constructed in one uniform plan. They raised the houses some three or four feet from the ground. In the early stages of modern development, most of them used bamboo and ordinary saplings for the posts (pillars).[39] In later development, to be precise, the frameworks of the house were of timber and the walls and floors were of bamboo matting, For the roof they used leaves of local species like *di, thilthek, siallu, laisua,* etc.[40]

The houses were usually not big. There was, in front, a large verandah called *sumhmun* where a mortar was kept to husk the rice with pestless. Inside the house was a fire-place, and on one side of it was a raised sleeping place. There used to be no windows, the only openings being at the front and at the back of the house. Opening of windows was reserved only for those who had performed *Thangchhuah.*

Marriage

The system or form of marriage among the Mizos right from inception was 'marriage by purchase'. This means girls were purchased by paying the price. The price varied from clan to clan. They were very careful in selecting partners and it was normally an arranged affair. In selecting a partner, parents exercised great care and looked into the family history as far as they could trace it.

After the official function ceremony was over, the girl was escorted to her husband's house in the evening. On her arrival the bride was welcomed by offering a cup of *zu* followed by rites performed by the priest. They prepared a public feast by killing fowls. This was called *rem-ar* meaning 'fowl of agreement'. After staying overnight the bride returned home early the next morning. On the second day, the father of the girl killed a female pig again for the villagers. When the day was over the girl was escorted back to the bridegroom's house to live there for good.

Zawlbuk

Zawlbuk, the nerve-centre of the Mizo society shaped the youth into a responsible adult members of the society.[41] Placed under the charge of a leader called the *Valupa*, the *Zawlbuk* fostered and nurtured a pure and uncorrupted life. The inmates of the *Zawlbuk* consisted of two distinct strata : Senior and junior groups. The latter supplied the *Zawlbuk* with firewood and water. The *Zawlbuk* also had three fold functions : First, it severed as a sleeping place and recreational centre for married and unmarried men. Secondly, it trained and disciplined young boys. Thirdly, it was an inn for a traveller. It was also a forbidden house for women.

Bawi System

This system appears to have existed from time immemorial among the Mizos. Therefore, it formed an essential part of Mizo society. Another system practised in the society was *Sal* meaning slavery.

There was a marked difference between the two. Anyone who surrendered himself to the Chief for any reason was known as *bawi*. But *sal* was a captive of war of the inter-clan feuds.[42]

Tlawmngaihna

What the Mizos most valued in life was *Tlawmngaihna* meaning moral discipline. A man was unselfish, zealous, courteous, considerate, courageous, industrious, kind, generous, preserving etc. was considered to have the spirit of *Tlawmngaihna*. If such a person was found in village he was honoured by offering a rice beer in a special cup made for it known as *tlawmngai No* at a special function organised for the purpose. At the function he was offered the drink first, followed by the Chief and the rest. This was the highest 'Award' in those days.[43]

Dress and Ornaments

In the early period, when the Mizos were in a less

advanced stage, they did not know how to manufacture cotton. How they manufactured cotton and used it for their clothing was a later development. Before they wore cotton material, men had worn what they called *Hnawkhal,* a coarse material made "from reeds or the bark of trees".[44] The *Hnawkhal* was replaced by a cloth made of cotton called *Puanhlap* (ordinary cloth). *Puanhlap* was they workday attire of men.

Women also wore a garment called *Siapsuap* made of the same material as that of the man's. After the *Siapsuap* of the women's apparel *Dawlrem Kawr* was added. It was named after a little chirping insect called *Dawlrem.* This was an improvement upon the existing attire. Later the women's workday dress consisted of *Hmaram-Pawnfen* (cotton petticoat) which was coloured in various designs. The most popular designs were the *Kawkpuizikzial,* and the *Lenhuangthuam* This dress was kept up by a cord known as *Kawngchilh,* and a spiral brass.

Not only women but men also wore *Saingho* (ivory) as earrings. The common ornaments they mostly used were *Saingho* and *thihna* (necklaces). As both men and women kept long hair alike, they also used *thimkual* (hair-pins) and *dawhkilh* (hair-sticks) respectively. Generally, these were made of bamboos. Men of distinguished character like *Thangchhuah* also wore a headdress like *Vakiria,* made and composed of parrots' feathers and porcupine' quills inserted into a bamboo ring. This head-dress was worn only on important occasions like the *Khuangchawi.*

Kut

"Kut" is a Mizo word for 'festival' or "feast". *Kut* became one of the common features of the social life of the Mizo people. Though its origin was lost in oblivion, some hold the view that *Kut* originated from *thlanrawkpa,* the famous legendary originator of the feast. But this theory was discarded by many. Therefore, the different clans performed it with slight alterations marking the difference of the performance from one village to another. There were three kinds of Kut : *Mim Kut, Pawl Kut,* and chapchar Kut. It may be conjectured that these Kuts had been observed while they were in Burma, specifically when they were in the valley between the *Run* (or Manipur) and the *Tiau* rivers."[45]

(1) *Mini Kut* : This *Kut* is the oldest *Kut Mim* is a kind of plant, the grain of which is taken. So this *Kut* is called after this *Mim*. It is also known as *Thitin,*[46] which means the departure of the dead. In the past the *Kut* was held in memory of the deceased. Fresh venetables, maize, bread (a sticky rice) etc. were offered on the occasion on the memories of the dead. Normally it lasted three days. On this occassion *Zu* was served and songs were also sung. From the third day the offerings that were edible were permitted to be eaten. The feast, also known as 'feast of weeping' is like the Christian feast of "All Souls Day".

(2) *Pawl Kut* : 'Pawl' means 'Straw'. Hence, *Pawl Kut* means a *Kut* held soon after the harvest was over. It was a sort of harvest thanksgiving.

This feast was meant for children. But men and women also joined them. On this occassion, each family prepared meat. For this reason, a week before the occassion, every one went hunting by setting traps. If they could not catch any other animal for its meat the family should kill some fowl. Eggs were also a compulsory item.

In the evening parents escorted their children with their food and meat and gathered there together at the memorial platforms on the outskirts of a village. Here they enjoyed what they called "Chhawnghnawt".[47] Children along with their mothers ate together and they tried to put their food and meat and egg into their friends' mouths, and so they ran one after another trying to put food into one's mouth inspite of their fullness. Youth also joined them. Parents also enjoyed this *Kut* with drinks. On this occassion even the poor should enjoy to their heart's content. This *Kut* lasted for a day.

(3) *Chapchar Kut* : *Chapchar Kut* is a contemporary of the *Pawl Kut.* It was set apart for adults only. This *Kut* was held immediately after the *jhum* cutting was over. Like *Pawl Kut,* in *Chapchar Kut,* they also went hunting. They set traps, and they also prepared enough *Zu* to last the feast. The *Kut* lasted for about a week. The duration depended Chiefly on the availability of *Zu* and food etc. Then on the evening of the third day, as was in Pawl *Kut,* a C*hhawnghnawh* was performed. Everyone was making merriment. The fourth day was known as *Zupui Ni* which was enjoyed with drinking *Zu.*

On the occassion, girls were dressed with their ornaments wearing their *puan* which they reserved for such occassions. Young men also did the same thing. As it was the happiest occassion in their social life, all eagerly looked forward to these days. During these days both men and women drank *zu.*

Both young boys and girls also participated by offering *Zu* to the dancing party. Since the *Kut* was considered the most important festival in the life of the Mizos, no couple should quarrel on these days and it was not permitted to have squabbles in the family.

Dances of the Mizos

One important feature of the social life of the Mizos is 'dance'. Dancing, in the early days, was one of the principal amusements in a village. Formerly, dances were performed only on certain festivals and on other important occassions. Mizos have the traditional dances. These dances are of many kinds, their occupying important place in the social life of the Mizos. We may now briefly describe some of these dances as follows :

***Khuallam* :** The most outstanding and colourful

dance of the Mizos is Khuallam. The origin is not known but it was connected with a series of ceremonies (Khuangchawi, Thangchhuah, Kut, etc.) performed by a man to attain a position of distinction in the society. On Khuangchawi ceremonies, the sacrificer invited his father-in-law, if he lived in a different village, to perform dance on this occassion. The invitation was called thingdum.[48] It was a dance performed by strangers. *Khual* means stranger or guest and *Lam* means dance. Hence Khuallam.

Cheraw Kan : Another colourful and distinctive dance is called *Cheraw Kan.* In cheraw, men sit facing one another holding the ends of bamboos in each hand on the ground, forming a number of squares. It is a dance of skill, and the dancers need to be alert so that an accident may be avoided. A dancing group is expected to spring in and out of the squares without being struck by the bamboos, keeping time to the music. Originally the dance was performed by man,[49] to wish a safe passage and victorious entry into the abode of the dead called 'Pialral' for a soul which just departed from this earthly existence.[50]

Solakia : Originally the dance was associated with hunting.[51] In solakia men and women dance in a big circle to the accompaniment of drum heats and a gong.

Chheih lam : *Chheih lam* is another cultural dance of the Mizos. It is also commonly known as *Zu hmun lam* as it was usually formed by the *Zu* drinking adults only. In ancient times, when *Chheih lam* was performed, the *zu* drinking men sat together in a circle singing a song of different tunes/lyrics with drum beats. One or two might take a turn to dance in the middle of the circle.

Tiger dance : This is not a common dance. In tiger dance a cloth was placed on the ground to represent a pig or goat.[52] To imitate a tiger, a youth of the village stalked the prey and jumped over the imaginary goat.

Musical Instruments

Songs must be accompanied by music. As such, Mizos have different kinds of musical instruments which, in those early days, they used to accompany their songs. Whenever they sang they had to include music; even when they performed the *Chheih lam* they used, the drums etc. Of these different musical instruments, gongs which were imported from Burma but adopted as indigeneous resources, occupied an important and significant place in the Mizo society. They are of different sizes. The larger gong is called *darkhuang* and the smaller ones are known as *darmang*. These gongs were commonly in use on the occasions of feasts known collectively as *Khuangchawi* or *Thangchhuah* feasts. Another instrument which is equally significant in the social life of the Mizos is the *Khuang* (drum). At a dance there was a regular beating of gongs and drums. *Khuang* is a barrel shaped drum made of wood, hollowed out with an axe. They used animal skin to cover both the faces and held it firmly with twisted cane string.

Besides these gongs and drums, there are six indigeneous Mizo musical instruments. They are-*Mizo Tingtang, Phenglawng, Rawchhem, Bengbung, Lemlawi* and *Tuium dar.*

The Mizo *Tingtang,* is called the *Tangta,* by the Lakhers and is a one-stringed violin. Its resonator is made out of a hollow gourd. In playing it, the instrument is held at the neck with the left hand, the fingers of which are used to make the notes by pressing on the string.[53] *Phenglawng* and *Rawchhem* are very similar in shape and size also. They are made of bamboo.

Games and Sports

In those early days were there no games and sports as we have today; but sometimes the society had certain occassions in which they had to show their strength and might.

Weight lifting was most popular. Every village had what was called *'Chawilung'* (stones used as weight lifting). They used to have a group competition as to who could lift up effortlessly. In every village either in the evening or in the daytime, young fellows were seen competing with one another.

There was group fighting from village to village, sometimes, over the carriage of a sick or dead person. When such occassions occurred both the opposing groups met at the boundary line and they began to fight until the other group was defeated. But such were rare occassions. This fighting was commonly known as *Inzawn chuh.*

Wrestling was another common game in which the male adults were involved. In the past mostly it was performed in the *Zawlbuk* as a matter of course. Here young men trained themselves by watching their elders, and by participating, Visitors to a village were often challenged. The main aim of each young man in a village was being the champion. Therefore, a successful wrestler fought up the line till he established a claim to challenge the local champion.

Mizo children have many games. We may now mention some of them. The favourite game for boys is *Inkawi hnawk* or *inhnawk.* It is played with beans; they hold the beans in one hand and they have to go through various stages for a complete round. The party who knocks away the other's beans most wins the game. There are two kinds of Kawi (bean) one is the ordinary and the other is called *Kawirit.* The game for girls is called *inkawibah.* There are three kinds namely—(1) *Bahpui,* (2) *Bahte* and (3) *In salman.* In this game they hold the bean with two hands and the bean is made to stand, whereas the bean of the boy's must lie. Like the boy's they have to undergo various stages till they win the game.

Hide-and-seek is a common game for both boys and

girls. Besides these games, there are many other games played by both boys and girls. Some of them are—*In-Ulen, Inkawl Vawr, Inbuh Vawr, Invai Lungthlak* etc.

Hunting

The Mizos were adventurous people. Whenever they had an occassion to go for hunting, they never missed the chance. The Mizo word for hunting is a *ramchhuak* (to go out to the jungle) but the real motive of *ramchhuak* was to hunt for elephants. They went hunting, sometimes, for almost three months. Their long absence from home, much inevitably, depended on their success or failure to get their prey. If they were successful, they organised a grand feast with great gaiety.

BAWI AND *SAL* IN EARLY MIZO SOCIETY

In early Mizo society, like in most other tribes, there were various institutions. According to Vaux, "Institutions are the various forms in which the social life of a people finds expression. The Institution themselves exist...for the sake of the society. Again, the institutions of a society will vary with time and place..."[54] The *bawi* custom was one of the oldest and also one of the most popular institutions. A *bawi* was an individual who was dependent upon a Chief by various reasons. According to Lewin, "*Boi* (*Bawi*)[55] is the term in their (Mizo) dialect which betokens of persons who had lost the right of individual freedom of action, but in all other respects, the word 'slave' would be inapplicable."[56] A similar view was given by B.C. Allen who wrote "... that in the regularly administered districts of Province, there are no practices or customs which have the slightest tinge of slavery apart from the *Boi* (*Bawi*) custom..."[57] The origin of the custom is not known but it is believed that it was as old as the society itself. Only a Chief could have a *bawi*.

Another institution very similar to that of the *bawi* custom was *Sal*. *Sal* is a Mizo term for slave. Vaux again defines slave as "a man who is bought and sold, who is a property of a master, who makes use of him as he likes."[58] Persons captured in wars or raids were called *sal.*[59] They were indeed the personal property of their captors. Hence, their position in the society was quite different and marriageable girls were taken captive and formed the bulk of *sal.*[60] This was the case in time of wars these groups of people were spared and captured them alive. The rest were killed.

The *sal,* like the *bawi* could buy their freedom by paying a big ransom which depended upon the demand of the captor. Every household could possess or keep as many *sal* as it could acquire. His fate solely depended on his possessor. The owner could sell him for a price or he could let him go scott-free. It is not known whether the system was common among the Mizos in the past or not, however, the same was common in the neighbouring State of Tripura where children were sold and exported to different parts of the country. A Chief who was captured in a war should not be treated as *sal,* but as a Chief, and only the Chief of a village should keep him in his house, where he should be treated as an equal.

The origin of slavery in ancient India is also very similar with that of the Mizos. It's origin may be traced with the word *dasa,* meaning originally a member of the peoples conquered by the Aryans in their first invasion of India. Many *dasas* captured in the battle were thus reduced to bondage and became slaves. Since then the word *dasa* began to denote a slave and has continued to do so till date.[61] The Mahabharata declares that it is a law of war that the vanquished should be the victor's slave and the captive would serve his captor until ransomed. A slave could buy back his freedom or be voluntarily released by his master. If he was an Aryan, he, like the Mizo Chief captured in a war, could return to his Aryan status[62]. Under the Graeco-Roman empire there were two kinds of slaves *viz.* 'debt-slave' and slave as such. This may have been the case everywhere where the institution of slavery was practised.

With this idea in view, an attempt an is made in this paper to discuss the *bawi* custom and its controversial abolition in Mizoram in 1927 and also to show how these two institutions became an important economic factors with reference to Chief in early Mizos society.

The Different Kinds of *Bawi*

In early Mizo society, there were three categories *of bawi viz. (i) Inpuichhung Bawi, (ii) Chemsen Bawi,* and *(iii) Tukluh Bawi.* According to some, there was one more category called *Fatlum Bawi.*[63] We may now examine them one by one.

(i) Inpuichhung Bawi : The most common and popular *bawi* was *Inpuichhung Bawi* (*Inpui* = main house, *chhung* = within). The term was applied to those who took refuge in the Chiefs house owing to poverty or driven by hunger. Widows, orphans and other who were unable to support themselves and had no one to support them formed the bulk of the class of *bowi.* A man could also become the *bawi* by compassion. If a man was too poor to perform his religious obligation due to poverty he might seek the helps of the Chief. If he did so, he became the *bawi* of the Chief by performing a ceremony called *Saphun.*[64] After this ceremony, the man and his family members became part of the Chief's family.

The Chief, sometimes, procured a wife for his *bawi.* In that case, the new couples had to serve the Chief for a period of three years and at the end of that period the couples would be free to leave the Chief if they so desired. However, the three year period would be extended by another period of three years in case the *buwi* married to a female *buwi.* Having set up a house of their own and settled as a separate family they were known as *Inhrang bawi* which literally means (In = house, hrang = separate) a *bawi* living in a separate house.[65] They were officially still *bawi* but only in name. Now, they were all freed from any tinge of *bawiship.* However, the youngest son would inherit *bawiship* but without any trace of *bawiship.* Regarding only the youngest son, who inherited the father's property a bawi, and the other children being entirely free, the customs and practices of the society differed from one Chief to another. While some Chiefs made the rule that the youngest son was a bawi others insisted that all the children were *bawi.*[66] The Chief was entitled to receive the marriage prices of the daughters. After all, in either case, the children were *Inhrang Bawi. Inpuichhung Bawi* was allowed to acquire a private property as well as his freedom by paying a *mithun* or its equivalent in cash or goods to the Chief.[67] This shows that the *bawi* under this category were enjoying a certain of freedom within and without the Chief's family. The relation between the Chief and his *bawi* was that if the Chief was in need of rice or any other assistance he could call on his bawi for help and vice versa.

It is interesting to note that the *bawi* was at liberty to move from his master and seek shelter in the house of another Chief if he was maltreated. This was allowed because of the fact that all the Chiefs then thought that they were the same family.[68] Though the custom was there, this rarely happened Chiefly because every Chief treated his *bawi* well for he knew that his importance and greatness solely depended on the number of *bawi* he possessed. So far as our knowledge goes, the only two cases of this kind were that of Suakpuilala and Vuttaia, the two most powerful Chiefs, who allowed their *bawi* to go to their respective relatives. Apart from the *bawi* being treated well, many a clever *bawi* had a chance to rise from being a *bawi* to being the Chief's most trusted adviser.

(ii) Chemsen Bawi : Another category of *bawi* in the society was *Chemsen Bawi.* The *Chemsen Bawi* were criminals who, after committing a crime of any nature, took refuge in the Chief's house for fear of revenge. If the criminal had a chance to touch the main post in the house of the Chief then he became a free man and no one, in the village was allowed to do any harm to him because he now belonged to the Chief.[69] Only the Chief could protect such a criminal. The avanger, if any, would be considered an enemy of the Chief if he continued to make attempts of vengeance. But he remained *bawi* for life. Debtors who were unable to repay their debts, thieves and other vagabonds also became bawi of this category in order to avoid punishments for the wrongs they committed. Civil disputes were also sometimes decided in favour of the party who were willing to become *bawi* of the Chief.

The *Chemsen Bawi,* like *Inhrang Bawi* lived in a separate house. Therefore, his position in the society was very similar to that of the *Inhrang Bawi* of *Inpuichhung Bawi.* However, there were two marked differences between the two. Firstly, the children of *Chemsen Bawi* were *bawi* as long as they lived. Secondly, *Chemsen Bawi* was under no obligation to work for the Chief but in return the Chief had every right to acquire the marriage prices of the daughters.[70] So, the measure of submission was much greater than that of the *Inpuichhung Bawi.*

(iii) Tukluh Bawi : The Bawi of this category were persons who, during the war or raid, had deserted their party and joined the victorious side by pledging that they and their descendants would obey the victor Chief. Like the other *bawi,* the *Tukluh Bawi* lived in a separate house.[71] The bawi also occupied a position similar to that of *Inhrang Bawi* in many respects.

Like *Inpuichhung Bawi* the *Tukluh Bawi* could purchase his freedom by paying *mithun.* Unlike the *Inpuichhung Bawi one mithun* would be enough to release all the family members in a household.[72] As a rule, the daughters of *Tukluh Bawi* were not *bawi* of any nature. So, there was no question of their marriage prices being received by the Chief.

The British administration recognised only

Inpuichhung Bawi because it was considered to be the most suitable which protected the weaker section of the people in the society. Shakespeare remarks thus......" and it would be extremely unwise to attempt to alter it."[73] *Tukluh Bawi* was also not formally recognised by the British but this category of *bawi* was ignored by them because their duties towards the Chief were comparatively so light that the *bawi* seldom claimed for their release. The *Chemsen Bawi* was not recognised by the British and whenever the *bawi* claimed protection he was released. It was, however, on the subject of *Inpuichhung Bawi* that controversy arose on the ground that the terms amounted to slavery. However, Lew in was right when he says, "The condition of these so-called slaves was very little different indeed from that of free people".[74] Parry also concludes, "I purposely refrain from calling these people (Chief's dependants) slaves....the term slave is a complete misnomer today, whatever it may have been in the past."[75]

Bawi **As An Economic Factor**

Bawi, as discussed, belonged to the Chief. Whether he lived with the Chief or in a separate house as in the case of *Inhrang Bawi, bawi* was all the same the *bawi* of the Chief. He was all for the Chief and in return, as indicated above, the Chief was all for the *bawi*. From this perspective, let us now examine how much the *bawi* contributed for the economic betterment of the Chief.

The *Inpuichhung Bawi* were part of the Chief's household and did all the works in return for their food and shelter. The Chief, like his subjects had his own *jhum*. So, the *bawi* cut and cultivated the jhum, and had to attend to his fish traps (*Ngawi*) and other traps. The female *bawi*-women and girls, like free men, fetched wood and water, and cleaned the daily supply of rice, weaved cloths and weeded the jhum also. Also, they looked after the Chiefs children. They had to do very little more work than they would have to if they were independent.

Moreover, they were free of all anxiety for their tomorrows. Also, they got their food, and some of them used the ornaments, guns and weapons of the Chiefs as theirs.[76] In this way, the *bawi* contributed enormous wealth to the Chiefs.

The *bawi* could become another source of economic prosperity for the Chief. The Chief sometimes procured a wife for his *bawi*. In that case, the new couple, as a rule, had to serve the Chief for a period of three years, and at the end of that period, the couple would be free to leave the Chief if they so desired. The period could, however, be extended by another period of three years in case the *bawi* was married to a female *bawi*. During this period the couple had to work for the Chief. In this way the couple brought economic prosperity to the Chief. Apart from this, the *bawi* could bring an economic boom to the Chief through different means. It may be noted that the Chief was entitled to receive the marriage prices of the daughters of the *bawi*. As we are aware, before the advent of the British and the introduction of money-economy to the people, the economic life of the people was so simple that the Chief relied on barter-economy : people exchanged their goods. The wealth of the Chief was also measured in terms of the number of *sial*[77] (*mithun*) he possessed. So *sial* played, and occupied, a significant place in the economic life of the Chief as well as the common man. Among them the value of property was judged in terms of *sial*. In the same way, the marriage price of the female *bawi* was also determined in terms of *sial*. Hence, in this way, the Chief became very wealthy because he received a number *of sial* as the marriage price of the *bawi's* daughter. In this way the price could bring economic fortunes to the Chief and other household members.

Sal as an Economic Factor

As pointed out before, the common people could keep as many *sal* as they could capture. He could also purchase from the other owners. The Chief hardly kept *sal* mainly because he had enough *bawi* to look after his welfare. But he also kept and possessed *sal* along with the *bawi*. Therefore, it is certain that *sal* did not contribute enormous wealth to the Chief as did by the *bawi* because the Chief normally kept a very few *sal*. From this point of view, *sal* became more meaningful to the common man than to the Chief.

Abolition of Bawi

By the Slavery Abolition Act, 1833, the British Government prohibited slavery in British Dominions, and in 1838 all the slaves throughout the British Empire were completely freed. With this background, the British came and occupied Mizoram in 1890. Consequently they found the *bawi* custom abhorrent and illegal. Their reaction was so swift that they freed any *bawi* who appealed for freedom by payment of a customary ransom to the Chief of a *mithun* or its equivalent of Rs. 40.[78] A majority of the *bawi* so redeemed under the condition belonged to the *Chemsen Bawi* and the *Tukluh Bawi*. Now, the main issue before the British administration in Mizoram was the case relating to the *bawi* who belonged to the *Inpuichhung Bawi*.

It may be pointed out that the Chiefs, too, had small differences of opinion among themselves over the *Inpuichhung Bawi* concerning the entitlement to the marriage prices of daughters of the *bawi* and the case of the youngest son who retained liability as a *bawi*.[79] These differences arose only through some Chiefs who were willing to modify the more extreme provisions of the customs in favour of their *bawi*. As noted earlier, the British administration recognised *Inpuichhung Bawi*. While doing this, the British took two factors into consideration. First, it was considered as the institution which not only protected the weaker section of the people in the society but also provided the extremely poor and down trodden a shelter. Secondly, the British knew that they needed the supports of the Chiefs in running the administration. Hence, they did not want to diminish the prestige of the Chiefs. Taking these two factors into account the British administration and the missionaries as two factors into account the British administration and the missionaries as well simply condoned the system without any objection from any quarter until 1904 in spite of the fact that the slavery Abolition Act, 1833 was in force. The main factor which influenced the missionaries not to take the *bawi* issue seriously was the belief that the system would soon disappear with the growing public conscience.[80]

For the first time in the history of Mizoram the system of *bawi* became an issue when the Missionary Conference held at Aizawl in 1904 took up the case for discussion. The conference then discussed that *bawi* should be given better treatment in the society.[81] As a result, they appealed to the district administration to introduce tangible change in the custom of *bawi*. In response to this appeal, the administration immediately took steps by inviting views from other officials serving in the district as to how a meaningful and effective change could be made on the custom without lowering much the status and prestige of the Chiefs in Mizoram.[82]

The British knew very well that the services of the Chiefs were so vital to effectively run the administration in Mizoram. This consideration thus influenced the district authorities not to take a hasty decision on the issue of *bawi* in Mizoram.

While the administration was taking positive steps with a view to modifying the *bawi* custom in line with the appeal made by the conference, the question of *bawi* became controversial when Dr. Peter Fraser, a missionary physician came to Mizoram in 1908. Fraser was so very critical about it, that he felt the custom which his missionary colleagues and the administration had condoned for many years must be abolished in Mizoram.

The issue became more serious when Fraser personally collected evidence that *bawi* were ill-treated in the society. He insisted that *bawi* should be freed in the name of the Lord Jesus Christ and King Edward.[83] The Chiefs defended that the *bawi* were not slaves in the true sense of the term and argued that there was no question of being released.

The situation deteriorated when the matter was taken up before the Assam Government. In short, the district administration won the case and Khawvelthanga, Chief of Maubuang who wholeheartedly supported Fraser was fined and his guns were seized. Fraser was also asked to leave Mizoram or sign the prepared undertaking that in future he should confine himself entirely to his missionary work, and that he should not interfere in the disputes concerning the Mizos customs,[85] Fraser flatly refused to sign the undertaking. The refusal caused him dear : his missionary work in Mizoram was abruptly suspended and he was ordered to leave Mizoram. So, he was temporarily expelled from the District.

After a short absence. Fraser came back and resumed his works in Mizoram. But he raised the same issue that the custom of *bawi* must be abolished out and out. Now, the issue became the matter of great concern for both the Government of Assam and India. While both the Governments were so keen in dealing with the matter, Dr. Fraser put more pressures to the Government and this infuriated the authorities. Consequently, he was expelled from the country for good. In the same way. Lt. Col. F.W.G. Cole, the Superintendent with whom Dr. Fraser had the dispute, was also asked to leave the country.

After the departure of Dr. Fraser, the subject of controversy was taken up and a settlement was effected. The points of settlement among other things may be given as :

(1) The use of the word *bawi* be discontinued.

(2) Rs. 40 or 1 *mithun* would redeem the whole family.

(3) A *bawi* might leave his master at will.

(4) Disputes over *bawi* would be settled in line with the Mizo custom as in the case of *Chawman* (fooding charge).

Following the settlement, the Government of Assam proposed a change for the future status of *bawi* in Mizoram. The proposal contained the following suggestions :

(1) A date be fixed after which the *bawi* contract could not be entered into.

(2) The Government would pay the customary ransom of Rs. 40/- if the *bawi* was freed.

(3) The Government should recover ransom from persons in whose behalf the same was paid.

(4) Persons so redeemed and released be at liberty to leave the Chief's house or to remain there as they wished.

(5) Let the Chiefs knew that they would be liable to bring to the court when the need arose.

However, S.N. Mackenzie, the Superintendent, strongly opposed the idea of redeeming the bawi on the ground that redeeming would encourage an increased beggary in the district and the redeemed would go again to the Chief. In spite of the objection raised by Mackenzie, the Government of Assam in 1927 then replaced the word *bawi* by a newly coined term "Chhungte" or "awmpuite" meaning "inmates of the house". Then, the term *bawi* was no longer allowed to be used in Mizoram. Nevertheless, the *bawi* issue reached the King of Great Britain who referred the petition of Fraser to the Parliament for discussion. Accordingly, the Parliament discussed the issue. Mary Winchester who was then restored to her relatives in London in 1872 was so instrumental to this effect. So, the Parliament passed that the *bawi* custom be abolished in Mizoram. As a result, the system came to an end in Mizoram in 1927. At last Fraser had won the case.

Concluding Remarks

The *Bawi* custom in early Mizo society was the system evolved through the ages and at that time it was a recognised institution. A man could became *bawi* under various reasons. The children of the *bawi,* like in ancient India, became *bawi* by birth but, like in other societies, they could buy back their freedom or be voluntarily released by their master. So, they may also be called domestic servants or personal attendants of the Chief. The system was sometime misconceived as *sal* or slave by those who are ignorant of the real condition and status of the bawi. The existence of the custom in early Mizo society was the beauty of the society itself because every section of the people found benevolence in the Chief. Had Dr. Peter Frazer, too, known the real concept of the system he would not have termed it as slavery. Instead he would have been inspired for its crusade.

Above all, an analytical study of *bawi* custom, however, reveals that the system was very similar to that of the custom called 'bonded labourer' the system commonly found and practised throughout India. A comparative study may further indicate not only the similarities between the two but it will be a valuable and significant study for further research.

HISTORY AND EVOLUTION OF EDUCATION IN MIZORAM THROUGH THE AGES[86]

Education in Mizoram in the modem sense of the word, may be said to date from the year 1893 when the British established a school after occupying the hills in 1890. Although the school was started by the British, the real foundation on education was laid by the Christian Missionaries who in the beginning faced a practical problem due to lack of a script in the native language. But the problem was soon solved by reducing the language to writing by adopting the Roman script.[87] In this connection it may be mentioned that according to the traditions, the mizos, like other tribes had a script written on an animal's skin which was, however, devoured by a dog due to their negligence.[88] In reducing the language to writing the role of Col. Lewin is so significant because he had already made an attempt in this venture even before the arrival of the missionaries into the hills.[89] The missionaries rather, continued and took up the work left by Col. of Lewin. And thus they did a great thing for the people. They not only brought a script into language but their vision and efforts thus began the process of formal education in Mizoram.

In this Chapter, the study is divided into three statues in order to make us properly understand the history of education during the period under review. The first stage describes what kind of education the Mizos had before the British. The second stage traces and discusses education under the British. The third stages tries to show the growth and the development of education under free India.

Education in Mizoram before the British

Before we proceed on formal education, a brief survey may be made on the nature of the traditional or indigenous education as practised by the native people before the coming of the British. This is required to have a glimpse on the continuity of education through the ages in Mizoram.

It is a fact that there was no formal education in the true sense of the term in Mizoram before the advent of the British, Further, it is a fact that modern system of education in India was brought by the British. Therefore, in Mizoram, like other places in India, the idea of schooling for children did not arise in the minds of the people. However, the indigenous methods of instruction were so systematic that in many respects they were more effective in terms of moulding the lives of the people in the society than the methods being applied under the system of formal education. Due to lack of a script, the language was oral and could not be communicated through writing, yet the education the children received was more practical as they learnt through actual participation in the works of the elders and parents. Now, let us discuss in brief the different agencies through which the natives undertook their education in the past.

Home : Like today, even in the past, the home was the most effective agency. Home is the oldest form of social organisation known to man. The child learnt the first lesson of citizenship in the family and received good training in discipline and self-control. Home was the place where the child learnt to obey authority and showed respect to the elders. This is very true till today. Home, in which the family members are closely knitted together with a high sense of mutual respect, responsibility and team spirit, is the potential teacher of the society.

Meal Time was the time when parents instructed the children about morality, civic sense etc. The father, being the head of the family, would distribute the work for the day.[90] So, the head of the family played the role of a teacher.

Zawlbuk, the "bachelors' house" was, perhaps, the most important agency so far as the indigenous education of the Mizos was concerned. It provided equal opportunities to the youth to learn co-operation, fellow-feeling, tolerance etc. It was the nerve-centre of the Mizo society and shaped the youth, into a responsible member of the society.[91] The *Zawlbuk* provided its inmates with a uniform system of code of conduct and discipline. The initial forced discipline exercised in the conduct and affairs of the *Zawlbuk* inmates took permanent root in their personality structure.[92] As a matter of fact, *Zawlbuk* inmates served as a standing army of the Chief who himself was the Commander-in-Chief. Thus, the boy grew up to become more useful for the society than for the family in which he was born. This gave rise to a very closely knitted Mizo society where each one was for all and *vice, versa.* Therefore, *Zawlbuk* was an important and indispensable informal education institution.

Tlawmngaihna, the Mizo ideal of manhood is a moral code or principle which meaningfully shaped the life of a Mizo youth in the past. The code covers all good qualities which a man is expected to possess.[93] *Tlawmngaihna* is so precious that in the past the people very much valued it and it is very deeply rooted in the Mizo society. In the past, *Tlawmngaihna* knitted different works of life together in a society without discrimination and prejudice. The desire to acquire the spirit of *Tlawmngaihna* thus ruled the hearts of every one because it was the highest award which everyone had a hankering to receive in his lifetime in one way or the other. A man who practiced the precepts of *Tlawmngaihna* was looked upon with admiration and highly respected in society. This is still true even today. Parry remarks thus, "Tlawmngaihna" therefore, deserves every encouragement, as if it were allowed to fall into disuse, it would be most detrimental to the whole of the tribe.[94]

Hunting was another area where a Mizo youth was trained as a responsible person in the society, Mizos loved hunting. They went for hunting for two purposes. Firstly, for religious purposes. Secondly, they did it as a sport and also for the meat.[95] Hunting for the chase of an elephant was the most favourite game of the people. They moved for many miles camping for days and months. During the whole period of hunting for an elephant the leaders of the group secretly observed each individual and made an assessment on the personality of each individual. Though secret, every one knew that he was being watched by his elders. Knowing this, all young men were so smart that each of them made the utmost efforts to surpass and outdo all the others in every thing they did. Therefore, hunting was yet another centre for learning and training through which the youths were disciplined and shaped as men.

Education Under The British

In Mizoram formal education was introduced by opening a school in 1893. The school was meant for the children of sepoys who were serving in Mizoram. A Military Police *havildur* was employed as a teacher and paid a staff allowance of Rs. 5/- per month in addition to his regular pay. Hindi was the medium of instruction. Similar schools were also opened at Lunglei and Demagiri, (*now* Tlabung). But before 1898, the school at Demagiri was under the school authority of the Chittagong Division.[96]

Meanwhile, it may be noted here that the two missionaries, James Herbert Lorrain and Frederick William Savidge, having reduced the language into writing, opened one school on 1 April 1894 with two pupils. Simultaneously they also started Bible Schools for which more attention was given. But the school was soon abandoned for they wanted to complete the translation work before they moved into their new assignment in Abor country, *now* the North Eastern State of Arunachal Pradesh.

It is a fact that education was not the main objective of the British administration. As such, the Government establishment school for the Mizo children only seven years after their coming. In 1896, A. Porteous, then Political Officer, submitted a proposal to the Secretary to the Chief Commissioner of Assam for sanctioning grant for the establishment of one school for the benefit of Mizo children.[97] In his proposal Porteous further suggested that very soon Bengali would make its way into use as the language of trade and official intercourse. He, therefore, strongly recommended that "the initial step of starting a Government School to teach Bengali in the first instance and later British, should be taken as soon as possible."[98] But the Government, as pointed out earlier, paid little attention to education Consequent upon this Porteous again in 1897 despatched a strong worded note to the authorities. There he writes : "I desire to point out that, although it is now seven years since Aijal (*now* Aizawl) was occupied, nothing whatever has yet been done by Government in the way of commencing to educate the Lushais."[99] Thus, on the basis of this despatch the Government school was established on 21 August, 1897, with Kalijoy Kavyatirtha as the Headmaster. The management of the school was put under a committee of three persons. The committee would submit proposals to the Superintendent for sanction of money for the management of the school.[100]

As noted before, the two missionaries were replaced by Rev. D.E. Jones of Welsh Mission. He was sent by the missionary authorities in London and arrived in Aizawl on 10 September, 1897. The two missionaries after staying together with D.E. Jones for months handed over the work to him on the last day of 1897 and went to England for furlough. D.E.Jones thus reopened the school on 28 February, 1898. Hence, from this day onward the management of the school was in the hands of the Welsh missionaries.

It may be pointed out that right from the beginning till 1902, the education in Mizoram was under the control of the Superintendent but managed by the department.[101]

In the history of education in Mizoram, the year 1903 is a milestone. In this year the Chief Commissioner visited Aizawl and he instructed the Superintendent to submit proposals to hand over the education of the district to the missionaries. Accordingly, on 1 March, 1903, all the Government schools on Mizoram were placed under the supervision of the mission.[102] The charge was taken over by Rev. E. Rowlands who was appointed an Honorary Inspector of all Government schools on 20 December, 1903. His considered experience in school management was expected to be beneficial to the cause of education in the district (*present* Mizoram State). The schools where the children of sepoys were studying would be transferred to the Mission only at such time when the children attained proficiency in Mizo language. But no religious instruction was to be imparted to the children studying in Government schools.[103] Thus the whole process was complete only in 1905-1906.

The number of schools was also, meanwhile, increased in the whole district when the Government permitted the District authority to open five new schools every year upto the maximum of 20 schools.[104] As a result, new village schools were opened and by 1903, there were 15 schools in North Mizoram. Of these schools 6 were in Aizawl town and the remaining schools were village schools.[105]

For the first time in the history of education in Mizoram, the school authorities conducted the Lower Primary Examination on June 1903. Out of 19 candidates 11 candidates came out successful.[106] The second examinations were held the next year and out of the total 29 candidates, the number of candidates who passed the examinations was 23.[107] To encourage the students the Government of Assam accorded sanction for the award of 8 Lower Primary Scholarships annually, the value of which was Rs. 3/- per month tenable for two years in the Upper Primary classes.[108] The scholarship would he awarded to the students on the result of their performance in the examinations to he held by the missionaries.'[109] The main purpose of the award was to help increase the number of Lower Primary Schools in Mizoram. Those, who qualified for the scholarship were to be sent out to start new schools in the villages. In

1913, three Upper Primary Scholarships for the whole of Mizoram were created. Accordingly, a special scholarship amounting to Rs. 4/- per month for two years was sanctioned. The awards were only for three boys. The awardees were to be nominated by the Superintendent. It was meant for the students of the Mission Middle British School at Aizawl.

In 1904, the Upper Primary School was introduced and the course of studies was also made. The course was prepared by the Director of Public Instruction in consultation with the Superintendent of the Lushai Hills.

Meanwhile, a new development took place in Lunglei Sub-Division. Savidge and Lorrain returned to Lunglei on 13 March, 1903 as Baptist Missionaries and they started opening of schools to train a few students to be teachers at village schools.[110] In February, 1904, the Chief Commissioner of Assam paid a visit to South Mizoram and Savidge was appointed on 9 October an Honorary Inspector of Schools for Lunglei Sub-Division. Thus the whole Mizoram was placed under two separate Inspectors of Schools.[111] The charge of education of the Lunglei Sub-Division was also transferred to the Baptist Mission and the process was completed in February, 1905.[112] This system continued till 1952.

The numerical growth of education in the form of schools between 1908 and 1947 was remarkable. In 1908-09 there were only 2 Middle British Schools (Upper Primary) and 15 Lower Primary Schools with 799 pupils on the rolls.[113] Within the next twenty years the number of schools and pupils was more than thrice of that number. The number of Lower Primary Schools (upto class III) was 114. The total number of students in the school was 3642.[114] There were 5 Middle British Schools with one Middle Vernacular School, and the number of Primary Schools was 221. For the same period the number of pupils on the rolls was 9606.[115] In addition to the existing Middle British Schools, the authorities opened in 1944 more Middle Schools known as Middle Anglo-Vernacular Schools at some selected villages. With this, when India attained independence in 1947, there were 254 Primary Schools and 11 Middle Schools in Mizoram.[116]

It may be interesting to note that a High School was established in 1944 amidst a great debate. Both the (government and the mission were against the idea of having a high school in Mizoram, the missionaries were satisfied if the Mizos could read the Bible whereas the Government was aware of the unemployment problem. McCall was of the view that higher education would create an elite group in the society.[117] In spite of a strong objection, however, in 1931, the Mizo Chiefs asked the Government to establish a High School and the matter was raised by H.W. Carter, a Baptist missionary at Lunglei, to the Hill Education Conference held at Shillong in 1935. The Lushai Student Association also submitted a memorandum to the Governor of Assam in 1941 and delegates were sent to Shillong to pursue the matter.[118] But the school was started by McDonald in 1944 as a reward for the role played by the Mizos in the Second World War. Thus the school was opened on 23 February, 1944 with 56 students. The first batch for matriculation appeared in the examination in March. 1948. The total number of candidates that appeared was 25, out of which 17 students passed successfully. In 1948 one more High School was established at Lunglei, followed by Gandhi Memorial High School at Champhai in 1950. St. Paul's High School was founded by the Holl Cross Society in 1954.

Education In Free India

The educational system and development underwent a radical change after India achieved independence. In 1947 the Government of Assam created two posts of Sub-Inspector of Schools for North and South Mizoram. The first incumbents joined their duties at their respective places in November 1949.[119]

The political development which took place in 1952 also affected the educational system in Mizoram. As noted earlier, the Lushai Hills District was formed as an Autonomous District Council on 25 April, 1952. As a result, certain powers were vested in the Council and this automatically changed the system of education. The post of Deputy Inspector of Schools was created and the first incumbent Lalchungnunga joined duty on 1 May, 1952, and the primary education was left in the hands of the Council. The Council thus appointed a body called "Primary Education Commission" with an objective to chalk out the modalities as to when and how the education would be taken over by the Council. There were 6 members in the Commission.[120] The Council also constituted a Board of 7 members to look after the Middle and Primary Leaving Certificate Examinations. The Board came into force on 1 August, 1954.[121] The Board had conducted examinations until the Mizoram Board of School Education was constituted in 1970. The Council authorities also formed an "Advisory levt Book Committee" to select and prescribe text books for use in the Primary and Middle Schools.[122] The Committee consisted of seven members.

Meanwhile, the number of schools increased tremendously. To cope with the rising number of schools, the administrative infrastructure was also built up. Thus in 1956 a post of Deputy Inspector of Schools for South Mizoram was created and posted at Lunglei.

In the history of education in Mizoram the year 1961 is yet another milestone. By this year the Assam Government handed over the primary education to the Council with effect from 1 August.[123] Accordingly, the Council appointed one Education Officer with supporting inspecting and ministerial staff, and looked after the Primary education. An Executive Member in charge of education was the head. The officer, Thanthuama of Kulikawn was assisted by the Sub-Inspector of Schools and the Assistant Sub-Inspector of Schools.[124] When the Council assumed responsibility, there were 629 Primary Schools, 113 Middle Schools, 10 High Schools and 1 Higher Secondary School. Correspondingly, there were 39950 and 6672 students in Primary and Middle Schools respectively. However, in High Schools and Higher Secondary Schools there were about 1864 students.[125]

In 1967 the whole district was divided into four Circles for convenience of administration. The Circles were Aizawl East, Aizawl West, Lunglei and Chhimtuipui. Each circle thus had its own Deputy Inspector of Schools.

Real progress and development in education was made only after Mizoram became a Union Territory in 1972. As a result, the structure of the whole educational set up was overhauled and reorganised through the newly formed Directorate of Education which began to function from 1 July, 1972. The Directorate was initially manned by a Director, a Joint Director and three other Deputy Directors. To implement various schemes, a number of State level officers were also appointed *viz. (a)* Science Promotion Officer, *(b)* Senior Research Officer, *(c)* Special Officer (Scout & Guides and Sports & Games) and *(d)* State Social Education Officer now called Joint Director, Adult Education.

Consequence upon Mizoram being upgraded to Union Territory was the revocation of the Mizo District Council Act of 1952. As a result, the Primary Education was taken back by the Government from 29 April. 1972. fins gave a sigh of relief to the teachers who could, not get their pay regularly under the District Council. It may be recorded that on the day the Primary education was taken over by the Government there were 425 Primary Schools with 60375 pupils. There were 184 Middle Schools with 19604 students. At the same time the number of High Schools was 90 and the strength of the students was 7840. Meanwhile, the number of Higher Secondary Schools, however, remained the same but the number of students rose to 421.[126] At the same time, the corresponding strength of the teachers in Primary Schools was 1310, 784 in Middle Schools, 395 in High Schools and 36 teachers in Higher Secondary Schools.[127]

Another landmark in the history of education in Mizoram was the constitution of the Mizoram Board of School Education (MBSE) in 1976. The Board was made under the Act of 1975. It became a statutory body on 25 March, 1976. The Board now looks after all the School Eeaving Certificate Examinations. Also with this, the term of the Advisory Text Book Committee came to an end. As a separate entity, the MBSE, first conducted the Primary and Middle School Leaving Certificate Examinations in 1977 and the next year the High School Leaving Certificate Examination was also conducted.

In June of the same year, the designation of Inspector of Schools was redesignated as District Education Officer. In the same way, the Deputy, Assistant and Sub-Inspector of Schools were also correspondingly redesignated as Assistant District Education Officer, Sub-Division Education Officer and Circle Education Officer. In 1983, Aizawl District was divided into two educational districts as Aizawl East and Aizawl West. With this, there are now four District Education Officers.

In order to improve the standard of Education in Mizoram, the Government passed a number of rules, regulations etc. Some of the important innovations may be mentioned as follows :

1. The Mizoram Aided High School and Middle School Management Rules, 1990.
2. Mizoram Aided School Contributory Provident Fund Regulations, 1990.
3. Mizoram Aided School (Employee's (Death-Cum-Retirement Gratuity Rules. 1990).

4. Mizoram Pre-Matric Merit Scholarship Rules, 1990.
5. Mizoram Grant-in-aid to Non-Official Voluntary Organization Rules, 1990.
6. Mizoram Middle School and High School (Provincialization) Rules, 1990.

On the basis of the recommendation of the National Policy on Education 1986, the Government of Mizoram also implemented a new scheme known as 'School Complexes', otherwise known as Comprehensive School Scheme'. For experimentation the committee selected 20 schools but the real implementation was done by the State Council of Educational Research and Training.[128] The scheme was introduced in Mizoram with effect from 31 January, 1991.[129]

In 1995 North Eastern Hill University (NEHU) handed over the plus 2 to the Directorate of School Education. This has increased the burden of education on the Department. As a result, Higher Secondary Schools were opened to accommodate those students who had passed matriculation. Now, according to the statistics, by the year 2000, there are 20 Higher Secondary Schools with 308 teachers and the number of students being enrolled is 6401.[130] Similarly, there are 370 High Schools with 2776 teachers and the number of students is 38570.[131] The number of Middle Schools has also increased tremendously. There are 757 Middle Schools with 50971 students and there are 4945 teachers.[132] Meanwhile, the number of Primary Schools is 1263 and the number of teachers is 4882 and there are 106, 165 students.[133] Besides these, there are a good number of Schools of different levels solely run by the Missions and the private owners. The number of such Schools is not included in the records being maintained by the Directorate.

Before we conclude, let us discuss in brief Adult

Education, Higher Education, Training Institutes and Pre-Primary Schools.

Adult Education, as it is understood, is an educational programme for adults outside formal education. Its main objective is to impart literacy to all illiterate adults.

In Mizoram, it was first instituted as Social Education Wing in 1972 and the term was substituted as 'Adult Education' on 2 October, 1978. In 1985, the post of Joint Director, Adult Education Wing was created. He is assisted by a number of Officers.

Regarding Higher Education in Mizoram, the first college called 'Aizawl College was founded on 15 August, 1958.[134] The first Principal was Rev. Bro. Godfrey, the Headmaster of St. Paul's High School. In 1958 the college was christened Pachhunga Memorial College, now called Pachhunga University College. At present there are 8 Government colleges including Pachhunga University College which is directly managed by the University, 10 deficit and 10 aided colleges in Mizoram. In all the Government Colleges, Science is one of the streams.

In 1979, the NEHU Campus was opened at Aizawl, and now Mizoram University, a Central University is being established.

There are a number of Training Institutes in Mizoram. The District Institute of Education and Training is a district level institute and the medium of instruction is Mizo. There are two such training institutes in Mizoram, one in Aizawl and the other is located at Lunglei.

The College of Teachers Education, known before as 'Mizoram Institute of Education' is the State level institute giving training to teachers with British as the medium of instruction. It is under the Directorate of Higher & Technical Education.

Meanwhile, the State Council of Educational Research and Training was set up in 1980 with a view to arranging and organising in-service training to teachers to produce and develop text books and other reading materials. It is now functioning as a separate establishment but the real control is in the hands of the Director of School Education.

Pre-School education is a recognised international phenomena. In Mizoram Miss K. Hughes started in 1926 which she termed as Class A and Class B. At the same time a Nursery School of Class A and B was also set up at Lunglei. With this small beginning, by 1972 there were 25 Pre-Primary Schools.[135] Now, with the mushroom growth of British Medium Schools in Mizoram, pre-schools are also amazingly increased. In Vernacular Schools they are called Class A and Class B but in British Medium Schools the same classes are called KG-I and KG-II.

Concluding Remarks

In Mizoram the education imparted to the people before the coming of the British was as important as modern education. The role of *Zawlbuk* was so significant an systematic that the education received from the *Zawlbuk* may thus be called 'formal education'. In introducing formal education the roles of the two agencies, the British and the Mission, are highly appreciated. But the two agencies had a different approach to education in Mizoram. Since education was not the sole objective of the administration it did not give it priority, thus leaving the whole management of education to the Mission. At the same time, the Missions had no further aim than making the native people to be able to read and write. To convert them into Christianity was their main objective. Therefore, they had no intention of opening schools beyond the Middle School standard.

The reminiscences of educational progress reveal that Mizos have a great passion for education and this has greatly surpassed the projections made by the State authorities in the field of education. It is a matter of pride that the Mizos have a high literacy percentage, even compared to the most developed States in India.

On the other hand, a very significant thing to be noted is a lack of what is called 'technical education' in Mizoram. Virtually the only technical education Mizoram has today is the Polytechnic Institute at Lunglei and the Women's Polytechnic in Aizawl. The Government of India established a Veterinary Science College in Aizawl a few years ago and this was with the financial assistance of the North Eastern Council, Shillong. In fact, technical education is the areas where the Government of Mizoram has to take a keen interest.

ROLE OF THE PRIESTS IN THE TRADITIONAL RELIGIOUS PRACTICES OF THE MIZOS

Religion, as it is understood is one of the most important and outstanding features of human life. It embraces the whole history of human existence and in all probability religion is virtually as old as humanity itself.[136] Therefore, the history of religion is the history of human development.

The unending search of man for explanation of natural processes beyond his observations convinced him to feel the need to establish friendly and beneficial relations with the living Reality thus overruling the mysterious phenomenon around him.[137] Yet his search for the Reality has no end. Instead the means, method and forms have multiplied from age to age. There lies the origin of religion which was motivated by fear of the unknown but whose presence is felt throught divine providence.[138]

Therefore, it is very difficult to understand the concept of traditional religion of every society because myriads of practices in the form of rituals and ceremonies are to be found. What is still true is that the idea of religion was similar among all so called Kuki tribes.[139] Hence, what is commonly found in the religious beliefs of the early race is that the religion consisted partly in animism, partly in veneration of ancestors and partly in the belief in a Supreme Being.[140] These were, in fact, the basic principles of every religion.

The Mizo religion, as was practiced in the past, too, had these characteristics, but a close examination clearly shows that the religion was more animistic in nature.[141] David Kyles thus expresses his view that the Mizo religion was animism.[142] At the same time, ancestor worship, otherwise known as *Mithirawp Lam* was another important aspect of Mizo religion. What is apparent is that the Mizos also believed in the existence of the Supreme Being who is considered as the God of all humanity and goodness.[143]

It is viewed that every primitive religion was more polytheistic in nature than monotheistic.[144] A study of the Mizo religion has confirmed this notion that the worshippers had to undergo many rituals. Hence, in line with the study conducted by experts[145] on religion, we may for all practical purposes, include in the Mizo religion all the sacrifices that requisitely obliged the symbolic services of the priests.

An attempt is made in this paper to examine the role of the two classes of the priests called *Sadawt* and *Bawlpu* in the primitive religion of the Mizos. But before we proceed any further, it may be good to highlight their position and the status in the society as well.

Puithiam

The priests, *Sadawt* and *Bawlpu,* were commonly called *Puithiam.* Both of them occupied important positions in the village hierarchy and they were the officials in the village administration next to the Chief's elders called *Upa.*

(i) Sadawt : He was a village priest and he belonged

to the Chief. Though the different clans in the village had their own clan-priests who were known as *Sadawt,* they were not as popular as *Lal Sadawt.*[146] The priest who was popularly known as *Sadawt* was only *Lal Sadawt.* All the other *Sadawts* employed by each clan were not at all on the limelight. Therefore, *Lal Sadawt,* may be termed as the 'high priest' of the Mizos and he was one of the most important functionaries in the village administration of the Chief.[147] He was responsible only with the rituals and ceremonies conducted by the Chief himself.

The priesthood of *Sadawt* was partly hereditary and partly selection. That is to say, that the village Chief had a prerogative power over the priesthood of any in the village. Therefore, *Sadawt* became a priest as long as he enjoyed the confidence of his mentor, the Chief.

Sadawt shared the lower end of the spine of the animal sacrificed as his remuneration. He was also remunerated on regular basis with the foreleg of the animal killed in the village.[148] As a general rule, *Sadawt* belonged to Hauhnar clan of the Lusei tribe.

(ii) Tlahpawi : *Tlahpawi* a helper of *Sadawt* was another functionary of some importance next to *Sadawt* in the village.[149] Being an assistant to *Sadawt, Tlahpawi* enjoyed equal status with that of *Sadawt* in the village hierarchy. Though the nature of his function is considered as secondary to *Sadawt* yet he could officiate the office of *Sadawt* in case the latter was unable to perform his duty and responsibility due to illness or other reasons. On the other hand, it is strongly urged that *Lal Sadawt,* could not function in any capacity as *Sadawt* without the presence of the former.[150] However, the latter could conduct any sacrifices with or without the former. Whatever may be the case, the fact is that the practice was different from village to village.

Tlahpawi performed the work of divination while the *Sadawt* offered sacrifice. In other words, he was a fortune—teller or a soothsayer for the sacrificer and his family members. This was an essential part whenever a sacrifice was offered. The instruments applied in the process were called *Tlahpawi.*

He enjoyed, like *Sadawt,* his position as long as the Chief had confidence in him. Also, being appointed by the Chief, *Tlahpawi* was usually a friend of the Chief. Only the Lusei clan had *Tlahpawi.*

(iii) Bawlpu : In regard to the sacrificial offering by the common people, the priest engaged was known as *Bawlpu.* Like the other priests, *Bawlpu* was also an important official in the village. As his concern was only with the common man's rituals, *Bawlpu* was considered as having a lower status in the village hierarchy than those of the *Sadawt* and the *Tlahpawi.*[151]

As his service condition demanded, whenever a man was sick *Bawlpu* was called for consultation in connection with the cause of the sickness. Though he was a priest, *Bawlpu* functioned as a physician or sage. He would feel the pulse of the sick to determine what caused the sickness and the trouble. Like a doctor, he would prescribe what kind of sacrifice the family should observe in order to appease the suffering and the trouble. The family should obey and follow whatever the *Bawlpu* said about the sickness.

In order to undergo the sacrifice *Bawlpu* accompanied by others, should go to the outskirt of the village called *Bawlhmun* or *Bawlmual.*[152] Every village had such a place for the purpose.

Bawlpu like *Sadawt* would not hand over the skill and technique of the incantations to anyone other than his own son or close relative who was considered capable of doing the job. It was usually handed down from father to son, and even then, he would do it so only when the father-priest was too old to perform his duty as *Bawlpu.*

Bawlpu was remunerated for his service in paddy.

The system of remuneration, however, varied from village to village, and it was again a matter of local arrangement. As a whole, the general practice was that even, household paid a paddy full of a basket called *fawng.* Another source of income in the form of remuneration was *faidam,*[153] a paddy of half basket given by the sacrificer himself when the ritual was performed.

There were some *Bawlpu* who knew the technique of breaking the practice of magic or witchcraft called *dawisut.* If the *Bawlpu* was employed for such a job he should be given a *mithun* (*sial*) because it was the job which required expertise and experience. But after sometime, the system was changed from paying a *mithun* to paying of Rs. 40/- instead. In this kind of crafty job the common people had confidence in the *Bawlpu* who belonged to the Hmar clans.[154] It was a general practice that *Bawlpu* hailed from non-Lusei tribe called *awze mi.* The only required qualification to become *Bawlpu* was the skill to chant incantations.

Role of the Priests

Now, we will have a review on the parts played by *Sadawt* and *Bawlpu.* But before we proceed any further, it may be proper to ascertain as to whether or not the sacrifices performed by *Bawlpu* are to be considered as a part of the Mizos religion. In this regard, all Mizo authors are found treating them as outside the purview of the Mizo religion simply because all do not have an analytical study of the Mizo religion. However, in the idea of Briton, religion may have a much wider meaning relating to human life. He says. "The aims of the worshippers may be selfish and sensuous, there may be an entire absence of ethnical intention, his rites may be empty formalities and his creed immoral, but this will be his religion all the same, and we should not apply to it any other name."[155] In the light of this view, we may say that all these sacrifices which required the services of both *Sadawt* and *Bawlpu* were the religion of the Mizos. In this study, too, we will include the sacrifices officiated both by *Sadawt* and *Bawlpu* as Mizo religion.

1. *Sakung*

The first stage in performing the religious rites in which the services of *Sadawt* was required was called *Sakung.* The ceremony was performed by a married son who, for the first instance, lived in a separate house of his own. It was something like an induction or initiation into the religion. In other words, the son was free to perform his own religion. To perform *Sukung.* The sacrificer had to kill one of his male pigs. It should be the biggest among them. This was called *Vawkpa sutnghak talh.* Before the pig was offered *Sadawt* conducted rituals by chanting incantations. When he finished the ceremony *Sadawt* killed the pig by piercing on the region opposite to the heart called *zakdawh* with a pointed bamboo weapon called *tul.* The incantation is as follows :

Sain aw ka Sahrial lo chhang ang che,
Sakunga thovin ka Sahrial lo chhang ang che,
Thlanchhaka thovin ka Sahrial lo chhang ang che,
Thlanthlanga thovin ka Sahrial lo chhang ang che,
Khawlaia thovin ka Sahrial lo chhang ang che,
Kawtpuia thovin ka Sahrial lo chhang ana che,
Leiruta thovin ka Sahrial lo chhang ang che,
Lailawia thovin ka Sahrial lo chhang ang che,
Thawhhmuna thovin ka Sahrial lo chhang ang che,
Bualchuma thovin ka Sahrial lo chhang ang che,
Zinglaia thovin ka Sahrial lo chhang ang che,
Chhuatphova thovin ka Sahrial lo chhang ang che,
Chhuatcheha thovin ka Sahrial lo chhang ang che,
Mualliana thovin ka Sahrial lo chhang ang che,
Nuntluak pang dama thovin ka Sahrial lo chhang
ang che,
Sabana thovin ka Sahrial lo chhang ang che.[156]

In addition to these lines Rev. Liangkhaia, however, added the following lines of incantation :

Lenpuia thovin ka Sahrial lo chhang ang che,
Tuala salu tarho chuan ka Sahrial lo chhang ang
che,
Muchhipa thovin ka Sahrial lo chhang ang che,
Mulena thovin ka Sahrial lo chhang ang che,
Fuanthara thovin ka Sahrial lo chhang ang che.[157]

When he finished chanting, *Sadawt* put the weapon at the outermost post of the house. It was tied up by a bamboo split (*raw hnang*) with the pointed side downwards. This was the place where the sacred part of the meat offered was kept. The skin of the forehead which was cut into three vertical lines and also into four horizontal lines was also kept at the very same place where the weapon was kept. This was called *Sathau.*

The ceremony lasted for three days and when these days were over, *Sadawt* went to the sacrificer's house early the next morning and ceremonially cleaned the house so as to remove the social inabilities of the sacrificer and his family members consequent upon the performance of the ceremony. Here, too, he chanted as :

"Thiang ang, thiang ang (chu mi) tuk thiang ang,
(chu mi) khua var ang,
Mi hnawh thiang ang, sa beih thiang ang,
Leisen chhuah thiang ang,
Thei thur er thiang ang,
Khual buk thiang ang,
Thin dai deh thians ang,
Phihlipa sil angin thiang vil vel ang.[158]

2. *Chawng* or *Chawnfang*

In performing the sacrifice of *Chawng* the sacrificer should offer two male pigs and a female pig to the spirit who was worshipped. Here, *Sadawt* performed his religious duty exactly as he did in Sakung by reciting the same incantations. This lasted for four days. However, the *Thlahpawi*—priest had a part to play. He had to conduct divination for each individual member of the house. As noted earlier, *Tlahpawi* ceremony was a method by which means the fate of an individual member of the family was forecast. To do so, Sadawt used bamboo splits, and the splits were to be broken by pulling them with force. If the breaking had a smooth cut then that should be taken as a bad sign for the person to whom the ritual was done. However, if the splits were broken unevenly then that was a good sign that the person would have a very prosperous life here on earth.[159] On the other hand, *thlahpawi* was not compulsory, and only some of the sacrificers would call for such needs.

3. *Dawino Chhui*

The third stage was *Dawino chhui* in which the subordinate sacrifices namely *Hnuaite, Hnnaite, Chung, Vausen* and *Lasi* were performed. Now, we will examine them one by one.

(a) Hnuaite : In *Hnuaite,* they worshipped *Lasi* a spirit believed to stay around the house.[160] It was believed to be giver of a blessing. To have this ceremonious ritual a female piglet was offered by the *Sadawt* with a chant as follows :

Hnuaite in ka zeltluang lo chhang ang che,
Charsut bula thovin ka zeltluang lo chhang ang che,
Kawmdawla tlrovin ka zeltluang lo chhang ang che,
Thuaidura thovin ka zeltluang lo chhang ang che,
Leithuah hraa thovin ka zeltluang lo chhang ang che.[161]

It is true and accepted that the religious practices were slightly different from one village to another. The difference is chiefly found in the chants and incantations. This may be due to the fact that *Sadawts* who recited the chants sometimes added more lines for their convenience and also for the convenience of the sacrificer. The incantation produced below is one clear example :

Hnuaitein ka zel tluang lo chhang ang che,

Thuaidura thovin ka zel tluang lo chhang ang che,
Banrel bula thovin ka zel tluang lo chhang ang che,
Thawmmawl bula thovin ka zel tluang lo chhang ang che,
Kaldung hnuaia thovin ka zel tluang lo chhang ang che,
Kalvanga thovin ka zel tluang lo chhang ang che,
Leithuah hra-a thovin ka zel tluang lo chhang ang che,
Thuah hnih thuah thuma thovin ka zel tluang To chhang ang che,
Chhimhmuna thovin ka zel tluang lo chhane ang che,
Kawmdawl hnuaia thovin ka zel tluang lo chhang ang che.[162]

(b) Hnuaipui : In *Hnuaipui,* a full grown female pig was sacrificed, and a spirit who, they believed, inhabited the lower region of the earth was worshipped. It was believed that the earth is composed often different layers. Hence, they addressed those spirits living in the tenth layer as *thuah hrat.*

Sadawt's service was involved as in the case of *Hnuaite* sacrifice, and he chanted the rituals as below :

Hnuaipuiin ka chhurpui lo chhang ang che,
Inrel hnuaia thovin ka chhurpui lo chhang ang che,
Kalvang hnuaia thovin ka chhurpui lo chhang ang che,
Banrel Bula thovin ka chhurpui lo chhang ang che,
Thawmmawl bula thovin ka chhurpui lo chnang ang che,
Palfara thovin ka chhurpui lo chhang ang che,

Lei thuah khat a thovin ka chhurpui lo chhang ang che,
Thuah hnih thuah thuma thovin ka chhurpui lo chhang ang che,
Thuahali thuahangaa lo thovin ka chhurpui lo chhang ang che,

Thuah sarih thuah riata thovin ka chhurpui ·lo chhang ang che,
Thuah kua thuah hraa thovin ka chhurpui lo chhang ang che,
Kawmdawl hnuaia thovin ka chhurpui lo chhang ang che,
Pi biakin lo chhang ang che,
Pu biakin lo chhang ang che,
Chhang ngaiin lo chhang ang che.[163]

Here, we find again a slight difference between the incantations produced above and below. The following is quoted from Rev. Liangkhaia.

Hnuaiin aw, ka chhurpui lo chhang ang che,
Lei thuah khat a thovin ka chhurpui lo chhang ang che,
Thuah thuma thovin ka chhurpui lo chhang ang che,
Thuah ngaa thovin ka chhurpui lo chhang ang che,
Thuah sarih a thovin ka chhurpui lo chhang ang che,
Thuah kuaa thovin ka chhurpui lo chhang ang che,
Thuah hraa thovin ka chhurpui lo chhang ang che.[164]

(c) Chung : *Chung* another sacrificial ceremony, was performed to appease the spirit who had a power over the sun and the rain. It was appeased with a piglet. *Sadawt* then chanted as :

Chungin aw ka zel tluang lo chharm ang che,
Van sanga lengin ka zel tluang lo chhang ang che,
Chumchi kara lengin ka zel tluang lo chhang ang che,
Romei kara chengin ka zel tluang lo chhang ang che,
Ni kara chengin ka zel tluang lo chhang ang che,
Thla kara chengin ka zel tluang lo chhang ang che,
Ni *zung* rawn zui che, ka zel tluang lo chhang ang che,

Thai *zimg* rawn *zui* che, ka zel tluang lo chhang ang che,
Ka tlung khana'n lo tum che, ka zel tluang lo chhang ang che,
Ka di hreha'n lo tum che, hreh hnih hreh thuma'n lo tum ang che;
Ka zel tluang lo chhang ang che.[165]

Again Rev. Liangkhaia gives a shorter incantation as follows :

Chungin aw, ka zeltluang lo chhang ang che,
Ni hnua lo thova, chungin ka zel tluang lo chhang ang che,
Ruahpat thova, chungin aw ka zel tluang lo chhang ang che,
Vanzawla thova chungin aw, ka zel tluang lo chhang ang che.[166]

(d) Vansen : In *Vansen,* they worshipped the spirit who was believed to live on the clouds and believed to be giver of abundant blessing. It was performed with a cockerel. *Sadawt* then cited as :

Vansenin ka hluikhuang lo chhang ang che,
Van sanga lengin ka hluikhuang lo chhang ang che,
Ni kara chengin vansenin ka hluikhuang lo chhang ang che,
Thla kara chengin vansenin ka hluikhuang lo chhang ang che,
Ni zung rawn zui che che, thla *zung* rawn *zui* che,
Ka tlung khana'n lo tum che,
Ka liang khana'n lo tum che, ka hluikhuang lo chhang ang che.[167]

Another incantation of the shorter version for the same sacrifice is produced as follows :

Vansenin ka Hluikhuang lo chhang ang che,
Romei kara cheng a vansenin lo chhang ang che,
Chumchi kara chenga vansenin lo chhang ang che.[168]

When the ritual was over. *Sadawt* offered the cockerel : cooked and ate it where a temporary hearth was erected at the water storage place. *Sadawt* then kept a part of the meat called *saserh* on the ceiling just over the water storage. The *Saserh,* apart from its liver and kidney, included every outer-part of the cockerel killed for the offering.

(e) Lasi : The spirit of hunting, believed to have a control over animals was worshipped with a female piglet. The intention of the worshipper was to receive a blessing from *Lasi* so as to become a skilled hunter. The method of offering the sacrifice was exactly the same as *Hnuaite. Sadawt* then chanted as follows :

Lasi in ka zel tluang lo chhang ang che,
Sikhawthanga'n ka zel tluang lo chhang ang che,
Sikhawvara'n ka zel tluang lo chhang ang che,
Hmawngfianga'n thovin ka zel tluang lo chhang ang che,
Khiang kaha thovin ka zel tluang lo chhang ang che,
Nizung rawn *zui* che.
Thlazung rawn *zui* che,
Ka liang kana'n lo tum che,
Nuntluak tumpui ang che,
Pang dam tumpui ang che.[169]

It was not a compulsory ceremony in *Dawino chhui.*[170]

4. *Sedawi*

Sedawi better known as *Sedawi Chhun* was one of the stages by which means the sacrificer of the feast would reach *Pialral.* As the title suggests, [*Se* is a short form of *sial* (*mithun*)] Sedawi was the feast first celebrated by killing a young male *mithun* having horns and ears of equal length.[171]

The skull of the animal sacrificed was kept on the forked pole of a chestnut tree, called *Seluphan* at least for three months. The manner in which they collected

Seluphan was ceremonially ritualistic. The sacrificer selected five men with some skill and one of the members should be a close relative of the performer. Then they went in to the jungles in search of the tree with the *Sadawt* as the leader. While going, they took with them a hen, food and *Zu*. When they saw the tree, then *Sadawt* began to spray *zu* from his mouth over the tree. He sprayed *Zu* against the tree three times. He then sat near the tree and began to chant :

Muchhepa fuk nan ka ti lo,
Sachhepa chuan nan ka ti lo:
Chalrawna lu chuan nan ka ti a ni.[172]

The ceremonial rites were over, the *Sadawt* again performed one more ritual by throwing pellets three times towards upper end of the tree. When he did the men beside him began to utter, "a khum e, a khum e" meaning the pellet flied over the tree.[173] This is not the end of the ritual. *Sadawt* then hit the tree with a *dao* followed by his friends. When the tree fell *Sadawt* would utter, "ka arhlui khuangin a thai thluk e," meaning "the fall was caused by my crowing cock".

When everything was ready, the party proceeded home. After reaching home the *Seluphan* was to be erected. But before placing it, a hole was to be made. For this purpose, *Sadawt* drew a circle on the ground by a porcupine quill and chanted the same verse as follows :

Muchhepa fuk nan ka ti lo,
Sachhepa chuan nan ka ti lo,
Chalvawma lu chuan nan ka ti a ni e.[174]

When he finished, *Sadawt* then hit the ground as if he had made the hole. Then the hole was dug and seluphan was erected. When it was erected *Sadawt* kept an egg at one end of the forked tree. Then *Sadawt* and his party entered into the house and continued to perform some more rituals by reciting the incantations as follows :

Zuva zovuai, zuva zovuai,
Sakunga thovin zuva zovuai,
Khuain zuva zovuai,
Khumpuia thovin zuva zovuai,
Thawhhmuna thovin zuva zovuai,
Chumchilha thovin zuva zovuai,
Bualchhuma thovin zuva zovuai,
Bualchhuma thovin *zuva* zovuai,
Chhuatcheha thovin zuva zovuai,
Chhuatphova thovin *zuva* zovuai,
Mualliana thovin zuva zovuai,
Nuntluak pangdama thovin zuva zovuai,
Sabana thovin zuva zovuai,
Zinglaia thovin zuva zovuai.[175]

However, according to B. Lalthangliana, the song verse was recited not by *Sadawt* but by the respective grandfathers of the sacrificer and his wife. He further says that another man who was a very close relative of the sacrificer also recited the verse.[176]

Having completed the chant, *Sadawt* again collected a small quantity of *Zu* by *haite* (a small gourd) and placed it between the wall and the outermost post. This was set aside for the spirit whom they worshipped in *Hnuaipui.* The same was repeated in *Chung, Vansen. Hnuaite* and *Lasi.*

What was essential in *Sedawi Chhun* was *Thlahual* a prayer for abundant blessings for the family members of the sacrificer *Sedawi Chhun* would have never been complete without *Thlahual* and it should not be misunderstand with another *Thlahual* performed to a person who was frightened by wild animals or some other incidents. *Sadawt* then prayed for each member of the family as follows :

Hual ang, hual ang,
(Ani) thla hual ang,
(Ani) hmui hual ang,
Mihnuai chhiaa thla tur hual ang,

Miral vana thla tur hual ang,
Mi thatin hual ang,
Sa kapin hual ang,
Fanu chawiin hual ang,
Fapa chawiin hual ang,
Fapa chawiin hual ang,
Buhpa chawiin hual ang,
Rareng chulin hual ang,
Chawhnu timin hual ang,
Kum sawmin hual ang,
Kum zain hual ang,
Turn vuiin hual ang,
Hai tarin hual ang,
Pi biakin hual ang,
Pu biakin hual ang,
Ka chham thelhin hual ang.[177]

The incantation was followed by killing a pig, and this was a compulsory item whenever a *mithun* was sacrificed.

In order to complete the process of *Sedawi Chhun*, the *Tlahpawi* ritual must be performed. It was done by *Tlahpawi*—the priest. As noted elsewhere, it was a process of divination by which means the fate of each family member was destined. The main objective of the ceremony was whether the person in the family would have a prosperous future in life or not. If the magical process indicated that the person would have a bright future, the prophesy should be taken seriously because it also destined life and death. Hence, it may be taken as the central theme of the Mizo religion.[178]

Tlahpawi was followed by another performance called *Sethlachhuah* which literally means the release of the spirit (*thla*) of *mithun* (*sial*). On the day when *sial* was sacrificed, *Sadawt* and the sacrificer or head of the performing party went to the outskirts of the village, and brought with them a spear called *sefei*, (a spear specially made to pierce *mithun*), a small quantity of *zu*, five leaves of a chestnut tree, a porcupine's quill and four feathers of a hen. These were the required instruments for conducting rituals. There the *Sadawt* erected an extremely a small house with stones; square in size. When the making was complete, the *Sadawt* laying the leaves on the ground inside the house and also holding the spears by his hand, then began to recite :

Chhuak ang, chhuak ang,
Chalvawma thla chhuak ang,
Ramhnuai lumin chhuak ang,
Sihzawl lumin chhuak ang.[179]

After the ritual was over, *Sadawt* and the sacrificer returned to the village and entered the house of the latter and the former then performed another ritual called *Thlahual.* Starting from the head of the family he called out the names one by one. The verse goes thus :

Hual ang aw, hual ang aw,
(Chu mi) thla hual ang aw,
Nipui dam chen hual ang aw,
Thlapui dam chen hual ang aw,
Fanu chawiin hual ang aw,
Fapa chawiin hual ang aw,
Khumpui lumin hual ang aw,
Tappui lumin hual ang aw.
Turn vuiin hual ang aw,
Haitarin hual ang aw,
Zawh zaw zovin hual ang aw,
Raveng chulin hual ang aw.[180]

From the song thus recited, it may be assumed that *Sadawt* was involved for the long and prosperous life of all the members of the family who observed the sacrifice.

Sadawt and the sacrificer, thus completing the *Thlahual* ceremony, came out of the house with the former appearing first. *Sadawt* had in his hand some *zu* and the sacrificer had a *sefei*-in his hand, too. With these, they proceeded towards the *seluphan* which the sacrificial animal was tied against. In the procession *Tlahpawi* also participated with *zu* in his hand, and *Tlahpawi* also did it in the same way as *Sadawt.* They sprayed *zu* three times each. *Sadawt* then sang as follows :

Khuain aw ka chalvawm lo chhang ang che,
Sakunga thova khuain aw, ka chalvawm lo chhang ang che,
Lailawia thova khuain aw, ka chalvawm lo chhaim ang che,
Thlanchhakathova khuain aw, ka chalvawm lo chhang ang che,
Thlanthlang a thovin khuain aw, ka chalvawm lo chhang ang che,
Khawlaia thova khuain aw, ka chalvawm lo chhang ang che,
Kawpuia thova khuain aw, ka chalvawm lo chhang ang che,
Leiruta thova khuain aw, ka chalvawm lo chhang ang che,
Bualchhuma thova khuain aw, ka chalvawm lo chhang ang che,
Zinglaia thova khuain aw, ka chalvawm lo chhang ang che,
Chhuatphova thova khuain aw, ka chalvawm lo chhang ang che,
Chhuatchcha thova khuain aw, ka chalvawm lo chhang ang che,
Mualliana thova khuain aw, ka chalvawm lo chhang ang che.
Lenpuia thova khuain aw, ka chalvawm lo chhang ang che.[181]

Sadawt and *Tlahpawi* sprayed *zu* again over the animal for three times each. Then, *Sadawt* dropped a small quantity *of zu* on the animal three times where the sacrificer had to pierce it. Before piercing the animal the sacrificer recited one more verse and entered into the house followed by *Sadawt.* The sacrificer should not turn back, otherwise it would be a bad omen.

On the day when *sial* was sacrificed, they also offered a young male pig ceremonially called *Pathian sa* literally meaning 'meat for God.' For the ceremonial process, a special fireplace was raised at the place between the fire-place and the front wall called *khumai*. The animal to be sacrificed was then killed by *tul*. There they cooked and ate. *Sadawt* then recited this :

Pathianin aw ka satluang lo chhang ang che,
Van sanga lenga pathianin ka satluang To chhang ang che,
Ni kara chenga pathianin ka satluang lo chhang ang che,
Thlakara chenga pathianin ka satluang lo chhang ang che,
Thian khawthanga'n ka satluang lo chhang ang che,
Pathian khuhtawngpa'n ka satluang lo chhang ang che,
Mi tin siamtu pathianin ka satluang lo chhang ang che,
Satui siamtu pathianin ka satluang lo chhang ang che,
Thingbul lungbul siamtu pathianin ka satluang lo chhang ang che,
Chhemdama thova pathianin ka satluang lo chhang ang che,
Chemkanga thova pathianin ka satluang lo chhang ang che,
A chhang ngaiin chhang ang che,
A hlang ngaiin hlang ang che.[182]

The Lusei clan performed this ceremony whenever they had a sacrifice with a *mithun*. The *Sedawi* ceremony lasted 7 days. After three months of *Sedawi Chhun*, the *Sadawt* cleansed the household from its social inabilities.

After the end of the three month period, the sacrificer had to perform another ritual called *selu lawh* when the skull of *sial* being kept as trophy at *seluphan* was removed and this was followed by *sethlakhung* performed by the sacrificer on the same day. As they did in the sethlachhuah, the performing priest and the sacrificer went to the place where *Sethlachhuah* had been held before. This time they brought with them *sefei* and *zu. Sadawt* thus chanted :

Khung ang, khung ang Chalvawma thla khung ang,
Sihpui lumin khung ang,
Kawtkai lumin khung ang,
Huang zawl lumin khung ang,
Inthuai lumin khung ang,
Thawmmawl lumin khung ang.[183]

After the ceremonial obligation was done, the proceeded home. When they reached home *Sadawt* put the spear near the *seluphan* and the container of *zu* called *zupeng* was also left nearby the *seluphan.* He then broke an egg with his hand and with that he rubbed the spear and began to chant :

Sil ang, sil ang Chalvawma tul sil ang,
Phihlipa sil sa angin var ang,
Ka artui angin var ang,
Ka buhfai angin fai ang.[184]

On this day, the sacrificer had to kill a male pig for the purpose of what is known as *Selulawhna.* The process and the chants recited were the same as in *Sakung.* Therefore, we will not repeat it here. While the skull of the animal kept at the *seluphan* was removed the priest chanted :

Turn ang, turn ang, Chalvawma lu tum ang,
Nuntluak tumpui ang,
Pang dam tumpui ang,
Buh leh bal tumpui ang,
Chawn leh lam tumpui ang,
Niin a ek khum ang che,
Thlain a ek khum ang che.[185]

When the ritualistic part was over, the skull taken

down was kept along with the other trophies. Then came the end of *Sedawi Chhun.*

5. *Sekhuang*

Sckhuang otherwise known as *Mitthirawp lam* was another area of sacrifice which required the service of *Sadawt.* When performed, the sacrificer had to make three small drums made of hollowed-out of wood producing three different notes or tones called *Talhkhuang.* It was to be kept at the *Seluphan.* For this kind of instrument they generally used two kinds of trees namely *Hnum* and *Fartuah.* Led by *Sadawt,* they went to the jungles looking for the trees. With him *Sadawt* took a dried skull of a he-goat with which he hit the tree before it was cut. While hitting the tree with the skull *Sadawt* uttered as *"Be," "B." "Be"* and continued to say, "Hei kei ni kihthluk in ni lo va, kel pa sil thluk in ni e, "meaning "you fell not because of us, but because of the hit caused by the goat." When they had finished making the drums the *Thangchhuah* feasters were entitled to play with the drums. Besides these persons, the wife of the sacrificer was entitled to beat them when she was going to bed.[186]

6. *Ngawn Chawn*

Ngawn Chawn, also known as *Hnum Chhe Hnawl,* was worshipped with a female pig. *Sadawt* conducted the rituals over the animal to be sacrificed but the animal was killed by *Tlahpawi Sadawt* then did the reciting of the chant as :

Hual ang, hual ang,
(Thanga) thla hual ang,
(Thangi) thla hual ang,
Khumpui lumin hual ang,
Tappui lumin hual ang,
Rareng chulin hual ang,
Buh reng chulin hual ang,
Nipui dam chen hual ang,
Thlapui dam chen hual ang,

Nun tluak pang damin hual ang,
Turn viau haitarin hual ang,
Thinga laknaah hual ang,
Tuia laknaah hual ang,
Thing leh khama tla lovin hual ang,
Tui leh luang a tla lovin hual ang.[187]

Sadawt then continued the process by chanting over the animal to be killed as :

Luh zoving e, luh zoving e,
Kan chhinchhak khua luh zoving e;
Kan chhimchhak khua luh zoving e;
Kan lengzaawl khua luh zoving e,
Kan minpui khua luh zoving e,
Kan rulhreu khua luh zoving e,
Laihanga e luh zoving e,
Kan bel telpui luh zoving e,
Nu puin 'aw' ti ua pa puin 'aw' ti ua
Laichinin 'aw' ti ua, Fa farin 'aw' ti ua,
Zawhzaw zovin 'aw' ti ua.[188]

When the ritual was over, the people sitting beside *Sadawt* said *'aw'* (yes) and they sprayed *zu* over the animal. The female pig to be offered was then killed by *Tlahpawi.* In case *Tlahpawi* was not available *Sadawt* could preside over the functions. The place where they killed the pig was at the water storage place.

They ate the meat of the animal offered on the floor of the house. When they finished eating, *Sadawt,* keeping a part of the meat and some other items in a broken gourd, and starting from the door at the back, began to recite as follows :

Chhia chhuak, chhia chhuak,
Kawmchara chhia chhuak,
Khumpuia chhia chhuak,
Tappuia chhia chhuak,
C'hhuat dunga chhia chhuak,
Khumhnuaia chhia chhuak.[189]

Then he continued to chant as *"Kuwngka hnuaia chhia chhuak"* meaning "go away the misfortunes through the lower part of the door," and kicked against the lower part of the door three times and went out of the house. The vessel by which he held the meat and some items was thrown away outside the village and he went home directly.[190] *Ngawn Chawm* was held for a day.

7. *Kawngpui siam*

This was another religious performance organized in public. The ritual sought for the village a prosperity on animals and enemies.[191] It was held or performed at the southern entry of the village. In case *Lal Sadawt* as was popularly known could not perform it due to any reasons, *Tlahpawl* could preside in his place. To perform the ritual they used a climbing plant known in Mizo as *Vawm hrui.* They made a ring-like circle with it and placed it on the road at the outskirts of the village. To perform it, three or five or seven numbers of people including *Sadawt* should go to the appointed place. The number of the participants should be that of an odd number. They took with them *zu* in a bamboo and a gourd. They also fetched with them ash and the animal for sacrificial offerings. The ash would then be placed inside the ring. Every year a pig and a hen were offered alternatively. Before offering the animal *Sadawt* then began to chant as :

> Hual ang, hual ang,
> Thanga thla hual ang,
> Thangate chhung hual ang,
> Mi thuai chhiahah tla lovin,
> Mi chem pelin hual ang.[192]

After the verse was over, *Sadawt* continued to recite another stanza as follows :

> Kawng ka siam e, kawngpui ka siam e,
> Mi lu Tawi nan ka siam e,
> Sa lu lawi nan ka siam e,
> Buh za lawi nan ka siam e,

Khua ding e, khua ding e,
Aizawl khua ding e,
Khua tlu e, khua tlu e,
Puia khua tlu e,
Chhawna khua tlu e.[193]

Besides the different stages apparently connected with the religion of the Mizos as narrated above, there are some other feasts and sacrifices like, *Khmangchawi Thangchhuah (In lam* and *Ramlam Thangchhuah), Zaudawh* etc. It seems that the priest-*Sadawt* had no part to play in these performances mainly because they were feast celebrated in publit. Even if *Sadawt* had a part to play it would he very marginal.

Now, we will turn to the second part of our study under review. Here, we will try to evaluate the role of the priest—*Bawlpu* in brief. At the same time, while reviewing the role of *Bawlpu* we will deal only with some significant sacrifices connected with sickness and misfortunes.

The services of *Bawlpu* were called for the sacrifice called *Ramhuai Hnena In Thawina* only. As noted earlier the Mizos broadly divided the so-called spirits into good spirits and bad spirits. All the rituals and sacrifices performed in connection with the bad spirits known in Mizo as *Ramhuai* were commonly called *Ramhuai Hnena Inthawina.* Therefore, Mizos offered sacrifices to divert or dissuade evil spirits from tormenting men and women.

The Mizos believed that every person had his or her appointed spirit who looked after him. When displeased, it caused sickness or other ailments, including, sometimes physical injury. Hence, the spirit must be propitiated. The sacrifice performed was named after the name of the animal killed. When a fowl was offered the sacrifice or ritual was named after the name of the animal killed. When a fowl was offered the sacrifice or ritual was named *Ar Khal* but it was *Kel Khal* when a goat was sacrificed.

8. *Khal*

There were a number of *Khals viz., Khal Tluang, Khal Pui, Khal Chung, Khal Chuam, Kel Khal, Ar Khal, Arpui Hang Khal, Vawkte Khal, Van Chung Khal, Lasi Khal and Sa Khal.* In *Khal* they worshipped the spirit believed to have settled somewhere on the hills. It was further believed that that spirit, by playing with the soul of a man, caused sickness or suffering. So, it was necessary to appease it. Hence, *Khal* was conducted.

In order to perform the ritual, if a goat was used, the animal was brought near the sick and *Bawlpu* began to chant as below :

> Khalin ka mualhawih hi (lal) lo chhang ang che,
> Turhpuia thovin ka mualhawih hi lo chhang ang che,
> Taua thoin ka mualhawih hi lo chhang ang che,
> Tauhala thovin ka mualhawih hi lo chhang ang che.[194]

I he following verse was also recited :

> Fanu chawiin rawn khal ang che,
> Fapa chawiin rawn khal ang che,
> Mi that, sa kapin rawn khal ang che.[195]

Whenever a *Khal* was performed, the members of the family should not communicate with any unknown guest for three day, nor should they visit smithy nor should they take any sour lemon.

9. *Bulthluk*

When people suffered from severe cold, *Bulthluk* was offered by killing a chicken and models of *mithun* made with clay and so many other articles called *bawlhlo* were needed for the rituals.

10. *Daibawl*

When *Bulthluk* was found ineffective another sacrifice called *Daibawl* was conducted. In *Daibawl* they tried to appease *Tuihuai,* or a bad spirit believed to have lived in the water. They also tried to appease it with a cock. It was performed at the outskirts of the village and touching of sacrificial implements was forbidden. Before killing animals to be sacrificed the *Bawlpu* uttered the words of salutation to the spirit :

Chibail!
Tuia miin ka hlui khuang lo chhang ang che,
Rama miin ka pui hang lo chhang ang che.[196]

According to K. Zawla, before proceeding to *Bawlhmun,* the *Bawlpu,* swinging the cock, chanted as follows :

Chibai! (He said aloud with his bagpipe called *rawchhem*)
Ramchawngnu a ti maw, Ramchawngpa a ti maw,
Ramchawnglala ram vua vua a ti maw,
Sumsem zawlah sum sem tang a ti maw,
Paisem zawlah pai sem tang a ti maw,
Ka rawh cheh a tha hlang tang a ti maw.[197]

After this ritual, the participants proceeded to *Bawlhmun* taking with them the cock, food and all the instruments required for the sacrifice. *Bawlpu* then chanted again as :

Chibai!
Ramchawngnuin ka hlui khuang lo chhang ang che,
Ramchawngpain ka hlui khuang lo chhang ang che,
Paisemin ka hlui kuang lo chhang ang che,
Thingbul a mi in ka hlui khuang lo chhang ang che,
Lungbul a mi in, ka hlui khuang lo chhang ang che,
Ka chham thelhin ka hlui khuang lo chhang ang che,
Thanga (The man who was sick) mantu hi lo haw rawh,
A In a ban tlan nan ka ti;
Hruia in hlin chuan phelh ula,
Lungin a delh chuan phawk ula,
Thingin a delh chuan phawk ula.[198]

Bawlpu continued to pray by naming all the sacrificial instruments as

Chibai!
Ka thembu a tha a ti, ka thei biak a tha a ti,
Ka rawcheh a tha a ti, ka maicham a tha a ti,
Ka leng lep a tha a ti, ka chang sial a tha a ti,
Ka darbu a tha a ti, ka ngaleng a tha a ti,
Tui bungpuinu, Thanga chawnbanah rawn vuan che,
I vuan thei lo vang.[199]

After this incantation was over, Bawlpu killed the cock by cutting off his head with a *dao.* Then he sprayed the blood over the instruments, and a portion of the meat was kept as sacred on the alter. The remaining portion was cooked and eaten there. While going home they collected water from the water-point. But they were not allowed to enter the house until they were sprinkled with the water by the people who were at home. That was the end of the *Daibawl* sacrifice.

11. *Khua leh Chawm*

This sacrifice was performed with a piglet, a black hen and a red cock when a child was attacked by convulsion. To perform the sacrifice the party, seven in number went to the appointed place and there they made a model of a female *Chawm* (a demon) and *Bawlpu* performed the rituals as follow :

Naufualnu, naufualpa, puk kilah lo tang ang che,
(Liana) lunglai mawlin lo thawk che,
Lui chhuk tumbu rawn satthlanu, satthlapa
I lo thawk thei tawh lo vang.[200]

When he finished the chant, *Bawlpu* killed the piglet and placed the uncooked liver into the mouth of *Chawmnu* and he also put some of them on her head. At the same time, a chicken was also offered for the spirit known as *Khua.*

The sacrifice was performed as a last resort. When all the devices had failed *Bawlpu* had to conduct this sacrifice but with a reluctantly heavy-heart. The sacrifice was performed at the outskirts of the village and selected the place where the sick hardly had a visit. As they did in *Daibawl* they made the two models of *Chawmnu* and *Chawmpa* who were adjoined with a small conical land-snail called *Piring*. *Bawlpu* then chanted using strong words of warning. After this, he cut the pig on its neck and allowed the blood to drop over all the sacrificial instruments placed on the alter, The livers and the kidnevs of the animal were given to *Chawm* and the remaining portion was cooked and ate there. All the sacred parts were, however, offered at the alter and then they left for home. It was forbidden to take the meat home.

Beside these sacrifices, there were other sacrifices *viz. Ui hring, Khuavang Hring, Arte Hring Ban* etc. All these were also connected with sickness and other ailments.

Concluding Remarks

The religion, presented and discussed as Mizos religion in this essay was basically the religion of the Lusei clans of the Mizos tribe. As a matter of fact, the religion, as practised among other clans of the Mizos tribes, was more or less the same and therefore they were mentioned as *dawisa kil za thei* which loosely means that many of the clans could share a common alter to worship among themselves.

Another aspect of the religion was that it was a family religion rather than a community religion because of the fact that it was observed and performed solely by an individual family with the support of other members of the community and it was held when a family needed. Only *Kawngpui Siam* may be called the religion worshipped in a community. From this point of view, the Mizo religion may, therefore, be termed as rituals and ceremonies performed in order to satisfy the moral obligations of an individual.

Lastly, as the religion in which so many spirits were worshipped the roles of the priests—*Sadawt* and *Bawlpu* were enormous. Every religious observance needed the services of the priests and therefore, they could hardly find a time to rest, especially the *Bawlpu* for he had a more busy schedule.

THE HISTORIC MOVEMENTS OF THE EARLY MIZOS

It is very interesting to make an attempt to study the movement of the early Mizos to their present habitat. It is very challenging, too, because till now no serious and systematic attempt was made nor any archaeological evidence found worthy to sustain that Mizos had undergone tremendous population movements in pre-historic times. However, the well-established fact is that population has moved from the earliest times to the present owing to causes such as drought, ethnic pressures, collecting food, seeking warmth and so on. Hence, it must be assumed that the Mizos had made movements along with other ethnic tribes and races for these same reasons just mentioned. However, our knowledge and available materials are too scanty to justify more than a guess about the early movements of the tribe. In spite of all these shortcomings, an attempt is made in this paper to investigate about the pre-historic and historic movements of the people with a view to throwing some light and as a step forward in the study under review.

The period of this study covers from the earliest times to the present, or until any written or recorded history of the people was made. Thus our study covers through the ages because at present it is too difficult to identify the period as ancient, medieval and modern as in the case of others. For this reason, in this attempt, the people will be referred to as Chin in Burma and Kuki in areas other than Burma. This is inevitable because the tribe did not form themselves as a homogenous race with a cultural entity.

The Early Habitat of the Mizos

In order to understand the movement of the people a consideration of their early settlements is essential. But before we proceed any further, it may be appropriate to state the views of scholars on the origin of the human race. Most scholars think that man made his first appearance in China. Burkitt says that the later stone age people made their movements from China to central Asia and thence to Europe.

It may, therefore, be conjectured that China is not only the home of early human race but also the home of the tribal peoples who are now scattered in the different places in southeast Asia, including north-east India. Therefore, while searching for the original habitat of the people our attention may be focussed on China, particularly the southern part, because our tradition points to it.

All societies have traditions about how they and the rest of mankind came into being. The Mizos too, have the Chhinlung tradition. This tradition claims Chhinlung as the original habitat of the Mizos. Chhinlung is said to be located somewhere in Szechuan Province, in southern China. The Chhinlung theory is more or less confirmed by scholars who have sub-divided the Tibeto-Chinese family into groups and sub-groups. In these divisions Mizos are grouped as a Tibeto-Burman family who speak the Tibeto-Burman language. The home of these peoples is not definitely known, but somewhere between Kansu in South China and Burma is believed to be their earliest known home. Hall believes that somewhere between Gobi desert and Northeast Tibet, also possibly Kansu, is the earliest known home of the Tibeto-Burman speaking peoples. This region, also known as 'buffer-state', forms part of Southern China where all the tribes are found and distributed widely over the mountainous area of Kweichow, Szechuan and Yunnan. In view of the settlement patterns of the tribal people, Southern China may be considered as the original homes of the tribal people including the Mizos. Thus, Prof. J.N. Phukan concludes : "The connections of the Mizos with the Burmese and the Shans in many of their cultural elements and civilization bring us to the theory that their late home of migration was Southern China bordering Myanmar where even today many tribes lead their traditional life." So, in all probabilities. Southern China and the entire fringe of the Eastern perimeter of the plateau between Kansu and Burma may be considered as the early home of the Mizos and the tribes now numerously found in Northeast India. These tribes were the descendants of early feudal rulers created by the Chinese emperors. They came to the South as the result of vast waves of population movements and also owing to Chinese pressures. In the period between 338 BC and 224 BC the tribal peoples moved *en masse* to the South owing to the war between the Chin and Ch'u. The imperial army of Ch'u put down the latter with a heavy hand and consequently this led to a large-scale dispersal of the populations of Szechuan and the other provinces in the south. But in subsequent years the people, after re-grouping themselves in various localities amid the hills and plains in Yunnan, set up a number of small principalities. One of these was that of Ngai-Zao founded by one prince called Chiu-lung.

The major wave of population movement of the tribal peoples to the South was also perhaps caused by the policy of Cheng, better known to history as Shih Huang (Wang) Ti (246-210 BC). Known as the Napoleon of China and founder of the Chinese empire, Shih Huang-Ti initiated real pressure on the tribes during the time when the construction of parts of the Great Wall was being vigorously performed. So, he was responsible for the great revolutionary development in China.

Early Migration of the Mizos-The Burma Phase

In this section we will deal with the entry into Burma by

the Mizos. The fact is that the people entered through different routes at different times and therefore, a search will be made to find out at least some truths on the coming of the Mizos from South China to Burma.

As noted elsewhere, the history of population movement has a long history because no tribe or race is static. Therefore, it is correct to say that the Mizos moved southward and arrived in Burma in course of time as the result of population movement. In order to form an idea as to the movement of the Mizos it is essential to follow the movement patterns of the Tibeto-Burman tribes and the Tai-Chinese peoples who were already prominent as tribes during the period under review.

According to Donnison, there were three main waves of population movements from China to Burma. The Tibeto-Burman tribes of Pyu, Arakanese, Kachin, Chin and a considerable number of smaller tribes were grouped in the first wave. The Mons of the Mon-Khmer races were put in the second wave. The third wave, however, included the Tai-Chinese peoples like the Shans or Tais, Karens and others. In order to understand the movement of the Mizos we will continue our brief survey on the movements of these peoples.

The earliest inhabitants of which any record exists in Burma were the Pyu, who reached Burma sometime in A.D 300. They were the natives of Burma through absorption. Next to the Pyu were the Mons of the Mon-Khmer group which arrived in Burma about the third century A.D and founded the kingdom with Pegu as its capital. They are now numerously found in Indo-China. They also became Burmese by assimilation.

Chins are akin to Mizos and in Burma Mizos were known as Chins. They were the earlier immigrants who lived in the Chin Hills of Burma before the Burmese proper settled in the plains. It is, therefore, suggested that the Chin people came to Burma in the second part of the ninth century A.D. But Luce puts the entry of the

Chins into Burma in the period between the fourth and the middle of the eighth centuries A.D. According to Lehman, Luce derived the fourth century from the fact that the Chins by this time had already used the word 'tangka' (coinage) which is believed to be the name of a Gupta coin of India. It is firmly believed that the coin was brought to the East by Samudra Gupta (c. 320-380 AD) in the middle of the fourth century. The eighth century date is, however, derived from the fact that the ancient land route used by the caravans and traders from China to India was not mentioned in literature. This convinces Luce to believe that the route was presumably closed after A.D. 300 until A.D. 750 and as such no major westward movement was noticed, otherwise it would have been recorded in the annals or literatures.[201] He, therefore, strongly believes and concludes that most of the hill people arrived in Burma between the two dates. Harvey has, however, believed that many of the immigrants must have settled in Burma before the Christian era.[202] It may, therefore, be concluded that the Chin people occupied the present Chin Hills before the end of the eighth century A.D.

The next tribes of interest after the Tibeto-Burma people were the Tai-Chinese group which includes, among others, the Shans and the Karens. Phayre observes that the Tai or Shans entered Burma early in the Christian era.[203] Gogoi puts the date as the sixth century A.D.[204] Thus, the Shans or Tai are believed to have completed their migration from China to Burma in the middle of the thirteenth century A.D. Sukapha, after leaving the Shan State of Maulung in Upper Burma about A.D. 1215 founded his Ahom Kingdom in Assam in A.D. 1228.

The Karen people were expelled from Yunnan by the Nau-Chao King Ko-Lofeng (A.D. 748-778) in A.D. 778.[205] Though the exact date is not known the Karens are said to have reached Burma in the beginning of the ninth century A.D. They came by way of the Mekong or Salween river into what is now known as the Shan State.

It may be interesting to note that the Karens reckon 1983 as their year of 2722. This means that they look to 739 B.C. as the year of their founding.[206] They had lived in Burma for many centuries. It was in the 18th century that the Karens began to cross Burma into Thailand. The Karen legends speak of coming from the land of 'Thibi Kawbi' which may indicate Tibet and Gobi desert. According to some, they originated farther to the west.

The Burmese proper entered Burma in the latter part of the ninth century A.D. and completed their migrations between A.D. 849 and A.D. 1044.[207] It is observed further that they probably began to migrate into Burma from the North-east in the ninth century A.D. and established their powerful kingdom with Pegu as its capital. Anawarahta (A.D 1047-1077) was the first great King of the kingdom.

From the account given above, it may be conjectured that the Mizos came to Burma alongwith the peoples who are akin to them. In all probabilities, Mizos are linked with the Chins by which name some scholars refer to the Mizos.

Early Migration of the Mizos—The North-East Phase

The present North-East India, formerly known as Assam (undivided), was inhabited by various racial elements. The region received wave after wave of immigrants from South-East Asia and elsewhere and for this fact, it may be considered as a museum of races.[208] While some elements of the inhabitants were probably indigenous, some other people were at times sent out from this region.

The earliest inhabitants of the region were the Kiratas, Cina and other primitive tribes.[209] In Sanskrit the term Kirata indicates the wild non-Aryan tribes living in the mountains particularly, of the Himalayas and the North-Eastern areas of India. They were connected with the Cinas or the Chinese.[210] The traditional meaning of the word Kirata are "those who *move-atanti* along the mountain sides, or in bad, dirty places, *Kira*.[211] MacDonald and Keith are of the view that Kirata is a name applied to people living in the cave of the mountains."[212] Therefore, it may be concluded that Kirata is a name applied to all peoples of Mongoloid origin who migrated from South-Fast Asia including Burma in course of time and found the region of the North-East India as their settlements.

The epics and the *Puranas* refer the 'Cinas' as Kuki-Chins or Lushai.[213] *The Geography of Ptolemy,* a work of about A.D 150 deals with the geography and peoples of other parts of Assam. But many of the words and places mentioned are difficult to identify. The word *Kirrhadae,* for example, is identified as *Kiratas*. In the same way another work of the Greeks. The *Periplus of the Erythrean Sea*.[214] which mentions about Assam in different descriptions also refers a number of tribes as *Kirrhadae*.[215] In this connection, the work of G.E Gerini, *Researches on Ptolemy's Geography,* is commendable. He rightly identifies Ptolemy's *Alosong* with Shillong and *Tiladai* with the Kuki-Chin.[216] Tiladai was located to the north of the Moirandos near the Garo Hills and Sylhet.[217]

In the *Mahabharata,* the *Puranas* and *Tantras* the ancient Assam is referred to as Pragjoytisha and Kamarupa respectively. The Mahabharata mentions one Bhagadatta as one of the four sons of Naraka. He was a powerful ruler who ruled in the west. *The Sabha Parvan,* from Hindu literature, relates the war between-Bhagadatta and Arjun. In the war, the latter defeated the former after eight days of war.[218] It also mentions that Bhagadatta had a host of *Kirats* and Chins and other numerous warriors who dwelt on the sea coast.[219] The Hindu literature like the two epics and so many others makes references to the Kiratas.[220] About the proper home land of the Kiratas, the *Visnu Purana* says that the

Kiratas are in the east of India.[221] Therefore, Chatterjee concludes, "the Kiratas were known to the Hindu world as a group of peoples whose original home was in the Himalayan slopes and in the mountains of the East...."[222] The history of the arrival in India (North-East India) of the various Mongoloid groups speaking dialects of the Sino-Tibetan family is not known but their presence in India was noted by the tenth century B.C when the Veda books were compiled.[223] The result of their participation in the history and culture of India in the areas where they had established themselves, has been their assimilation and absorption with the other peoples.

The migrations of the Mongoloid tribes to Assam took place through the North-Eastern and Southern routes of Assam from Burma. They entered Assam through the courses of the riser Brahmaputra, Chindwin, Irrawaddy, Salween, Mekong and Menam. Some of them also entered Assam through mountain passes of Assam and Burma through the north-east and southeast. When they arrived in Assam the Mon-Khmer tribes had already occupied some hilly regions hut they had been driven out later by the newly arrived tribes into different directions.[225] Therefore, some occupied the foot hills of the Himalayas from Sadiya to the Punjab in the West, and the rest occupied the hills of Assam such as the Garo Hills, Naga Hills, Lushai Hills, Khasi Hills and so on. It was only after their distribution and occupation of particular areas that they came to be known as Nagas, Bodos, Mizos. Khasis and so on and the areas of their occupation were known by their tribal names.[226] The Sesatae of the Periplus and the Besadae of Ptolemy were also the same hill people of Assam allied to the Garos, Nagas and the Lushai-Kukis or the Mishmis.

Early Migration of the Mizos—The Mizoram Phase

Like the previous movements, the migration of the Mizos from Burma or the North-East took place in three phases and as such, the people were for the sake of convenience identified under the three names as 'Old-Kuki,' 'New-Kuki' and the 'Lushai'.

The 'Old Kuki' of Hrangkhawl, Biate, Langrawng, Pangkhua and Mug (Mawk) was the first batch in migration. They were followed by the so-called 'New Kuki' and the 'Lushai' followed them as the third batch in migrations. We do not know, like the previous movements of the people, when they came to Mizoram but what is known definitely is that the first two batches had been pushed, causing them to go as far as what is now known as Tripura State of India and the present day Bangladesh. A good number of Mizos are still living in Bangladesh. But the history of their migration indicates that the first two immigrants, or at least some of them migrated back to Hiramba and made their settlements at the hills now known as North-Cachar Hills District of Assam.

Soppit brings the date of their migration to the middle of the sixteenth century A.D.[227] But this conclusion may be disputed on account of the fact that mention is made in the annals of Tripura under the Raja Chachag or Roy Chachag who is said to have flourished about A.D 1512.[228] Chachag or Roy Chachag.[229] was the military commander of Dhanya Manikya who ascended the throne of Tripura in A.D. 1490. In A.D. 1513 the Raja issued a coin in his name and in the coin it is written as conqueror of Chittagong."[230] During his reign a quarrel arose between him and the Kukis over the possession of a white elephant. The Kukis occupied the deep forest lying to the East of Tripura and the West of Lushai Hills.[231] The *Rajamala*, the Chronicle of the Tripura Rajas, also mentions the Kukis. The Chronicle speaks about the services rendered by the Kukis to the Tripura kings.[232] The Chronicle also narrates how the Raj Kumar fell in love with a Kuki woman.[233]

There is also evidence to indicate that the Mizos, under the name Kuki, had already arrived in Tripura late in the twelfth century A.D. In the history of Tripura mention is made that once Raja Dharmadahar of Kailagadh invited Nidhipati, a Kanauj Brahmin to his court and granted him an estate, known in history as Brahmottar land. The inscription in the copper plate marking the event bears the name of Kuki-land. The land bounded in the east of Longoi (Langkaih) river and the date is mentioned as A.D. 1195.[234] The theory is that the Kukis, who are known in Tripura as Halam, sneaked into Tripura due to ethnic pressures, possibly perhaps, long before the coming of Palian and Zadeng ruling clans of Zahmuaka who had been pushed down by the Sailo Chiefs of the same ancestor. They entered Tripura not from Lower Burma, but from Upper Burma passing through the area now known as Mizoram.

The New Kukis are believed to have come from the same route followed by the Old Kukis. We cannot place them far behind the Kukis of the first batch. Hence, they are said to have arrived in the land in the period between fourteenth and fifteenth centuries A.D.[235]

The last batch of migration, which were identified as 'Lushai', like the first two groups, consisted of many clans. The most prominent among them was the Lusei tribe of the Sailo clan. They were the direct descendants of Thangura who is believed to have existed in A.D. 1580. As noted before, Palian and Zadeng groups came before the Sailos and they are said to have come in A.D 1610.[236] The Sailo clan are believed to have migrated to Mizoram beginning from the second half of the seventeenth century and might have continued till the beginning of the nineteenth century. McCall has asserted that Lallula occupied Mizoram around A.D. 1810.[237]

THE MIZO UPRISING : A SIGNIFICANT EVENT IN THE HISTORY OF CHIEFTAINSHIP IN MIZORAM

When the advent of the British in the area, now Mizoram,

was around the corner, a remarkable event took place. The people revolted against the autocratic and whimsical rule off the Sailo Chiefs who became masters of the whole of Mizoram after crushing all their rival Chiefs and held undisputed sway over all sorts of clans. The event, locally known as *Lal Sawi*, was a popular uprising against the despotic rule of the Chiefs in which almost all the commoners were involved. The movement spread from one village to another like wildfire. The uprising halted the smooth running of the administration of the Chiefs. The result was however short-lived and brief because the unity among the common people could not last long. For this reason the Chiefs restored themselves to their previous positions without much difficulty. The restoration of the Chiefs was immediately followed by the advent of the British. Here, an attempt is made in this paper to give a brief account of the uprising thus highlighting the whole episode.

Causes of the Uprising

When the wounds off the war between the Eastern and the Western Chiefs were hardly healed this uprising arose to muddle the positions of the Chiefs. As the uprising was Chiefly directed against the Chiefs, the causes are also not far to seek. Though the incident happened in a later period of the reigns of the Chiefs the woes of the people were not of recent origin. It may, therefore, be assumed that the oppressive rule of the chiefs was solely responsible for what happened in Mizoram. The causes of the uprising may be briefly described as follows.

Nobody can say for certain as to how and when Chieftainship originated. Its revolution appears to have grown out of the collective needs of the group life. Inter-clan feuds which were common among the Mizos also appear to have been responsible for the rise of Chieftainship, its origin may be traced Chief. In those days, a man's wealth was measured by the valuable items he possessed. For example, if a man had many *mithuns* he was considered a wealthy man and was respected in the village. Likewise, a man who had a gong, whether big or small, was considered a wealthy man. Thus the valuable property like silver, beads, gongs, *mithun* etc. would always find their way to the Chief's house. He seized them for greed.[241] So, under such prevailing and uncertain situation the people had no choice but to revolt against the Chief.

Secondly, the Chief had officials to whom the people paid tributes. The officials were, the *Upa,* the *Tlangau,* the *Ramhual,* the *Zalen,* the *Puithiam* and the *Thirdeng.* The *Khawchhiar,* a village writer was the creation of the British. These officials helped the Chief in his day to day administration. The *Puithiam,* a priest, was concerned only with the religious rites. The people were obliged to pay tributes or dues to them in addition to regular payment to a Chief. The dues became heavy and burdensome to a common man. Thus, having enjoyed a higher status than the common people in the society the officials sometimes misused their position which embittered the common man. Upas, acting as a link between the Chief and the ruled always lived a comfortable life. Sometimes they demanded favours from the people even without the Chief's knowledge. For this reason, the *Upas* and officials were the target of attack together with the Chief when a political party was formed in 1946.

Thirdly, in fact, the people were the life line of the Chief. They were the tax payers. Every family was bound to pay *Fathang* or paddy tax after harvesting was over and the amount of which was varied from time to time depending, however, on an individual Chief. Generally, every resident paid the same quantity. The Chief was also entitled to receive *Sachhiah* or meat tax. Whenever wild animal was shot or trapped the Chief shared its hind leg. In case a villager failed to pay this due, he was liable to a rigorous punishment to the extent of being expelled from the village or death penalty. But after circulation of money the Chief, if he chose, could impose a fine of Rs. 40/-. He also received *Chi chhiah* or salt tax. When a salt well was found in a village a party had to pay to the Chief a share. In addition to this share, each member of the party must pay a certain quantity out of his own share. The Chief then got the biggest share. The village Chief also received a share out of wild honey collected by villagers. This was called *Khuai chhiah* or bee tax. Anyone who collected wild honey without prior permission from the Chief was liable to a fine of Rs. 40/-. If a *mithun* was sold to a person belonging to another village the man had to give Rs. 2/- more as a due payable to the Chief. This was called *Sekawt hawn man.* Again, the villagers had to construct or repair the Chief's house, free of cost. For this, the people did not pay anything in kind or cash but they spent, sometimes, many days for the Chief. This in turn affected the economic life of the villagers. This was called *Lal in sak chhiah.* Besides these taxes, the Chief sometimes realised taxes from the people on certain items. The taxes imposed upon the common people became unbreakable and failure of payment could lead to a serious action upon the concerned person. Thus the people looked for a chance to do away with these obnoxious taxes.

Fourthly, the Chief's action which the people most hated was locally known as *ram.*[242] By it, the Chief used to seize the property of a man who disobeyed his orders. The victim was also liable to expulsion from the village. The Chief could send any of his subjects away from his village without giving any reason thereof. At the same time, every family had the right to leave a Chief to join another village. In a normal situation, the Chief was obliged to accept the migration of his subject, but before he left he should clear his dues, and again in certain cases, the Chief was not bound to oblige. Sometimes a villager did try to escape from a village for fear of the Chief. In that case he risked his own life because in case the new Chief did not accept him, his life was completely in danger. Every Chief in fact required more houses, as his strength was measured by the number of houses he possessed.

Fifthly, the Chief sometimes showed partiality to his subjects. This policy badly affected the general life of the people. In theory, the Chief was the custodian of every citizen. All men were equal before him. But in real practice, he was fully partial. There was a big gap between the rich and the poor. In times of danger he would employ the services of those whom he did not favour. However, on certain occassions where the Chief's favour could be earned he would select only the one whom he favoured most. There was distinction between the rich and the poor, the brave and the coward etc. He did not welcome a family that could not cultivate enough paddy for a year. Nor was there a place for a lazy man. If a grown up man was found loiterng in the day time ho would he asked as to why ho was at home. Thus for all such reasons, the hatred against the Chief gathered momentum when the Sailo Chiefs became masters of the whole Mizoram in the latter period of their rule. Thus, the Sailo Chief's did not show any signs that they were better than their predecessors.

Outbreak of the Uprising

The commoners wanted to liberate themselves from the yoke of the Chief for a long time. They failed to achieve it because unity among them could not become an entity. Now, being united they had to resort to the course of the uprising. The uprising first broke out in Lalkhuma's village at Lungchhuan[243] and soon spread to the villages of his brother Lungliana and Lalvunga, the descendants of Vuta. The uprising was plotted by Lalkhuma's subjects who stayed overnight in the river making a fish trap.[244] There they drew up the plan for the attack. The movement soon spread to the Chiefs of South Mizoram, descendants of Rolura. Almost all the Chiefs were attacked and subdued. It also affected Bengkhuaia who captured Mary Winchester. The Chief belonging to the descendants of Manga also experienced the outrage of the uprising. Fortunately, however, the villages of Lalsavunga's descendants did not rise up and it is not known why these people did not revolt. It is believed, however, that the Chief did not rule excessively or perhaps the people lacked the courage to stand up. Whatever the reasons might have been, the fact is that the Chiefs and their subjects lived together peacefully while the other parts of the hills were burning.

The Weapons Used

During this uprising, guns and other lethal weapons were not used except that only two shots were fired. These were also done under compulsion. They used pledges as useful weapons. Unity was also an important weapon. Physical assault of the Chiefs was not heard of, and instead they were asked to take pledges. However, before a Chief was asked to do so the people came together and took pledges themselves to unite together for their cause. They collected water in a basin and everyone present there was given a piece of firewood with one end burnt. Putting the fire into the water one said, *"Lal lama ka tan leh chuan he mei ang hian ka thi ang"*, meaning *"I will die like this fire if at all I support the chief again"*.[245] Everyone took the oath. This was done so that they could stand united.

After taking the pledge the commoners turned towards the Chief. The Chief was called upon to take the pledge promising never to behave to the people as before. As his subjects did, water was collected in a container and the Chief was given a firewood with one end burnt and made to dip it into the water and say *"Ka lalna hi he thingthu ang hian mil rawh se"*, meaning *"Let my Chieftainship be extinguished like this fire."*[246] All the Chiefs' officials and their supporters were also asked to do the same.[247] However, in some villages, the Chiefs were asked only to reorganise their administrative set up so as to make atmosphere tangible for the commoners. Yet in some places, the commoners, after removing the Chief, made their own choice of a new Chief.

Resurgence

After this event, there were some villages without Chiefs. But the gap period was not long. Two factors were responsible for the resurgence of the Chiefs. In the first place, unity of the people could not remain in tact for long. Unity, the mainstay, was lacked. In the second place, there was the tussle amongst the various clans over the question of Chieftainship. They could not remain without a Chief nor could they choose one among themselves. Therefore, the people had no option but to restore the Chieftainship to the rightful Chiefs.

Now, the situation again became favourable to the Chiefs for unity among the people was breaking. To worsen the fragile situation, an incident took place in Lungliana's village at Hmawngkawn. A Paihte girl was maltreated by another tribe. As a result, clan-feuds began to erupt making the commoners a divided house. Hence the Paihte clan reversed their stand and sided with the Chief.[248] Thereupon, the Chief, Lungliana, without any delay, reacted with an attempt to revive his position. He was aware that he alone could not do anything at the moment. He therefore sent a secret message to Lianphunga informing him to come over and loot his subjects. Lianphunga, taking Lalhluma along with him, proceeded to Lungliana's village. When the villagers knew that Lianphunga and his party were coming over to the village to help the Chief they gathered together to stop him and they put up a bamboo barricade. When the party arrived at the barricade they were informed not to proceed beyond it. They also warned him that crossing the barricade would mean death to him and to his party. At this juncture having found no allernative Lalhluma jumped over the crowd and said. "*Keimah Lalhluma Lallula tupa sarthi rual ka ni loe,"* meaning "I, Lalhluma, grandson of Lallula will not die of unnatural death, shoot me."[249] Two shots were tired at him but luckily both the shots failed to explode. Luahmanga, who had fired one of the shots and having found his position hazardous, jumped out of the crowd and said. *"Lai lam ka pawm leh ta. Ka mei thawlh a nung leh ta e* "meaning "I do accept the Chief and my fire is also lit again".[250] When he declared this, all the others who were armed with guns also withdrew their guns. There began a complete break down of unity among the commoners. Now the Chiefs in different places declared, *"Kan mei thawlh a nung leh ta"* meaning "Our dead fires are lit again".[251] The news of the Hmawngkawn incident soon spread far and wide. The deposed Chiefs then restored themselves in their own places. Having consolidated their positions the Chiefs began to take action against the ringleaders. But before the Chiefs could fully recover themselves from these shocks the whole situation took a new turn. The advent of the British and their subsequent administrative interference in the affairs of the Chiefs reduced the latter to merely depend on the mercy of the British.

MIM KUT OF THE MIZOS

Festivals, are external expressions of social behaviour, and are integral parts of every society. In the past, people performed rituals to appease deities of the fields, forests, mountains, water, etc. People also sometimes solemnised rituals to promote fertility. Rituals were based on beliefs and the main aim of these was to enlist super-natural protection against evil spirits.[252] Scholars, therefore, have been trying to link the two as the origin of festivals. Primitive peoples thus connected death, battle, hunting, agriculture, etc., with festivals. Whatever the case may be, festivals form one of the essential ingredients of all cultures. Therefore, every society, whether primitive or civilized, has festivals which are celebrated in one form or the other.

Like any other communities in the world, the Mizos as a community, too have festivals performed in their own system as a part of their cultural expressions. Thus, in Mizo language 'festival' is a common term which simply means *Kut*. Mizos have three festivals *viz. Mim kut, Pawl kut,* and *Chapchar kut.*[253] The origin of each of these festivals is connected with legend and *Mim Kut* is the oldest of the three.

In this essay, an attempt is made to study one of the festivals of Mizos locally called *Mim Kut* with reference to their social life as depicted by the well-known Mizo folktale.

Its Origin

Mim Kut is anyway, a harvest festival of a particular grain locally called *Mim*. It is harvested sometime in the month of August and September. The seeds are eaten as food. In the past, when there was scarcity of paddy or rice caused by a natural calamity like famine, people fed on the grain. The festival was so-called because it coincided with the harvesting time of the arain. The festival is otherwise known as *Tahna Kut* meaning "festival of weeping" because the festival was solely held in remembrance of the departed souls.[254] The festival may be compared with the feat of "All Souils' Day" being celebrated by the Catholic Church on 2nd November.

Though the origin of the festival is lost in oblivion, it is connected with legend and the legend is given in the tale narrated as follows :

"Long long ago there lived two lovers named Tlingi and Ngama. As lovers, they met each other in some places known only to them. One day they agreed to meet near a hillock which both knew.

In those days, their village was at war with another village and therefore no one would reveal her or his presence by making a noise when she or he was in the forest.

As Tlingi reached the tryst she sat quietly at a place where she could not be seen easily by anyone who passed by. Ngama came to the other side of the hillock and he too sat quietly and waited the arrival of his lover. So, they sat and waited not knowing they were so close to each other all the time.

Each of them while waiting thought that she or he had to wait only for a few moments, however, the waiting lasted days and months. Then Tlingi died of love-sickness. Ngama planted flower bearing trees where she was buried and he visited the grave very often.

After the death of Tlingi, Ngama could not eat and so he became thin and weak. One day, unable to bear the pangs of separations Ngama was in trance, and he went to the *Mitthi Khua*[255] where he met his beloved who was very thin. Tlingi and Ngama were very happy that they had met each other again.

Ngama found that the house where Tlingi lived needed repair and so they went into the forest to collect building materials. Trees which Tlingi thought to be big were not so big in the eyes of Ngama. The big animals of Tlingi were only small insects to Ngama. Thus, Ngama reasoned that the difference in sight was due to the fact that one was a spiritual being while the other was a human being. Ngama then recovered from his trance, and became a normal human being again. He then promised to feed Tlingi with the first crops he reaped from the field."[256]

From that day onward the Mizos offered food and other crops ceremonially to their dead kith and kin. This may be hard to believe, but this is how the origin of the "festival" is traced.

Importance

The tale just narrated, clearly indicates that the two important components of Mizo culture *viz.* festivals and rituals were inseparable elements. This explains the importance of the festival itself in the social life of the people. In the primitive life of the people nothing was more precious than "festivals" and "religion". So, their religious and social life expressed through their festivals thus went hand in hand. They became part and parcel of the social practice of the people.

In those early days, there was no date fixed for holding the festival. However, it must be held within *Mim Kut Thla,* a local name for the month of September. The Chief and his *upas* (advisers) decided the time well in advance and this was made public through the village crier. From the time when it was made known that the festival would be held, every family prepared itself to have enough drink for the festival. And in the same way, people should collect various items of crops to be offered for the dead. It was believed by the people that all the departed souls revisited the families on this occasion and shared the items offered for them.[257]

When the time came, the authority in the family performed rituals by offering a small quantity of cooked food along with the crops at the raised platform specially erected for the purpose near the place where bamboo water-containers are kept. The place is locally known as *tuium hun hmun.* The items offered then became sacred and no member in the family should touch them. But after four days, all became cleansed again for human consumption.

The festival lasted four days. On the first day when family rituals were performed and over, parents of some families came together and drank rice-beer locally known as *zu,* for the whole day. Drinking was inevitably accompanied by singing of lamented songs. This was the main event of the day. Merrymaking of any sort in any manner was prohibited. Children were no exception to this rule. The next three days were also observed as days of mourning and penance. No one in the village was allowed to do manual work, nor any kind of squabble permitted in the family. Divorced couples, if any, had to reconcile. Then finally, the festival was over.

Concluding Remarks

Though according to Mizo terms *Mim Kut* is a festival, a close examination reveals that it obviously lacks certain important elements of a festival. Though drinking and singing mark the occassion with festivity, yet they were done without any gaiety. In the social life of the people it was common that drinking accompanied by singing formed an important part on any occasion. This was again to be accompanied by dance performance. The same thing was seen when death occurred. From this point of view, the *Mim Kut* festival in which drinking and singing songs of lamentation were performed was not much different from the common daily life of the people. Moreover, the two important characteristics of the festival *viz.* dancing and feasting, were totally lacking. In the same way, as noted elsewhere, merrymaking was totally unpermitted. The festival was rather associated with mourning and penance. Thus, taking all these accounts into consideration *Mim Kut* may be termed as a ritual performed with no festivity. Further, it may be suggested to the extent that the festival was nothing more than ancestor worship. But this is not the view of the people.

On the other hand, if we look at the other side of the coin, the festival does not lack all the essential elements of festivals. Thus, the festival may he termed as a seasonal festival with limited participation. Moreover, the festival may be called a family or a small community festival performed with a purpose. Alter all, according to the Mizos, *Mim Kut* is one of their festivals and it will remain so in the days to come.

ZAWLBUK AND ITS ABOLITION : A SIGNIFICANT EVENT IN THE HISTORY OF THE MIZOS

Zawlbuk, a Mizo word for 'bachelor's house' had occupied a high degree of social magnitude in pre-British Mizo society. It was a place where youths were shaped into responsible adult members of the society. It also sustained and provided a pure and uncorrupted life among the members of the society. N.E. Parry the Superintendent of the then Lushai Hills accredited the importance and the contributions of the *Zawlbuk* to the Mizo society in the following words : "I ascribe much of the indiscipline among the Lakhers to the fact that they have no bachelor's house or equivalent to the Lushai *Zawlbuk*".[258] It was the nerve-centre of the Mizo society.

Theories

There are two theories on the origin of the *Zawlbuk*. One probable theory is that in early times it was a common affair among the tribal people to attack the people of another tribe for some reasons. This led to inter-tribal feuds endangering the peaceful living of the common people. More detrimental than this barbarious act was an inter-clan feud which commonly occurred among the tribes for want of being dominant over the other. Therefore, killing of an enemy became a legalised deed among them; the man who brought home the head of an enemy was admired and respected as a 'warrior' Thus, fighting between two Chiefs or villages became a common phenomenon. For this reason, it became a necessity for all young men to sleep together in one common place in order to protect the village from the enemy. To meet such possible attack, a collective action with prompt moves was more desirable. This could be done when all the adult members of a village slept in one place. Hence, the *Zawlbuk* institution originated.

The other theory suggests that when people were less in number the entire village used to live together in one big house as an enlarged family due to two reasons : traditionally a village was situated on the hill top and this involved scarcity of flat land enough for the construction of houses. They, therefore began to build a big and long house enough to accommodate the entire village to live in; secondly there they stayed together for fear of attack from another village.

These theories of origin are also considered responsible for the practice of head-hunting among the Mizos.

Origin

The origin of *Zawlbuk* may be traced from China where "Long Houses" or "Communal Houses" were found among the tribes who were dominantly settled in the Southern provinces. Besides these houses, bachelor's houses (and among some of the tribes, girl's houses), were separately maintained in which only adolescent boys of twelve or thirteen years of age as minimum were allowed to sleep. The bachelor's house was strikingly different from communal houses.[259] In the bachelor's house only adult members of the village lived, whereas in a communal house an entire village lived together.[260]

It may be conjectured that the bachelor's house custom was brought down by the tribes who migrated to the different parts of Southeast Asia including India where various tribes of Tibeto-Burman speaking people are found. It was found mainly among the patrilineal tribes and became a practice however, even among the matrilineal Indonesians.[261] Both the Khasis and the Garos, however, lack the bachelor's house. It may be noted that among the Mon-Khmer speaking people only the Palaung had both the communal house as well as the bachelor's house. The same system was also practised by the Nagas who called it *Morung*.[262] We may, therefore, assume from this statement that the Mizos had brought the *Zawlbuk* custom down from China centuries ago. This conclusion also suggests the original habitat of the Mizos. The Pawi (Lai) and the Lakher (Mara) tribes now mostly concentrated in the Southern part of Mizoram also lack a similar institution, the reasons for which are not definitely known. The Pawi, however, claim that being a dominant clan or tribe they do not find any reason to have the *Zawlbuk* institution. In the case of the Lakhers (Mara) they may belong to the Mon-Khmer speaking people among whom such an institution was not found.

A Brief Description

Every village had a *Zawlbuk* but it was the choice of a village to maintain more than one. In big villages, however, there were more than one. It is said that in Selesih village there were more than 7 *Zawlhuks* located at the most central place in the village. It was constructed in a manner facing towards the Chief's house and not tar off from it. It had a verandah at the entrance. Next to it was a wall not touching the floor by about three feet, and made without a door. At about five feet inside the wall another wall of about three feet was raised. A log as big as the whole village could carry and sufficient to cover the entire breadth of it was collected from the forest and placed on the raised wall after peeling its bark. This tog was popularly known as 'bawhbel'. Every village had a hankering to have the biggest 'bawhbel' which was considered a show of pomp.[263] A smaller village with less population could place two logs over the other in a stable position. The open space between the 'bawhbel' and the wall was used as a place for stocking firewood. The level of the floor was paved down by about two feet just inside the 'bawhbel'. This was done in view of defence purposes.

At the far end of the *Zawlbuk* there used to be a raised platform about six feet wide and one foot high covering the whole breadth of the *Zawlbuk*. This portion known as 'Bahzar' or 'Dawvan' was used as a sleeping place. The wall at the back portion was made like the wall at the entrance. The space thereby leaving an opening between the two walls was known as 'awkpaka.'. A fire place was placed at the centre of the *Zawlbuk* and was filled up with earth right from the ground. The floor was strongly built as the dwellers used it to provide them facilities for various indigenous physical exercises like wrestling etc. Therefore, the floor was strongly woven in a particular design known as 'chhuatpuitah'. The walls were woven too in a different design known as 'bawhtah' thereby making the walls very strong. The size of the *Zawlbuk* was big enough to accommodate all the young men and young folks of the village.

The Hierarchy of the *Zawlbuk* Group

In fact, the Chief of the village was the *de facto* head of the *Zawlbuk* by virtue of the position he held. He did not, however, interfere in its day to day administration. The administration was managed by the leader of the *Zawlbuk* called 'Valupa' appointed by the Chief. The inmates selected one among themselves who was recognised and considered as having an undisputed quality. The *Valupa* was the second most powerful man in the village next to the Chief. He was respected and obeyed by all people due to the qualities he possessed. He commanded the *Zawlbuk* dwellers who collectively acted as the Chief's army. Sometimes, the Chief had to yield to him for he directly commanded the *Zawlbuk* dwellers. He was assisted by his trusted friend chosen from among the inmate. The adult members of the *Zawlbuk* dwellers formed another group. They were the common men in the village.

It was the duty and responsibility of all the boys of the village who had attained 11 years of age to supply firewood to the *Zawlbuk* every evening.[264] If anyone was found tailing to do so, severe action was taken against him and he might he forced to collect fire-wood from the jungle that night itself. Sometimes the boy was ordered to supply ten bundles of wood in addition to his usual supply the next day, as punishment. No parents dared come forward to oppose the order given to their wards. Therefore, in order to avoid such harsh punishment inflicted upon a boy, each one brought the firewood to the *Zawlbuk* with the knowledge of one witness. One of the *Zawlbuk* dwellers was made monitor to check whether the boys did accordingly. Such boys were known as 'thingnawifawm'. Besides, one boy was engaged to supply the *Zawlbuk* with drinking water, He should keep at least three bamboo containers ready for use and was also responsible for keeping the *Zawlbuk* clean, and making the fireplace at the *Zawlbuk* hearth every evening. He was free however, from supplying firewood. The duty was done in rotation among the boys. These groups were fed by giving them shares[265] as a reward, in times of "Chawngchen" and 'Khuangchawi' feasts held in the village. Women were prohibited to enter the *Zawlbuk* and seeing a woman entering even in a dream was also taken as a bad omen.

Admission

To admit one as an adult member of the *Zawlbuk* one had to undergo a queer test after claiming for membership. The claim was verified by the *Valupa* or any of his assistants whom he entrusted to do the job by pulling out the longest hair from his pubic region and that hair was to be long enough to circle around the established size of a bamboo pipe. If the boy was found qualified he would be classified as an adult and the *Valupa* would formally admit him as member of the *Zawlbuk* by making an announcement in the presence of the other members.

Function

As a social institution, the *Zawlbuk* had three main functions. It was used as a sleeping place for the young unmarried men of the extended family to stay until they got married. After marriage, the young man left the *Zawlbuk* and returned to the home of his parents. It was a common practice that the married man could stay on in the *Zawlbuk* till a child was born. To avoid injury to an unborn child the parents should not engage in sexual intercourse after the fifth month of pregnancy. For this reason a married man might again take up temporary residence in the *Zawlbuk* could be used as a recreational and training centre. It was the custom of the young men to court girls when the had free time. This was done generally at night after the evening meal. It was the usual practice of the dwellers to first visit the *Zawlbuk* before going for courting. Here, the new entrants were asked to do wrestling and other indigenous games as training. Sometimes, the experts in wrestling were engaged in such feats as a show for the trainees. Again, one was challenged by the other, in a manner as to who would be the champion in a particular game. Other various indigenous games were also played in the *Zawlbuk*. When the 'Chapchar Kut' festival was about to come they practised dances in the *Zawlbuk*. As it was used as a training place, the *Zawlbuk* was also used as a place where insolvent villagers were disciplined. It was the second place of imparting discipline and good manners, the first being the home where parents instructed their children at meal times to be good citizens of the society. It has been customary among the Mizos to look for a house in the neighbourhood to stay over night. On such occasions the *Zawlbuk* served as an inn or guest house for male visitors. Besides, the *Zawlbuk* formed an ideal place for emergency cases like during the raid from another village etc. The young men slept in the *Zawlbuk* and could, therefore, without any delay be called in any emergency. Here lay the real need of the *Zawlbuk* in the village.[266]

Abolition of the *Zawlbuk*

Like many other social customs, the *Zawlbuk* could not stand the force of changes which took place after the coming of the British resulting in its abolition. Four factors may be accounted for the abolition of the *Zawlbuk* in the Mizo society. The four forces were : in the first place, the introduction of the British administration contributed for the abolition of the *Zawlbuk*. The sole authority over the *Zawlbuk* in a village was the village Chief. With the coming of the British the Chief's authority was reduced very much by making him dependent. He had to exercise powers only at the behest of the British, this directly affected the discipline in the *Zawlbuk* administration. The law and order in the *Zawlbuk* apparently deteriorated. Though its existence was recognised, its place in the society was seriously undermined by the people. A small spark was enough to make a big fire and the *Zawlbuk's* end as parents found it difficult to cope with because sometimes the *Zawlbuk* inmates were too harsh in action towards an individual and supply of firewood to *Zawlbuk* was too burdensome for the parents whose involvement was often required when their wards were sick. In the second place, Christianity was a real hindrance to the proper functioning of the *Zawlbuk*. The practice of Christian virtues slowly eradicated the indigenous practices and customs. The importance of the institution was inevitably neglected by the new and aware society. Its extinction was, therefore, inevitable when formal education was introduced among the Mizos. Informal education had to be replaced by formal education. Of all the forces, this was the most important one because parents were prepared to send their children to school where the children would gain more. They felt that they could control their children better at home than what the *Zawlbuk* could provide.[267] Lastly, the movement for the abolition was quickened by the people who took part in the war service. When World War I broke out many Mizo young men were recruited to war service. These people returned with a changed outlook. Representing almost every village, these War servicemen thus made remarkable contributions towards adopting a modem way of living. People, thus began to feel that the best way to improve their future lot was to break away from their indigenous ways of living.[268] In this way the idea of continuing with the *Zawlbuk* it began dying out in course of time in the minds of the people themselves.

At the same time, definite attempts were made by some of the British residents to continue the *Zawlbuk* institution in Mizoram. The idea was spearheaded by N.E. Parry the Superintendent of the then Lushai Hills who championed the cause of the Mizo customary laws. When he assumed office in 1926 the *Zawlbuk* had a deserted look in almost every village, and it was almost non-existent in a few villages the institution had already been abandoned. Parry, deeply moved by the role it had played in the Mizo society, therefore, issued a Standing Order to all the Chiefs directing them to revive the *Zawlbuk* in Mizoram in the following words :

> "I had noticed that in a few villages
> the *Zawlbuk* is no longer maintained.
> All Chiefs are hereby informed that
> every Lushai Village must keep up a
> *Zawlbuk*. Circle Interpreters will report
> to me any villages that have no *Zawlbuk*."[269]

He further ordered the Chiefs who had already abandoned the *Zawlbuk* to rebuild it in the following words :

"Please order all circle Interpreters toreport villages which have no *Zawlbuk*. The following villages, I know, have no *Zawlbuk* and should be ordered to build one before the 31st March 1926 :

1. Paliana
2. Hrangchhuana
3. Lalzidinga".[270]

Meanwhile, in Southern Mizoram attempts were also made by the Christian Missionaries to revive the institution. Rev. F.J. Raper, of the Baptist Mission, took keen interest in reconstructing the *Zawlbuk*. He mobilised the youth to keep up the values which the society attained through it. Being a District

Commissioner for Boy Scouts in Mizoram he provided material assistance to the *Zawlbuk* inmates. He helped them by giving them materials like petromax, carrom boards etc. with a view to innovating their minds for the *Zawlbuk* which was losing its credibility.

In spite of these efforts, the view of the people on *Zawlbuk* could not be changed. When A.G. McCall succeeded Parry the same voice was insistently raised by the people. Conceding to their views McCall then convened a Public Meeting on 1 January 1938 at Aizawl (Thakthing) to evolve a concrete policy on the *Zawlbuk* in Mizoram.[271] In this meeting McCall was fully convinced to revoke Parry's order in 10 days time. From this historic decision the *Zawlbuk* fell into complete disuse and in course of time it became an institution of the past in the history of the Mizos in Mizoram.

REFERENCES

1. Vanchhunga, *Lusei leh a vela hnamdangle,* Zoram Printing Press, Aizawl, 1955, p. 225.
2. A.G. McCall, *Lushai Chrysalis,* Lusac Co., London, 1949, Reprinted (2004) Spectrum Publications, Guwahati/ New Delhi, p. 109.
3. E.T. Dalton, *Descriptive Ethnology of Bengal,* Govt. Printing Press, Calcutta, 1872, p. 45.
4. Sangkima, "*Zawlbuk* And Its Abolition". *Proceedings* of the North-East India History Association, Seventh Session, Association, 1986, p. 306.
5. Edwin M. Loeb And Jan M.O. Broek, "Social Organization And the Long House in South-East Asia", *American Antropologist,* Vol. 49, Jan-March, 1947, No. 1, p. 414.
6. *Ibid.,* p. 418.
7. T.H. Lewin, *Progressive Coltoquial Exercises in the Lushai Dialect 'Dzo' or Kuki Language with vocabularies and Popular Tale,* Calcutta Central Press Company Ltd. Calcutta, 1874, p. 80.

8. Lalrinmawia, "Bawi Custom And Its Abolition in Lushai Hills", *Historical Journal Mizoram,* November 1990, p. 3.
9. Animesh Pay, *Mizoram : Dynamics of Change,* Pearl Publishers, Calcutta, 1982, p. 35.
10. A.G. McCall, *op. cit.*, p. 122.
11. T.H. Lewin, *Wild Races of South-Eastern India,* W.H. Allen & Co., London, 1870, p. 50.
12. J. Shakespear, *The Lushei-Kuki Clans,* Macmillan & Co. Ltd., London, 1912, Reprinted (2004) Spectrum Publications, Guwahati/Delhi, p. 49.
13. N.E. Parry, *The Lakhers,* Macmillan & Co. Ltd., London, 1932, p. 13.
14. T.H. Lewin, Progressive Colloquial Exercises, *loc. cit.*, p. 80.
15. J.E. Webster, "Tippera", *Eastern Bengal District Gazetters,* Pioneer Press, Allahabad, 1910, p. 19.
16. Edward Balfour, *Encyclopaedia Asiatica,* Vol. V, Cosmo Publication, New Delhi, 1976, (Reprint) p. 618.
17. Sangkima, "Social Life of the Mizos : Some Aspects", *Proceedings of the North-East India History Association,* Jagiroad, 1991, p. 236.
18. N.E. Parry, *A Monograph on Lushai Customs And Ceremonies,* Tribal Research Institute, Aizawl, (Reprint), 1976, p. 6.
19. Rev. Liangkhaia, *Mizos Awam Dan Hlui,* Thakthing Bazar, Press, Aizawl, 1984, p. 26.
20. L.B. Thanga, *The Mizos,* United Publishers, Guwahati/ New Delhi, 1978, p. 15.
21. *Ibid.*
22. Nuchhungi, *Mizos Nanpang Infiamna,* J.B. Press, Lunglei, 1963, p. 35.
23. V.L. Siama, *Mizo History,* Lalrinliana & Sons, Aizawl, 1978, p. 10.
24. Lalrimawia, "Economy of the Mizos (1840-1947)", *Studies in the History of North-East India,* North-East India History Association Publication, 1986, p. 166.

25. H.N.C. Stevenson, *The Economics of the Central Chin Tribes,* Tribal Research Institute (Reprint) 1986, p. 12.
26. E.O. James, *History of Religion,* The British University Press Ltd., London, 1964, p. 2.
27. Rev. Liangkhaia, "Mizo Sakhua" *Mizo-Ziarang,* Mizo Academy of Letters, Aizawl, 1975, p. 1.
28. Rev. Saiaithanga, *Mizo Sakhua,* Maranatha Press, Aizawl, n.n.p. 2.
29. Rev. Liangkhaia, "Mizo Sakhua", *op. cit.,* p. 1.
30. C. Vanlalauva, *Religious Beliefs And Customs Among the Mizos,* (unpublished Thesis) Guwahati University, 1978, p. 162.
31. Hrangthiauva & Lalchungnunga, *Mizo Chanchin,* Lalrinliana and Sons, Aizawl, 1978, p. 68.
32. J.H. Hutton, "Head-Hunting", *Man in India,* vol. X, No. 4, December, 1930, p. 208.
33. H.B. Rowney, *The Wild Tribes of India,* Thosi, Delapue & Co., London, 1882, p. 183.
34. J.H. Hutton, *op. cit.,* p. 211.
35. John Rowlings, "On the Manners, Religion and Laws of the Cucis or Mountaineers" *Asiatic Researches,* Vol. II, Cosmo Publications, New Delhi, (Reprint) 1979, p. 14.
36. "Shifting Cultivation in North East India", North East India Council For Social Science Research, Shillong, 1976, p. 3.
37. John Macrare, 'Accounts of the Kookies or Lunotas' in *Asiatic Researches,* Vol-VII, Cosmo Publications, New Delhi, 1979 (rep) p. 183.
38. A.G. McCall, *Lushai Chrysalis,* Lusac & Co., London, 1949, Reprinted (2004) Spectrum Publications, Guwahati/New Delhi, pp. 165-166.
39. Seletthanga, *Pipu Lenlai,* Lianchhungi Book Store, Aizawl, 1978(4th edition) p. 6.
40. R.G. Woodthorpe, *The Lushai Expedition 1871-1872,* Tribal Research Institute, Aizawl (reprint 1978), pp. 79-80. See also the fascimile reprint of the original

U.K. edition, reprinted by Spectrum Publications, Guwahati/Delhi in 1981.

41. (Mrs) N.Chatterji, *Zawlbuk As A Social Institution In The Mizo Society,* Tribal Institute, Aizawl, 1975, p. 80.
42. Thomas Herbert Lewin; *Progressive Colloquil Exercises in the Lushai dialect,* Calcutta, Central Press Company Ltd.
43. Pastor Challiana, *Pi Pu Nun,* Trio Book House, Aizawl, 1978 (Reptd.) p. 12.
44. L.B. Thanga; *The Mizos,* United Publishers, Guwahati/ New Delhi, 1978, p. 15.
45. Hrangtiauva & Lalchungnunga, Mizo *Chanchin,* Lalrinliana & Sons, Aizawl, 1978, p. 68.
46. *Ibid.*
47. *Chhawnghnawt,* It was a feast. On *Chupchur Kut* and *Pawl Kut* occassions the children and young people held feasts together in the village square or near the memorial platforms. The feast was enjoyed thoroughly. Children and young men stuffed meat and rice into one another's mouths amidst merriment.
48. K. Zawla, *Pi Pute leh An Thlahte Chanchin,* H.A. Press, Aizawl, 1981 (3rd edition) pp. 39-40.
49. C. A. Soppit, *A Short Account of the Kuki-Lushai Tribes on the Sorth East Frontier,* Tribal Research Institute, Aizawl, 1976, p. 20.
50. *Enchanting Mizoram,* Published by the Govt. of Mizoram, 1977.
51. A.C. Ray; *Mizoram,* Publication Division, Ministry of Information and Broadcasting, Govt. of India, 1972, p. 13.
52. C.A. Soppit, *op. cit.,* p. 21.
53. N.E. Parry, *The Lakhers,* Firma KLM(P) Ltd. Calcutta, 1976, p. 183.
54. Ronald De Vaux, *Ancient Israel—Its Life and Institution,* Darton Longman & Todd, London, 1974 (Edition), p. viii.
55. Bracketted words are mine. (*Author*)
56. T.H.Lewin, *Progressive Colloquial Exercises In The*

Lushai District Of The Dzo or Kuki Language With Vocabularies And Popular Tales, Calcutta, Central Press Company Ltd., 1874, p. 80.

57. Aizawl Record Room (ARR). From B.C. Allen, Chief Secretary to the Chief Commissioner of Assam To Secretary to the Government of Bengal, *Letter* No. 4902P. Shillong, the 15th August, 1916.
58. Ronald De Vaux, *op cit.*, p. 80.
59. Proceeding of the seminar organised by Mizo History Association *Historical Journal Mizoram,* Vol. 1, Book I, 1982, pp. 6-7.
60. J Shakespeare, *The Lushei Kuki Clam* (P-I), Tribal Research Institute (Rep 1975, p.49.) Spectrum Publications, Guwahati/Delhi (2004) Single volume fascimile reprint.
61. J.E. Webster, “Tippera”. *Eastern Bengal District Gazetteer,* Pioneer Press, Allahabad, 1910, p. 19.
62. Dev Raj Chanana, *Slavery In Ancient India,* People’s Publishing House, New Delhi, 1990 (Reprint) p. 19.
63. Sangkima, *Slavery In Ancient India,* a talk at AIR, Aizawl on 24.6.2001 as an IGNOU Programme.
63. *Saphun* literally means (sa=religion, *phun=to* adopt) to adopt the religious custom of another clan. This means ‘change of clan’ and this should be solemnised with a ceremony involving the local priest. The priest.... by the Chiefs.
65. A.G.McCall, Lushai *Chrysalis, TRI* Aizawl, 1997, p. 123. Spectrum Publications, Guwahati/Delhi (2004) Single vol. fascimile reprint.
66. J. Shakespeare, *op.cit.*, p. 47.
67. *Ibid.*, p. 46.
68. *Ibid.*
69. Sangkima, *Mizos : Society And Social Change,* Spectrum Publications, Guwahati/Delhi, 1992, p. 40.
70. A.G McCall, *op. cit.,* p. 122.
71. *Ibid.*
72. J. Shakespeare, *op. cit.*, p. 48.

73. *Ibid.*
74. T.H. Lewin, *Wild Races of South-Eastern India,* W.H. Allen & Co. London, 1870, p. 50.
75. N.E. Parry, *The Lakhers,* Tribal Research Institute, Aizawl, (reprint) 1976B. The bracketted words are mine.
76. J. Shakespeare, *op. cit.*, p. 46.
77. *Ibid.,* see also A.G McCall; *op. cit.*, 124.
78. A.G. McCall, *Ibid.*
79. Sangkima, *op. cit.*, p. 127.
80. J. Meirion Lloyd, *On Every High Hill,* Liverpool (n.d) p. 62.
81. ARR, From J. Shakespeare, Superintendent Of The Lushai Hills to Giles, Sub-Divisional Officer, Lungleh, letter No. 1104G Dated Aijal the 7th January, 1905.
82. *Ibid.*
83. A.G. McCall; *op.cit.*, p. 127.
84. R. Vanlawma, *Ka Ram Leh Kei* (*My country And I*) Zalen Printing House, Aizawl, 1972, pp. 43-44).
85. A.G. McCall, *op. cit.*, pp. 127-128.
86. Mizoram, the erstwhile Lushai Hills was occupied by the British on 4 May, 1890. The Lushai Hills was granted the status of an autonomous District Council in 1952, and in 1954 the same was renamed as Mizo District. By the North-Eastern Areas Reorganisation Act, 1971, the District was elevated to Union Territory on 21 January, 1972 and was given a new name, 'Mizoram'. In 1986, Mizoram was upgraded to the status of Statehood with Aizawl as capital. Mizoram now has eight Districts.
87. J.H. Lorrain, *Dictionary of the Lushai Language,* The Asiatic Society, Calcutta, (Reprint), 1973, p. (v).
88. K. Zawla, *Mizo P Pule Leh An Thlahte Chanchin,* Zomi Book Agency, Aizawl, (Reprint), 1993, p. 5.
89. A *letter* by J.H. Lorrain to Col. T.H. Lewin dated 25th April, 1899.

90. Pastor Challiana, *Pi Pu Nun,* Trio Book House, Aizawl, 1978, p. 3.
91. (Mrs) N.Chatterji, *Zawlbuk As A Social Institution In The Mizo Society,* Tribal Research Institute, Aizawl, 1975, p. 3.
92. Laltanpuii, "Salient Features of the Culture of the Mizos and It's influence on Education". Paper read for M.Ed. Degree at NEHU, Mizoram Campus in 1981.
93. Sangkima, *Mizos : Society and Social Change,* Spectrum Publications, Guwahati/Delhi, 1992, p. 43.
94. N.E.Parry, *A Monograph On Lushai Customs And Ceremonies,* Tribal Research Institute (Reprint), Aizawl, 1976, p. 21.
95. Sangkima, *op. cit.*, p. 44.
96. *Ibid.*, p. 87.
97. Aizawl Record Room (ARR), From Porteous to the Secretary to the Chief Commissioner of Assam. Letter No. 211 dated Fort Aijal the 22 June 1896, and No. 227 dated the 17th July, 1896.
98. ARR, *Ibid.* Letter No. 677 dated Fort Aijal the 28th January, 1897.
99. (ARR), *Ibid.*
100. (ARR) : From Superintendent to the Commandant, Military Police, Letter No. 1150 dated Aijal the 18th February, 1899.
101. M. Prothero, *Report On The Progress Of Education In Assam During The Years 1897-1898 And 1901-1902,* Government Press, Shillong, 1902, p. 38.
102. (ARR), Form J.Shakespear, Superintendent of Lushai Hills to The Secretary to the Chief Commissioner of Assam, letter No. 962G. Dated Aijal, the 26th February, 1903.
103. (ARR), *Ibid.* Letter No. 962 G. Dated Aijal, the 26th February, 1903.
104. (ARR), From Secretary of the Chief Commissioner of Assam to the Director of Public Instruction. Assam Letter No.459 P-T-99 87G. Dated Aijal the 19th November, 1903.

105. *Mizo Ieh Vai Chanchin Bu* (A Magazine) October, 1903.

 (A) Name of Aizawl Schools : (1) Boy's M.E.School (2) Thakthing (3) Hrianghmual (4) Rahsi Veng (5) Mirawng Veng (6) Maubawk

 (B) Name of Village Schools :

 (1) Khandaih(Phullen)(2)Maite (3) Phulpui (4) Khawrihnim (5) Biate(6) Lungtan (7) Khawreng (8) Ngopa (9) Zukbual.

106. Lalbiakliana, *Mizoram Zirna Chanchin* (History of Education), Social Education Wing, Aizawl, 1979, p. 26.

107. (ARR), From Director of Public Instruction, Assam to the Secretary to the Chief Commissioner of Assam, Letter No. 1077 p. dated Shillong, 22nd February, 1904.

108. (ARR), From Secretary to the Chief Commissioner of Assam to the Director of Public Instruction of Assam, Memo No. 2166 dated Shillong, the 4th April 1903.

109. (ARR), From Secretary to the Chief Commissioner of Assam to the Director of Public Instruction Letter No. 660, p. I-8216 dated Shillong the 19th September 1904.

110. *The Annual Report of Baptist Missionary Society On Mizoram* 1901-1938, p. 8.

111. (ARR), From Secretary to the Chief Commissioner of Assam to the Director of Public Instruction. Assam, Letter No.660 p. 1-8216 dated Shillong the 19th September 1904.

112. (ARR), From Major J. Shakespear, Superintendent, Lushai Hillsto the Secretary; Chief Commissioner of Assam. Letter No. 1275 G.-dated Aijal the 18th—20th February 1905.

113. Sangkima, *op. cit.*, p. 92.

114. *Administrative Report of the Lushai Hills 1927-28* Govt. of Assam, Shillong, 1928.

115. Lalrimawia, British Policy to the Education of the Lushais upto 1947, *Historical Journal Mizoram*, Vol. I, 1982, p. 27.

116. B. Poonte; *District Hand Book* (Mizo District), The Lock Printing Press, Aizawl, 1965, p. 11.

117. A.G. McCall, *The Lushai Hills District Cover*, Maranatha Press (Reprint), Aizawl 1980, p. 225.
118. J.V. Hluna, *Education And Missionaires in Mizoram*, Spectrum Publications, Guwahati/Delhi, 1992, p. 142.
119. Lalchungnunga, Progress and Development of Education in Mizoram (1947-1982). *Historical Journal Mizoram*, Vol. I, 1982, p. 4.
120. Lalbiakliana, *op. cit.*, p. 39.
121. *Ibid.*, p. 40.
122. *Ibid.*
123. Lalchungnunga; *op. cit.*, p. 5.
124. C. Lalkunga; *History of Mizo Education*, Hnamte Press, Aizawl, 1979, p. 21.
125. *Ibid.*, p. 19.
126. *Statistical Hand Book Mizoram 1974*, p. 177.
127. *Ibid.*, pp. 182-185.
128. Baldev Mahajan, Srilekha Majumdar and F. Lallura; *Educational Administration in Mizoram*, New Delhi, 1994, pp. 31-35.
129. Government of Mizoram; Notification No. B. 12019/7/89-EDN, 31 January, 1991.
130. Directorate of School Education; *Provisional Abstract of School Statistics, 1999-2000*, pp. 1-4.
131. *Ibid.*
132. *Ibid.*
133. *Ibid.*
134. Bro. Aurrele Tessier; "Reminiscences" *Silchar Diocese Silver Jubilee Brochure, 1977*, p. 71.
135. Lalbiakliana, *op. cit.*, p. 54.
136. E.O. Jones, "Prehistoric Religion. "*Historia Religionum* (Religion of the past) (Ed) C.Jouco Bleeker and Geo Widengren, Leiden, 1969, p. 23.
137. E.O. Jones, *History of Religion*, London, 1964, p. 29.
138. David Bidney, "The Ethnology of Religion and the Problem of Human Evolutin", *American Anthropologist*, (Ed.) Sol Tax, Vol. 56, No. 5, Part 1, October, 1954, p. 2.

139. Horation B. Rowney, *The wild tribes of India,* London, 1882, p. 187.

140. Kenneth Scott Latourette, *The Development of China,* New York, 1964, p. 18.

141. Sangkima, "Social And Cultural History of the Mizos : An outline of Pre Colonial Period, "PIALRAL (*A Historical Journal of Mizoram*) Vol-4, December, 1995, p. 53.

142. David Kyles, *Lorrain of the Lushai.*

143. A.G. McCall, *Lushai Chrysalis.* TRI, Aizawl (Reprint), 1977, p. 68, Speetrum Publications. Guwahati/Delhi 2004 fascimile reprint.

144. David Bidney, *Loc.Cit.*

145. Works of the following authors may be very helpful in order to understand the concept of religion in general and primitive religion in particular-Durkheim, E.B Taylor, E.E Evans-Pitchard, John B.Noss, Ruth Benedict.

146. Rev. Saiaithanga, *Mizo Sakhua,* Maranatha Press, Aizawl, n.d, p. 10.

147. N.E Parry, *Lushai Custom—A Monograph On Lushai Customs And Ceremonies,* Tribal Research Institute, Aizawl (Reprint) 1976, p. 8.

148. Pastor Challiana; *Pi pu Nun,* Trio Book House, Aizawl, 1978, p. 40.

149. Mizo *Sakhua,* Tribal Research Institute, Aizawl, 1983, p. 14.

150. *Ibid.* p. 15.

151. (Mrs) N.Chatterji, *The Mizo Chief And His Administration,* Tribal Research Institute, Aizawl, 1975, p. 11.

152. B. Lalthangliana, *Pi pu Chhuahtlang,* Hrangbana College, Aizawl, 1998, p. 176.

153. Rev. Saiaithanua; *op cit.,* p. 10.

154. *Ibid.*

155. Daniel G. Brinton, *Religions of Primitive Peoples,* G.P. Putram's Sons, London, 1897, p. 27.

156. *Mizo Sakhua, op. cit.,* p. 22.

157. Rev. Liangkhaia, Mizo *Chanchin.* Academy of Letters, Aizawl, 1976, p. 24.
158. *Mizo Sakhua, op. cit.,* p. 24.
159. *Ibid.,* pp. 53-55.
160. Hrangthiauva and Lalchungnunga; *Mizo Chanchin,* Lalrinliana & Sons, Aizawl, 1978, p. 277.
161. Rev. Liangkhaia, "Mizo Sakhua", *Mizo Zia-Rang,* Academy of letters, Aizawl, 1975, p. 27.
162. *Mizo Sakhua, op. cit.,* p. 40.
163. *Mizo Sakhua, op. cit.,* pp. 45-46.
164. Rev. Liangkhaia, *loc. cit.*
165. *Mizo Sakhua, op. cit.,* p. 42.
166. Rev. Liangkhaia, *loc. cit.*
167. *Mizo Sakhua, op. cit.,* p. 44.
168. Rev Liangkhaia, *loc. cit.,* p. 6.
169. *Mizo Sakhua, op. cit.,* pp. 41-42.
170. Brig. Ngurliana, "Mizo Sakhaw Kawngpui, "*Historical Journal Mizoram,* Vol. VIII, 1998, p. 35.
171. C. Chawngkunga, *Sukhua.* Dep. of Art And Culture, Aizawl, 1997, p. 41.
172. *Ibid.*
173. *Ibid.*
174. *Mizo Sakhua, op. cit.,* p. 49.
175. *Ibid.,* pp. 50-51. Also C.Chawngkunga, *op. cit.,* p. 42.
176. B. Lalthangliana, *op. cit.,* p. 205.
177. *Mizo Sakhua, op. cit.,* pp. 52-53.
178. *Ibid.,* p. 56
179. *Ibid.,* pp. 57-58.
180. *Ibid.,* p. 58.
181. *Ibid.,* pp. 59-60.
182. *Ibid.,* pp. 62-63.
183. *Ibid.,* pp. 65-66.
184. *Ibid.,* p. 66.

185. *Ibid.*, p. 67.
186. *Ibid.*, p. 78.
187. *Ibid.*, p. 98.
188. *Ibid.*
189. *Ibid.*, pp. 99-100.
190. *Ibid.*, p. 100.
191. Hrangthiauva and Lalchungnunga, *op. cit.*, p. 30.
192. K. Zawla, *op. cit.*, p. 65.
193. *Ibid.*
194. Pastor Challiana, *op. cit.*, p. 34.
195. *Ibid.*, p. 35.
196. *Ibid.*
197. K. Zawla, *op. cit.*, p. 56.
198. *Ibid.*
199. *Ibid.*
200. Pastor Challiana, *op. cit.*, p. 36.
201. *Ibid.*
202. G.E. Harvey, *op. cit.*, p. 4.
203. Arthur P.Phayre, *History of Burma,* London, 1883, p. 12.
204. Padmeswar Gogoi, *op. cit.*, p. 10.
205. H.I. Marshall, *The Karen People of Burma,* Columbus University, Ohio, 1922, p. 12.
206. Paul and Elaine Lewis, *Peoples of the Golden Triangle,* Thames and Hudson, London, 1984, p. 70.
207. D.G.E. Hall, *op. cit.*, p. 122.
208. P.C. Choudhury, *The History of Civilization of the People of Assam to the Twelfth Century AD.*, Guwahati, (Reprint) Spectrum Publications, 1987, p. 75.
209. N.D. Chaudhury, "The Early Inhabitants of North-East India with Special Reference to Mizoram." Paper presented in the International Seminar on the *Studies on the Minority Nationalities of North-East India—The Mizos* held on 7-9 April 1992 at Aizawl, Mizoram.

210. S.K. Chatterji, *Kirata-Jana-Krti,* The Asiatic Society, Calcutta, 1974, p. 26.
211. *Ibid.*, p. 28.
212. *Ibid.*, p. 27.
213. N.D. Chaudhury, *op. cit.*, p. 1.
214. The work is done by W. Vincent. W.H. Scoff also writes the *Periplus.*
215. P.C. Choudhury, *op. cit.*, p. 28 (Foot Note).
216. *Ibid.*, pp. 31-35.
217. *Ibid.*, p. 34.
218. Edward Gait, *A History of Assam,* Guwahati, 1926, p. 10.
219. *Ibid.*, p. 34.
220. For detailed discussion kindly refer to *Kirata-Jana Krti* by S.K. Chatterjee, *op. cit.*, pp. 30-36.
221. *Ibid.*, p. 34.
222. *Ibid.*, p. 35.
223. *Ibid.*, p. 16.
224. P.C. Choudhury, *op. cit.*, p. 83.
225. G.A. Grierson, *Linguistic Survey of India,* Vol-1, Delhi (Reprint) 1967, pp. 41-48.
226. P.C. Choudhury, *op. cit.*, p. 84.
227. G.A. Soppit, *A Short Account of the Kuki-Lushai Tribes etc.* Aizawl, (Reprint) 1976, p. 7.
228. E.T. Dalton, *Descriptive Ethnology of Bengal,* Calcutta 1972, pp. 110-111, G.A. Grierson, "Kuki-Chin Group", *Linguistic Survey of India, op. cit.*, p. 1.
229. A.C. Bhattacharya, *Progressive Tripura,* New Delhi, 1930, p. 19.
230. N.R. Roychoudhury, *Tripura Through the Ages,* 1983, p. 17.
231. A.C. Bhattacharya, *op. cit.*, p. 19.
232. Rev. James Long, *Analysis of the Rajmala or the Chronicles of Tripura* (Reprint) 1955, p. 8.
233. *Ibid.*, p. 7.

234. Suhas Chatterjee, "Early History of the Mizos", *Proceedings of the North-East India History Association* (NEIHA), Guwahati, 1988, p. 102.

235. Sangkima, "Some Sources of Early Mizo History : A Chronological Study." NEIHA *Proceedings*, Jorhat, 1993, p. 91. A detailed discussion of the early history of the Mizos is given in this article.

236. *Ibid.*, p. 92.

237. A.G. McCall, *op. cit.*, p. 35.

238. R. Vanlawma, "Mizo Lake Leh A Khua Leh Tui", *Mizo Zia-Rang,* Mizo Academy of Letters, Aizawl, 1975, p. 62.

239. A.G. McCall, *Lushai Chrysalis,* 1977 Reprint, p. 37. Also fascimile reprint (2004) Spectrum Publications, Guwahati/Delhi.

240. *Ibid.*

241. *Ibid.*

242. N.E. Parry, *A Monograph on Lushai Customs and Ceremonies,* TRI (Reprint), 1976, p. 2.

243. R. Vanlawma, *Ka Ram Leh Kei,* Zalen Cabin, Aizawl, 1989, (Reprint), p. 37.

244. Rev. Liangkhaia, *Mizo Chanchin,* Mizo Academy of Letters, Aizawl, 1976, p. 85.

245. *Ibid.*

246. R. Vanlawma, *op. cit.*, p. 38.

247. *Ibid.*

248. Rev. Liangkhaia, *op. cit.*, p. 86.

249. *Ibid.*

250. R. Vanlawma, *loc. cit.*

251. *Ibid.*

252. Birendranath Datta, *et al. A Handbook of Folkloce Material of North-East India,* Guwahati, 1994, pp 150-154.

253. Sangkima, *Mizos Society and Social Change, Guwahati/* Delhi, Spectrum Publications, 1992, pp. 62-63.

254. Pastor Challiana, *Pi Pu Nun,* Aizawl, Reprint, 1978, p. 5.

255. According to their beliefs Mizos classified the abode of the dead as *Pialral* and *Mitthi khua*. The former was meant only for *Thangchhuah,* one who performed great feasts in his life time. The latter place was considered as the resting place of the souls of all ordinary men.

256. The translation of the tale is solely based on "The Folktales Of Mizorm", by Laltluangliana Khiangte. Aizawl, 1997.

257. B. Lalthangliana; *Pi Pu Chhuahtlang,* Aizawl, 1998, p. 88.

258. N.E. Parry, *The Lakhers,* Firma KLM, Calcutta, 1976, Reprint, p. 28.

259. Edein M. Loeb and Jan O.M. Brock, "Social Organization And The Long House In Southeast Asia" in *American Anthropologist,* Vol. 49, No. 1, 1947, p. 414.

260. *Ibid.*

261. *Ibid.,* p. 418.

262. G.M. Godden, "The Nagas And Other Frontier Tribes Of North East India", *Journal Of Anthropological Institute Of Great Britain And Ireland,* Vol. XXVII, 1897, p. 47.

263. V.L. Siama, *Mizo History,* Lalrinliana & Sons, Aizawl, 1978, p. 28.

264. Zatluanga, *Mizo Chanchin,* Khuma Printing Press, Aizawl, 1966, p. 82.

265. It was the custom and right of the *thingnawifawm* (boys) to ask for their share from the giver of the east. They demanded it by shaking the house of the host. They were fed only when the adults had finished. If there were not left-overs, fresh rice and meat were prepared for them.

266. Sangkima, *Mizos : Society And Social Change (1890-1947),* Spectrum Publications, Guwahati/Delhi.

267. A.G. McCall, *Lushai Chrysalis,* Lusac & Co., London, 1947, p. 211. Reprint (2004) Spectrum Publications, Guwahati/Delhi.

268. N. Chatterji, *Zawlbuk As A Social Institution In The Mizo Society*, Tribal Research Institute, Aizawl, 1974, p. 30.
269. Aizawl Record Room, Order No. 116D/26.1.1926.
270. *Ibid.*, Order No. 118/2.2.1926.
271. Zatluanga, *op. cit.*, p. 84.

4 Women and Politics in Mizoram Through the Ages

Like most societies, the Mizo society is patriachal whereby women are by nature inferior to men. In the past, the status and position of women in the society were not only lower but far more precarious than their male counterparts. The same was the case of their role in the polity of early Mizo society too.

In the early Mizo society, there was no political system as such. A village Chief was the supreme administrative head within the limits of his territory. His word was law. In short, the whole political process was completely dominated by male chauvinism. However, woman had a chance to become a ruler if her husband had deceased. This had become the case until 1947.

With the advent of the British there was, however, a slight change in the political system of Mizoram. Mizoram was annexed in 1890 and this required the British to make more efforts to consolidate their position. The tasks were however not achieved in 1895 when the rising of "Eastern Lushais" under Kairuma and his allies was completely suppressed.[1] Now, having been consolidated, the British had to choose either options for their further course of action : to abolish or to retain the institution of Chieftainship in Mizoram. They opted for the latter. Thus Chieftainship was retained with reduced powers. Thus dawned a new system of administration in Mizoram.

The year 1947 is a landmark in the political history of Mizoram. In this year the District authorities granted the people to form a political party. In the same year, the first women's organization called "Mizo Hmeichhe Tangrual" (MHT) was founded by a group of women in Aizawl. Through this organization women began to take part in local politics. Their main objective in getting involved in politics was to promote the status of women in the society. Since then, their participation in active politics in Mizoram has been a permanent feature. Therefore an attempt is made in this chapter to examine how far women have been taking part in the police of Mizoram through the ages. The discussion is broadly divided into two parts. In the first part of the discussion the part played by womenfolk in the administrative system before the British is investigated. This investigation covers the period upto 1946. In the second part of the discussion, the role of women in the political process of Mizoram after 1946 will be examined.

Role of Women Before 1946

A careful examination of the part played by womenfolk in the political system of Mizoram before the advent of the British reveals that women did not have rights to rule as rightful heirs. This speaks how women had a part in the administration. A further study, however, shows that though rightfully barred by custom, women became rulers or Chieftainesses only when they had a chance. Such a chance generally emerged when the reigning Chief died. They acted as regents and we find a number of such cases. We may now discuss those who reigned on behalf of their minor sons *i.e.* those who had to occupy the vacant throne left by their fathers on account of death.

Let us first discuss Lalhlupuii, wife of Lalngura, Chief of Sentlang. The village was completely devastated by Col. Lister in 1850. Lalngura is said to have died in 1855, when his only son Vanpuilala was about 4 or 5 years of age. Lalhlupuii then reigned as regent. The regency may have lasted for more than 13 years. It may also be longer than this assumed date, because she had to act as a regent for her nephew Lalhleia, the only son of Vanpuilala. During her regency she was fully supported by his *Upas* (Advisers)[2]. Vanpuilala died in 1869[3] when he was around *20* years of age.[4]

Upon the death of Vanpuilala, his people were divided into two factions between his mother and his widow who was the sister of Pawibawia. Lalhlupuii lived at Darlawn and the widow lived at Khawlian. The latter claimed regency on behalf of her infant son Lalhleia. In the dispute Pawibawia supported his sister whereas Lalhlupuii in consequence sought the assistance of Kalkhama who had moved his village across Tuiruang river where he set up a village on the same ridge as that of Darlawn. This greatly increased the areas controlled by Suakpuilala and his sons. Now they ruled over the lands between the Tut and the Tipaimuk rivers.[5] However, the action of Lalhlupuii very much infuriated Vuta who was very anxious to move his village south of Darlawn. The enmity brought the two into clash.

At about this time, there was another powerful Chieftainess in the person of Pibuki, mother of Suakpuilala. Her husband was Manga and she was the daughter of Lalrihua. We know very little about her reign, yet we know that she ruled over Durtlang.[6] She might also have been a ruler of Muthi village.[7] She was a kind and wise ruler.

It appears that Suakpuilala had at least two sisters who had two separate villages. Ruttlungpi (Rothangpuii) perhaps ruled over Muthi village.[8] Vanhnuaithangi was another sister of Suakpuilala. About the time of Lister's expedition she married Ngursailova, son of Lalchokla (Lalsutla). They settled in Sylhet *now* in Bangladesh. His village communities were peopled by Mizos and other adherents of Vanhnuaithangi.

In course of time, the couples quarrelled and later they divorced. Vanhnuaithangi returned to Mizoram with her followers, and she established a new village in about 1860. The separation thus led to a dispute between Suakpuilala and his brother-in-law over the price of the bride but the dispute was patched up in 1862 when Ngursailova proposed to have a raid on Sylhet.[9]

Vanhnuaithangi ruled over the village called Thilthek with 200 houses. Her village had 180 fighting men with about 20 guns.[10] It is also reported that the men of Vanhnuaithangi village came into collision with forces of Baker's expedition in 1869. The encounter took place on the bank of the Gootur (Tut river).[11]

Darbilhi was another important personality in the history of Mizoram. She was the daughter of Zahuata, Chief of Thingsat village. She was married to Nochhuma, son of Khualsawia. Her husband died in 1882. A.S. Reid said that when the expeditions of 1889 took place Nochhuma had been dead for seven years.[12] She succeeded her husband at Darzo. The lady was great and famous. She was a wise ruler, too. During the Chin-Lushai Expeditions (1889-1890) Darbilhi was very helpful for the British because she had already had a mutual relations with the British. But she seemed to have taken alarm at the capture of Lalthuama, son of Vandula and fled to the village of one Dopura.[13]

One of the objects of the expeditions was to reassure Darbilhi that she had no reason to be alarmed. When the forces arrived at Darzo on the afternoon of 4th February, 1890, they were well received by her, and then the two parties took an oath of friendship.[14] Capt. Shakespeare represented the British Government. On the occasion she was very instrumental in reaching an understanding between the southern Chiefs and the British. It may, however, be noted that while Darbilhi had cordial relations with the British, some other Chiefs were very busy in fighting against the British.

Contrary to Darbilhi in terms of relations with the British was Ropuiliani who, like other Chieftainesses, succeeded her husband Vandula. Provoked and hardened by the cruel killings of her own sons and relatives Ropuiliani formed a formidable force against the British and therefore she adopted the most stringent and unpalatable policy towards them.[15] When she assumed she was a potential danger to the British because she was fully recognised by the descendants of her late husband as a ruler. So, she was a person whose leadership was badly needed by the people.

Because of her strong anti-British policy Ropuiliani was charged as a problem Chieftainess and accused her of playing a clandestine role in inciting other Chiefs of the south. As a result, the Government sent expedition against Ropuiliani and her son Lalthuama in 1893, under the command of Capt. Shakespeare. This time the Government was determined to crush the Chiefs who were still unsubdued. In short, Ropuiliani and her son Lalthuama were arrested and taken to Lunglei, and then deported to Rangamati on 8th April, 1894. Then she died the next year on 3rd January 1895. Her capture had a good effect in pacifying the other Chiefs.

Besides these, there were some other Chieftainesses who were equally formidable to the British as their deceased husbands. Some of them may be mentioned.

We do not know when she assumed power, Neihpuithangi widow of Vuta, was such a great personality. She was one of the allies of Kairuma who caused a great rising called "Eastern Rising". When the British demanded, she surrendered 12 guns out of the 50 guns demanded.[16] It is also reported that Pawibawia's mother (Saituali?) was also a great ruler. She had 180 houses.[17] She is reported as having 110 fighting men with 30 guns[18]. Mention may also be made about the widow of Lalsavunga, his daughter Darhlupuii, Darchhohpuii, widow of Thangpuia and widow of Thansanga.

Since Ropuiliani's sons did not live long, the

deceased sons were succeeded by their respective wives. They were-Darsuakpuii widow of Hrangphunga, Suaki widow of Sangliana and Sumkungi widow of Lalthuama.[19] In fact, they ruled under the supervision of Ropuiliani.

Background of Political Development

Before we proceed to the second half of this chapter it may be necessary to briefly highlight the background of political development in Mizoram. This is required to bridge the two discussions. In Mizoram political consciousness was first witnessed during the first half of the twentieth century A.D.. For this awakening some factors were responsible. In the first place, the attempt of N.E Parry to revive the almost obsolete *Zawlbuk* was responsible.[20] The common people considered this action as an attempt by Parry to perpetuate the Chiefs rule in Mizoram. Secondly, political events outside Mizoram also contributed to the political awakening of the people. Some leaders considered politicking as the shortest possible way to remove the autocratic rule of the Chiefs.[21] Fourthly, another contributing factor was the formation of what is known as "Chiefs' *Durbar*" by A.G. McCall in 1931. The main purpose of the *'Durbar'* was to prevent interference of local officers in the functioning of the Chiefs.[22] Fifthly, the Second World War also contributed. In the war some Mizos performed commendable jobs. This made McDonald happy. So, when he was asked for the formation of a political party he had no difficulty in granting permission. Accordingly the first political party called "Mizo Union" (MU) was formed on 11th April 1946, followed by the United Mizos Freedom Organization (UMFO), a faction of the MU party. With this background in view now we will turn to the next discussion.

Role of Women After 1946

We have inadequately highlighted how women played a

part in the administration of the State before 1946. The nature of women's participation in the polity formation before and after 1946 was distinct from each other, because of the fact that there was a wide period of gap between the two.

In order to understand the role of women in an emerging politics in Mizoram, mention may be made, as already noted above, of the women's organization called Mizos Hmeichhe Tangrual. Formed on 16th July, 1946 with a view to promoting the status of women in the society, the organization was a contemporary of the Mizo Union Party. Organised itself on the pattern and model of the party, the Tangrual resembled the Mizo Union Party in many ways. Thus, the women leaders were boldly inspired to take active part in politics. In this connection three factors may be mentioned.

In the first place, the leaders of the two organizations were intimate with one another because most the leaders of both the organizations were partners or closely related with one another. This intimacy led both the parties (groups) to work together for the furtherance of their objectives. Secondly, the women leaders were firmly convinced that their objectives would best be implemented in a better and proper way if they took active part in local politics. As a matter of fact, many of their demands could be implemented only with the political decision taken by the appropriate forum. From this point of view the participation of women in politics was a necessity. Thirdly, the whole current political developments clearly favoured women to be involved in local politics.

Under such circumstances, the women leaders were firmly convinced to join the political party for their betterment in future. In this connection the role of the organizations was very imperative. Knowing very well what was going on around them, the Tangrual organization took a very significant decision in this matter, in its meeting held on 23rd August, 1947. The resolution says, *"He pawl hian a tul a tih ang apiangin politics a khawih thei ang".*[23] meaning "This organization will take part in politics whenever it deems fit."

In the meantime, the uncertain political future of the Mizos became certain with the visit to Mizoram by the so-called Bardoloi Sub-Committee, to take stock of the political situation in Mizoram. The main objective of the visit was to formulate what kind of autonomy would be given to the Mizos when India got independence after the departure of the British from India. The District Conference appointed six members to meet the Committee. Lalziki Sailo, a female, was one of the members. In 1921 she was adopted by one British Lady Missionary named Miss Edith Mary Chapman. She was taken to England three times in 1925-1926, 1931-1932 and 1936-1937. She had her education in Calcutta, Madras and New Delhi.[24] Being brought up by the Missionaries she was very good in British. Like other women of the day, she was also forced into the arena of politics. Interestingly, however, her autobiography is completely silent about her involvement in politics.

The Mizo Hmeichhe Tangrual also met the Sub-Committee and discussed the would be status of women in the society after Independence.[25] The Sub-Committee was also met by some other organizations.

In July 1947, L.L. Peters succeeded McDonald as the first Superintendent of a free India. When he reached Aizawl the political situation was tense because of the feuds between the two factions of the Mizo Union. The parties were divided into the Mizo Union proper and the Mizo Union "Right Wing". In order to abate the tension he convened a meeting of prominent leaders in Aizawl. The meeting's report was published and this, to a great extent, subsided the political atmosphere in Mizoram at that time.

The most important part of the recommendation was the formation of a District Council in hill districts with powers of legislation and administration over certain subjects.[26] Following the recommendation, the Government of Assam set up for Lushai Hills what was known as "Advisory Council" to look after the welfare of the people before the District Council was established. The Advisory Council reserved two seats for women each for Aizawl town and Lunglei town.[27] The Tangrual had repeatedly requested the authorities to include their representatives in the Council. The members were to be elected on the basis of democratic norms of adult franchise.

In the elections that followed four women candidates contested—two each from Aizawl and Lunglei towns. In Aizawl, the official candidate of the women's organization was Zami, and she was supported by the Mizo Union. The official candidate was challenged by its own President, Lalsangpuii. As she had an interest in contesting the election the committee in its sitting on 21st February, 1948 had a serious and painstaking discussion on the issue. Lalsangpuii was alleged to have made publicity in the media called *Zoram Thupuan* accusing the committee members in nominating someone other than her. Then Lalsangpuii was asked to make her position clear whether she would to vacate her post in case she contested the forth coming elections.[28] In the meeting itself she told the members that she would not contest the election.[29] Yet the meeting resolved with some reservations that if the President wanted to contest the elections she should inform the General Secretary of her decision by 6th March, 1948. Then, the President informed the Committee of her decision to contest in the election.[30] The matter was again discussed in the meeting and resolved that the President should vacate her responsibility of President until the election results were declared; and during her vacation the Vice President would take charge of being President. She would be accepted back as President only if she was not elected.[31] The issue thus perverted the smooth functioning of the organization for quite sometime thereby causing dissension and friction among the members.

As planned, the elections were held on 15th April, 1948. The contest were very keen and interesting not mainly because the official candidate was challenged by its own President but because it was the election where women for the first time took part in. In this connection, it may be noted that even before the elections were held Lalsangpuii had a bettor chance because of the fact that in Aizawl town the UMFO party had the backing of the rich and the intellectual groups. This gave an advantage point to Lalsangpuii. For this reason the result was a foregone conclusion that Lalsangpuii would be elected. So, when the real election took place the result was that Zami, the official candidate of the Tangrual was badly defeated. But outside Aizawl town the UMFO party fared badly. Almost all the seats were won by the Mizo Union party. The election had serious repercussions upon the organization. Consequently, the organization was then divided as factions of Aizawl South and Aizawl North because the members in Aizawl North appeared to be the supporters of Lalsangpuii who also had her residence in that area Secondly, the two factions went to the Court in connection with the expenditure on elections. Lalsangpuii and her supporters borrowed Rs. 116.40 from Chhotelal Seth and Co., a Marwari business house in Dawrpui area in Aizawl North. They took the money in the name of the organization, yet nothing was known by the leaders at headquarters when they received the letter to repay the amount. Then the matter was taken up in the law court. As a result, the Court ordered Lalsangpuii and her company to return the borrowed amount.[32] Thirdly, the women leaders now made another request to the Mizo Union leadership to appoint a woman member in lieu of Lalsangpuii in the committee because they could no longer accept Lalsangpuii as their representative and they contested that her place in the Mizo Union was also automatically ended.[33] As requested the Mizo Union leadership appointed two women representatives in the committee.

With these elections, the whole process for the formation of the Advisory Council was over. The main task before it was to prepare the ground for the coming of the District Council. The members tried to discuss the "Draft Regulation", for the District Council but no serious discussion could take place owing to the problems created by the members of the Mizo Union. At last, the Government of Assam, though its advisor Nari K. Rustomji, authorised the Advisory Council to have administrative powers on certain items. The last meeting was held on 11th February, 1950 and it passed a number of resolutions concerning the District Council which was likely to come in the very near future.

When the time came, the Government of Assam constituted the District Council on 26th April, 1952 on the basis of the recommendations of the Bardoloi Sub Committee. The Council had 24 members of which 18 were to be elected and the remaining 6 were to be nominated. The Constitution of the Mizo District Council was a dream-come-true to the women leaders. As a women's organization their main concern was the upliftment of their position in the society. They were also concerned with the participation in the District Council with a view to improving their position.[34] Their third concern was to take part in the village level administration.[35] They also talked among themselves about a "greater Mizoram," they wanted the District Council to have certain provision for its future expansion in terms of membership so that the Mizos living in Cachar and Manipur areas might have a chance to send their representatives in the future.[36] The women leaders also made it clear that they strongly opposed the possible formation of the Regional Council in Mizoram. The matter was discussed by the Northern Division in its meeting held on 7th October 1948.[37] They further resolved to bring the matter to the notice of the Superintendent. In the view of the leaders the formation of the Regional Council could have a bad impact upon the functioning of the organization.

As stated earlier, the women leaders were very much concerned with having representative in the District Council. They needed someone to present their case in the Council. For this reason, they repeatedly passed resolution after resolution asking the authorities to give them seats in the Council for women. Sometimes they demanded two seats and sometimes they asked for three seats. Since its inception till the District Council was instituted in 1952 the organization discussed this issue as one of its agendas in the Assembly of Division or Local level meetings. But when the formation of the District Council became an accomplished fact, the organization in its General Assembly held on 7-9 February 1951 made its position clear. In the Assembly the members selected by secret vote three names as possible candidates in the forthcoming District Council. The selected persons were Hmingliani, Thankimi and Varziki.[38] This was done to give an impression to the people that the women members in the District Council were the real nominees of the women folk. Finally, Hmingliani and Thankimi were in the list after dropping one of the three by the Assembly, on the pretext that they would not be given more than two seats. The decision of the Assembly was conveyed to the Government.[39] With regards to the Village Council, in the special Assembly held in 1952, the members unanimously resolved to contest the election.[40] However, the decision was reviewed in its General Assembly held at Thakthing *Zawlbuk,* Aizawl on 30 October 1953. The Assembly modified as such that it was generally agreed to contest the forthcoming Village

Council elections but only candidate who would have a winning chance, should contest the elections.[41]

Meanwhile, the District Council was inaugurated at Reid House. Aizawl on 26 April 1952 by Bishnuram Medhi, the then Chief Minister of Assam. The first session was also held in the same house. The oath-taking ceremony was performed by S.N. Barkataki, the then Deputy Commissioner of the Lushai Hills District. But to the surprise of every member of the Tangrual organization the nominated member of women was none other than Lalziki Sailo who was not a member of the organization. As a matter of fact, the nomination was a bolt from the blue for aspiring women who had been troubling themselves for years. All their hopes and aspirations were for a time vanished, for their own candidates were not chosen.

As to why Lalziki Sailo was nominated in the first Mizo District Council, opinions are differed. According to Lalziki, she was nominated by Lalmawia of the UMFO leadership.[42] This may be to a certain extent true but in the elections the UMFO did very badly. Only one candidate out of 18 elected members, Pachhunga was elected from the UMFO.[43] As a matter of rule, the party having majority members had the right to nominate members. In the idea of Hmingliani, ex-President of Mizo Hmeichhe Tangrual, Lalziki Sailo was nominated by the Governor of Assam.[44] This may be true because Lalziki Sailo was a popular figure not only among women folk, but also among the Mizo community because of her political as well as educational background. As, stated before, she was brought up by the Missionaries and she had also done programmes in the British Broadcasting Corporation (BBC). She was popular among the officials for her fluency in British. When asked about her role in the Council meeting she said she did not make any remarkable contributions in terms of participation in the debate as well as championing the cause of women. She said her main handicap was the language used in the Council debate. Being brought up by the missionaries her mother tongue was British. So, she could not be effective in the House on account of the language problem. Being unable to express herself properly in Mizo, she preferred to stay away from participation in the debate.

However, a new page in the history of the Tangrual was opened when its President Hmingliani was nominated as member of the second Mizo District Council. She was nominated not because of her position as President of the organization but her nomination was made through secret ballot among the members of the Central Working Committee of the Organization. She got the highest vote by securing six votes among them.[45] She was the wife of R. Thanhlira,[46] one of the most popular and prominent men among the Mizos. During her tenure as a member of the District Council, Hmingliani played a very significant role in trying to cause changes in the customary law of the Mizos through legislation. In this connection, mention may be made that as the result of efforts by the Tangrual organization a significant change was effected by the District Council. According to this change women were allowed to inherit property by "Will" if properly executed with witnesses.[47] But when it was practised practical problems cropped up owing to objections raised by males. Thus Court cases became common and as a result, the District Council authorities thought of reverting the decision. This agitated the women functionaries.[48] Here the presence of Hmingliani as member was very significant. She tried her best to convince the authorities not to go back to the old system.

Because of her utmost effort no change was made regarding inheritance. As a result of this, women have a right to inherit family property.[49] This is one of the greatest achievements made by Hmingliani as an individual and as member of the women's organization.

In 1962 at the end of the term of the second District Council, Hmingliani was again, nominated for the third Mizo District Council but this time, she surrendered the seat to her colleague Malsawmi of Zarkawt, Aizawl.[50] Since then women as a group of an organised functionary gradually alienated themselves from active politics and as a result of disturbances following the outbreak of 1966, the whole political atmosphere was not normal. Hence, the organization completely divorced politics in its life and activities. Moreover, the whole set up of women's organizations was badly hurt by the political upheaval of 1966 thereby causing the Mizo Hmeichhe Tangrual to lose its position as an organization representing women in the society.

In 1966 the Mizo National Front declared independence from India. As a result, the working of the District Council was also very much crippled. Thus, during the period from 1962 to 1972 till Mizoram was elevated to the status of Union Territory (UT) no woman was elected to the District Council nor was any woman nominated as its member.

Following the upgradation of the Mizo District Council to U.T. the Assembly elections were held on 12th April, 1972. In these elections no party had any woman candidate. But when the Ministry was formed the ruling party, the Mizo Union, nominated Miss Saptawni, the Headmistress of Presbyterian Church Girls' School, Aizawl. It is not known whether or not she made a mark in her tenure as Member of the Legislative Assembly (MLA) with regard to the upliftment of women in the society.

During this period new political parties were in the offing. On 17th April, 1975 a new party known as People's Conference (PC) was formed with Brig. Thenphunga Sailo as it President. Apart from the General Secretary there were six Secretaries. One of them was Thansiami.[51] She is still with the party now known as

Mizoram People's Conference (MPC). The change of the party name was necessary for the new registration in the Election Commission of India.

At about this time, yet another new political party was formed. The party was called the Mizo Democratic Front (MDF).[52] Miss Sanglianchhungi was the President. This is a landmark in the political history of Mizoram for a woman took the leadership of a political party. Further, this clearly indicates that women are not inferior to men in terms of leadership in the political field.

In 1975 a new political history was made in India. The Prime Minister Indira Gandhi declared emergency throughout India. In Mizoram too, the opposition leaders were put behind the bars. Brig. T. Sailo, the President of the P.C. Party and his colleagues were sent to Tezpur jail in Assam. Sanglianchhungi and some of her colleagues were also arrested and put in the District Jail at Aizawl. Sanglianchhungi may be the second Mizo woman who was interned for political reasons after Chieftain Ropuiliani who was arrested and imprisoned at Rangamati jail (*now* in Bangladesh) in 1894 by the British. Ropuiliani sacrificed her life for the cause of her countrymen, the Mizos, in 1895.[53]

Sanglianchhungi also made history in Mizoram. When she was in the prison cell the general elections to Parliament (Lok Sabha) were held on 11th March 1977. Sanglianchhungi contested the elections from her interment on the MDF (Independent) ticket and used 'tiger' as her election symbol.[54] In the political history of Mizoram she may be the first and the last woman who contested the Lok Sabha elections from behind the bars. Till now no other woman or man is found doing the same.

The elections to the second Legislative Assembly were again held on 1 7th and 20th May 1978. In the elections only one woman candidate contested. She was Thanmawii of the P.C. Party. She fought her elections from Serchhip Constituency and she was elected by securing 1824 out of the total votes of 6380.[55] She was the lone woman contender out of the total candidates of 113 and she was the first elected woman member in the Mizoram Legislative Assembly. Sanglianchhungi did not contest the elections.

The P.C. Party, won the elections, and formed the Ministry but it lasted only six months. Due to the split in the party a re-election was necessary. On 10th November 1978, Mizoram was placed under the President's Rule. As a result, new elections were again held on 24th and 27th April 1979. This time Thanmawii contested again and she was elected from Aizawl East constituency by securing 2177 votes. Sanglianchhungi also contested as an MDF candidate but she got only 148 votes.[56] She contested from the constituency of Aizawl West. The Ministry was formed again by the P.C. party with Brig. T. Sailo as Chief Minister for the second time. The third Legislative Assembly had two women members with K. Thansiami joining the Assembly as a nominated member. She was the second woman who entered the Assembly as a nominated member after Saptawni who made her debut in the House in 1972.

In the 1984 elections Thansiami was elected on the ticket of the P.C. party. This time, the Ministry was formed by the Congress party and Rokungi was a nominated member. She did not complete her term on account of the agreement signed by the Government of India and the MNF outfit in 1986. Following this agreement a new Ministry was formed as an interim Government with Laldenga as the Chief Minister for an interim period of six months. Accordingly, in 1987 elections were held again as scheduled and Lalhlimpuii was elected on the MNF ticket and the MNF got a majority and the Ministry was formed with Laldenga as the Chief Minister for the second time. Lalhlimpuii was inducted as a Minister. She is the first woman Minister in the Mizoram Legislative Assembly.[57]

Like the first P.C. Ministry, the MNF Ministry lasted only two years and the new Ministry was formed by the Congress with the support of some MNF members who dissented and formed the MNF (Democratic). This Ministry completed the remaining three years.

In the 1992 elections no woman candidate contested. In the same way, in 1998 elections while 33% seat reservation for women was being debated, no major party in Mizoram allotted seats to women except the Mizo National Front (Nationalist), a faction of the MNF party. Veronica K. Zatluangi contested in the name of the party at Vanva constituency in Lunglei District away from her home constituency in Aizawl South-I. The major parties like the Congress, MNF and MPC failed to give any candidacy to women. In the Congress party there were some hot and serious aspirants but not a single seat was given to women in spite of strong pressure from the women's wing. Altogether there were seven women contestants. The other six candidates were P.C. Thachhungi (Lok Sabha) who contested from Tlungvel Constituency, Lalrinmawii (BJP) contested from Aizawl North-I, K. Thansiami (JD) contested from Aizawl South-I, Rothangpuii (Lok Sakti) who contested from Serchhip Constituency and Lalthanzami who also contested from Serchhip Constituency. No candidate was serious except Veronica K. Zatluangi who had left her service on voluntary retirement. After all, the elections of 1998 are remarkable in the history of women in Mizoram mainly because a record number of women contested. No candidate was elected and the number of votes they got were all confined within three digit figures.

Concluding Remarks

It is a fact that women are by status inferior to their male counterparts in the Mizo society. In early society, they were also debarred from the right to succeed. In spite of this, there were instances where women succeeded their deceased husbands on the throne and they became rulers or Chieftainesses not as a matter of right but as a matter of chance. Yet, they proved that they were equally competent as their husbands whom they succeeded.

It may further be observed that women have not been totally segregated from political manouvering at any period of time. In the early period, as noted above, they took part in the administration whenever they had any chance. However, the nature of their participation in the system of administration was quite different when a political party was formed. They joined active politics only because of their desire to uplift the status of Mizo women in their society.

Our study, however, reveals that there was a great change in the nature of women's participation in politics after 1966. After this period, women as an organization totally divorced politics. Those who later joined political parties, did so as individuals. They played important parts by becoming members of the women wing of the party. No restriction or distinction is made against women in this field of activity. However, the role being played by them is still very unsatisfactory. From this view point, it is very difficult to predict the political future of women in Mizoram.

ROPUILIANI : HER ROLE IN THE STRUGGLE AGAINST THE BRITISH IN MIZORAM

There were a number of Chiefs and Chieftainesses famous for their active participation in the struggle against the advent of the British in Mizoram. Ropuiliani was one such personality.[58] Like many Chiefs, she sacrificed her own life for the good cause of the Mizos in general and of her own men whom she served and governed in particular. In bravery and gallantry, she outwitted many Chiefs in the resistance against the British. Provoked and hardened by the ruthless killing of her own sons and relatives, Ropuiliani stood in the way of the British by forming a formidable opposition.

She did not lack any of the qualities which men had. She was not an ordinary woman by virtue of her wit and tactics. She tried to preserve with all cause the sanctity of her position which she inherited from her husband, Vandula. She asserted her patriotism by relentlessly fermenting all her efforts and abilities and in dislodging the British in their attempts to suppress the Chiefs and their subjects.

Ropuiliani inherited the feeling of hatred for the British from her husband Vandula and her father Lalsavunga. Both father and husband were the old enemies of the British.[59] Before he died, Vandula, the husband, had opposed the British in their attempts to suppress the Mizos. Lalsavunga, the father, too, was one of the Chiefs against whom the Cachar Column of the Lushai Expedition 1 871-72 was directed.[60] It is therefore strongly believed that Ropuiliani had stored enough grounds for an anti-British feeling.

Before he died, Vandula was the head of all the Haulawng Chiefs. Not only that, he was a recognised leader among them and also extended his influences upon the Shendus. Before applying a strong arm policy against Vandula the British had tried hard to induce him, but in vain. They could not persuade him to come to their side even through his own brother Seipuia was an ally of the British. Failing to convince him, the British considered Vandula an enemy. When Ropuiliani assumed sovereign authority she was deeply influenced by the legacy left by her late husband towards the British. The attitude of the British towards her and her allies also remained unchanged. Thus and in the same manner. Ropuiliani also adopted the most stringent and bitter policy towards the British.

It is not known when Ropuiliani succeeded her husband but when she assumed power she became a danger to the British in their future plans. She had an absolute command over all the descendants of her late husband. This was imperative because after Vandula the Haulawngs were without any able ruler. They needed a leader badly in their resistance against the advent of the British. It was their first duty to choose between the two choices. In the first place, she should follow the policy adopted by her late husband, and in the second place, she had to follow a policy of reconciliation deviating from the legacy of her husband. In the end, she chose the former one which she adhered to till her death. Now confrontation with the British became her sole aim in life. Therefore an attempt has been made in this chapter to assess the role of Ropuiliani who offered stiff and intense resistance to the British whose supremacy was later recognised over all of the erstwhile Lushai Hills.

Her Role

To assess the role played by Ropuiliani in her conflict with the British we must examine the various circumstances in which she became involved with the British. As a confrontationist and anti-imperialist, Ropuiliani did not give in herself to the British as a friend and as collaborator with any slightest tinge. There was not a single event or incident in which Ropuiliani was directly involved but she was involved in all the incidents for which successive operations were sent, for she controlled the situation.

The first incident for which a military expedition of 1889 was despatched took place near Rangamati in the Chittagong Hill Tracts. This event took place on 3rd February 1888 in which Lt. J.F. Stewart and his party were killed. It was Hausata who killed them. The incident provoked the British and an expedition was sent in 1889. The despatch was inevitable for it was the duty of the British, to protect the men living within their declared boundary, and not to avenge the murderers would be a breach of faith.[61] Murray, who was one of the team members, declared the British policy in the strongest terms and said : "Every white man is held to be a Chief.[62] "The Government of Bengal was determined to take action against the Chiefs whom they considered responsible for the murder.

In fact, the Government identified the responsible Chiefs but Lalthuama, the youngest son of Ropuiliani, was also accused as having hands behind the murder by harbouring one of the killers.[63] Later, through investigation, it was found out that Lalthuama had certain complicity with the murder of Lt. Stewart. Actually, the Government had suspected the loyalty of Lalthuama and that he had complicity in the murder of Lt. Stewart. The Government had also suspected the loyalty of Lalthuama and Ropuiliani for quite some time.[64] In another incident in which the bugler was murdered, Lalthuama encouraged by his mother, was again suspected as having given guides to the Shendus who killed a bugler. This was made known to the British by Seipuia, brother of Vandula. He, however, said that the men supplied by Lalthuama were taken by force.[65]

The military operation was reinforced by despatching another detachment popularly known as the Chin-Lushai expedition of 1889-1890. This time it was done on a bigger scale. The operation was destined to accomplish the tasks which had been assigned to the previous one and to take control of the whole situation caused by the incidents that were taking place during the intervening period. In short, the expedition achieved its objects by bringing the trio who killed Stewart and his party to book.[66] In spite of its achievements, the operations of 1889-90 were extended with a view to completing the punishment of the raiding villages, and subduing the Chiefs who still put up resistance under the leadership of Ropuiliani or the Haulawngs, confirming the authority of the British Government over the tribes in the east who were still unsubdued, and opening up of communications across the hills on the

Burma side. As a part of operations permanent posts were established at Fort Tregear (South Vanlaiphai) and at Lungleh (*now* Lunglei) and a Political Officer was appointed there. During the winter of 1890-91 an additional post was built at Lalthuama's village[67] with a view to subduing him and his mother Ropuiliani along with other Chiefs who were also making trouble for the British through the influence of the latter. The operations thus intimidated them and the situation became calm for a while.

As a result, the year 1890 was quiet. No untoward incident took place. However, the lull which followed was short-lived. The years of 1891 and of 1892 were marked by fresh outbreaks across the Hills. The 1891-1892 rising was partly political and partly economic. As political, the trouble in the South arose as a result of injudicious action on the part of Murray who paid a visit to Zakapa's village. Murray and his party did not anticipate that any opposition would be offered to them. The party was attacked and they had to run for their lives.[68] A punitive expedition was hurriedly organised but failed to capture the Chief. But the operations were on to bring all the Chiefs to a submission who had refused to do so in earlier time. Among them were included Ropuiliani, Lalthuama and their collaborators who had open hostility with the British.[69] Captain Hutchinson's military detachment made a considerable headway in dealing with the revolting Chiefs. Besides the Haulawng Chiefs, Dokulha who had a hand in the murder of Lt. Stewart was captured and he was sentenced to transportation for life to the Andaman Islands and he finally died there.[70] Again, this abated the situation for a while.

The economic grievances of the people in general and the Chiefs in particular were responsible for the outbreaks in 1892. The establishment of new posts at Lunglei and at Fort Tregear and an additional temporary post at Lalthuama's village was giving the Chiefs an extra burden for they had to supply labour at the expense of their subjects. This was an interference on the part of the British in the internal affairs of the Chiefs. Whether the Chief was loyal or disloyal to the British he had to render labour and to give tribute. Labourers were required to go from villages, on 8 or 9 days' journey in return for a reasonable rate of pay. This system was not acceptable to the people as a whole and it was not consonant with their custom either. W.B. Oldham, the Commissioner of the Chittagong Hill Tracts was of the view that the system enforced in 1892 in the South was the sole cause of the troubles in the last four years. According to him it was a worthless kind of system with which the Government interfered. He said, "It was the sole cause of troubles in 1892 as it is of those pending."[71] The system in 1892 cost the Bengal Government alone over 3 lakhs, and over 2 lakhs in 1893. Inspite of the economic impact on the Government, the Government of Bengal did not allow it to fall into disuse Yet Oldham insisted that the continuation of the system would retard the objective the British Government had in view, including pacification and the creation of a labour supply system.

It appears that the rising of 1892 was the creation of the British themselves. Though outwardly situations seemed quiet, the Government was not hopeful of any rapid and peaceful settlement with Lalthuama and his mother because, besides the economic restraints as a result of impressed labour and tribute, as pointed out earlier, their clans were ruthlessly victimised during the rising itself. Hardened at heart by her experiences Ropuiliani inflicted a stiff resistance to the British inspite of her growing age. Again, when all the other Chiefs of his clan had laid down their lives Lalthuama was the only Chief left to continue his father's policy towards the British. But he was under the complete control of his mother Ropuiliani. She asserted her influence upon him and acted as a remote control. She directed Lalthuama in all his attempts to offend the British. In the eyes of the British, therefore, Ṛopuiliani and her son Lalthuama equally shared the responsibility for all the untoward incidents against the British. The British charged both Ropuiliani and Lalthuama as problem Chiefs for their clandestine role in inciting the other Chiefs of their own clan to ignite tension between them and the Chiefs. To make the situation worse, the British Government realised later that in all the activities of Lalthuama against the British, the involvement of his mother, Ropuiliani was confirmed. To their great dismay, Lalthuama married a daughter of Lianphunga who was the enemy of the British.[72] The British highly considered the marriage as a plot to destabilise the whole situation. As a result, Captain Shakespeare led a punitive expedition against Lalthuama and his mother. While countering the hostility, Shakespeare was besieged at Chhipphir of Vansanga's Village. But he was able to hold out only through the help of Lalluava of Bualpui. Throughout his campaign in the South, Shakespeare received considerable support from Dara, an interpreter.

The Government was not hopeful of any permanent and peaceful settlement with the Chiefs until the powers of the Haulawng Chiefs and their collaborators were crushed. Towards the end of 1892 there was a sign that peace might come at least in the South as the powers of some hostile Chiefs were broken and scattered. But the prospect for peace was overshadowed by a fresh revolt in the middle of the year 1893. It was learnt that Lalthuama and his mother Ropuiliani, with Dokhoma, a northern Chief, were again conspiring another revolt. They wanted to show that they were not happy and satisfied with the British for their aggressive attitude towards them. They were the last to be subdued. The incident took place when some *coolies* and an interpreter were attacked. The authorities took immediate action with a view to containing the revolt within the South.

To suppress the rising, an expedition was despatched under Capt. Shakespeare. Before the movement was mobilised C.W. Davis, the Political Officer, North Lushai Hills, was also consulted. The despatch consisted of more than five hundred and fifty troops and more than 400 military police. It was done jointly with the Northern Column. The mission was intensely directed against Lalthuama and his mother Ropuiliani under whose leadership and clandestine atrocities were actively organised. The Government this time was determined to crush the powers of the Chiefs who were still unsubdued.

The forces approached Ropuiliani's village under the darkness of the night to surprise her and her son. After crossing the Mat river and at dawn the next day the village was reached while it was still dark. Without any resistance, the party captured Ropuiliani and her son Lalthuama. Their subjects too were rapidly disarmed and their weapons were confiscated.[73] With the capture of Ropuiliani and her right-hand man, Lalthuama, the Haulawng Chiefs of Vandula's descendants lost their leader and they were now without a leader.

The party returned to Lunglei with their seized weapons. Ropuiliani and her son Lalthuama were also taken along. They were imprisoned there but the British did not feel safe to keep them at Lunglei and feared that their presence there might escalate the situation. Therefore, they decided to take them outside Mizoram. This was informed to their higher authority[74] and accordingly, the Government of Bengal directed the local authority to deport the prisoners to Rangamati, the headquarters of Chittagong Hill Tracts. Thus, the prisoners were deported to Rangamati from Lungleh on 8th April 1894. But Ropuiliani could not survive the shock of prison life and she died on 3rd January, 1895[75] at a fairly old age. She was very weak when admitted into hospital on 18th April 1894 and her health was deteriorating when she was attacked with dysentery for a few days. This, perhaps, hastened her end. When she died her dead body was brought home in a coffin and Lalthuama was also allowed to accompany the dead body home. This followed his release from imprisonment thereby allowing him to settle at his own village. It is hardly possible to determine her real age but when she died Ropuiliani looked over 70 years of age. In prison, the jail authority treated them as State prisoners, guarded by wardens, and not by Police constables.

Results of the Capture

Now, with the capture of Ropuiliani it became easier for the British to subdue the Chiefs of lesser importance. The subjects of Ropuiliani and Lalthuama were rapidly disarmed. Messages were despatched to neighbouring villages informing them to surrender their arms. The response was rapid for tear of further intimidation. From Ropuiliani's village alone the British extracted 100 guns within a week. In all they collected more than 500 guns including those from villages other than Ropuiliani's.[76]

The general condition of the country was quiet. The people also abandoned the idea of resistance although isolated outbreaks might have occurred here and there. And to contain such separate sporadic outbreaks a small number of Police Force would suffice.

Another significant achievement of the expedition was the capture of Lalchheuva, son of Rothangpuia, wanted for murder. Another capture which had a significant effect in pacifying the country was that of Vansanga who kept up the spirit of hospitality among the Mizos.

POSITION AND STATUS OF WOMEN IN TRADITIONAL MIZO SOCIETY

An old British saying :

"A woman, a dog, and a walnut tree,
the more you beat them the better they be."

An old Mizo saying :

> *"Crab's meal is not counted as meat as women's word is nor counted as word : Bad wife and bad fence can be changed. But unthreatened wife and unthreatened grass of the fields are both unbearable."*

Every society, however primitive, has a social organization. Within the framework of this organization there are different levels formed by different classes of people like men, women, children and others. Each of these different strata having specific responsibilities at times unite for some purposes and have to perform different functions in various capacities in the society. With the exception of the matriarchal society, every society treats women as an inferior lot to men. Therefore, we may say with evidence that everywhere in the world, primitive or civilized, the way the society treats women is more or less similar in all respects. This holds true even in today's so-called *'advanced society'*.

This social view on women also coincided with the view held by the Church in the early Christian era, on women. In the early Church, women were not credited as equal to men. From the Church point of view, women should not enjoy the same status with men in matters relating to powers and responsibilities in the Church organization. Nor should they preach in and outside the Church. Instead, they should remain silent listeners. Thus, St. Paul (c. A.D. 5-67), one of the fathers of the early Church wrote with command : *"The women should keep silence in the Church. For they are not permitted to speak.... If there is anything they desire to know, let them ask their husbands at home. For it is shameful for a woman to speak in the Church."*[77] It is not definitely known why St. Paul pronounced such dictum. But what we find from this statement is that even in the Christian community where individual freedom is advocated women were discriminated against. Almost an identical view is found in an old Mizo saving which reads : "Women and crabs do not have religion." This saying implies, it seems, what Paul dictated to the Corinthians as just indicated.

The Mizo society is a patriarchal society where male dominance is prevalent. As such, in the period under review women were not treated as equal to their male counterparts. In spite of this fact, women occupied a comparatively high position in the family in terms of responsibilities particularly in matters relating to household affairs. At the same time, their responsibilities in the family and participation in social oblizations were markedly different at different stages. With this background in view, an attempt is made in this paper to throw some light on the position and status of women in the traditional Mizo society. The study is divided into two heads; women in the family and women in society.

Women in the Family

In early Mizo society there were two agencies which moulded the social life of the people. They were the family and the *Zawlbuk*. The family as an agency of the society played a very important role in moulding the social life of the Mizos. In one sense, the family surpassed the *Zawlbuk* in terms of importance because the family acted as an institution where all the family members were taught manners whereas the *Zawlbuk* administration dealt with only its' male inmates. Therefore, the family occupied a high place in the Mizo society.

In spite of certain prerogatives recognised in the society the husband, being head of the family, exercised unfittered and autocratic dominance over his wife and other members of the family. The wife, being second in order of preference, and purchased by-price, however, had no legal right to claims in the family. Her status was so wretched that while submitting herself to her husband she should endure and execute all the responsibilities in the family but without authority.[78] So the demand by the family only enabled the woman to accept her place in the family.

With regards to.birth, both male and female children were treated with equal joy. In fact some parents felt happier to have a female child for the fact that the prospects of getting support from a female child were more promising than that of the male one who would soon leave the house for the *Zawlbuk.* These expectations lured the parents. When a male child was born he was hailed and blessed by the *Upa* (elder) as *"Mipa huaisen Sai kap tur"* which means *"a valiant, the would be elephant killer"* At the same time the birth *of a* female child was greeted with the words, *"Se man tur"* meaning *"one who would cost a mithun."*[79]

Right from her childhood days the tiny girl made herself available to the parents. She assisted her parents as much as she could. She had to take care of her younger brothers and sisters, draw water, cook and do any other works whatever the family needed. Sometimes, accompanying her mother she fetched firewood. In this way, the girl helped her parents when she was still young.

When the girl attained adulthood she was assigned with different nature of work. She had to accompany her parents in the *jhum* thereby doubling her responsibilities in the family. Working the whole day at the jhum along with others she found no time for taking rest even when she reached home late in the evening. She had to spend the whole night with various engagements. It was customary among married and unmarried women to engage themselves with cotton works. Besides, the unmarried women had to perform a well-established social custom by receiving youngmen who came to spend time in amusing themselves after toiling the whole day at *the jhum.* This custom is called *Inleng* (courting). When the next day dawned she had to rise early to start life afresh for the whole day. In the early morning she proceeded to the spring (waterpoint) to fill empty bamboo tubes with water, finish unhusking the rice by pounding in a mortar and cook the breakfast. She should have finished all these tiring jobs before sun rise while the husband and the other male members were still asleep. Then after the meal the real work for the day began. All these pre-day engagements were performed by the young woman and the mother in the house. If the mother had no daughter she had to single out these duties.

As a matter of fact, woman in normal busy times hardly took rest. When weeding season was over, there Autumn season set in. This was the season when men engaged themselves with hunting. Those who did not go for hunting they roamed about without helping the family. But for womenfolk it was the busiest season of the year.

During this pleasant season the Mizo woman sets her daily routine in two features. The first part of her work in a given day was to fetch firewood from the jungle. It was her duty to stock firewood for the next rainy season. The other part included making of clothes for the coming winter. So it was no wonder to hear the mother shouting with a shrill voice calling the children who were playing around her for help. In this way the woman in the family managed the whole household affairs without fatigue.[80]

Inspite of all this tireless sacrifice rendered to the family, the wife still found herself very insecure in the family as her membership was likely to be terminated at any time by her husband by saying *ka ma che* meaning *"I divorce you"*. As pointed out earlier, by custom she had no rightful claim over the properties in the family except those brought along with her as *Thuam* (dowry) at the time of her marriage. The children belonged to the father and even the right to inheritance was denied to her. Further, it may be noted that the wife was customarily bound not to call the husband by name in the presence of others.

The position of a woman in the family could be elevated for some reasons. In the first place, it was a common practice among men to go hunting whenever they were free. They usually were away from home for months. During the long absence of the head of the family, the mother took overall charge to manage the home affairs. Her words were to be obeyed. Even after his return from hunting the husband could manage to adjust himself with what was going on at home. In the second place, the wife's influence increased in the family if the husband became handicapped, caused by some accident. In the third place, the wife assumed charge in the family when the husband died. If such a situation happened in the family it confined itself within that family alone.

Women in the Society

Like in the family, women took active part in the community life of the society. However, her participation had a limit, confining her within certain areas only. As the society was community-based, therefore each section of the people had a part to play in it according to the duty assigned to each section. As such, a boy had a role to play, so also a girl had to perform other duties. Likewise, men and women had to act in different manners too, when required.

For instance, the boy rendered compulsory services to the community by supplying firewood to the *Zawlbuk*, but the girl was free from this service. Her services were confined only to the household affairs. During festivities and other community feasts held in a village only the boys of *Thingnawitawm* (supplier of firewood to the *Zawlbuk*) could participate, but in minimal degrees.

In the festivals like *Pawl kut* and *Chapchar kut*, however, both male and female children participated with some enthusiasm. The *Pawl kut*, meant for the children, was occasionally celebrated in the beginning of the year.

The occassion was marked by gaiety and happiness. Amidst rejoicing, children of all ages came out at the open ground and held a public feast called *Chhawnghnawt* which took place at the outskirts of a village. Men and women also joined them. When the feast was held, the participants tried to put food into each other's mouth. The same thing was repeated when the *Chapchar Kut* was held. On the *Pawl kut* occassion both male and female babies were adorned differently. The female baby was attired with red feathers fixing them with her hair by beeswax on the crown of her head. The male baby was also dressed in the same way but with a tuft of goat hair dyed red.[82]

Now, the girl experienced another stage of life when she graduated to adult responsibility. She began to live an independent life but under the protection of the parents. At this stage she had nothing to worry about because she could take active part in the social activities without any inhibitions. But in this transition she found her life quite changed for the simple reason that her participation in the social life was at risk. Here, whether or not she liked to be involved in the social activities, she was bound by social obligations, if she failed to perform these social functions she would be nowhere in the society. She would be disdained as a social outcast. However, she became self-contented when she was treated socially on equal tooting with her male counterparts.

As mentioned earlier, the girl was the hope of her parents. As long as she remained unmarried her parents left everything in her care. Since the livelihood of the community wholly depended on agriculture-based cultivation, success in life rested chiefly on intensive labour. Therefore, it was customary for the girl to have a working partner called *Lawmpa* throughout the year. In such partnership the girl held the reins in order to make the partnership a lasting one. If the male partner left her it would be a great shame on the part of the girl, bearing all blemishes and loss, for physically he was more preferable to her in terms of working ability. Thus, in order to maintain a long lusting partnership the girl should keep up all sorts of courtesy and manners towards her male partner. Mutual appreciation had to stay between them. In order to do so the girl was customarily bound to take all the belongings of the man under her case. Thus she had to wash his dirty clothes, mend the work day attire, carry all his working tools to and for long with the food for mid-day meal. She had to supply him *tuibur al* and *meizial* (cigarettes). By doing all this the girl performed only one part of her social obligations.[83]

After the day's toil at the field, as already pointed out the girl had to find time for meeting the courting party. As it existed, the Mizo society was a free society wherein the opposite sexes were allowed to mix freely. Such permissiveness sometimes resulted in social laxity which ended in doom for the girl. In such cases, it was the girl who would lose her reputation and prestige in the society.

The married life of a woman was another aspect which clearly revealed the status of woman in the Mizo society. In those early days, the parents were very careful in selecting a partner for their daughter. They looked into the family history as far back as they could trace. In case the boy felt like taking the girl in marriage, he would testify the worthiness of the girl by intensifying his courting methods. At the same time, it was the duty of the girl to preserve the sanctity of her womanly nature. This courting period normally took not less than three lunar years. Even if the girl found him acceptable as a husband, she would not yield to him in the pre-marital period or before the lapse of the said period.[84] If no serious lapses occured on either side then marriage would take place. In any case, the parents should have taken the consent of the girl before the process of marriage was finalised.

The girl was purchased and the price was distributed among the relatives of both paternal and maternal lines. The bride came to the husband's house with *Thuam* (dowry) which consisted of *Thival* (bead with 3 strings) or *Thifen* (bead with one string) or an amber bead worth not less than Rs. 20/- or cash not less than Rs. 20/-.[85] If *Thuam* was not brought, her price would be increased by Rs 20/-. Besides *Thuam*, the bride was expected to bring along with her a *Pawnpui* (quilt) and a *Thul* (a basket container or box). But these were not counted as *thuam*. Provided these symbolic properties were prepared at her husband's house the price would be less by Rs. 20/-.

As *thuam* belonged to the bride the husband had no right to dispose any of it without her consent. It could be disposed of only in times of famine and otherwise but only with the consent of the bride.[86]

In case of long and precariotis illness the bride was entitled to give away all her properties during her life time. Divorce or separation on any reason was a serious matter which badly affected the social life of the divorce. In case the bride was divorced she had no claim except on her own properties. If the divorce was however due to adultery she had nothing to claim including her own properties. The marriage price was also to be given back to the man.[87] It so happened that a husband sometimes abandoned his wife and children. In such an event, social protection was provided to a life. She should retain ail the properties and it was upto her to accept him hack in case he returned. As already referred to elsewhere, all the children legitimate or illegitimate belonged to the father. The mother was, however, entitled to receive the price called *Numan* (for being the mother Rs. 4/- or an article or animal of that value).[88]

Regarding social participation, the unmarried woman and the small girl, enjoyed a wide range of freedom. In social festivities like *Khuang Chawi. Chawngchen* etc. the woman took active part. It will not be an exaggeration to say that no festival could be held without the participation of women. On such occassions no restriction was imposed upon her even to the extent of indulging in drinking *Zu.* The *Sumdeng Zu* was the drink prepared specially for both the unmarried man and woman.[89]

At normal times a woman did not indulge in drinking for it was considered a shameful practice. The wives of a Chief and his eiders were however, free to take drinks side by side with their male counterparts. On certain occassions, when together amusing themselves, they consumed *Zu* without any restraint. When they were under the excess influence of the drink their family life was at risk, sometimes even ending in divorce.

Smoking was also found very common among the Mizos. Children of both sexes began smoking very young. Women of all ages smoked much. A pipe smoked by a woman was called *Tuibur.* As a good wife she should possess *tuibur al* (impregnated nicotine water) all the time. In those early days, *tuibur al* was used in their daily life as we now commonly use tea in welcoming visitors. The diligent and active bride was expected to keep it in her possession at all times in order to supply to the family members and the visitors when needed. Otherwise she would be considered as unworthy wife.[90]

In performing religious and other sacrificial rites woman did not have a part to play. All these rites were performed by male members only. A woman could not become a priest called *Bawlpur* or *Sadawt.*

Woman and death are said to have a connection in some ways. In those early days, when a woman died while giving birth, she was said to have died of *raicheh.* In such an event, all the villagers should stay at home tearing that the spirit of the dead woman would enter their house causing death to one of its occupants. In case a husband died it was the duty of a wife to perform a rite called *thlaichhiah* for a period of three lunar months. Only after this rite was observed for the said period, the wife was customarily free from any marital restrictions. She was free to leave the house or to remain if she chose. If she chose, she had a right to stay on in her husband's house as long as she pleased. When a spinster died, like a bachelor, a special grave was prepared as a mark of respect and honour to her.

Concluding Remarks

The various accounts just described bring out only certain important aspects of women's position in the Mizo society as found in the period under review. The study may impress us to form an idea that women were discriminated in the family life as well as in the social life of the Mizos. If one looks at the society of that period from today's situation and judges accordingly one would definitely conceive many discrepancies against women. But a careful examination reveals that no sign is seen against maltreatment of women in the society on grounds of sex. In a male dominated society like that of the Mizos, we cannot expect women to enjoy equal status with men in all respects because the division of labour had already demarcated the lines where both men and women should limit their respective responsibilities. This means that both of them were accordingly assigned duties in the society separately without disturbing each other. If women were considered as having more workload than their male courterparts in and outside the home then they only carried out their responsibilities in the family and the society. This characterised the nature of the society in which the Mizos lived.

In accordance with the natural phenomenon, women were socially restrained from certain obligations. No single woman was allowed to visit the *Zawlbuk* which they presumed was a bad omen for the *Zawlbuk* dwellers. This was justifiable on the ground that the *Zawlbuk* was not used as a common dwelling place for both men and women; it was reserved purely for men only.

An unmarried woman was free to choose her life partner under the system of civil contract soluble at the will of both the parties. As indicated earlier her position was that she could be divorced by her husband for a simple reason but in such a case she was bound by a social protection by allowing her to have claim on property if the ground was not adultery. But in divorce, she had nothing to claim for the property. This is still in force.

It may therefore be summed up that women in the Mizo society held respectable responsibilities without any social discrimination, and were placed in a respectable place. As a matter of fact, women were the backbone of the society. Therefore. Mrs. Chatterji was right when she wrote : "...the sums of women in their society was in no way interior to that of man and she suffered none of those derogatory and discriminatory treatments as may be found in some of the more advanced societies".[91]

REFERENCES

1. Bengal Sectt. Political A, November, 1896, Progs. No. 16-17.
2. Lalthanliana, *Mizo Chanchin,* Vanbuangi Gas Agency, Aizawl, 2000 p. 506.
3. R.G. Woodthorpe, *The Lushai Expedition 1871-1872* (Reprint) Spectrum Publications, Guwahati/Delhi, p. 29.
4. Alexander Mackenzie, *The North Eastern Frontier of India* (Reprint) Mittal Publications, Delhi, 1979, p. 425 (Appendix E).
5. *Ibid.*
6. *Ibid.*
7. Lalthanliana, *op. cit.*, p. 440.
8. Alexander Mackenzie, *op. cit.,* p. 424.

9. *Ibid.*, p. 428.
10. H.R. Browne, *The Lushais 1898-1989,* (Reprint) Firma KLM Pvt. Ltd., 1978, p. 18. See also Lalthanliana, *op. cit.,* p. 449.
11. Foreign And Political Department Report 1874. On Eastern Boundary of Hill Tippera, p. 5.
12. A.S. Reid, *Chin Lushai Land,* (Reprint) Firma KLM Pvt. Ltd., 1976, p. 196.
13. *Ibid.*
14. *Ibid.,* p. 197.
15. Sangkima, Ropuiliani : Her Role In the Struggle Against The British In Mizoram", *Historical Journal Mizoram,* Vol. vi, 1996, p. 11.
16. Sangkima, *Mizos : Society And Social Change,* Spectrum Publications, Guwahati/Delhi, 1992, p. 76.
17. According to Suhas Chatterjee she had 180 houses, *Mizoram Under British Rule,* Mittal Publications, Delhi, 1985, p. 110. According to H.R Browne she had 150 houses, *op. cit.*, p. 21.
18. H.R Browne, *op. cit.*, p. 21.
19. Lalsangzuali Sailo, *Lalnu Ropuiliani,* Hnamte Press, Aizawl, 1999, p. 10.
20. Order No. 116D/26/1/1926.
21. Sangkima, "The Process Of Merger Of Mizos Hills With India, paper read in the National Seminar held on 26-27th November, 1998 at Assam University, Silchar.
22. A.G. McCall, *Lushai Chrysalis,* Reprint (2004) Spectrum Publications, Guwahati/ Delhi, pp. 245-246.
23. The *Minute* No. 1 of 23rd August. 1947.
24. J.V. Hluna, *Education And Missionaries in Mizoram,* Spectrum Publications, Guwahati/Delhi, 1992, pp. 164-165.
25. The *Minutes* of 29th April 1947.
26. Sangkima, "The Process of Merger of Mizo Hills with India," paper read in the National Seminar held on 26-27 November, 1998 at Assam University, Silchar.

27. Chaltuahkhuma, *Political History of Mizoram,* Aizawl 1981, p. 61.
28. The *Minutes* of 3.3.1948.
29. *Ibid.*
30. *Ibid.*
31. The *Minutes* of 6th March 1948.
32. The *Minutes* of 19th January 1951.
33. The *Minutes* of 22nd May 1948.
34. The *Minutes* of 10th August 1948.
35. The *Minutes* of 10th October 1948.
36. The *Minutes* of 19th August 1948.
37. The *Minutes* of 7th October 1948.
38. The *Minutes* of 7-9th February 1951.
39. *Ibid.*
40. The *Minutes* of 30-31th October 1951.
41. The *Minutes* of 30th October 1953.
42. Lalziki Sailo interviewed on 23.11.1998.
43. Chaltuahkhuma, *op. cit.,* pp. 78-79.
44. Hmingliani interviewed on 23.11.1998.
45. The *Minutes* of 2nd February 1957.
46. Raymond Thanhlira had his education at St. Anthony's College, Shillong. He was the President of Mizo Union Party and for short periods in the 1950s and 1960s : Member of Parliament (Rajya Sabha) (1952), Member of Assam Public Service Commission, Chairman of Assam Public Service Commission. He also qualified for Assam Civil Service but did not join.
47. Hmingliani, "Mizo Hmeichhe Din Hnuin", *Mizo Hmeichhe Tangrual Souvenir,* Aizawl, 1986, p. 13.
48. Biaksiami, *Mizo Hmeichhe Tangrual,* Aizawl, 1982, p. 11.
49. *Ibid.*
50. The *Minutes* of 7th April, 1962.
51. Chaltuahkhuma, *op. cit.*, p. 123.

52. *Ibid.*
53. Sangkima, "Ropuiliani-Her Role In The Struggle Against The British In Mizoram, "*Historical Journal Mizoram,* Vol-VI, Aizawl, 1996, pp. 11-17.
54. Chaltuahkhuma, *op. cit.*, p. 125.
55. *Ibid.*, p. 128.
56. *Ibid.*
57. Laltanpuii, *Mizo Hmeichhe zinga Politics ngaihsakna.* Talk broadcast on All India Radio, Aizawl in 1990.
58. The Sailo Chiefs of the North Lushai Hills were the descendants of Rohnaa and they were known after him or his great son Lallula. Lalsavunga, father of Ropuiliani, was one of the great grandsons of Lallula. Vandula, husband of Ropuiliani, was the grandson of Rolura after whom the Sailos of South Lushai Hills were descended and known. Sometimes, British writers referred to them as Howlongs (Haulawngs). The problem of Vanhnuailiana, son of Lalsavunga, specially with regard to his relation with Ropuiliani will remain unsettled without further research on the subject.
59. Suhas Chatterjee, *Mizoram Under The British Rule,* Mittal Publications, Delhi, 1985, p. 21.
60. Sir Robert Reid, *The Lushai Hills,* Firma KLM Private Ltd. Calcutta, Reprint, 1976, p. 49.
61. *Ibid.*, p. 3.
62. *Ibid.*
63. A.S. Reid, *Chin—Lushai Land,* Firma KLM Private Ltd. Reprint, 1976, p. 192.
64. Suhas Chatterjee, *op. cit.*, p. 192.
65. A.S. Reid, *op. cit.*, p. 192.
66. J. Shakespeare, "Note on the Lushai Hills, Its inhabitants and Administration since 1888", Dated Manipur, 22nd March 1905. Hereafter referred to as *Note on the Lushai Hills.*
67. H.J.S. Cotton, "Historical Note on the question of the jurisdiction of the British Government of the Chittagong and South Lushai Hill Tracts", Darjeeling, the 12th May 1893.

68. A.S. McCall, *Lushai Chrysalis,* Reprint (2004) Spectrum Publications, Guwahati/Delhi p. 60.
69. A.S. Reid, *op. cit.*, p. 191.
70. J. Shakespeare, *Note on the Lushai Hills.*
71. W.B. Oldham, Commissioner of the Chittagong Hill Tracts to H.J.S. Cotton, Chief Secretary to the Government of Bengal, Chittagong, the 24th July, 1895.
72. A.S. Reid, *op. cit.*, p. 195.
73. L.W. Shakespeare, *History of the Assam Rifles,* Spectrum Publications, Guwahati/Delhi, Reprint, 1981, p. 104.
74. Suhas Chatterjee, *loc. cit.*
75. From R.W. Murray, the Superintendent of the Chittagong Jail to the Magistrate of Chittagong, No. 23 Dated Chittagong the 6th January, 1895.
76. J. Shakespeare, *Note on the Lushai Hills.*
77. *The Holy Bible,* 1 Corrinthian, Chapter 14 : 34-35.
78. Challiana, Pastor, *Pi Pu Nun,* The Trio Book-House. Aizasl, 1978, p. 2-3.
79. *Ibid.*
80. John Rowlings, "On the Manners. Religion and Laws of the Cu'ci's or Mountaineers of Tripurs. "*Assiatic Researches,* vol. II, Cosmo Publications, New Delhi, Reprint, 1978, p. 144.
81. Hrangthiauva and Lalchungnunga, *Mizo Chanchin,* Lalrinliana & Sons Aizawl, 1978, p. 55.
82. Zatluanga, *Mizo Chanchin,* Khuma Printing Press, Aizawl, 1966, p. 20.
83. Hmingliani, *"Mizos Hmeichhe Din hmun", Mizo Hmeichhe Tangrual Souvenir,* Aizawl, 1986, p. 11.
84. *Ibid.*
85. *Mizo Hnam Dan* (Mizo Customary Law), Published by the Mizo District Council, Aizawl, 1957, pp. 8-9.
86. *Ibid.*
87. N.F. Parry, *'A Monograph on Lushai Customs and Ceremonies',* Tribal Research Institute, Aizawl, Reprint, 1976, p. 49.

88. *Mizos Hnam Dan, op. cit.,* p. 46.
89. Challiana, Pastor, *op. cit.,* p. 46.
90. Seletthanga; *Pi Pu Lenlai,* Lianchhungi Book Store, Aizawl, 1978, p. 25.
91. (Mrs.) Chatterji, *Status of Women in the earlier Mizo Society,* Tribal Research Institute, Aizawl, 1975, p. 2.

5 Mizoram : From District to a State

Introduction

The Lushai Hills was conquered by the British in stages. The trend of British annexation in Lushai Hills was the same as that in Naga Hills. The Lushai tribals (now known as Mizos) continued to raid British territories. Punitive actions followed every raid and in course of time the entire Lushai Hills was conquered by the British. The Chief Commissioner of Assam proposed to the Government of India in 17th July 1987 to transfer South Lushai Hills from Bengal to Assam. He also proposed to merge Demagiri with South Lushai Hills. He suggested the merger of North and South Lushai Hills into a single district of Assam with headquarters at Aizawl and Major Shakespeare as its first Superintendent and Political Officer with effect from 1st October 1897.

The two districts were accordingly united and placed under Assam with effect from 1st April 1898. The administration of the district was vested in the Chief Commissioner, the Superintendent and his assistants and in the Chiefs and headmen of the villages.

The district was declared as an excluded area as per the provisions of Government of India Act, 1935. It was a district of Assam, when India became free in 1947.

Formation of District Council

Lushai Hills took full advantage of the provisions of the Sixth Schedule of the constitution and the Lushai Hills District Council was formed alongwith other District Councils of hill districts of Assam.

Early Political Activities

Mizo Union was the first political party of Mizoram, which was established on 9th April 1946. The party was started by R. Vanlawma the founder general secretary for solving, many local problems of the district; which are listed below :

(i) Unlike any other districts of the country this district has a Superintendent as the head of the Civil and Police administration. Thus the functions of the District Magistrate (or Deputy Commissioner) and Superintendent of Police were-merged in one and were handled by the same officer. This made some of the Superintendents autocratic and oppressive specially when state administration blindly supported them.

(ii) The Mizos had chieftainship. Their chiefs had autocratic powers and they were often supported by the Superintendent in outragious acts.

(iii) The Lushai Hills district was denied representation in legislature, because it was an excluded area.

The Mizo union pledged to work for the *(i)* abolition of Chieftainship, *(ii)* representation of the Mizos in the State and Central legislature and *(iii)* improvement of the social and economic conditions of the Mizos.

The party had large following. Later on there was split in the party and a section merged with Indian National Congress. The other group became secessionist.

The U.M.F.O. was established by Lalmavia. He was an ex-army-man, who later on joined Burmese Civil Service. He wanted that Lushai Hills should join Burma. He could not succeed in enlisting the active support of U Nu in his scheme. After that he started U.M.F.O. and worked for the secession from India. The popularity of

Mizo Union, which wanted to stay in India, demoralised Lalmavia. Ultimately, he became the supporter of the North-Eastern Hill State within Indian Union and merged his party with East India Tribal Union.

There were many other parties in Mizoram, but Mizo National Front or M.N.F., which was a latecomer in Mizo—political scene played crucial role in the formation of Mizoram State.

Mizo Participation in Hill State Movement

A section of Mizos became protagonists of North Eastern Hill State at a later stage, but most of them wanted more autonomy under Sixth Schedule. When members of the executive councils of the autonomous District Councils of Assam met at Shillong on 16th June 1954 under the chairmanship of B.M. Roy, the Chief Executive Member of United Khasi and Jaintiya Hills District Council to consider the formation of Hill State, the views on separate hill state were not acceptable to the Chief Executive Members of the Lushai Hills and North Cachar Hills District Councils. They wanted to have more autonomy for the District Councils rather than a hill state. They never thought in this direction for considerably long period.

When All Party Hill Leaders Conference was formed in 1960, then the political leaders of Mizoram also joined it. They fought 1962 general elections from APHLC ticket and got elected. However, most of them did not follow APHLC directive and therefore did not resign their assembly seats after the election. One of the candidates who resigned on the party directive lost his seat to MNF candidate in the 1963 bye-election. When APHLC delegation met Central Home Minister in November 1960 to discuss their demand for the creation of hill-state, then one of the objections raised by the latter was that the Hill areas were not geographically contiguous to one another. Saprawnga was representing Mizo Hills district as a delegate. He spontaneously reacted that Mizo

Hills may back out from Hill State demand in that case and it should get a state of its own. Perhaps this sparkled the imagination of Mizos to have a state of their own and the day came very soon when Mizos were no more with the APHLC and it became the party of the Meghalayans only.

The Rise of Mizo National Front

Whenever bamboos flowers and bear fruits, the number of rats multiply enormously and crops are eaten by them, creating famine situation resulting into starvation deaths. It happens almost after every fifty years in Mizoram and Mizos call it *Mautam Tampui* (mau = bamboo, tampui = havoc of famine). In 1959 also *mautam tampui* occurred in Mizoram. The Assam Government was given advanced warning about the famine, but they failed to take timely and adequate measure to combat the worsening situation. There were starvation deaths and this angered Mizos. The Mizo Cultural Society founded by John F. Maniliana tried to help the starving people, but could not do much in this direction. Mizo National Famine Front was formed in 1959 to organise relief work. R. Dengthuama and Laldenga were president and secretary respectively of the new organization. Mizo National Famine Front was converted into Mizo National Front, a political party on 22nd October 1961—with Laldenga and R. Valawma as its first elected president and secretary respectively.

Laldenga was inspired by the Phizo and the N.N.C. The formation of Nagaland state encouraged him to launch armed rebellion in Mizoram. He modelled MNF on the lines of NNC. Later on, a break away group of MNF, turned itself as MNC *i.e.* Mizo National Council like Naga National Council.

Laldenga was a primary school teacher before World war second and a Havildar clerk during the war. He joined District Council office as an accountant in 1952. He resigned his job of accountant so that to escape the charge of misappropriation of District Council funds. He was defeated in District Council elections in early sixties.

Laldenga was a fine orator and he had a mesmerizing gaze. He took full advantage of the following factors to make MNF popular :

(i) MNF under the leadership of Laldenga took full advantage of people's anger against Assam Government for not taking adequate famine relief measures in spite of prior warning.

(ii) It took full credit for fighting the famine and helping the suffering people.

(iii) The District Council and the Mizo Union leaders who were controlling the District Council had initially very good relation with the Congress. However, they were very angry with B.P. Chaliha, Assam Government and I.N.C. party after their prior advice about famine relief work were ignored by the latter. Laldenga fully utilized the rift between the Mizo Union and the Congress and the angry statements of the District Council and Mizo Union leaders against Assam government for the halting and inadequate relief measures.

(iv) The Mizo Union and the Congress parties were responsible for the abolition of Chieftainship. It is alleged that the compensations were not given to the chiefs observing equity. Educated chiefs got more in comparison to uneducated ones. Although government paid handsome compensation, many chiefs spent the money in no time and became paupers. The pauperization of chiefs made them angry with the government and the Mizo Union. MNF under the leadership of Laldenga easily enlisted the support of the disgruntled chiefs.

(v) MNF enlisted the support of discharged men of the 2nd battalion of the Assam regiment, who were dis-satisfied because regiment was disbanded without making any provision for their re-habilitation. They formed the part of underground army of M.N.F. later on.

(vi) Lack of proper economic planning left a large section of people unemployed and dissatisfied. They became supporters of MNF in due course.

(vii) Lack of dynamism and proverbial vacillation on the part of the Chief Minister and his playing politics in Mizo Hills affairs helped the MNF. The Chief Minister pampered MNF in order to make Mizo Union weak, inspite of being informed about the treasonable activities of the MNF.

(viii) MNF continued to talk of non-violent methods to be adopted by them. On the other hand, their efforts for armed rebellion continued unabeted. The government was caught unaware when MNF staged armed rebellion. They could realise very late that they were hood-winked and the talk of constitutional and non-violent Gandhian methods by Laldenga had no meaning for him.

(ix) The Mizos also did not like Assamese as the official language and Mizo Union joined APHLC on this issue.

(x) Pakistan continued to help Mizo rebels by giving them military training and by supplying them arms and ammunitions.

Under above circumstances, Laldenga's open preaching for independence found receptive ears and hearts and he was never stopped from doing so by the Assam government. The almost open and very long international border with Burma and East Pakistan helped MNF in organizing insurgency.

A point which is important and pertinent and needs to be mentioned here is, that our governments have always followed wrong modus operandi in tackling such problems, which used to send wrong signals that violence may pay and one may reach the corridore of seat of power through violence. The MNF and Laldenga really came to the seat of power through violence and rebellion.

The MNF fought District Council and Assembly elections during 1962 and after that also, but mostly lost the battle to Mizo Union. Even Laldenga lost District Council elections. They, however, could win a bye-election in 1963. The Mizo Union always wanted to stay in India and Mizos voted for it. It was due to mishandling of Mizo affairs that MNF could win a section of Mizos for secessionist cause.

The MNF openly preached secession and no action was taken against it. In a memorandum submitted to the Prime Minister on 30th October 1965, it said—

"Mizos from time immemorial lived in complete independence without foreign interference. Chiefs of the different clans ruled over separate hills and valleys with supreme authority and their administration was very much like that of Greek city states of the past..............they are a distinct nation, created and moulded and murtur by God and Nature. The Mizos had never been under Indian Government.............."

"Solely (due) to their political immaturity, ignorance and lack of consciousness of their fate, the representatives of the Mizo Union choose integration with free India."

"During fifteen years of contact and association with India, the Mizo people had not been able to feel at home with Indians, or in India, nor have they been able to feel that their joys and sorrows have really ever been shared by India. They do not feel, therefore, Indians. Being created a separate nation, they can not go against the nature to cross barriers of nationality. They refused to occupy a place within India as they consider it to be unworthy of their national dignity and harmful to the interests of their posterity."

"The only aspiration and political cry is the creation of Mizoram, a free and sovereign State to Govern herself to work out her own destiny and to formulate her own foreign policy."

"Though Mizos are head-hunters and belonged to a martial race, they will adopt non-violent methods if independence is not granted."

Armed Rebellion

The MNF was not only preaching independence, but was also preparing to achieve it through armed revolt. They recruited and trained thousands of persons, many of them ex-armymen, for violent struggle and just in four months time after submission of above mentioned memorandum, they captured Aizawl and issued the Declaration of Independence, which sounded somewhat like Declaration of American War of Independence. It reads as given below :

"In the course of history, it becomes invariably necessary for mankind to assume their social, economic and political status to which the laws of Nature's God entitle them. We hold this truth to be self-evident that all men are created equal and that they are endowed with inalienable fundamental human rights and dignity of human persons and to secure these rights, governments are instituted among men deriving their just powers from the consent of the governed, and whenever any form of government becomes destructive of them, it is the right of the people to alter, change, modify and abolish it and institute a new government laying its foundation on such forms as to them shall seem most likely to effect their rights and dignity. The Mizos created and moulded into a nation and nurtured as such by

Nature's God, have been intolerably dominated by the people of India in contravention to the laws of nature."

A bomb exploded at the electric veng, Aizawl on 28th February, 1966. After a few hours, on 1st March 1966, an hour after midnight, the Aizawl sub-treasury was attacked and Rs. 64,000.00 and some arms and ammunitions were looted. Actually three plateless jeeps and a truck were parked in front of the sub-treasury and armed men overpowered the treasury guards and looted it. They put out the Aizawl Telephone Exchange and declared independence.

The revolt was properly planned and it broke out simultaneously in all the important towns of Mizo Hills. Kolasib, Champai, Saireng etc. were captured on March, 3 and Lunglei on March 5, 1966. The sub-treasury was also looted at Lunglei. The S.D.O. (Civil) was captured. The Assam Rifles at Lunglei was also over-powered.

The Mizo Hills district was completely captured by the rebels. Assam Rifles and Assam Police failed to meet the situation. Army had to be called in.

The rebels also formed their under-ground government Mizoram Sawrkar, as they called it—with a president, a parliament, a speaker, and the council of ministers. They declared the establishment of National Judiciary (National Refinement Court) and National Army, (Mizo National Army).

The formation of four Divisions, each under a Chief Commissioner, and four Sub-Divisions in each Division, each under a Deputy Commissioner was announced. All received to uniform salary of Rs. 15.00 per month.

We find a parallel in the modus operandi of underground movement in Nagaland and Mizoram. Laldenga and MNF copied everything, with slight modification here and there, from Phizo and NNC :

There were many factors, which helped Laldenga and MNF in getting an upper hand in Mizo Hills affair.

We have already discussed those points. What helped MNF most was the apathy of Assam government Thousands of people participated in the uprising and things were planned meticulously. It is most surprising that Assam Government remained highly ignorant and inactive and was caught napping when even the final scene of the drama was being enacted.

Counter-measures and Pacification

The Army was called in aid of the civil power. The Government of Assam declared Mizo Hills district as a disturbed area under the Assam Disturbed Areas Act, 1955. The Armed Forces (Assam and Manipur) Special Power Act, 1958 was also applied. The MNF was declared as an unlawful organization on 6th March 1966, by Government of India and was banned under Defence of India Rules.

The army started its operation as soon as it was requisitioned. It captured Aizawl on 5th March 1966 and moved towards Lunglei under air cover. The Lunglei was spared from being bombed on the intervention of Church leaders and it was captured without resistance. All the towns were re-captured by army within a month. The MNF vice-president requested D.C. to arrange talk between the Government and the rebels-on 7th March 1966. The D.C. asked them to surrender.

The hard-core of MNF retired to deep valleys and inaccessible hills and forests after army captured all the towns. The army also proposed to the Government of India to hand over the district to the Defence Ministry. The Government of India did not agree. Then army worked out Operation Security by regrouping of villages. The aim of the grouping of the villages was :

- *(a)* to facilitate effective military operation against the rebels.
- *(b)* to segregate them from the masses,
- *(c)* to provide protection to the villagers,

(d) to facilitate economic development,

(e) to provide social services to all, and

(f) to provide communication facilities.

The army claimed that the grouping of villages helped the villagers. It certainly helped them and also helped army in combating insurgency.

However, villagers suffered a lot of hardship during the regrouping. It is alleged that compensations were given to few persons only. The shifting was compulsory rather than voluntary and the villagers had to suffer physically and psychologically while leaving their old villages and parental homes inspite of their migratory habits. Mizoram had a large number of very small villages scattered through out the hills and not connected by roads and it was not possible for the army to protect them unless they were re-settled near the roads. This was the logic behind the regrouping of villages.

Although back-bone of the underground movement was broken by army operation, insurgency continued. The army had to continue counter-insurgency measures for prolonged period. The government stepped up development efforts and social welfare activities. This had the desired effect and a large number of underground came overground. There was split in MNF and most of the intellectuals deserted it. There was confusion and demoralization in the rank and file of MNF. The people wanted peace. The emergence of Bangladesh deprived the underground of their support base.

Union Territory Status

The desirability of awarding union territory status was felt by many people after the start of under-ground activities. Mizoram was awarded Union Territory Status on 21st January 1972 as per the provisions of the North-Eastern Areas (Reorganization) Act, 1971. Mizoram also got its Legislative Assembly and Council of Ministers as per the Act of 1971. The first two Ministries led by the Congress and the People's Conference tried to bring MNF to conference table. There efforts bore fruit and an accord was signed between the Union Home Secretary and MNF Chief Laldenga on 1st July 1976. The agreement could not be implemented due to some reason, leading to another phase of insurgency, counter-insurgency and pacification.

The talks were called off in 1978 and MNF stepped up its hostile activities against security forces, civil officials and non-Mizos. This resulted into ban on MNF and its allied organization and arrest of Laldenga on 8th July, 1979.

Fresh effort by Mizoram Pradesh Congress (I) resulted in resumption of talks and dropping of charges against Laldenga after 1980, but the talks broke down due to Laldenga's demands of greater Mizoram and constitutional safeguards for Mizoram of Jammu and Kashmir type.

The Congress (I) Ministry headed by Lalthanhawla came to power in Mizoram in 1984, Lalthanhawla was committed to the cause of peace, harmony and development. MNF also wanted the resumption of peace talks. Laldenga was called back from London to Delhi on 29th October 1984. After a lot of deliberations and series of discussions and consultations, a memorandum of settlement was signed on 30 June 1986 by R.D. Pradhan, Central Home Secretary; Laldenga, MNF Chief and Lalkhama Chief Secretary, Government of Mizoram.

After the peace accord MNF deleted the clause of "Independence and secession from India" and other objectionable clauses from its constitution. The underground MNF and MNA personnel surrendered with arms and ammunitions. The Government of India took steps to confer statehood on Mizoram and to rehabilitate the surrendering personnel of the MNF and MNA. The ban on MNF was lifted. MNA was disbanded.

The Statehood

The State of Mizoram Act, 1986 and Constitution (53rd Amendment) Act conferred Statehood on Mizoram. An interim Congress-MNF coalition government was formed on 21st August 1986 with Laldenga as Chief Minister and Lalthanhawla as Deputy Chief Minister as per the understanding between the Government and MNF. The Chief Minister Lalthanhawla resigned earlier after the State Act was passed to facilitate the formation of the new coalition Government.

The journey of Mizoram from a district to a state took 39 years. It is one of the smallest states of the Indian Union both in terms of area and population but has a bright future and a lot of promise for Mizos and India as a whole.

Champhai District

District HQ : Champhai

Distance from State Capital (In KM) : 194

Sub Divisions : Champhai, Khawzawl, Ngopa

Town of the District : Champhai

Major Language : Mizo, English, Hindi

Demographic Features

Area, No. of Household, Population & Literacy Rate According to 2001 Census

Area (Sq. km.)	*No. of house holds*	*Population*			*Decadal variation % 1991-2001*	*Literacy Rate (%)*
		Total	*Male*	*Female*		
3185	22059	108392	55756	52636	29.90	91.20

Source : Economic Survey Manipur 2007-08.

Population By Religion (Census 2001)

Christian	*Hindu*	*Muslim*	*Sikhs*	*Buddhist*	*Jains*	*Religion not stated*	*other*
105061	2248	432	24	163	6	209	249

Source : Economic Survey Manipur 2007-08.

Distribution of Population by Social Group (2001 Census)

ST Population	*SC Population*	*Others*
104924	0	3468

Source : Economic Survey Manipur 2007-08.

Agriculture

WRC Statistics of Champhai

2006-2007			2007-2008		
No. of WRC farmers	*Area of WRC cultivated (Ha.)*	*Area still to be developed (Ha.)*	*No. of WRC farmers*	*Area of WRC cultivated (Ha.)*	*Area still to be developed (Ha.)*
2630	2557	2113	2630	2374	2113

Source : Economic Survey Manipur 2007-08.

Sericulture

Sericulture Villages and No. of Families Engaged

No. of Sericulture Village		*No. of Families Engaged*		*Area under Sericulture Plantation (in Ha.)*		*No. of Sericulture Farm*	
2006-07	*2007-08*	*2006-07*	*2007-08*	*2006-07*	*2007-08*	*2006-07*	*2007-08*
25	25	1600	1600	900	950	2	2

Source : Economic Survey Manipur 2007-08.

Production of Cocoons, Silk Yarn and Seed Distributed

Mulberry (in MT.)	2006-07	8
	2007-08	7
Muga (in MT.)	2006-07	0
	2007-08	0
Eri (in MT.)	2006-07	0
	2007-08	0
Oak Tasar (in lakhs)	2006-07	1.50
	2007-08	1.00
Silk yarn (in MT.)	2006-07	0
	2007-08	0
No. of seed/cutting distributed to Farms (in '000')	2006-07 2007-08	2068 1745

Source : Economic Survey Manipur 2007-08.

No. of Sericulture Farms, Area and Reeling Units

No. of Sericulture Farms		*Area in Ha.*		*No. of Reeling Units*	
2006-07	*2007-08*	*2006-07*	*2007-08*	*2006-07*	*2007-08*
2	2	900	950	0	0

Source : Economic Survey Manipur 2007-08.

Livestock & Poultry

Livestock and Poultry Population (Quinqennial Livestock Census) 2007-08

Cattle	Crossbred	572
	Indigenous	6556
	Total	7128
Buffaloes		3183
Mithun		1105
Sheep		564
Goats		706
Horse and Ponies		831
Pigs		36705
Clogs		4139

Fowls	265884
Ducks	502
Turkey	3
Others	2
Total	**320752**

Source : Economic Survey Manipur 2007-08.

No. of Institutions and Veterinary Personnel During 2007-08

Hospitals	1
Dispensaries	7
Rural Animal Health Centre	13
Artificial Insemination Centres	2
Doctores/Surgeons	11
VFA/SUFA/JM/JEO/PI/LS etc.	28

Source : Economic Survey Manipur 2007-08.

Fishery

Fish Seed Production and Distribution during 2006-07

Production of Fish Seed (in lakh Nos.)	*Distribution of Fish Seed (in lakh Nos.)*
1953	20

Source : Economic Survey Manipur 2007-08.

No. of Nurseries and Fish Ponds in 2007-08

Nurseries/	*Fish Ponds*		
Hatcheries	*Govt.*	*Private*	*Total*
0	0	775	775

Source : Economic Survey Manipur 2007-08.

Area of Fish Ponds and Production Fish

Area of Fish Ponds (in Ha.)		*Production of fish (in Qntl.)*	
2006-07	*2007-08*	*2006-07*	*2007-08*
135.00	146.00	1953	1950.00

Source : Economic Survey Manipur 2007-08.

Industry

No. of Small Scale Industries Registered During 2007-2008

Unit Registered	15
No. of persons employed	40
Amount of Investment (Rs. in lakhs)	40

Source : Economic Survey Manipur 2007-08.

Electricity

Cumulative No. of Village Electrified

As on 01.04.2007	*As on 01.04.2008*
76	80

Source : Economic Survey Manipur 2007-08.

Health

Medical Institution and No. of Bed Strength

Government Hospital	*Bed (as on 01.04.2007)*	*Bed (as on 01.04.2008)*
Civil Hospital	60	60

Source : Economic Survey Manipur 2007-08.

No. of Births and Deaths Registered

(January-December)

Births (Nos.)			*Deaths (Nos.)*		
2005	*2006*	*2007*	*2005*	*2006*	*2007*
2082	2205	2608	441	466	486

Source : Economic Survey Manipur 2007-08.

Tourism

Number of Tourist Spot and Tourist Lodge in Champhai

No. of Tourist Lodge		*No. of Highway Restaurant*		*No. of Picnic Spot*	
2006-2007	*2007-2008*	*2006-2007*	*2007-2008*	*2006-2007*	*2007-2008*
4	5	1	1	0	0

Source : Economic Survey Manipur 2007-08.

Banking

No. of Commercial Banks in Champhai

Name of Bank	*Number*
SBI	1
MCAB	1
MRB	8
Total	**10**

Source : Economic Survey Manipur 2007-08.

Police

Number of Police Stations, Out Posts, Check Posts, Wireless Stations

Police Stations		*Out Posts*		*Check Posts*		*Wireless Stations*	
2006-07	*2007-08*	*2006-07*	*2007-08*	*2006-07*	*2007-08*	*2006-07*	*2007-08*
3	3	1	1	1	3	6	6

Source : Economic Survey Manipur 2007-08.

7 Kolasib District

District HQ : Kolasib

Distance from State Capital (In KM) :

Sub Divisions : Kolasib, Vairengte, Kawnpui

Towns of the District : Kolasib, Vairengte

Major Language : Mizo, English, Hindi

No of blocks : 2

No of villages inhabited : 33

Demographic Features

Area, No. of Household, Population & Literacy Rate According to 2001 Census

Area (Sq. km.)	*No. of house holds*	*Population*			*Decadal variation % 1991-2001*	*Literacy Rate (%)*
		Total	*Male*	*Female*		
1382	14053	65960	34562	31398	35.20	91.30

Source : Economic Survey Manipur 2007-08.

Population By Religion (Census 2001)

Christian	*Hindu*	*Muslim*	*Sikhs*	*Buddhist*	*Jains*	*Religion not stated*	*other*
59098	4237	1995	31	177	2	114	306

Source : Economic Survey Manipur 2007-08.

Distribution of Population by Social Group (2001 Census)

ST Population	*SC Population*	*Others*
59221	17	6722

Source : Economic Survey Manipur 2007-08.

Agriculture

WRC Statistics of Kolasib

2006-2007			*2007-2008*		
No. of WRC farmers	*Area of WRC cultivated (Ha.)*	*Area still to be developed (Ha.)*	*No. of WRC farmers*	*Area of WRC cultivated (Ha.)*	*Area still to be developed (Ha.)*
1712	2929	1412	1709	3515	1339

Source : Economic Survey Manipur 2007-08

Sericulture

Sericulture Villages and No. of Families Engaged

No. of Sericulture Village		*No. of Families Engaged*		*Area under Sericulture Plantation (in Ha.)*		*No. of Sericulture Farm*	
2006-07	*2007-08*	*2006-07*	*2007-08*	*2006-07*	*2007-08*	*2006-07*	*2007-08*
20	20	750	750	450	500	4	4

Source : Economic Survey Manipur 2007-08.

Production of Cocoons, Silk Yarn and Seed Distributed

Mulberry (in MT.)	2006-07	6
	2007-08	7
Muga (in MT.)	2006-07	2.30
	2007-08	2
Eri (in MT.)	2006-07	2.0
	2007-08	2
Oak Tasar (in lakhs)	2006-07	0
	2007-08	0
Silk yarn (in MT.)	2006-07	0
	2007-08	0
No. of seed/cutting distributed to Farms (in '000')	2006-07	1408
	2007-08	2515

Source : Economic Survey Manipur 2007-08.

No. of Sericulture Farms/Area and Reeling Units

No. of Sericulture Farms		*Area in Ha.*		*No. of Reeling Units*	
2006-07	*2007-08*	*2006-07*	*2007-08*	*2006-07*	*2007-08*
4	4	450	500	0	0

Source : Economic Survey Manipur 2007-08.

Livestock & Poultry

Livestock and Poultry Population (Quinqennial Livestock Census) 2007-08

Cattle	Crossbred	2017
	Indigenous	3947
	Total	5964
Buffaloes		112
Mithun		11
Sheep		43
Goats		2244
Horse and Ponies		0
Pigs		25132
Dogs		1936

Fowls	93023
Ducks	2843
Turkey	58
Others	0
Total	**131366**

Source : Economic Survey Manipur 2007-08,

No. of Institutions and Veterinary Personnel During 2007-08

Hospitals	1
Dispensaries	4
Rural Animal Health Centre	8
Artificial Insemination Centres	5
Doctores/Surgeons	11
VFA/SUFA/JM/JEO/PI/LS etc.	17

Source : Economic Survey Manipur 2007-08.

Fishery

Fish Seed Production and Distribution During 2006-07

Production of Fish Seed (in lakh Nos.)	*Distribution of Fish Seed (in lakh Nos.)*
10093	80

Source : Economic Survey Manipur 2007-08.

No. of Nurseries and Fish Ponds in 2007-08

Nurseries/ Hatcheries	*Fish Ponds*		
	Govt.	*Private*	*Total*
1	2	1508	1510

Source : Economic Survey Manipur 2007-08.

Area of Fish Ponds and Production Fish

Area of Fish Ponds (in Ha.)		*Production of fish (in Qntl.)*	
2006-07	*2007-08*	*2006-07*	*2007-08*
695.50	704.50	10093	4852.50

Source : Economic Survey Manipur 2007-08.

Industry

No. of Small Scale Industries Registered During 2007-2008

Unit Registered	14
No. of persons employed	35
Amount of Investment (Rs. in lakhs)	32.2

Source : Economic Survey Manipur 2007-08.

Electricity

Cumulative No. of Village Electrified

As on 01.04.2007	*As on 01.04.2008*
27	27

Source : Economic Survey Manipur 2007-08.

Health

Medical Institution and No. of Bed Strength

Government Hospital	*Bed (as on 01.04.2007)*	*Bed (as on 01.04.2008)*
Civil Hospital	52	60

Source : Economic Survey Manipur 2007-08.

No. of Births and Deaths Registered

(January-December)

Births (Nos.)			*Deaths (Nos.)*		
2005	*2006*	*2007*	*2005*	*2006*	*2007*
1412	1471	1773	270	271	269

Source : Economic Survey Manipur 2007-08.

Tourism

Number of Tourist Spot and Tourist Lodge in Kolasib

No. of Tourist Lodge		*No. of Highway Restaurant*		*No. of Picnic Spot*	
2006-2007	*2007-2008*	*2006-2007*	*2007-2008*	*2006-2007*	*2007-2008*
4	5	1	1	0	0

Source : Economic Survey Manipur 2007-08.

Banking

No. of Commercial Banks

Name of Bank	*Number*
SBI	3
MCAB	1
MRB	6
Total	**10**

Source : Economic Survey Manipur 2007-08.

Police

Number of Police Stations, Out Posts, Check Posts, Wireless Stations

Police Stations		*Out Posts*		*Check Posts*		*Wireless Stations*	
2006-07	*2007-08*	*2006-07*	*2007-08*	*2006-07*	*2007-08*	*2006-07*	*2007-08*
4	4	1	1	2	2	12	11

Source : Economic Survey Manipur 2007-08.

8 Mamit District

District HQ : Mamit

Distance from State Capital (In KM) : 112

Sub Divisions : Mamit, Kawrthah, W. Phaileng

Towns of the District : Mamit, Kawrthah, W. Phaileng

Major Language : Mizo, English, Hindi

Demographic Features

Area, No. of Household, Population & Literacy Rate According to 2001 Census

Area (Sq. km.)	*No. of house holds*	*Population*			*Decadal variation % 1991-2001*	*Literacy Rate (%)*
		Total	*Male*	*Female*		
3025	12253	62785	33114	29671	2.70	79.10

Source : Economic Survey Manipur 2007-08.

Population By Religion (Census 2001)

Christian	*Hindu*	*Muslim*	*Sikhs*	*Buddhist*	*Jains*	*Religion not stated*	*other*
50563	2404	1096	24	8579	17	6	96

Source : Economic Survey Manipur 2007-08.

Distribution of Population by Social Group (2001 Census)

ST Population	*SC Population*	*Others*
58950	18	3817

Source : Economic Survey Manipur 2007-08.

Agriculture

WRC Statistics of Mamit

2006-2007			2007-2008		
No. of WRC farmers	*Area of WRC cultivated (Ha.)*	*Area still to be developed (Ha.)*	*No. of WRC farmers*	*Area of WRC cultivated (Ha.)*	*Area still to be developed (Ha.)*
410	892	1097	392	173	1075

Source : Economic Survey Manipur 2007-08.

Sericulture

Sericulture Villages and No. of Families Engaged

No. of Sericulture Village		*No. of Families Engaged*		*Area under Sericulture Plantation (in Ha.)*		*No. of Sericulture Farm*	
2006-07	*2007-08*	*2006-07*	*2007-08*	*2006-07*	*2007-08*	*2006-07*	*2007-08*
5	5	263	263	150	250	2	2

Source : Economic Survey Manipur 2007-08.

Production of Cocoons, Silk Yarn and Seed Distributed

Mulberry (in MT.)	2006-07	2
	2007-08	1
Muga (inMT.)	2006-07	0.30
	2007-08	0
Eri (in MT.)	2006-07	0
	2007-08	0.20
Mulberry (in MT.)	2006-07	17
	2007-08	12
Silk yarn (in MT.)	2006-07	0
	2007-08	0
No. of seed/cutting distributed to Farms (in '000')	2006-07	836
	2007-08	0

Source : Economic Survey Manipur 2007-08.

No. of Sericulture Farms, Area and Reeling Units

No. of Sericulture Farms		*Area in Ha.*		*No. of Reeling Units*	
2006-07	*2007-08*	*2006-07*	*2007-08*	*2006-07*	*2007-08*
2	2	150	250	0	0

Source : Economic Survey Manipur 2007-08.

Livestock & Poultry

Livestock and Poultry Population (Quinqennial Livestock Census) 2007-08

Cattle	Crossbred	135
	Indigenous	1972
	Total	2105
Buffaloes		208
Mithun		0
Sheep		77
Goats		1780
Horse and Ponies		8
Pigs		23351
Dogs		2662

Fowls	109823
Ducks	499
Turkey	2
Others	0
Total	**140517**

Source : Economic Survey Manipur 2007-08.

No. of Institutions and Veterinary Personnel During 2007-08

Hospitals	0
Dispensaries	4
Rural Animal Health Centre	14
Artificial Insemination Centres	1
Doctors/Surgeons	4
VFA/SUFA/JM/JEO/PI/LS etc.	15

Source : Economic Survey Manipur 2007-08.

Fishery

Fish Seed Production and Distribution During 2006-07

Production of Fish Seed (in lakh Nos.)	*Distribution of Fish Seed (in lakh Nos.)*
7530	75

Source : Economic Survey Manipur 2007-08.

No. of Nurseries and Fish Ponds in 2007-08

Nurseries/	*Fish Ponds*		
Hatcheries	*Govt.*	*Private*	*Total*
2	1	1029	1030

Source : Economic Survey Manipur 2007-08.

Area of Fish Ponds and Production Fish

Area of Fish Ponds (in Ha.)		*Production of fish (in Qntl.)*	
2006-07	*2007-08*	*2006-07*	*2007-08*
520.00	529.00	7530	3200.60

Source : Economic Survey Manipur 2007-08.

Industry

No. of Small Scale Industries Registered During 2007-2008

Unit Registered	4
No. of persons employed	12
Amount of Investment (Rs. in lakhs)	5.3

Source : Economic Survey Manipur 2007-08.

Electricity

Cumulative No. of Village Electrified

As on 01.04.2007	*As on 01.04.2008*
72	75

Source : Economic Survey Manipur 2007-08.

Health

Medical Institution and No. of Bed Strength

Government Hospital	*Bed (as on 01.04.2007)*	*Bed (as on 01.04.2008)*
Civil Hospital	50	50

Source : Economic Survey Manipur 2007-08.

No. of Births and Deaths Registered

(January-December)

Births (Nos.)			*Deaths (Nos.)*		
2005	*2006*	*2007*	*2005*	*2006*	*2007*
1206	1356	1729	258	286	230

Source : Economic Survey Manipur 2007-08.

Tourism

Number of Tourist Spot and Tourist Lodge in Mamit

No. of Tourist Lodge		*No. of Highway Restaurant*		*No. of Picnic Spot*	
2006-2007	*2007-2008*	*2006-2007*	*2007-2008*	*2006-2007*	*2007-2008*
3	4	0	0	0	0

Source : Economic Survey Manipur 2007-08.

Banking

No. of Commercial Banks

Name of Bank	*Number*
SBI	3
MRB	6
Total	**9**

Source : Economic Survey Manipur 2007-08.

Police

Number of Police Stations, Out Posts, Check Posts, Wireless Stations

Police Stations		*Out Posts*		*Check Posts*		*Wireless Stations*	
2006-07	*2007-08*	*2006-07*	*2007-08*	*2006-07*	*2007-08*	*2006-07*	*2007-08*
5	5	1	1	0	1	14	14

Source : Economic Survey Manipur 2007-08.

9 Lawngtlai District

District HQ : Lawngtlai

Distance from State Capital (In KM) : 296

Sub Divisions : Lawngtlai, Tuichhak, Chawngte

No. of block : 2

No. of villages inhabited : 174

Population below poverty line : 10116 (families)

Towns of the District : Lawngtlai, Chawngte

Major Language : Mizo, English, Hindi

Demographic Features

Area, No. of Household, Population & Literacy Rate According to 2001 Census

Area (Sq. km.)	*No. of house holds*	*Population*			*Decadal variation % 1991-2001*	*Literacy Rate (%)*
		Total	*Male*	*Female*		
2557	13902	73620	38776	34844	35.80	64.70

Source : Economic Survey Manipur 2007-08.

Population By Religion (Census 2001)

Christian	*Hindu*	*Muslim*	*Sikhs*	*Buddhist*	*Jains*	*Religion not stated*	*other*
32877	1910	230	73	38410	88	32	0

Source : Economic Survey Manipur 2007-08.

Distribution of Population by Social Group (2001 Census)

ST Population	*SC Population*	*Others*
70234	5	3381

Source : Economic Survey Manipur 2007-08.

Agriculture

WRC Statistics of Lawngtlai

2006-2007			*2007-2008*		
No. of WRC farmers	*Area of WRC cultivated (Ha.)*	*Area still to be developed (Ha.)*	*No. of WRC farmers*	*Area of WRC cultivated (Ha.)*	*Area still to be developed (Ha.)*
587	1475	1184	546	712	1032

Source : Economic Survey Manipur 2007-08.

Sericulture

Sericulture Villages and No. of Families Engaged

No. of Sericulture Village		*No. of Families Engaged*		*Area under Sericulture Plantation (in Ha.)*		*No. of Sericulture Farm*	
2006-07	*2007-08*	*2006-07*	*2007-08*	*2006-07*	*2007-08*	*2006-07*	*2007-08*
30	30	840	840	550	650	0	0

Source : Economic Survey Manipur 2007-08.

Production of Cocoons, Silk Yarn and Seed Distributed

Mulberry (in MT.)	2006-07	4
	2007-08	3
Muga (in MT.)	2006-07	0
	2007-08	0
Eri (in MT.)	2006-07	0
	2007-08	0
Oak Tasar (in lakhs)	2006-07	0
	2007-08	0
Silk yarn (in MT.)	2006-07	0
	2007-08	0
No. of seed/cutting distributed to	2006-07	0
Farms (in '000')	2007-08	0

Source : Economic Survey Manipur 2007-08.

No. of Sericulture Farms, Area and Reeling Units

No. of Sericulture Farms		*Area in Ha.*		*No. of Reeling Units*	
2006-07	*2007-08*	*2006-07*	*2007-08*	*2006-07*	*2007-08*
0	0	550	650	0	0

Source : Economic Survey Manipur 2007-08.

Livestock & Poultry

Livestock and Poultry Population (Quinqennial Livestock Census) 2007-08

Cattle	Crossbred	183
	Indigenous	2943
	Total	3126
Buffaloes		147
Mithun		0
Sheep		125
Goats		5231
Horse and Ponies		0
Pigs		24901
Dogs		4200

Fowls	92601
Ducks	906
Turkey	4
Others	38
Total	**131279**

Source : Economic Survey Manipur 2007-08.

No. of Institutions and Veterinary Personnel During 2007-08

Hospitals	0
Dispensaries	1
Rural Animal Health Centre	4
Artificial Insemination Centres	1
Doctors/Surgeons	3
VFA/SUFA/JM/JEO/PI/LS etc.	9

Source : Economic Survey Manipur 2007-08.

Fishery

Fish Seed Production and Distribution During 2006-07

Production of Fish Seed (in lakh Nos.)	*Distribution of Fish Seed (in lakh Nos.)*
7100	20

Source : Economic Survey Manipur 2007-08.

No. of Nurseries and Fish Ponds in 2007-08

Nurseries/ Hatcheries	*Fish Ponds*		
	Govt.	*Private*	*Total*
0	0	1053	1053

Source : Economic Survey Manipur 2007-08.

Area of Fish Ponds and Production Fish

Area of Fish Ponds (in Ha.)		*Production of fish (in Qntl.)*	
2006-07	*2007-08*	*2006-07*	*2007-08*
490.70	492.00	7100	3500.30

Source : Economic Survey Manipur 2007-08.

Industry

No. of Small Scale Industries Registered During 2007-2008

Unit Registered	3
No. of persons employed	10
Amount of Investment (Rs. in lakhs)	7

Source : Economic Survey Manipur 2007-08.

Electricity

Cumulative No. of Village Electrified

As on 01.04.2007	*As on 01.04.2008*
71	68

Source : Economic Survey Manipur 2007-08.

Health

Medical Institution and No. of Bed Strength

Government Hospital	*Bed (as on 01.04.2007)*	*Bed (as on 01.04.2008)*
Civil Hospital	30	30

Source : Economic Survey Manipur 2007-08.

No. of Births and Deaths Registered

(January-December)

Births (Nos.)			*Deaths (Nos.)*		
2005	*2006*	*2007*	*2005*	*2006*	*2007*
1772	1877	2146	326	291	349

Source : Economic Survey Manipur 2007-08.

Tourism

Number of Tourist Spot and Tourist Lodge in Lawngtlai

No. of Tourist Lodge		*No. of Highway Restaurant*		*No. of Picnic Spot*	
2006-2007	*2007-2008*	*2006-2007*	*2007-2008*	*2006-2007*	*2007-2008*
2	3	0	0	0	0

Source : Economic Survey Manipur 2007-08.

Banking

No. of Commercial Banks

Name of Bank	*Number*
SBI	2
MCAB	1
MRB	1
Total	**4**

Source : Economic Survey Manipur 2007-08.

Police

Number of Police Stations, Out Posts, Check Posts, Wireless Stations

Police Stations		*Out Posts*		*Check Posts*		*Wireless Stations*	
2006-07	*2007-08*	*2006-07*	*2007-08*	*2006-07*	*2007-08*	*2006-07*	*2007-08*
5	5	2	2	0	0	5	6

Source : Economic Survey Manipur 2007-08.

10 Lunglei District

District HQ : Lunglei

Distance from State Capital (In KM) : 235.0

Sub Divisions : Lunglei, Hnahthial, Tlabung

Towns of the District : Lunglei, Hnahthial, Tlabung

Forest Cover (%) : 9.97

Major Language : Mizo, English, Hindi

Major Plantation : Rubber, Coffee

Demographic Features

Area, No. of Household, Population & Literacy Rate According to 2001 Census

Area (Sq. km.)	*No. of house holds*	*Population*			*Decadal variation % 1991-2001*	*Literacy Rate (%)*
		Total	*Male*	*Female*		
4536	27889	137223	71402	65821	23.10	84.20

Source : Economic Survey Manipur 2007-08.

Population By Religion (Census 2001)

Christian	*Hindu*	*Muslim*	*Sikhs*	*Buddhist*	*Jains*	*Religion not stated*	*other*
109204	4612	775	63	22429	28	14	98

Source : Economic Survey Manipur 2007-08

Distribution of Population by Social Group (2001 Census)

ST Population	*SC Population*	*Others*
130768	33	6422

Source : Economic Survey Manipur 2007-08.

Agriculture

WRC Statistics of Lunglei

2006-2007			2007-2008		
No. of WRC farmers	*Area of WRC cultivated (Ha.)*	*Area still to be developed (Ha.)*	*No. of WRC farmers*	*Area of WRC cultivated (Ha.)*	*Area still to be developed (Ha.)*
1176	463	1104	1139	651	1089

Source : Economic Survey Manipur 2007-08.

Sericulture

Sericulture Villages and No. of Families Engaged

No. of Sericulture Village		*No. of Families Engaged*		*Area under Sericulture Plantation (in Ha.)*		*No. of Sericulture Farm*	
2006-07	*2007-08*	*2006-07*	*2007-08*	*2006-07*	*2007-08*	*2006-07*	*2007-08*
16	16	900	900	400	500	2	2

Source : Economic Survey Manipur 2007-08.

Production of Cocoons, Silk Yarn and Seed Distributed

Mulberry (in MT.)	2006-07	4
	2007-08	6
Muga (in MT.)	2006-07	0
	2007-08	0
Eri (in MT.)	2006-07	1.50
	2007-08	1.8
Oak Tasar (in lakhs)	2006-07	0
	2007-08	9
Silk yarn (in MT.)	2006-07	0
	2007-08	0
No. of seed/cutting distributed to Farms (in '000')	2006-07	600
	2007-08	1370

Source : Economic Survey Manipur 2007-08.

No. of Sericulture Farms, Area and Reeling Units

No. of Sericulture Farms		*Area in Ha.*		*No. of Reeling Units*	
2006-07	*2007-08*	*2006-07*	*2007-08*	*2006-07*	*2007-08*
2	2	400	500	0	0

Source : Economic Survey Manipur 2007-08.

Livestock & Poultry

Livestock and Poultry Population (Quinqennial Livestock Census) 2007-08

Cattle	Crossbred	1293
	Indigenous	2360
	Total	3653
Buffaloes		112
Mithun		0
Sheep		4
Goats		2799
Horse and Ponies		65

Pigs	37384
Dogs	6215
Fowls	175412
Ducks	183
Turkey	0
Others	0
Total	**225827**

Source : Economic Survey Manipur 2007-08.

No. of Institutions and Veterinary Personnel During 2007-08

Hospitals	1
Dispensaries	6
Rural Animal Health Centre	20
Artificial Insemination Centres	14
Doctors/Surgeons	18
VFA/SUFA/JM/JEO/PI/LS etc.	49

Source : Economic Survey Manipur 2007-08.

Fishery

Fish Seed Production and Distribution in During 2006-07

Production of Fish Seed (in lakh Nos.)	*Distribution of Fish Seed (in lakh Nos.)*
4512	50

Source : Economic Survey Manipur 2007-08.

No. of Nurseries and Fish Ponds in 2007-08

Nurseries/	*Fish Ponds*		
Hatcheries	*Govt.*	*Private*	*Total*
1	2	1038	1040

Source : Economic Survey Manipur 2007-08.

Area of Fish Ponds and Production Fish

Area of Fish Ponds (in Ha.)		*Production of fish (in Qntl.)*	
2006-07	*2007-08*	*2006-07*	*2007-08*
312.50	314.20	4512	4501.00

Source : Economic Survey Manipur 2007-08

Industry

No. of Small Scale Industries Registered During 2007-2008

Unit Registered	33
No. of persons employed	105
Amount of Investment (Rs. in lakhs)	120

Source : Economic Survey Manipur 2007-08.

Electricity

Cumulative No. of Village Electrified

As on 01.04.2007	*As on 01.04.2008*
138	132

Source : Economic Survey Manipur 2007-08.

Health

Medical Institution and No. of Bed Strength

Government Hospital	*Bed (as on 01.04.2007)*	*Bed (as on 01.04.2008)*
Civil Hospital	190	190

Source : Economic Survey Manipur 2007-08.

No. of Births and Deaths Registered

(January-December)

Births (Nos.)			*Deaths (Nos.)*		
2005	*2006*	*2007*	*2005*	*2006*	*2007*
3325	3516	3609	771	736	794

Source : Economic Survey Manipur 2007-08.

Tourism

Number of Tourist Spot and Tourist Lodge in Lunglei

No. of Tourist Lodge		*No. of Highway Restaurant*		*No. of Picnic Spot*	
2006-2007	*2007-2008*	*2006-2007*	*2007-2008*	*2006-2007*	*2007-2008*
6	7	1	1	0	0

Source : Economic Survey Manipur 2007-08.

Banking

No. of Commercial Banks

Name of Bank	*Number*
SBI	6
MCAB	1
MRS	8
Total	**15**

Source : Economic Survey Manipur 2007-08.

Police

Number of Police Stations, Out Posts, Check Posts, Wireless Stations

Police Stations		*Out Posts*		*Check Posts*		*Wireless Stations*	
2006-07	*2007-08*	*2006-07*	*2007-08*	*2006-07*	*2007-08*	*2006-07*	*2007-08*
6	6	2	2	0	1	8	8

Source : Economic Survey Manipur 2007-08.

11 Saiha District

District HQ : Saiha

Distance from State Capital (In KM) : 378

Sub Divisions : Saiha, Tuipang

Towns of the District : Saiha, Tuipang, Sangau

Major Language : Mizo, English, Hindi

Demographic Features

Area, No. of Household, Population & Literacy Rate According to 2001 Census

Area (Sq. km.)	*No. of house holds*	*Population*			*Decadal variation % 1991-2001*	*Literacy Rate (%)*
		Total	*Male*	*Female*		
1399	11109	61056	31242	29814	33.60	82.20

Source : Economic Survey Manipur 2007-08.

Population By Religion (Census 2001)

Christian	*Hindu*	*Muslim*	*Sikhs*	*Buddhist*	*Jains*	*Religion not stated*
59618	1112	209	3	73	2	39

Source : Economic Survey Manipur 2007-08.

Distribution of Population by Social Group (2001 Census)

ST Population	*SC Population*	*Others*
58742	12	2302

Source : Economic Survey Manipur 2007-08.

Classification of workers (2001 census)

(a) Cultivators : 18211

(b) Agri-labourers : 36240

(e) Small & Marginal Farmers : 6227

Agriculture

WRC Statistics of Saiha

2006-2007			2007-2008		
No. of WRC farmers	*Area of WRC cultivated (Ha.)*	*Area still to be developed (Ha.)*	*No. of WRC farmers*	*Area of WRC cultivated (Ha.)*	*Area still to be developed (Ha.)*
321	387	453	422	376	861

Source : Economic Survey Manipur 2007-08.

Sericulture

Sericulture Villages and No. of Families Engaged

No. of Sericulture Village		*No. of Families Engaged*		*Area under Sericulture Plantation (in Ha.)*		*No. of Sericulture Farm*	
2006-07	*2007-08*	*2006-07*	*2007-08*	*2006-07*	*2007-08*	*2006-07*	*2007-08*
20	20	500	500	350	450	1	1

Source : Economic Survey Manipur 2007-08.

Production of Cocoons, Silk Yarn and Seed Distributed

Mulberry (in MT.)	2006-07	4
	2007-08	4
Muga (in MT.)	2006-07	0
	2007-08	0
Eri (in MT.)	2006-07	0
	2007-08	0
Oak Tasar (in lakhs)	2006-07	0
	2007-08	0
Silk yarn (in MT.)	2006-07	0
	2007-08	0
No. of seed/cutting distributed to	2006-07	0
Farms (in '000')	2007-08	0

Source : Economic Survey Manipur 2007-08.

No. of Sericulture Farms, Area and Reeling Units

No. of Sericulture Farms		*Area in Ha.*		*No. of Reeling Units*	
2006-07	*2007-08*	*2006-07*	*2007-08*	*2006-07*	*2007-08*
1	1	350	450	0	0

Source : Economic Survey Manipur 2007-03.

Livestock & Poultry

Livestock and Poultry Population (Quinqennial Livestock Census) 2007-08

Cattle	Crossbred	217
	Indigenous	3717
	Total	3934
Buffaloes		822
Mithun		0545
Sheep		44
Goats		803
Horse and Ponies		201

Pigs	21856
Dogs	2160
Fowls	103979
Ducks	128
Turkey	11
Others	315
Total	**134798**

Source : Economic Survey Manipur 2007-08.

No. of Institutions and Veterinary Personnel During 2007-08

Hospitals	1
Dispensaries	4
Rural Animal Health Centre	8
Artificial Insemination Centres	4
Doctors/Surgeons	6
VFA/SUFA/JM/JEO/PI/LS etc.	10

Source : Economic Survey Manipur 2007-08.

Fishery

Fish Seed Production and Distribution in During 2006-07

Production of Fish Seed (in lakh Nos.)	*Distribution of Fish Seed (in lakh Nos.)*
2820	60

Source : Economic Survey Manipur 2007-08.

No. of Nurseries and Fish Ponds in 2007-08

Nurseries/	*Fish Ponds*		
Hatcheries	*Govt.*	*Private*	*Total*
0	2	491	493

Source : Economic Survey Manipur 2007-08.

Area of Fish Ponds and Production Fish

Area of Fish Ponds (in Ha.)		*Production of fish (in Qntl.)*	
2006-07	*2007-08*	*2006-07*	*2007-08*
197.30	200.50	2820	2834.00

Source : Economic Survey Manipur 2007-08.

Industry

No. of Small Scale Industries Registered During 2007-2008

Unit Registered	3
No. of persons employed	12
Amount of Investment (Rs. in lakhs)	7.5

Source : Economic Survey Manipur 2007-08.

Electricity

Cumulative No. of Village Electrified

As on 01.04.2007	*As on 01.04.2008*
53	55

Source : Economic Survey Manipur 2007-08.

Health

Medical Institution and No. of Bed Strength

Government Hospital	*Bed (as on 01.04.2007)*	*Bed (as on 01.04.2008)*
Civil Hospital	62	62

Source : Economic Survey Manipur 2007-08.

No. of Births and Deaths Registered

(January-December)

Births (Nos.)			*Deaths (Nos.)*		
2005	*2006*	*2007*	*2005*	*2006*	*2007*
1252	1432	1484	364	400	367

Source : Economic Survey Manipur 2007-08.

Tourism

Number of Tourist Spot and Tourist Lodge in Saiha

No. of Tourist Lodge		*No. of Highway Restaurant*		*No. of Picnic Spot*	
2006-2007	*2007-2008*	*2006-2007*	*2007-2008*	*2006-2007*	*2007-2008*
4	3	0	0	0	6

Source : Economic Survey Manipur 2007-08.

Banking

No. of Commercial Banks

Name of Bank	*Number*
SBI	1
MCAB	1
MRB	3
Total	**5**

Source : Economic Survey Manipur 2007-08.

Police

Number of Police Stations, Out Posts, Check Posts, Wireless Stations

Police Stations		*Out Posts*		*Check Posts*		*Wireless Stations*	
2006-07	*2007-08*	*2006-07*	*2007-08*	*2006-07*	*2007-08*	*2006-07*	*2007-08*
2	2	4	4	2	0	7	6

Source : Economic Survey Manipur 2007-08.

12 Aizawl District

District HQ and State Capital : Aizawl

Distance from State Capital (In KM) : 0.0

Sub Divisions : Aizawl Sadar, Sakawrdai, Saitual

Towns of the District : Aizawl, Darlawn, Saitual, Tlangnuam, Phullen, Aibook

Forest Cover (%) : 59.49

Major Language : Mizo, English, Hindi

Major Minerals : Crude Oil, Coal, Lime Stone

Major Plantation : Tea, Rubber, Coffee

Tourist Spots : Aizawl, Bung, Tamadil, Dampa, Murlen

Demographic Features

Area, No. of Household, Population & Literacy Rate According to 2001 Census

Area (Sq. km.)	*No. of house holds*	*Population*			*Decadal variation % 1991-2001*	*Literacy Rate (%)*
		Total	*Male*	*Female*		
3756	64753	325676	166877	158799	38.10	96.50

Source : Economic Survey Manipur 2007-08.

Population By Religion (Census 2001)

Christian	*Hindu*	*Muslim*	*Sikhs*	*Buddhist*	*Jains*	*Religion not stated*	*other*
303893	14508	5185	106	576	30	208	1170

Source : Economic Survey Manipur 2007-08.

Distribution of Population by Social Group (2001 Census)

ST Population	*SC Population*	*Others*
303641	182	21853

Source : Economic Survey Manipur 2007-08.

Agriculture

WRC Statistics of Aizawl

2006-2007			*2007-2008*		
No. of WRC farmers	*Area of WRC cultivated (Ha.)*	*Area still to be developed (Ha.)*	*No. of WRC farmers*	*Area of WRC cultivated (Ha.)*	*Area still to be developed (Ha.)*
411	366	942	453	440	942

Source : Economic Survey Manipur 2007-08.

Sericulture

Sericulture Villages and No. of Families Engaged

No. of Sericulture Village		*No. of Families Engaged*		*Area under Sericulture Plantation (in Ha.)*		*No. of Sericulture Farm*	
2006-07	*2007-08*	*2006-07*	*2007-08*	*2006-07*	*2007-08*	*2006-07*	*2007-08*
40	40	1800	1800	1100	1200	4	4

Source : Economic Survey Manipur 2007-08.

Production of Cocoons, Silk Yarn and Seed Distributed

Mulberry (in MT.)	2006-07	17
	2007-08	12
Muga (in MT.)	2006-07	1.01
	2007-08	0.50
Eri (in MT.)	2006-07	0.30
	2007-08	0
Oak Tasar (in lakhs)	2006-07	0
	2007-08	0
Silk yarn (in MT.)	2006-07	4.00
	2007-08	4.30
No. of seed/cutting distributed to Farms (in '000')	2006-07	2532
	2007-08	5040

Source : Economic Survey Manipur 2007-08.

No. of Sericulture Farms, Area and Reeling Units

No. of Sericulture Farms		*Area in Ha.*		*No. of Reeling Units*	
2006-07	*2007-08*	*2006-07*	*2007-08*	*2006-07*	*2007-08*
4	4	1100	1200	1	1

Source : Economic Survey Manipur 2007-08.

Livestock & Poultry

Livestock and Poultry Population (Quinqennial Livestock Census) 2007-08

Cattle	Crossbred	5891
	Indigenous	1486
	Total	7377
Buffaloes		263
Mithun		107
Sheep		86
Goats		1576
Horse and Ponies		142

Pigs	74340
Dogs	12435
Fowls	309312
Ducks	1445
Turkey	246
Others	431
Total	**407760**

Source : Economic Survey Manipur 2007-08.

No. of Institutions and Veterinary Personnel During 2007-08

Hospitals	1
Dispensaries	6
Rural Animal Health Centre	30
Artificial Insemination Centres	20
Doctors/Surgeons	44
VFA/SUFA/JM/JEO/PI/LS etc.	80

Source : Economic Survey Manipur 2007-08.

Fishery

Fish Seed Production and Distribution in During 2006-07

Production of Fish Seed (in lakh Nos.)	*Distribution of Fish Seed (in lakh Nos.)*
2190	60

Source : Economic Survey Manipur 2007-08.

No. of Nurseries and Fish Ponds in 2007-08

Nurseries/	*Fish Ponds*		
Hatcheries	*Govt.*	*Private*	*Total*
1	3	842	845

Source : Economic Survey Manipur 2007-08.

Area of Fish Ponds and Production Fish

Area of Fish Ponds (in Ha.)		*Production offish (in Qntl.)*	
2006-07	*2007-08*	*2006-07*	*2007-08*
151.20	155.40	2190	2100.00

Source : Economic Survey Manipur 2007-08.

Industry

No. of Small Scale Industries Registered During 2007-2008

Unit Registered	53
No. of persons employed	156
Amount of Investment (Rs. in lakhs)	189

Source : Economic Survey Manipur 2007-08.

Electricity

Cumulative No. of Village Electrified

As on 01.04.2007	*As on 01.04.2008*
98	101

Source : Economic Survey Manipur 2007-08.

Health

Medical Institution and No. of Bed Strength

Government Hospital	*Bed (as on 01.04.2007)*	*Bed (as on 01.04.2008)*
Civil Hospital	350	350
T.B. Hospital	50	50
Non-Government Hospitals		
Greenwood Hospital	66	68
Adventist Hospital	30	40
Nazareth Hospital	43	45
Bethesda Hospital	80	80
Aizawl Hospital	33	77
Care Hospital	17	17
Grace Nursing Home	36	36

Source : Economic Survey Manipur 2007-08.

No. of Births and Deaths Registered

(January-December)

Births (Nos.)			*Deaths (Nos.)*		
2005	*2006*	*2007*	*2005*	*2006*	*2007*
8088	9264	8283	2021	2030	2201

Source : Economic Survey Manipur 2007-08.

Tourism

Number of Tourist Spot and Tourist lodge in Aizawl

No. of Tourist Lodge		*No. of Highway Restaurant*		*No. of Picnic Spot*	
2006-2007	*2007-2008*	*2006-2007*	*2007-2008*	*2006-2007*	*2007-2008*
8	8	0	0	3	2

Source : Economic Survey Manipur 2007-08.

Banking

No. of Commercial Banks

Name of Bank	*Aizawl*
SBI	8
UCO	1
Vijaya	1
IDBI	1
UBI	1
Axis	1
Syndicate	1
CBI	1
BOB	1
PNB	1
MCAB	5
MRB	23
MUCO	1
Total	**46**

Source : Economic Survey Manipur 2007-08.

Police

Number of Police Stations, Out Posts, Check Posts, Wireless Stations

Police Stations		*Out Posts*		*Check Posts*		*Wireless Stations*	
2006-07	*2007-08*	*2006-07*	*2007-08*	*2006-07*	*2007-08*	*2006-07*	*2007-08*
8	8	3	3	0	0	26	22

Source : Economic Survey Manipur 2007-08.

13 Mizoram at a Glance

Geographical Area (Sq. Km) : 21,087

Geographical Location	
Longitude	92°.15'E to 93°29'E
Latitude	21°.58' N to 24°.35' N
Length	
North to South	277 kms
East to West	121 kms
International Borders	
With Myanmar	404 kms
With Bangladesh	318 kms
Inter State Borders	
With Assam	123 kms
With Tripura	66 kms
With Manipur	95 kms
Administrative Set Up	
No. of District	8 nos.
No. of Autonomous District Council	3 nos.
No. of Sub Division	23 nos.
No. of R.D. Block	26 nos.
No. of Villages (2001 Census)	
Inhabited	732 nos.
Uninhabited	108 nos.

Source : Economic Survey Mizoram : 2008-09.

Population (As per Census 2001)

Sl. No.	*Particular*	*Unit*	
1.	**Total Population**		
	Persons	Nos.	8,88,573
	Male	Nos.	4,59,109
	Female	Nos.	4,29,464
	Rural	Nos.	4,44,567
	Urban	Nos.	4,41,006
2.	**Decadal Population Growth (1991—2001)**		
	Absolute	Nos.	1,98,817
	Percentage (%)	%	28.8%
3.	Population Density	Per Sq. Km	42
4.	**No. of females per 1000 males**	Nos.	935
5.	**0-6 Population**		
	Persons	Nos.	1,43,734
	Males	Nos.	73,176
	Females	Nos.	70,558
6.	**Literacy**		
	Persons	Nos.	6,61,445
	Males	Nos.	3,50,105
	Females	Nos.	3,11,340
	Rate	%	88.8
7.	**Total Workers**		
	Main workers	Nos.	3,62,450
	Marginal workers	Nos.	1,04,709

Source : Economic Survey Mizoram, 2008-09.

General Review

1. Mizoram is expected to achieve a growth of 6.46% during 2008-2009. The growth in GDP at the national level during 2008-09 is estimated at 7.1 percent.

2. The per capita income of Mizoram for the year 2008-2009 is estimated at Rs. 29,576. At the national level, the per capita income is estimated to be around Rs. 38,084. It is estimated that by 2009, the State Population will reach 10,96,622.
3. Agriculture and Allied sector contributes about 14% of the State Income. Agriculture proper (Crop Husbandry) contributes about 7% of GSDP.
4. The Industry Sector contribution to GSDP is about 20%.
5. Tertiary Sector (Service) remains the driver of the State economy by contributing about 65% of GSDP.
6. For the first time, Estimates of District Domestic Product (DDP) is attempted with the reference year 2005-06. Aizawl District has the highest DDP and highest Per Capita Income.
7. The year 2008 receives rainfall of 2175 mm while 2500 mm is the average annual rainfall in the State.
8. Bamboo flowering locally called “Mautam” has caused scaling down of agricultural operations in the State. The total production of paddy decreased from 420,901 M. Tonnes during 2006-07 to 15,688 M. Tonnes during 2007-08.
9. The per capita availability of milk per day in Mizoram worked out to be 51 gms, while the Indian Council of Medical Research recommends 240 gms of milk per day for an individual to keep up his/her health in good condition.
10. There was a sharp increase in floriculture production during 2007-08. About 71,94,000 cut flowers were produced as against 30,90,992 during 2006-07. Out of the total meat production (including Broiler meat) Pork accounted for the highest quantity with 64.34 percent followed by beef with a share of 16.89 percent, broiler meat accounted for 17.49 percent of the total meat production.

11. Fish production both from culture sector and riverine sector is estimated to be 3750 M.T. which can meet only 3.70 kg per capita against the total requirement of 11 kg thus leaving a shortfall of 7.30 kg per capita which comes to 7,426 MT.
12. Based on "State of Forest Report-2003" published by Forest Survey of India, Ministry of Environment & Forests, Forest covers 18,430 sq. km. (*i.e.* 87.42 percent) of the State's Geographic Area, out of which 84 sq. km. is very Dense Forest, 7,404 sq. km. is Moderately Dense Forest and Open Forests cover 10,942 sq. km.
13. Only 5% of the total energy demand of the State is met within the State and the remaining 95% is imported. The power peak load requirement of Mizoram for 2007-08 is 60 MW but the total installed capacity is only 37.17 MW. The Potential availability hydro power of Mizoram is estimated at 2425 MW, out of which only less than 2% is utilized and more than 98% of hydro potential available is lying unutilized.
14. 137 villages in the State are still without electricity. Per capita power consumption is 173.26 KWH.
15. By the end of 2007-08, the total length of classified roads under PWD was 5225.31 Kms. The total length of the road by the end of the previous year (2006-07) was 4571.12 Kms registering an increase of 634.19 Kms during one year. The total length of National Highway under Border Roads Organisation (BRO) in Mizoram upto 2007-08 was 558.00 Kms. Thus, the total length of road network of classified roads both under PWD and BRO by the end of 2007-08 was 5,783.51 Kms out of which 3,938.95 Kms (68.10 percent) were surfaced road and the rest 1,844.56 Kms (31.90 percent) were unsurfaced.
16. The progressive number of Motor Vehicles registered

upto December, 2008, both private and Government was 63,028.

17. There are 107 branches of financial institutions in the State consisting of 36 commercial banks, 60 branches of Mizoram Rural Bank and 11 branches of Mizoram State Cooperative Apex Bank. The branches of commercial banks and MRB in the State account for 89 percent of the total branches in the State. The population served per branch comes to around 8,304 while the national average is 15,000.

18. The credit-deposit ratio (CDR) increased from 56.52% on 31st March 2007 to 57.10% on March 2008 which is still low as compared to the national average of 75%.

19. Mobile Phone connections as on October 2008 stood at 2,85,272 while there were 1,71,296 connections as on December 2007.

20. Up to 2007-2008 there were 3,432 number of schools at different level of education in the State. The teacher pupil ratio are : Primary (1 : 17), Middle (1 : 8), High School (1 : 11) and Higher Secondary (1 : 13). Out of 3432 Schools, 54% are managed by Government.

21. The total number of Colleges and other higher educational institutions in the State during 2007-08 was 27 with the total enrolment of 6,136.

22. By February 2009, there are 10 Government hospitals, 12 CHCs, 57 PHCs and 366 Sub-Centres. Doctor population ratio is estimated at 2,913.

23. There are 154 Rural Habitations in a Non-Covered Status of Water Supply and 13 towns still left to be covered with water supply for achieving National Norm of minimum Water supply level for Urban Areas *i.e.* 70 lpcd.

24. Under NLCPR, DONER sanctioned 79 projects in respect of Mizoram since 1998-1999 with the total

approved cost of Rs. 63,392.81 lakhs of which 50 projects were completed. The State Government is taking up 41 NEC schemes within the approved cost of Rs. 233.06 crores during 2007-08 in which Rs. 54.80 crore has been released. Fund Received during 2008-09 till February 2009 was Rs. 14.73 crore.

25. While the approved outlay for Annual Plan 2008-09 is Rs. 1,00,000.00 lakh, the revised outlay is Rs. 104,774.92 lakhs. Since, the size of the Annual Plan for 2009-10 has not been fixed, Rs. 1000.00 crores which is the previous year outlay is tentatively proposed in which Rs 100.00 crores is tentatively earmarked for implementation of New Land Use Policy (NLUP).

26. The fiscal deficit has been improved over the years but deteriorated to Rs. 329.22 crore in 2007-08 (Pre-Actuals) which is 8.34 per cent of GSDP. The level of fiscal deficit in 2008-09 (BE) remains at Rs 131.49 crore which is 3 per cent of GSDP. Due to deterioration of the fiscal position the possibility of placing the fiscal deficit to 3% of the GSDP by 2008-09 as required under FRBM Act may seems to be a herculean task.

27. There is a revenue surplus of Rs. 193.63 crore during 2007-08. The level of collections in State's Own Revenues in 2008-09 is expected to improve much beyond the BF level. While the State's revenues continued to be dominated by inflow of resources from the Centre, the contribution of the State' own resources has been improving over the years.

28. Debt as a percentage of GSDP in 2007-08 pre actual is 90.54% which is expected to be reduced at 84.50% in 2008-09 (BE). Expenditure on interest payments for 2008-09 (BE) is Rs. 203.13 crore which is 9.16 per cent of the total revenue receipts.

Source : Economic Survey Mizoram 2008-09.

Serchhip District

District HQ : Serchhip

Distance from State Capital (In KM) : 112

Sub Divisions : Serchhip, N. Vanlaiphai, Thenzawl

Town of the District : Serchhip

Major Language : Mizo, English, Hindi

No. of blocks : 2

No. of villages inhabited : 58

Demographic Features

Area, No. of Household, Population & Literacy Rate According to 2001 Census

Area (Sq. km.)	*No. of house holds*	*Population*			*Decadal variation % 1991-2001*	*Literacy Rate (%)*
		Total	*Male*	*Female*		
1421	10116	53861	27380	26481	17.60	95.10

Source : Economic Survey Manipur 2007-08.

Population By Religion (Census 2001)

Christian	*Hindu*	*Muslim*	*Sikhs*	*Buddhist*	*Jains*	*Religion not stated*	*other*
52495	531	177	2	87	6	39	524

Source : Economic Survey Manipur 2007-08.

Distribution of Population by Social Group (2001 Census)

ST Population	*SC Population*	*Others*
52830	5	1026

Source : Economic Survey Manipur 2007-08.

Agriculture

WRC Statistics of Serchhip

2006-2007			2007-2008		
No. of WRC farmers	*Area of WRC cultivated (Ha.)*	*Area still to be developed (Ha.)*	*No. of WRC farmers*	*Area of WRC cultivated (Ha.)*	*Area still to be developed (Ha.)*
1500	1353	368	1568	1353	293

Source : Economic Survey Manipur 2007-08.

Sericulture

Sericulture Villages and No. of Families Engaged

No. of Sericulture Village		*No. of Families Engaged*		*Area under Sericulture Plantation (in Ha.)*		*No. of Sericulture Farm*	
2006-07	*2007-08*	*2006-07*	*2007-08*	*2006-07*	*2007-08*	*2006-07*	*2007-08*
20	20	640	640	300	400	2	2

Source : Economic Survey Manipur 2007-08.

Production of Cocoons, Silk Yarn and Seed Distributed

Mulberry (in MT.)	2006-07	3
	2007-08	5
Muga (in MT.)	2006-07	0
	2007-08	0
Eri (in MT.)	2006-07	0
	2007-08	0
Oak Tasar (in lakhs)	2006-07	0
	2007-08	0
Silk yarn (in MT.)	2006-07	0
	2007-08	0
No. of seed/cutting distributed to	2006-07	516
Farms (in '000')	2007-08	1370

Source : Economic Survey Manipur 2007-08.

No. of Sericulture Farms, Area and Reeling Units

No. of Sericulture Farms		*Area in Ha.*		*No. of Reeling Units*	
2006-07	*2007-08*	*2006-07*	*2007-08*	*2006-07*	*2007-08*
2	2	400	500	0	0

Source : Economic Survey Manipur 2007-08.

Livestock & Poultry

Livestock and Poultry Population (Quinqennial Livestock Census) 2007-08

Cattle	Crossbred	436
	Indigenous	1263
	Total	1699
Buffaloes		985
Mithun		171
Sheep		31
Goats		571
Horse and Ponies		128

Pigs	23692
Dogs	1825
Fowls	84116
Ducks	39
Turkey	9
Others	0
Total	**113266**

Source : Economic Survey Manipur 2007-08.

No. of Institutions and Veterinary Personnel During 2007-08

Hospitals	0
Dispensaries	3
Rural Animal Health Centre	9
Artificial Insemination Centres	3
Doctors/Surgeons	5
VFA/SUFA/JM/JEO/PI/LS etc.	18

Source : Economic Survey Manipur 2007-08.

Fishery

Fish Seed Production and Distribution During 2006-07

Production of Fish Seed (in lakh Nos.)	*Distribution of Fish Seed (in lakh Nos.)*
1382	25

Source : Economic Survey Manipur 2007-08.

No. of Nurseries and Fish Ponds in 2007-08

Nurseries/	*Fish Ponds*		
Hatcheries	*Govt.*	*Private*	*Total*
0	1	646	647

Source : Economic Survey Manipur 2007-08.

Area of Fish Ponds and Production Fish

Area of Fish Ponds (in Ha.)		*Production of fish (in Qntl.)*	
2006-07	*2007-08*	*2006-07*	*2007-08*
95.15	98.30	1382	1200.00

Source : Economic Survey Manipur 2007-08.

Industry

No. of Small Scale Industries Registered During 2007-2008

Unit Registered	80
No. of persons employed	224
Amount of Investment (Rs. in lakhs)	192

Source : Economic Survey Manipur 2007-08.

Electricity

Cumulative No. of Village Electrified

As on 01.04.2007	*As on 01.04.2008*
32	32

Source : Economic Survey Manipur 2007-08.

Health

Medical Institution and No. of Bed Strength

Government Hospital	*Bed (as on 01.04.2007)*	*Bed (as on 01.04.2008)*
Civil Hospital	50	50

Source : Economic Survey Manipur 2007-08.

No. of Births and Deaths Registered

(January-December)

Births (Nos.)			*Deaths (Nos.)*		
2005	*2006*	*2007*	*2005*	*2006*	*2007*
996	1020	1266	235	217	211

Source : Economic Survey Manipur 2007-08.

Tourism

Number of Tourist Spot and Tourist Lodge in Serchhip

No. of Tourist Lodge		*No. of Highway Restaurant*		*No. of Picnic Spot*	
2006-2007	*2007-2008*	*2006-2007*	*2007-2008*	*2006-2007*	*2007-2008*
2	2	1	1	0	0

Source : Economic Survey Manipur 2007-08.

Banking

No. of Commercial Banks

Name of Bank	*Number*
SBI	2
MCAB	1
MRB	6
Total	**9**

Source : Economic Survey Manipur 2007-08.

Police

Number of Police Stations, Out Posts, Check Posts, Wireless Stations

Police Stations		*Out Posts*		*Check Posts*		*Wireless Stations*	
2006-07	*2007-08*	*2006-07*	*2007-08*	*2006-07*	*2007-08*	*2006-07*	*2007-08*
2	2	2	2	0	0	4	4

Source : Economic Survey Manipur 2007-08.

15 Mizoram : Today and Tomorrow

Mizoram lies in the north east end of India, much of its southern part sandwiched between Bangladesh and Myanmar. It is situated between 21.56 to 24.31 degrees north latitude and 92.16 to 93.26 degrees east longitude, extending over a land area of 21,087 square kilometers. The Tropic of Cancer passes by the capital city. Aizawl. The length of the state from north to south is 277 km. At the broadest from east to west, it is 121 km.

Its major length in the west borders the Chittagong Hill Tracts of Bangladesh, spanning 318 km. In the east and the south, its border with the Chin Hills and Northern Arakans of Myanmar extends to about 404 km. On the Indian side, Mizoram is bounded by the states of Assam, Manipur and Tripura. The length of its borders with these states extends over 123 km, 95 km. and 66 km, respectively.

Districts-8; Sub-Divisions 15; Development Blocks 22; Villages-817; Towns 22; City 1. There are no City or Town Councils. These are administered by Local administration Department (LAD) of the State Government. Autonomous District Councils 3, namely, the Chakma, Lai and Mara District Councils in the southern region.

Geography Natural Resources

The mountain ranges in Mizoram run from north to south and largely taper from the middle of the state towards the north, the west and the south. The ranges in the west are steep and precipitous while where those in the east are somewhat gentler. The average height of the hills in the west is 1000 meters, gradually rising to 1,300 meters in the east. There are several mountain peaks of medium height. The highest peak in Mizoram is Phawngpui (Blue Maountain), which is 2,157 m. high and is located in the southeastern part of the State. A list of hill ranges, peaks and rivers in Mizoram is included in Appendix A.

Mizoram is interspersed with numerous rivers, streams and brooks. The important rivers in the northern part of the state, flowing northwards, are the Barak (Tuiruang) and its tributaries, the Tlawng (Dhaleshwari), the Tuirial (Sonai) and the Tuivai. The Tuivawl, a tributary of the Tuivai, is another important river in the area. The Barak, the Daleshwari, the Tuivai and the Sonai are navigable for considerable stretches. The Daleshwari in particular had been the main entry and exit routes for Mizoram through the ages. Forest produce like timber and bamboo are floated down the river from the interior of the hills to the plains of Cachar in Assam while food, consumer goods and merchandise are brought by boats from the Assam plains to the hills of Mizoram. Before fair weather road from Silchar in Cachar district of Assam to Aizawl was constructed during World War II, the administration depended entirely on this river for transportation of men and material. The Barak and the Tuivai constitute the borderline between Manipur and Mizoram and the two territories have through the centuries shared the facilities provided by these rivers.

The most important river in the southern region of the state is the Chhimtuipui (Kolodyne) with its four main tributaries—the Mat, the Tuichang, the Tiau and the Tuipui. The Kolodyne flows into Mizoram from Myanmar and turns west first and then southward within Mizoram and reenters Myanmar. Though interrupted by rapids, some stretches of the river in Mizoram are navigable.

The Khawthlangtuipui (Karnaphuli) and its tributaries—the Tuichawng, the Phaireng, the Kau, the Deh and the Tuilianpui—form the western drainage system. The Karnaphuli enters Bangladesh at Demagiri; at its mouth sits the port city of Chittagong.

Much of the potential of the river systems and water resources in Mizoram remains largely unexploited. The utilization of the hydro-potential for generation of energy, for example, in whatever form, large scale, mini or micro, is still fractional. There has been a modest improvement in the supply of drinking water but the sector lacks rational and systematic approach. The current condition of water transportation is less than retrogressive, partly because of the non-availability of transit facilities through Bangladesh.

There are three small plains in the state scattered over the mainly hilly terrain. The plains have thick layers of rich alluvial soil. The largest of these plains is the Champhai Plains, 10 km long and 5 km wide, and is situated near the Myanmar border, 150 km to the east of Aizawl. Another plain area is at Vanlaiphai, 90 km away to the southeast of Aizawl. It is 10 km long and 3/4 km wide on average. The third such area is at Thenzawl, 100 km south of Aizawl. These plains have been put mainly to paddy cultivation. In addition, there are several small level grounds beside some of the rivers, which have been developed for wet rice cultivation.

The common rocks found in Mizoram are sandstone, shale; silt stone, clay stone and slates. The rock system is weak and unstable, prone to seismic influence. Soils vary from sandy loam and clayey loam to clay, generally mature but leached owing to steep gradient and heavy rainfall. The "soils are porous with poor water holding capacity, deficient in potash, phosphorous, nitrogen and even humus. The pH shows acidic to neutral reaction due to excessive leaching." (Environment & Forest Department Report 2003). Appendix B contains more detailed information on geological conditions and minerals of Mizoram.

According to the report (2003) of the Department of Environment and Forests, 83 per cent of the total area of the state (21,087 sq. km.) is covered by forests. However, due to the traditional practice of shifting cultivation called *'jhuming'* uncontrolled fire, unregulated felling and arbitrary allotment of land to individuals, two-third of the area is reported to have been partly depleted and degraded.

The different types of land cover in Mizoram as estimated by Landsat Imagery are shown below : (Sources : Department of Environment and Forest).

Different Types of Land Cover in Mizoram

Type of Land Cover	*Area (in sq. km)*
1. Closed (good) forest	4,190
2. Closed forest affected by shifting cultivation	13,520
3. Forest degraded by shifting cultivation	2,600
4. Non-forest	640
5. Water bodies	140
Total	**21,090**

Bamboo

Mizoram has abundant natural bamboo resources. Around 57 per cent of the area of the state is covered by bamboo forests, located in the areas ranging in height from 400 m to 1500 m above the mean sea level. These forests are situated mainly in the river banks and abandoned jhum lands, forming a dominant secondary vegetation.

Both the clump forming and non-clump forming bamboos are found in most parts of Mizoram. The exception is the high land parts of the eastern region. There are 20 species of bamboo in the state, of which Melocanna baccifera, locally called 'Mautak', is the dominant. Forming no clumps, it is a fast spreading bamboo. The culms grow up to 8-10 m tall and are extensively used for construction of houses in the rural areas, especially for walling and flooring, and temporary dwelling of various sorts. They are also used for furniture, fencing, weaving and pulping, but are not yet processed for industrial use. During rainy season, the shoots form an important item of food for the population. At present, the State Government claims to have received annually Rs. 8 million in revenue mainly from bulk sales of unprocessed bamboos. This is done through the *Mahal* system, a practice of contracting out the rights of harvesting bamboos to individuals or firms on payment of nominal royalties.

The dominant bamboo in North East India, the Melocanna baccifera is said to have a life cycle of 48 years, at the end of which it flowers and bears fruits and dies. The fruits when eaten by rodents apparently increase the fertility of the latter, resulting in an explosion of the rat population in a short time. Once the bamboo fruits are exhausted, the rats turn to eating whatever food grains available in the farms or in storage, causing severe depletion of food supplies for the population and resulting in famine. Such occurrence on two occasions in the past has been recorded in Mizoram. The next flowering of the bamboos is forecast to occur in 2007.

Climate

Mizoram as a whole receives an average rainfall of about 3000 mm a year, with Aizawl getting 2380 mm and 3,178 mm for Lunglei in the south. Rainfall is usually evenly distributed throughout the state. During rains the climate in the lower hills and river gorges is highly humid and exhausting for people, whereas it is cool and pleasant in the higher hills even during the hot season. A rather peculiar characteristic of the climate is the incidence of violent storms during March-early May.

Strong storms arise from the north-west and sweep over the entire hills, often causing extensive damages to 'kacha' (temporary) dwellings and flowering perennials.

Temperature varies from about 12 degrees C in winter to 30 degrees C plus in summer. Winter is from November to February, with little or no rain during this period. Spring lasts from end February to mid-April. Heavy rains start in June and continue up to August. September and October are the autumn months when the rain is intermittent.

Socio-Political Structure

Historical Background

Except for those written after the advent of the British in the late 18 century, there is no recorded history of the Mizos. Some of the tribes living outside of Mizoram prefer to call themselves 'Zomis or simply Zos'; 'mi' affixed to these terms means 'people or persons'. The British variously referred to them as Lushais, Kukis (old or new Kukis, depending on the period of their contacts with the tribes) and Chins in Myanmar. All modern historians belonging to the various tribes, however, agree that all the tribal groups inhabiting the immediate neighborhood of the present state of Mizoram—in such areas as in Myanmar, Bangladesh, Tripura. Assam and Manipur—once belonged to the same proto-tribe. They often refer to themselves collectively as 'Zo Hnahthlak', people of Zo ancestry, origin or progeny.

While some of the tribes living outside Mizoram such as the Hmars, the Paites, the Thadous or Kukis, etc. still prefer to assert their sub-group identities for practical political or other reasons, the trend toward integration in a larger identity is gradually gaining strength. This growing awareness of belonging to a larger identity has the potential to upset in future the balance of the existing political demarcations in the sub-region.

Despite the absence of recorded history, most researchers conclude that the Mizos came to their present abode from southern China, possibly Yunnan province, by gradual migration through northern Myanmar. Dietary practices, customs, traditional values, legends, oral history, folklore and linguistic affinity are some of the bases on which these investigations are conducted. Although there can be no certainty about the period in which the Mizos migrated to the present Chin Hills in Myanmar, it is generally believed that this took place about four to five hundred years ago. However, the Mizos of Mizoram appear to have arrived at their present settlement relatively recently, perhaps in the late 17th or early 18th century. Animesh Ray, a researcher of considerable thoroughness, put it in the early 18th century (Mizoram, India—The Land and The People Series 1993). As their oral history attests,, the last wave of the migration of the Mizo tribes from Myanmar to India took place at about the time, or soon after, the institution of hereditary chieftainship gradually overtook their earlier practice of warrior chieftainship. Once hereditary rulers were installed, genealogy, even if orally passed on, became a reliable record of sort. Based on the genealogy of the chiefs, "early 18th century" appears to be the most likely period.

Traditional Institution

Although other Mizo tribes adopted and practiced hereditary chieftainship, the Sailo Chiefs of the Lusei or Lushai tribe were the most durable, perhaps, because they were the most enlightened. At any rate, their mode of governance became the norm for rural administration in much of the Mizo or Zo inhabited areas in pre-independent North East India. The British did little to interfere with the system of administration practiced by the Chiefs, except in rare cases of extraordinary misrule. Instead, they devised ways to ensure maintenance of law and order and social order through the Chiefs.

Indeed, this practice of "indirect administration" was formally provided for in the Government of India Act, 1935, and on the basis of this Act, an official order, named "Excluded and Partially Excluded Areas Order,' defining the areas to be covered, was issued by the King in Council on March 3. 1936.

The following paraphrase of an order issued by the Superintendent of Lushai Hills in 1898 also makes this clear :

1. Every Chief is responsible for all that goes on in his village. All orders affecting a village shall be sent to the Chief through the Circle Inspector (an official appointed by the British to liaise with the Chiefs).
2. Every Chief shall adjudicate all civil disputes between people of his village. He shall also dispose of all criminal cases, except those in which a person is killed or badly wounded. A Chief's order would not be interfered with unless he had acted in bad faith.
3. The Chiefs are responsible for ensuring that records are kept of the following :
   (i) All births and deaths in the village;
   (ii) All movements of people into or out of the village; and
   (iii) All changes the licensed guns.

The authority of the Chief, though nearly absolute within his domain which may consist of one or more or a group of villages, was often restrained in practice by the Council of Elders (Upas), an advisory body appointed by the Chief to assist him in the performance of his duties. The members of this Council were usually so selected by the Chief as to represent and safeguard the interests of the different clans or sub-tribe groups among his subjects. Captain T.H. Lewin, a former British Administrator in Lushai Hills, was so impressed by the administrative system of the Mizo Chiefs that he described it as "a democracy tempered by despotism" worthy of being "classed among the visions of Utopian philosophy." (Exercises in The Lushai Dialect 1874).

In return for his services, the Chief was entitled to : (1) Fathang—six bushels of rice grain from every household; (2) Sachhiah (Meat Tax)—anyone who bagged a four-legged big game must present him one of the hind legs; and (3) whenever his house required to be repaired or rebuilt, his subjects would do it for free.

Institution of Zawlbuk (Bachelor's Quarters)

Apart from the dispensation of the Chief and his Elders, the main instrument for ensuring discipline, instilling moral education, maintenance of law and order and the smooth functioning of the society was the institution of Zawlbuk. The exact date when this institution came about cannot be pinpointed. It is, however, certain that this tradition came to be established after the Mizos entered India and the Chief felt secure enough to regulate the management of social order for his subjects.

Though everyone was responsible to make sure that theft and other crimes were not committed, there had to be an organizing agency that was capable of ensuring this. This is what the Zawlbuk did. All boys from the age of about 10 to till they were married and had one or two children were required to sleep at Zawlbuk, a large dormitory like structure usually located in the middle of the village. This is where the boys were trained to fit themselves into society. Before a boy attained puberty, he was taught to shoulder his responsibilities for the community such as fetching water, collecting wood for use at the Zawlbuk, cleaning the Zawlbuk and its surrounding, and tending the Zawlbuk fire, which was used for lighting as well as for warmth. All the traditional values that the community held dear were passed on to the youth via the Zawlbuk life by way of practical demonstration.

A Historical Background

By the early thirties, Christianity, which entered Mizoram for the first time on January 11, 1894 via the Welsh Missionaries, had become the religion of the overwhelming majority of the Mizos. The Church had set up schools and rudimentary health services. Literacy was spreading fast. A few young Mizos had even gone to universities. At the same time, common people had begun to give up their old ways. Western ways of dressing and thinking had begun to spread, especially among the young men. Social life centered on the ways of Zawlbuk had gradually disappeared and had been replaced by that revoked around the Church. Through the organizing activities of the Church they began to understand the advantages of forming groups for focused goals.

The mass movements of the times for independence in mainstream India, too, inspired in a few young men as yet undefined ideas about possibilities in politics. And they started thinking in terms of organizing themselves for common purposes. Thus was born the first district wide and secular organization, Young Mizo Association (originally named Young Lushai Association after the name of the District) on June 15, 1935. A missionary initially headed the association; and its objectives were entirely non-political, namely, 1) to use leisure for beneficial activities; 2) to serve for the welfare of the people and 3) to promote Christian way of living. In the same year was founded the Mizo Zirlai Pawl (Mizo Students Union) with a motto : 'Unity is strength.' Its aim was to promote understanding, cooperation and unity among all Mizo students, regardless of whether they lived in Mizoram or outside. Both organizations grew rapidly and soon became effective vehicles for the promotion of fellow feeling and unity amongst the young Mizos of various regions.

World War II and the anticipation for Indian independence during the same period were really that set the Mizos to think about politics. Once Burma fell to the Japanese, they became the frontline. Near panicking British administrators mobilized the Chiefs and the people to pledge loyalty to the Imperial Crown and to resist the advance of the Japanese army at all costs. Even before the war, a large number of young Mizos had enlisted in the British Indian Army and many of them were now fighting alongside the British. And, naturally, the families and friends of these soldiers were inclined to side with the British.

At the same time, increasingly tense were the anxieties of the Mizos for their future in the new dispensation that was to follow independence of India. It is also obvious that the then British administrators of Mizoram had given them more than a hint that the Mizos could still have the option to opt out of the three dominions (India, Pakistan and Burma) to be created by the Independence of India Act, 1947 even as late as on August 14, 1947. Copies of the relevant documents are in Appendix C. These documents as well as the Resolutions of the Chin-Lushai Conference held at Fort William, Calcutta in 1892 (also in the same appendix) were to form later the bases on which the Mizo National Front (MNF) 'declared' independence for Mizoram and resorted to insurgency in March, 1966.

Political Parties

Thus, the objectives of the first two political parties formed immediately preceding independence also reflected the anxieties and debates of the times.

The Mizo Union, formed on 9 April 1946, was first named Mizo Common People's Union, reflecting the anti-Chiefs sentiments of the common people. Many had suspected that the British, working with the Chiefs, were trying to encourage a policy of isolated independence for Lushai Hills or Mizoram. The District Conference that had been convened in January 1946 by the then Superintendent, A.R.H. McDonald to advise him on future administrative set up for the Hills had had half of its members composed of Chiefs, in the face of opposition by the commoners. To enlist the support of the elite and the enlightened and liberal chiefs, the name of the party was changed to Mizo Union. However, it remained a party of the common people.

As independence was drawing near, there were sharp differences of opinion regarding the future of Mizoram. Though the Mizo Union was in favour of staying within India, a secessionist group came up in the Party favouring merger with Burma. (Their long term goal though not specified appeared to be independence. The draft of the Burmese Constitution had included the right to secession by the States within ten years vide Chapter X). The group, supported by most of the Chiefs, broke away from Mizo Union and formed a party called the United Mizo Freedom Organisation (UMFO) on 5 July 1947.

In 25 January 1947 the Constituent Assembly of India (the drafting body of the Indian Constitution) appointed an Advisory Committee on minorities, tribal areas and related matters under the chairmanship of Sardar Vallabhbhai Patel. The Committee in turn constituted a Sub-Committee chaired by Gopinath Bardoloi for the northeastern tribal areas and the Excluded and Partially Excluded Areas. This became popularly known as the Bardoloi Sub-Committee and the members co-opted from Mizoram were Ch. Saprawnga and Khawtinkhuma, representatives of the Mizo Union.

On the basis of various memoranda submitted to it by political groups, including McDonald's District Conference and the Mizo Union, Bardoloi Sub-Committee in its Report to the Constituent Assembly suggested a special setup for the tribal areas. It recommended that the tribal people should be free from any fear of exploitation or domination by the advanced section of the people from the plains and that they should have full freedom with regard to their traditions, customs, inheritance, social organizations, village administration, etc. The pattern of administration recommended for the tribal areas in the North East thus took shape in the Sixth Schedule to the Constitution.

Early Elected Bodies and Related Activities

After independence, as a prelude to the District Council, a 35 member Advisory Council was created and the elections to the Council were held on 15 April 1948. The Mizo Union captured all the seats, except two won by the UMFO. The Mizo Union soon came into conflict with Superintendent L. L. Peters, who was openly siding with the Chiefs over the latter's role in future administration. The Mizo Union then launched non-cooperation movement in December 1948, which lasted till February 1949 and for months thereafter in some far-flung areas.

District Council : As envisaged by the Sixth Schedule to the Constitution of India, which was adopted on 26 January, 1952, six autonomous districts with District Councils came up in Assam—the Mizo District Council being one such district. Regional Council was set up in the Pawi-Lakher Region in southern Mizoram. The Advisory Council had been dissolved in November 1951 and the election to the District Council was held on 4 April 1952. The total strength of the Council was 24, of which 18 were to be elected and six nominated. Out of 18 seats, 17 were won by the Mizo Union and one by UMFO. The District Council was inaugurated by Bishnuram Medhi, Chief Minister of Assam on 25 April 1952.

Under the Constitution, the District Council has law making powers concerning :

(1) Management of land and forests other than reserve forest;

(2) Use of canal or water for the purpose of agriculture;

(3) Regulation of the practice of *jhum;*

(4) Establishment of village or town committee and matters relating to village or town administration including public health and sanitation.

(5) Appointment or succession of chiefs or headmen;

(6) Inheritance of property;

(7) Marriage and divorce; and

(8) Social customs.

The District Council also has the power to constitute village councils and courts, appoint its officers and to prescribe procedures.

The Regional Council exercises all these functions within its area. There are certain exclusive jurisdictions of the District Council, which covers primary schools and the medium of instruction for them, dispensaries, markets, cattle pounds, ferries, fisheries, roads and waterways. The District or Regional Council has financial powers to levy taxes, fees, tolls, etc. over the subjects it is empowered to legislate. It also has the power to control or regulate money lending or trading by non-tribals within its area.

The first budget of the Council in 1952-53 was Rs. 17,175—which was mainly for establishment. From the start, the Council suffered from chronic financial inadequacy despite a grant announced by Prime Minister Jawaharlal Nehru during his visit to Mizoram in October 1952.

Village Councils and the Abolition of Chieftainship : Through the sustained pressure of the Mizo Union, the Assam Government passed the Lushai Hills (Acquisition of the Chief's Rights) Act in 1954. In August 1954, the rights and interests of 259 Chiefs in the District Council area were taken over by the Council and the Regional Council assumed those of 50 Chiefs in the Pawi-Lakher Region. Village Councils were constituted to perform basically the same functions as hitherto discharged by the Chiefs and their *Upas*. The Mizo Union won the election to all the Village Councils, which was held on 24 July 1954, thus vindicating its stand for the abolition of chieftainship.

Demand for a Hill State : As they experienced some measure of autonomy within the confines of the Assam state, the Hills people started demanding for more. In 1953, the United Mizo Freedom Organisation (UMFO) passed a resolution demanding the formation of a hill state consisting of Manipur. Tripura, the Autonomous Districts of Assam and the North Eastern Frontier Agency (now Arunachal Pradesh). The attempt to impose the Assamese language as the official language of the state and the alleged discrimination by the Assam government against these areas were other reasons advanced. The resolution was one of several submitted to the States Reorganisation Commission (SRC), which was visiting Assam in 1954. (The Commission was charged to look into demands in various parts of India for re-demarcation of state boundaries or reconstitution of new states and to make recommendations to the Government of India). The Mizo Union also cited 'Assam's discrimination' against hill people as the source of the clamour for a separation from Assam and demanded for the integration of the Mizo inhabited areas of Manipur and Tripura with Mizo district.

The SRC did not recommend creation of a Hill State; instead urged a review of the powers and the functioning of the district councils. The Nagas had boycotted the SRC. Most tribal leaders and their people were unhappy with its recommendations. The leaders met at Aizawl in 1955 and formed the Eastern India Tribal Union (EITU) to demand the creation of a hill state comprising the hill districts of Assam. The UMFO merged with KITU. As some parties like the Mizo Union did not join the EITU, a more inclusive forum to work for the same demand was set up at a meeting of hill leaders at Shillong on 6 and 7 July 1960. The forum was called All Party Hill Leaders Conference (APHLC), which resolved at its meeting at Haflong in November 1960 that the hill districts should separate from Assam and form an eastern frontier state.

In 1961, Assamese became the official language of the state, amid vociferous protests by hill leaders. Disillusionment felt by the hill leaders with the government in Delhi and with the state authorities in Assam, in particular, crystallized into bitter opposition to their continued inclusion within Assam.

On its part, the Central Government offered what was termed the Scottish Pattern of autonomy, which still fell far short of the autonomy expected by the hill people, let alone, statehood. The Mizo Union boycotted outright the Commission designated to work out the details of the Pattern as it stuck to a demand for statehood for the Mizo populated areas. No Mizo leaders could afford to be moderate any longer. The more radical they appeared, the more they appeared to gain in popular support.

The Mizo National Front (MNF) and Insurgency

Such was the situation in Mizoram when Laldenga, the founder of the Mizo National Front, came on the political arena in 1961. Opportunely for him, a famine brought about by an explosion of rat population resulting from the flowering of bamboos (called *mautam)* had ravaged the entire Mizoram hills two years earlier. Resentment against the Assam government for its "delayed and negligent" famine relief operations was high. A number of voluntary bodies sprung up to provide relief to the famine stricken people. The Mizo National Famine Front launched by Laldenga in 1960 was one such an organization, which achieved a striking success in enlisting volunteers. The Front dropped the word "Famine" from its name and, on 22 October 1961, became the Mizo National Front (MNF), a political party with an avowed aim of achieving an independent and sovereign Mizoram. (A copy of the Memorandum submitted to the Prime Minister of India, demanding independence, is at Appendix D). The party grew rapidly, especially amongst the youth. By 1963, it managed to gain in a bye-election two seats of the State Assembly vacated by the Mizo Union as well as 145 Village Councils. However, the Mizo Union retained its primacy in the rural areas, winning 220 Village Councils.

Insurgency : Once the MNF declared 'independence' as its goal, it followed that it would have to resort to armed struggle to try and force the Indian government to concede independence to Mizoram. After preparing for three years, on 28 February 1966, the MNF volunteers commenced an armed struggle for independence and attacked different Government stations all over Mizoram. On 1 March it declared independence for Mizoram. Laldenga and sixty others signed the declaration, which appealed to all independent countries to recognize 'independent' Mizoram. With some lulls m the fighting, the rebellion 'officially' lasted 20 years, till the MNF armed cadres laid down their arms upon the signing of the so-called Peace Accord in 1986, technically termed 'Memorandum of Settlement." (Appendix E).

A brief assessment of the insurgency movement as a whole, however, may be relevant. The primary question that has often been raised is whether Laldenga actually intended to lead the MNF into an open rebellion against the government of India. It has been argued that he was exploiting the disgruntled youth of the time in order to propel himself into political prominence. An ex-serviceman and ex-clerk of the District Council, suspended for misappropriation of funds, Laldenga had been a political nobody. He was no doubt an exceptionally charismatic demagogue. On the other hand, there was no doubt that most of the MNF cadres, particularly the educated, had been fully aware of the inevitability of a protracted armed struggle and had been prepared for it, believing that independence would ultimately be a possibility. Even if Laldenga had not intended it originally, his own followers would have made rebellion inexorable. The question for him then really became how and when to end the insurgency.

According to Biakchhunga, who served as Chief of the MNF Army from 1971 to 1978 and then briefly acted as President, citing the urgency to "make contacts with foreign powers" Laldenga and his family along with a small escort left Mizoram for East Pakistan on the night of the uprising itself, *i.e.* 28 February 1966. He came back to Mizoram for about a week in December of that year to attend the first MNF Parliament Session at Sialsir village. These were the two occasions on which Laldenga was personally present in Mizoram throughout the duration of the rebellion. At the Parliament Sitting, Laldenga handed over the entire task of running the underground government that had been set up by the MNF to the Vice-President. Lalnunmawia, who kept his charge from December 1966 to May 1969. During this period, the bulk of the MNF underground activists remained within Mizoram. They then moved south to Chittagong Hills in East Pakistan in early 1969. On 20 May 1969, Laldenga again took over the Presidency of the MNF from Lalnunmawia. Since then, most of the rebel activities were carried out on specific missions directed from outside India. Hnam Kalsiam or Nation Building, Biakchhunga 1996 and personal interview with him).

Soon after Laldenga reclaimed the overall charge of the movement, he secretly sent Rozama and Vanlalngaia, ranking Intelligence Officers of the MNF, as emissaries to make contact with the officials of the Indian government. Though these messengers were arrested by the Indian Police at Karimganj on 5 July 1969, before they could reach Delhi, the result of their interrogations by the Police was bound to have been conveyed to the Indian Intelligence. It may thus be safely assumed that the Indian authorities became aware of Laldenga's readiness to end the insurrection on a bargain. Vanlalngaia said to this writer on 11 August 2004, "On that fateful day when Laldenga dispatched us to make peace overtures to the Indian officials, I realized that the struggle for independence ended then and there." This was around the time the 'sub-state' of Meghalaya, comprising the Garo Hills and the Khasi and Jantia Hills, was being formed. Mikir hills and North Cachar Hills were given option to join the sub-state. It became apparent that Meghalaya, without firing a single bullet, would soon attain full statehood. The future of Mizo Hills, however, significantly remained to be decided.

As for Laldenga's "mission" to mobilize foreign governments for aid to the MNF movement, on account of which he had absented himself for nearly three years from the scene of the real struggle, his performance seemed rather dismal. The Inter Services Intelligence (ISI) of Pakistan, which was always looking for an opportunity to fish in India's troubled political waters, naturally facilitated his move to East Pakistan and later to West Pakistan or rather Pakistan after the creation of Bangladesh. Even the ISI did not seem to lavish him with funds. The current Chief Minister of Mizoram, Zoramthanga, then Private Secretary to Laldenga, often speaks today in public speeches of the times when they had to "pray" all night to God to provide them with needed funds and of how miraculously they were always provided. The reason behind the ambivalence of the ISI towards the MNF must have arisen from the suspicion that Laldenga was not resolute in the struggle he had initiated, a suspicion that was beginning to exasperate the educated cadres of the MNF soon after the move to East Pakistan. China's assistance to MNF either in the form of weapons or training seemed nominal. It was also apparently a one time affair and, according to

Biakchhunga, it was discontinued due to "difficulties of communication."

It became clear that from late 1969 onwards, Laldenga was secretly searching ways to make contact and commence negotiations with the government of India. However, this was about the time India was preoccupied with the liberation movement in East Pakistan and later with the birth pangs of Bangladesh. Apparently, the impending fall of East Pakistan greatly demoralized the MNF leadership. Zoramthanga, the then Private Secretary to Laldenga, even proposed on 16 December 1971 that they might surrender to the advancing Indian forces at Subalong. (Biakchhunga). The main forces of the MNF were also later occupied in settling down in the Arakan Hills of Myanmar, as they could no longer stay in independent Bangladesh. As Laldenga and his personal staff were on their way to Islamabad, former Vice-President, Lalnunmawia and a Minister, R. Zamawia were deputed on 18 December 1971 once again to sound out the Indian authorities for peace talks.

It was only since November 1973, after Laldenga settled down in Pakistan, that regular contacts between the MNF and Indian authorities begun. In a letter to Prime Minister Indira Gandhi dated 20 August 1975, Laldenga stated, "Since November 1973, my officials have been meeting your representatives to discuss the question of restoration of peace and normalcy in Mizoram..." In this letter, he asserted that the solution of the Mizoram problem could be found within the framework of the Indian Constitution and revealed that his senior colleagues did not know as yet his overtures to the Indian government. He requested "the utmost secrecy" be kept about his peace moves and sought the help of the government in persuading his radical colleagues to come to the negotiating table.

The story after this in a nutshell was that of Laldenga

and his coterie working together with the Indian Intelligence in the attempt to "persuade" the "radical elements" in the MNF to accept a settlement within the Indian Constitution. Those who could not be persuaded were pressured or sidelined or marginalized. However, it took much effort and time before the entire MNF outfit could be brought around to agree to cease fire. Settlement could perhaps have come earlier, but for the fact that the political situation within Mizoram from 1979 to 1984 was such that no arrangement could be made for Laldenga to become the Chief Minister without election, the minimum prize that he would have wished for, for giving up arms. During this period, the People's Conference Party, a regional political party, was in power and the Chief Minister, Brigadier (Rtd) Thenphunga Sailo would not give up his office unless he was defeated in an election.

It was only after the Indian National Congress (I), a party that could be directed and controlled from Delhi came to power in 1984 that the prospect for peace in Mizoram became bright. The then Chief Minister, Lal Thanhawla offered to vacate his office in favour of the MNF chief Laldenga if that would facilitate the peace negotiations, much to the relief of the people who were by now extremely frustrated at the protracted negotiations.

After resumption of talks in late 1984, the two sides finally came to a settlement in early 1986. The Memorandum of Settlement was signed on 30 June 1986. The text of the accord is at Appendix E.

As provided for in the agreement between the Indian National Congress and the MNF, upon the signing of the peace accord Laldenga was installed as the Chief Minister of Mizoram on 21 August 1986. Before the signing of the record. Laldenga had amended the constitution of the MNF making it a political party. The MNF became a regional party in Mizoram.

Major Political Parties : Indian National Congress

The District Branch of the Indian National Congress was established by A. Thanglura on 11 April 1961 when Mizoram was still one of the districts of Assam. Its presence in Mizoram remained uneventful and lacking in influence till the election to the fourth and last District Council in April 1970, in which the Congress won 10 out of 18 elected seats. In the election to the newly created Union Territory of Mizoram held in April 1972, it won six seats whereas the Mizo Union got 21 seats out of the 27 elected members. Soon after this election, the Mizo Union, which had formed the government in the Union Territory, decided to merge with the Congress. Since then, the party has been playing a leading role in the affairs of Mizoram, either as the ruling government or in opposition.

For the first time the Congress came on its own into power in Mizoram in the 1984 election to the UT Assembly. It won 20 seats against 8 by the PC. Lal Thanhawla, the President of the party, became the youngest Chief Minister in the country on May 5. 1984. Upon the conclusion of the peace settlement between the MNF and the central government, however, Lal Thanhawla vacated the Chief Minister's office and the MNF President. Laldenga became the Chief Minister on August 21, 1986. He became the Deputy Chief Minister instead.

After a short break, the Congress again formed the Mizoram government, upon winning the sixth Assembly election in 1989 with 23 MLAs out of the 40 seats. The last time the Congress came into power was in the election to the Assembly held on November 3, 1993. It contested the election jointly with the Mizoram Janata Dal, a name briefly assumed by the People's Conference party led by Brig. T. Sailo. The two parties together won 24 seats as against 14 by the MNF and two Independents. Though the People's Conference Party or Janata Dal withdrew from the coalition government after 5 months, with the support of eight MLAs who defected from the MNF and the PC, the Congress government managed to serve its full term. In the State elections held after this, in 1998 and 2003, the Congress won only 6 and 12 seats respectively and thus had to be in opposition. To some justifiable extent, the Congress has been blamed for bringing corruption into the politics of Mizoram. Its refusal to continue development plans initiated by its predecessor Ministry, the Sailo government, is responsible for the lack of infrastructure in Mizoram. And these are the main reasons for its failure to come back into power. Credit must be given to the introduction by the Congress of the New Land Use Policy (NLUP), a plan to replace the practice of jhuming by settled cultivation, even though it was largely unsuccessful. The concept behind the policy has highlighted the seriousness of the problem.

Lal Thanhawla remains the President of the Party and as the leader of the largest group of MLAs (12) in opposition, he is the official Leader of the Opposition in the State Assembly. At present, the party is the second largest political party in Mizoram.

Mizo National Front (MNF)

Founded on 22 October 1961 as a revolutionary party to fight for independence of Mizoram by Laldenga, it was transformed into a normal political party on the day of the signing of the peace accord between it and the government of India. Upon the death of Laldenga, Zoramthanga was elected President of the party and remains so till today.

For the first time, the MNF contested the 1987 election and won with a 25 member's majority. Congress won 13 and PC two. Its rule was, however, short-lived. As two of its MLAs broke away from the party on August 9, 1988, the Ministry was reduced to a minority and the Assembly had to be dissolved. After a brief President's

Rule, another election was held on January 21, 1989, in which the Congress replaced the MNF government.

In the next two terms of the State Assembly, the MNF remained in opposition and staged a come back only in the 1998 election. It fought the election jointly with the MPC and the two parties together won 33 seats. Zoramthanga, the MNF leader, was installed as the Chief Minister while the MPC President, Lalhmingthanga, became the Deputy Chief Minister. As the MNF on its own has a majority in the legislature, the MPC members were evicted from the Ministry within less than a year. In the last Assembly election held on November 20, 2003, the MNF won 21 seats; and in alliance with two independents and 1 former MPC member, it formed the present Ministry. It thus remains the largest political party in Mizoram.

Corruption in high places appears to be less rampant in the present MNF government than it was in the time of the Congress. However, its practice of openly bestowing favours to loyal party workers is its drawback. While such a practice may earn votes at the time of elections, it prevents the government departments from fully focusing on development works. It has also yet to work out a thorough going plan for infrastructure development, for example, in the energy sector, without which no effective development programmes can be pursued in Mizoram.

Mizoram People's Conference (MPC)

Upon retirement from the Army in early 1974, Brigadier Thenphunga Sailo set up a Human Rights Committee to monitor and record human right abuse and excesses committed by the security forces, especially on the innocent civilians, in the course their operations against the insurgents. The reports prepared by this group were brought to the notice of the central government, with the result that the security forces became more careful and less high-handed in their operations. The Human

Rights Committee became very popular and many people hailed Brigadier T. Sailo as a father figure and protector.

With a view to playing an effective role in the affairs of Mizoram, the Committee thought of setting up a political party and convened a general conference of people of all walks of life. The conference decided to form a political party named 'People's Conference' (PC) on April 17, 1975. Brig. T. Sailo was elected the first President. It was the first party in Mizoram, which clearly defined its objectives, particularly with regard to development plans for the territory. Its candidate, Dr. Rothuama won the 1976 Parliamentary election with an impressive margin.

In the second election to the Mizoram Assembly, PC won 23 out of 30 seats and its President Brig. T. Sailo became Chief Minister on June 2, 1978. However, due to internal dissension, the PC government fell; the Assembly was dissolved and President's Rule had to be imposed on November 11, 1978. After five months of President's Rule, fresh elections to the Assembly were held again. This time also, the People's Conference won a majority of 18 MLAs and new Ministry headed by Sailo was sworn in on May 8, 1979. The ministry served its full term of five years but was ousted in the 1984 election by the Congress (I). For the first time in Mizoram, the Sailo government embarked upon infrastructure development for energy, transport and communications, rail links, etc. Despite the continuing insurgency situation, it managed to lay substantial foundation for future development work. However, these development foundations have not been consistently pursued by successive ministries till today.

The PC party was later renamed Mizoram People's Conference (MPC) party. Apart from briefly sharing power in coalition ministries with the Congress(I) in 1994 and with the MNF in 1998, it has not been in power since 1989. With only two MLAs in the current legislature, it looks destined to disappear from the political landscape.

(The present writer convinced the President of Mizo Union and key advisers of the advantages that might accrue then from merging with an all India party. He also drafted the terms of the merger).

Social Organisations : YMA : The Young Mizo Association

The YMA, which was founded in 1935, with a total membership of 145004 in 2003 in the northern zone alone, is still thriving. Its membership is open to both officials and non-officials. All political parties cultivate its support, though it has managed to remain to be seen as neutral and non-political. Its role in the preservation of traditional values and useful customs, and even in the maintenance of law and order is pivotal. Its approach to issues concerning the community is often conservative and at times tends to infringe on individual liberties.

Mizo Hmeichhe Insuihkhawn Pawl (MHIP)

This Association of Mizo Women was founded in the early 50s and has spread all over the slate. Its available membership figure for the 5 districts of northern Mizoram in 2003 was 1,57,302, making it probably the largest NGO in India. Its motto is : To help others, though in the course of lime, it has tended to concentrate on women issues. The YMA and, MHIP are the two main NGOs, which are engaged in effective social work and charitable activities in the rural areas. As leaders of large and influential organizations, the leadership of these associations in the urban areas tends to waste time and energy in irrelevant popular activities.

Mizoram Upa Pawl (MUP) or Mizoram Senior Citizen's Association

Founded in the early 80s, she association in 2003 had 50400 members in the northern zone of Mizoram. The membership is open to men and women above the age of

50. Its aim is to preserve traditional values and to work for the welfare of senior citizens.

Mizo Zirlai Pawl (MZP) or Mizo Student's Association

The association was established in 1935 and has since gained preeminence as the forum of the youth, it was originally concerned with the interests and welfare of the Mizo students, especially m the endeavour to create understanding and unity among them. In addition, it has now transformed into a non-partisan political pressure group on various issues affecting not only the student community but also Mizoram as a whole. Its leaders have also increasingly used it as a staging ground for entry to full time participation in politics.

The Churches

The Mizos take pride in proclaiming that their community is 100 percent Christian. Christianity is indeed omnipresent m the life of the community.

This is amply demonstrated by the fact that no community activities can commence without what is termed *'hunserh,'* a brief dedication service where some verses of the Bible is read, followed by a prayer for blessings on the particular activity of the occasion.

The established Churches are the Presbyterians in the north and the Baptists in the South. The Roman Catholic Church is also present and is slowly gaining adherents. There are a few other denominational groups with widely differing number of followers. The Churches organize their activities under various wings such as the youth, women, children and a common social front. In addition to the regular Church Services, a number of camping crusades are held every year.

The liberal minded often allege that too much time is wasted on religious activities. The imposing presence of religion in the life of the community also appears to promote conformity while, in real terms, it does little to reform the daily lives of its adherents. As the result, uprightness in appearance and form without inner reform, indeed, hypocrisy seems to bee slowly becoming a norm in Mizo society.

Economic Profile

The economic life of the Mizos has always been centered around *jhum* or shifting cultivation. During the rule of the chiefs, the chiefs distributed jhum land ever year from the land under their control to their subjects. The Village Councils now do the allocation of jhum land by letting the villagers draw lots. The sizes of the plots used to be usually between 1.5 and 3 hectares per family, depending on the number of able-bodied persons in a family. However, as land available for *jhuming* is becoming less due to allotment of lands to individuals, plot sizes in recent years have become smaller. Besides, the earning per man day in this practice of farming is so low that many young people now prefer to work as wage earners in services and other sectors.

Jhum sites selection in done in November/December and by mid February, felling of the vegetation in usually finished. The dried vegetation must be set on fire preferably before the early rains in mid March. After the unburned debris of trees and bamboos are cleared, the plot is ready for cultivation.

The crops grown in the plots are mixed Paddy remains the principal crop and others that are inevitably grown are common vegetables and pulses for household consumption. Nowadays, cash crops such as ginger, tumeric, bird's eye chilly, oil seeds, maize, sugar cane, etc. are grown. A variety of spices, herbs, flowers, fruits and oil seeds like sesame, soybeans and mustard and cotton can grow well in Mizoram. The basic problem is the method of farming the land, that is, the practice of shifting cultivation, which causes depletion of forests and biodiversity, soil erosion as also a complex of environmental damages. Crop yields from unleveled lands cannot be very high either and new scientific thinking says that it is better to improve them through scientific methods than through replacement with plantations which represent an alien interaction into a scientific pro-environmental as well as silk zone. It is important to better jhum restrict its spread and involve micro-credit agencies and give better alternative markets. The jhumias is poor and marginalized. His work and that of his fellow—to be and improved. That lives and income grow, instead of condemning them with the prejudice of government and insensitive "encouragements". Alternative arrangements such as settled farming have not worked. This remains the basic task facing the governments that has yet to be structurally dealt with. Attempts to change the practice of jhuming through the programmes initiated by the Congress under the New Land Use Policy and by the present MNF government under the Mizoram Intodelh (Self Sufficiency) Project (MIP) have so far made no substantial difference.

Indicators of Current Status

The following selected facts and figures may help in assessing the current economic standing of Mizoram :

Population—891058; females per 1000 males : 938; persons per square kilometer : 42; rural population : 53.9 per cent. (2001 Census).

Food grains production—paddy : 109,205 MT; maize : 14879 MT and pulses : 4986 MT. (2002-2003).

Per capita income—Rs. 7517 (1993-94 in current prices). Compare this with an all India average of Rs. 7185.

Employment breakup—farmers (mainly *jhuming*) 66 per cent; manufacturing—5 per cent and government employees, trading and services—29 per cent.

Sources of the domestic product of the State—40 per cent from farming, 15 per cent from manufacturing and 45 per cent from government employees, trading and services.

According to the central Planning Commission, those who were in 1993 below the poverty line (BPL) in Mizoram were 26 per cent (about 200000) whereas the State government reckoned it to be 56.07 per cent.

Literacy is 89.49 per cent as compared to all India's 52 per cent. While in literacy among the states of India Mizoram is placed second after Kerala, the drop out rate from Grades I—V in 1994-95 was 63 per cent. This clearly shows that the number of those who are able to go to High Schools is quite limited. For examples, in Aizawl District the number of enrolment in Primary Schools in 2001 was 33874, those who went on to High Schools was 18389 and those went to Higher Secondary Schools was 5705. This is largely in an urban area where the schools are relatively well equipped with teaching staff and instruments. The corresponding figures for Champhai District, mostly rural area, are—Primary School. 14577. High School, 4947 and Higher Secondary School, 402. (Figures for the whole State are not yet available).

Resources

Mizoram has no known mineral resources, which are commercially exploitable. The few surveys that the Geological Survey of India and the Oil and Natural Gas Commission have conducted so far did not find any. In addition to human resources, the only natural resources of Mizoram are its fertile but fragile soil, forests, sub-tropical climatic condition in slopes of varied elevation and highly conducive to growth of various fruits, flowers and crops, and its numerous rivers. About these natural resources have already been detailed.

Infrastructure

As noted earlier, Mizoram is critically deficient in infrastructure development particularly in the physical kind. The few initiatives taken by the Sailo Ministry in 1979-84, especially in the power sector, have remained unimplemented. A brief account of what has been done in this sector will show the actual state of affairs.

Energy

The potential in this sector is enormous, particularly in the generation of electricity by means of the hydropower. Beside the active investigations that were conducted on hydropower projects such as fuirial (60 MW), Tuivai (210 MW) and Serlui-R (12 MW), the Bairabi Hydel Project (120 MW) on the Tlawng or Daleshwari River had been ready for execution in the early 80s in the tenure of the Sailo Ministry. The successor Ministries continued to ignore the project. It has now been revised with a reduced capacity of 80 MW. With the new policy of commercialization of large hydro projects in India, however, the State government faces a serious funding problem, unless the central government makes exception for Mizoram.

The North East Electric Power Corporation (NEEPCO) has taken up Tuirial and Tuivai, but progress is slow. Only 12 percent of the electricity produced by these projects will be owned by the State and the rest of its requirement will have to be purchased. The Power Department is currently undertaking five Mini Micro Hydel Projects : Tuirial-B (12 MW); Maicham (11 MW); Tuipanglui (3 MW) : Kau-Tlabung (3 MW) and Lamsial (500 KW).

The Power Projects under investigation are : Kolodyne I—120 MW (completed and pending for techno-economic clearance); Kolodyne II—300 MW;

Tuipui—30 MW; Bairabi II—50 MW; Tuichang—30 MW; Turini 60 MW and Tuivawl—50 MW.

The current position regarding supply and consumption of electric power is : Estimate of requirement : 102 MW as against existing supply of 72 MW; Electricity generated by the State : 22 MW (Diesel—16 MW and Mini/Micro—6 MW); Purchased from neighbouring States : 50 MW and shortage : 50 MW.

Transports System

The length of the network of roads in the State as on March 31, 2001 was 4122.37 kilometers, which included 328 kilometers of National Highways constructed and maintained by Border Road Organisation (BRO). Motor-able roads connected 704 villages and the road length per 100 square kilometers was 19.54 km. (The Draft Five Year Plan for 2002—2007). Not only is construction of roads in the hilly terrains difficult, maintenance of these roads is extremely expensive. Often there are days when some areas remain inaccessible due to blockage of roads by landslides or other damages caused by heavy rains. Except for the National Highways and a few leading roads, much of the road length in Mizoram is unusable for load bearing heavy vehicles.

The man supply route for Mizoram is the National Highway-54 from Silchar in Assam to Aizawl and beyond. If this road is blocked even for a few days, many consumer goods become scarce. The other roads linking Mizoram with Manipur and Tripura are not yet pliable by heavy vehicles on a regular basis. Even otherwise, these States cannot supply the requirements of Mizoram as they are equally remote from the centers of manufactured goods as Mizoram is.

Mizoram's hilly terrain limits the scope of rail and air links. There are not many stretches of level land where long runways can be made. On December 12, 1998, the first airport was opened at Lengpui, near

Aizawl, where medium-sized jet aircraft can land and take off. No facilities for transportation of air cargo are available yet. Nor is there any flight landing facility. The entire airport building is over-large, over-expensive and underutilized. It is another example of the Center's partnership and local—without a proper cost-benefit analysis. The only rail link to Mizoram is by a narrow gauge railroad, which terminated at Bairabi, a town situated at the bank of Daleshwari, 3 km. from Assam border. Surprisingly, the urgency of development and expansion of this lone rail link does not seem to register with the present authorities.

Two Inland Waterways, on the Karnafuli river between Chittagong and Demagiri in Mizoram and on the Daleshwari river, that were in much use during the British rule became virtually unused after the partition of India. After the construction of the Kaptai Dam on the Karnafuli in Bangladesh, a huge area around Demagiri has been submerged. This created a good potential for inland water transport in the area, provided understanding in the matter can be reached between the governments of Bangladesh and India. The Tlawng or Daleshwari joins the Barak in Cachar and was used by the Mizos for travel and transportation down to areas, which have become Bangladesh, and even to Shillong and the plains of Assam in India. Except for floating down forest produce like bamboo and timber, Mizoram hardly uses this route any more, perhaps, due to uncertain transit facilities beyond Cachar.

The Barak river and a long stretch of its tributary, Tuivai, was also much used by the inhabitants of northeast Mizoram and the southeast area of Manipur for supply and travel route. Due to insurgent activities across the rivers on the Manipur side, the use of these waterways has become erratic. The Kolodyne in South Mizoram can also, perhaps, be harnessed for transit to Akyab in Myanmar, once the projected hydro dams on it are constructed.

Yet 4.7 million Rupees was earmarked for development of inland water-ways in the plan for 2002-2007—a reflection of poor planning and perception and especially when one consider the huge investment in air links.

Communications

As the network of post offices depends for the dispatch of mails on the physical transport system, its services are relatively slow. Non-courier mails from Delhi take a week or more to reach Aizawl while Speed Post takes about 3 to 4 working days. The population per Post Office in 1993-94 was 1920. As of June 2003, there were nine telephone exchanges in Mizoram with working connections in the Secondary Switching Area, numbering 54255 subscribers. The telephone equipment currently has the capacity for 73120 connections. Mizoram is now linked by an underground optic fibre wires. The telecom system still does not have the capacity for information highway. During the year preceding June 2003, 1027 new Internet connections were provided.

Water Supply

Water supply during the dry season has always been a special problem of Mizoram. The villages were traditionally situated on hilltops, as a part of the strategy for defence against on coming enemies. The practice has still continued. Thus, the only viable way to provide water supply to these settlements is to pump river water to a reservoir located on a high point above the settlements and distribute the water by gravity. This is being done for the urban areas and some selected villages. With the chronic shortage of electric power supply, it will be a long way before adequate supply of water, if at all, can be arranged for the people of Mizoram.

The Department of Public Health Engineering, which is responsible for water supply and sanitation, also promotes tapping of underground water by means of hand pumps. A number of these pump sets have been distributed yearly. With severe depletion of underground water during dry season, this is a poor supplement to water supply work. Harvesting of rainwater is a practice long known in Mizoram. Since there is usually excess of rainwater during the rainy season, with improved collection, storage and distribution facilities, rainwater can be gainfully harvested and substantially augment the water supply during the dry season. The government of Mizoram has yet take meaningful initiatives in this direction.

Human Resources

The department of School Education and that of the Higher and Technical Education are in charge of human resource development. Like in the rest of India, a scheme for quality education for all (Sarva Shiksha Abhyian) was introduced in 2003 in Mizoram. Under this scheme, all children in the age group of 6 to 14 years are expected to attend school. In 2003 there were 8.985 out of school children from this age group as compared to 17.99 in 2002 representing a signal progress. For the age group of 15 to 35 years, a new project Called 'Eradication of Residual Illiteracy' (ERIP) has been introduced. With the implementation of these two projects, the State expects to achieve full literacy by 2007.

The main weakness of the education system has been the continuing lack of technical equipment and quality for science and technical education in school level. This has cumulatively resulted in a very low proportion of scientists and technologists among the educated Mizos. There is also a distinct lack of what might be termed scientific temper among the intellectuals. At present, except for veterinary sciences, there is no degree level school for engineering or medical subjects. The Mizoram University which opened in 2001, has not been able to introduce courses in physical sciences.

The Present Position of Educational Institutions in Mizoram

Primary Schools : 1225, Middle Schools : 777, High Schools : 408, Colleges : 30, Polytechnics : 2; Teachers Training Institutes : 2, University : 1. There is a University of Veterinary Sciences run by the central Government. There is also a Regional Institute for Nursing, Laboratory Technicians and Pharmacology owned by the North East Council (NEC). There are a few departmentally managed, diploma levels, vocational training institutes for information technology, mechanics, etc.

Public Health

In terms of persons per public health care establishments, Mizoram may have the most health care facilities among the States of India. With 14 hospitals in the State, the number of persons per hospitals bed in 191 was already 627, the lowest among the North East States. The next lowest, Arunachal's was 755 as compared to all India for 1324 persons. But this is about quantity, not quality. The main problem affecting the health care system in Mizoram, like in education, is the lack of equipment, medicines and specialists, compounded by erratic and fluctuating electric power supply. Without adequate diagnostic, radiological and other laboratory facilities, the most competent physician cannot be effective. Because of this persisting problem, most patients with complicated cases, especially those who require sophisticated surgery, had to be referred to private medical institutions outside Mizoram in such places as Guwahati, Kolkata, Vellore, Chennai, Delhi and Bombay. This not only creates easily avoidable hardships for the people, but is also a serious drain on the finances of the State since so many of its employees undergo medical treatment outside the State. The fact that patients who need bandages or syringes have often to buy them from private suppliers outside the hospital amply demonstrates the seriousness of the situation.

The government is currently constructing a hospital designed to serve as Referral Hospital, to be so equipped and staffed as to obviate the necessity of sending patients to places outside the State. With the basic foundation of the health care system in disarray as it is now, it is doubtful if the government will be competent enough to manage such a hospital.

The number of health care centers managed by the government are as follows : Subsidiary Health Centers : 351; Primary Health Centers : 58; Community Health Center : 9.

Banking and Finance

The common people in Mizoram seldom use banking instruments for their financial transactions. They mostly use cash money. Those who use banks do it mainly for saving or term deposits. Taking loans from banks against collaterals is also popular. The number of 'bad loans' is said to be high, particularly those loans extended by the first financial institution set up by the State, Zoram Industrial Development Corporation (ZIDCO).

ZIDCO was set up by the State government in collaboration with the Industrial Development Bank of India (IDBI) to foster the start up and the growth of industries in Mizoram. Another semi-financial institution, Mizoram Khadi and Village Industries Board (KVI) in 1986, was set up to promote various types of small scale and cottage industries. These two institutions extend credits to individuals and cooperative bodies for starting small industries. Part of the funding for the loans they service comes from the central credit institutions for development.

There are two central government sponsored financial institutions. North Eastern Development Finance Corporation (NEDFI) and National Bank for Agriculture and Rural Development (KABARD), which have recently opened branch offices in Mizoram with junior official representatives. These two have yet to make substantial contribution to the development of Mizoram. Full Hedged banks that are operating in Mizoram are : State Bank of India (SBI); Vijayya Bank; United Commercial Bank; Mizoram Cooperative Apex Bank; Mizoram Rural Bank and Mizoram Urban Cooperative Bank. The Credit-Deposit ratio in 1996 was 16.

The banks in Mizoram were not authorized to deal in foreign currency exchange until recently. The State Bank of India is now authorized to do so.

Selected Economic Sectors with Prospects : Agriculture

The major agricultural crops, total yield for each crop in 2002-2003 in metric tons, and the area sown in hectares are given below :

	yield	*Area sown*		*yield*	*Area sown*
	metric ton	*hectares*		*metric ton*	*hectares*
Paddy (jhum)	67.076	41,356	WRC	33,725.0	12,905.0
HYV	8,404	2,806	Maize	14,879.0	7,489.0
Pulses	4,986	4,666	Oilseeds	5,285.0	7,132.0
Tapioca	1,330	232	Sugarcane	7,443.0	1,370.0
Potato	726	369			

As already explained elsewhere, shifting cultivation of rice is uneconomic and has no future. Alternative crops that have already been identified as suitable for Mizoram, especially horticultural crops, must be encouraged.

Horticulture

Systematic promotion of horticulture in Mizoram is recent, although plantation of fruits like orange, hatkora (of citrus family) and pineapples has been in long practice. Mizoram has been identified to be ideal for a variety of horticultural crops. The State government is now making a thrust in this sector. The crops with potential are briefly described in the following :

Production in 2002-2003 :	*Area in Ha.*	*Production : MT*
Fruits	21,150	57,858
Plantation Crops	3,478	6,844
Vegetables	7,581	40,970
Spices	7,058	36,439
Roots & Tubers	850	5,286

A. Fruits : Grape : *Bangalore Blue* is cultivated in an area of about 1,000 Ha. in the eastern high altitude area. The yield is 70-80 quintal/acre. Passion Fruit : Cultivated so far in about 2,000 hectares, it is said to grow well again the eastern region. Orange : Mandarin was popular but has declined owing to disease. It is being revived with improved seedlings. Banana—growing is getting large scale and is now marketed in Meghalaya and Assam. The variety of banana grown in Mizoram is perhaps the best in the world.

B. Spices : Turmeric—Lakadang variety as well as the traditional turmeric, native to the place, grows well. The native turmeric called 'Ai-eng' can grow as shrubs in wooded sites and can be left wild for a few years. Its roots do not deteriorate but multiply and the quality appears to improve. Promotion of this crop is at the initial stage. Only 2785 MT was harvested in 2002-2003. Ginger—has been increasingly grown, but with frequent price fluctuation, its prospect is uncertain. It also causes serious soil erosion. In 2002-2003, 47,821 MT was harvested. (This was obviously not included in the spices production listed herein earlier). Chillies—a variety of chillies has been grown. Bird's Eye chilly is indigenous to Mizoram and is the most sought after for export.

C. Plantation : Arecanut—is grown in the western and northwestern lowlands. It does not yet meet local consumption.

D. Flowers : Rose-grows well and has good prospects but not enough yet for export outside the State. Anthurium—was tried for mass production only in 2002. It is already sold as cut flower in metropolis of other States. It can be harvested in six months and appears to be better in quality than those grown in other States. Bird-of-Paradise (BOP)—was introduced two years ago. It was expected to flower in 3 years, but has done so this year. It seems to have a bright future.

Other varieties of horticultural crop being tried are black pepper, cardamom, jatropha carcus, vanilla, etc. Medicinal herbs, native to Mizoram, have also yet to be identified and the case of growing others to be explored.

Forest-Based Industry

Apart from processing horticultural crops when it has in optimum quantities, the most suitable industrial sector for Mizoram appears to be forest-based. Bamboo in particular is plentiful and is easily renewable. At present, due to the shortage of electric power, large-scale industrial plants cannot be set up.

Others

In 2002, there were 1500 cottage and small-scale industries operating and producing goods worth Rs. 370.5 million. There were 4258 registered small industries in 2003. (Mid Term Appraisal of Five-Year Plan). Animal Husbandry, Fishery, Sericulture and Tourism sectors are not yet in the take-off stage.

Tourism, however, seems to have a good potential, if international standard infrastructure and facilities can be provided. Mizoram can be projected as a unique and exotic tourist destination.

Relations with Neighbouring Regions

Apart from the inter-States interactions initiated by the North Eastern Council (NEC), the present political leadership of Mizoram does not maintain much interaction with its neighbours. This may be partly because the current party in power, the MNF, is a regional party with no direct links to other parties. However, with several problems in common with the other States in the region, such as security, law and order, infrastructure needs, health care, etc., close coordination with them cannot but be useful.

Relations with Assam

One outstanding problem with Assam is the issue of the northern boundary of Mizoram with the Cachar District of Assam. The present demarcation was specified by Section 6 of the North Eastern Areas (Reorganisation) Act. 1971. Vide Section 4.2 (1) of the Peace Accord signed with the Government of India in 1986 the MNF Party accepted it. And the then Congress government of Mizoram countersigned the Accord, implying that the State government also accepted it. The MNF and the Congress are the only two political parties, which came into power after the 1986 Accord. Since their hands are tied by the Accord they had signed, they are not in a position to dispute the boundary arrangement.

However, from the time of the Mizo District Council in the 1950s till the early 1980s, the authorities in Mizoram as well as the general public had been objecting to what was fixed first as the de facto boundary of the then District and later of the Union Territory of Mizoram. The UT government even constituted a 'Fact Finding Committee' in 1973 on the matter. The 'Summary Finding' of that committee stated, "The Mizos are unsatisfied with the line and manner in which their

Northern Boundary with Cachar was fixed arbitrarily by the British and are likely to remain so for generations to come, unless and until it is refixed based on certain reasonable grounds like historical, traditional and occupational backgrounds. From the study of the boundary fixation herein related, it is clear that there was such a line and in its final form is represented by the Inner Line of 1875."

This is not a live political issue at present, but the general public has still not accepted the boundary. NGOs like YMA and MZP have been keeping the issue alive by raising it in public and the media. And the State government may one day be forced to dispute the boundary in the future.

Under the existing Inner Line regulations, Indians other than Mizos as well as foreigners are required to obtain Inner Line Permit (ILP) before entering Mizoram. There is therefore no problem of migration from Assam into Mizoram. There is, however, a large floating population of masonries, carpenters and construction workers from Assam, particularly the Kaimganj area of Cachar, scattered all over Mizoram. Some who came without ILP or overstayed their Permit or commit crime are occasionally deported by the authorities.

As Mizoram's entire supply of manufactured and essential goods and construction materials comes from or through Assam, it cannot afford to disrupt its relationship with Assam. No trade figures are available, as interstate trades are not recorded. The entire surplus of cash crop produces of Mizoram, such as chilies, ginger, cotton, oilseeds and other product like orange and grapefruits are sold to Cachar. Way back in 1994, a group called 'Hnam Chhantu' (a group campaigning for self reliance for Mizoram) conducted a research on the extent of the dependence of Mizoram on food products of Assam. The food items selected were vegetables, cooking oil, fish and eggs. They found that the city of Aizawl alone consumed these items in one month, which cost at the time over Rs. 28 million.

Relations with Manipur

Mizo tribes or people of Mizo origin inhabit the southern and western hill areas and some parts of the northern region of Manipur. These people freely come and go. As insurgent groups have been active in these hills areas, a number of people from the area, especially the South District of Manipur, fleeing from the disturbed area, have been migrating to Mizoram. The migrants are largely accommodated and face no difficulty in integrating into the society. A National Highway from Aizawl crosses into the southeast of Manipur and there are thrice weekly flights of Indian Airlines between Aizawl and Imphal. There is a steady flow of people on both sides.

Two small insurgent outfits, based in Manipur, are occasionally active in the northern part of Mizoram. The Zomi Revolutionary Army (ZRA) claims to work for the reunification of what it terms 'Zomis' or tribes of Zo origin and is active in the Paite inhabited area of northeast Mizoram. The Hmar People Convention (Democratic) or HPC (D) demands the curving of Hmar Autonomous District Council in the Hmar tribe occupied area of mid north Mizoram and occasionally launches its activities either from Cachar Hills of Assam or southwest Manipur. Their leader, Lalhmingthang, hailed from Khawlian village of Mizoram and now usually resides at Lakhipur in Cachar District. The ZRA personnel are mostly-drawn from Paites of south Manipur while those of the HPC (D) is a mixture of Hmars from Manipur and Mizoram. Some times, the insurgents of the Manipur valley, the Meiteis, also cross over to northern Mizoram and encounter the security forces.

The Nagas demand the integration of all the Naga inhabited areas of India. If this is agreed to by the Government of India, a large chunk of northern Manipur will have to be integrated into Nagaland. In that event, the Mizo tribes of southern Manipur are likely to fight for incorporation into Mizoram. The Meitei insurgents foresee this and are steadily asserting their writ over the area. This is a possible future issue that can seriously complicate the relationship between Manipur and Mizoram.

Relations with Tripura

Mizoram and Tripura are, perhaps, the least interactive of neighbours. Some 7000 Brus, a non-Mizo ethnic group, fled from western Mizoram to Tripura in 1998 and are now encamped as refugees in two locations there. They are being looked after by the central government, though their presence could strain the services sector in the area. The refugees' claim that the Mizos tried to force them to convert into Christianity and that they had to flee Mizoram for fear of being persecuted. The Mizos amongst whom the Brus had lived and the State government vehemently denied this. They in turn claim that false rumours spread by vested interest working against Christianity in Mizoram alarmed the Brus and they migrated to Tripura of their own accord. During the last election to the Legislative Assembly of Mizoram in November 2003, there was an unsuccessful attempt by the Opposition parties and some NGOs to block the postal ballots cast by these refugees.

The Tripura Chief Minister alleged in 2003 that there were some training camps in Mizoram of the insurgent groups fighting against his government such as the All Tripura People's Liberation Organisation and the All Tripura Tiger Force. Given the mobility of the mostly hill men fighters operating against the Tripura government and their familiarity with the jungles of the 66 km. long border with Mizoram, it is quite possible that they sometimes set up shelters on the Mizoram side of the border. The present Chief Minister of Mizoram, Zoramthanga, a former rebel leader, has often been accused by the Opposition Parties of secretly enlisting the support of insurgents such as HPC (D) and ZRA and of abetting the transportation of weapons by the National Socialist Council of Nagaland (Isaac-Muivah) or NSCN (I-M) through Mizoram. These accusations have not been proved or conclusively substantiated, as there has not been constituted a formal enquiry to look into these matters.

Across the state boundary in Tripura is the Jampui Hills range, which is peopled by the Mizos in about a dozen villages. These people look towards Mizoram for their cultural succour. A number of the educated among them migrated to Mizoram and some of them occupy high official posts. They make no political demand and provide a potential useful bridge between the two States, though they have not been used as such so far.

There is no direct air link with Tripura. Two fairly good roads link the two States. There are markets along the road across Kanhmun (Mizoram) on both of the border. Some manufactured goods of daily needs and local agricultural products are traded in these markets. Some goods smuggled from Bangladesh especially processed baby foods and used clothes pass into Mizoram at this border. The trade between the two States is negligible.

External Relations : Relations with Bangladesh

In the scheme with which India has so far conducted its relationship with Bangladesh, the interests of the North East States, particularly of Mizoram, do not seem to figure prominently. (A copy of declassified Note on Indo-Bangladesh Relations is at Appendix F). This is perhaps due to the fact that the spirit and the level of bilateral cooperation have not attained the stage where detailed sub-regional concerns can be accommodated. It can also be because the Mizoram government has not made concrete structural proposals to the Government of India for beneficial relationship between the State and Bangladesh. Some officials and non-official trade representatives including the Chief Minister have recently made visits to Bangladesh with the ostensible purpose of improving the officially non-existent trading relations. Without agreed border trade posts and transit arrangements at the level of the two national governments, and improved land transport system in the border areas, there can be no meaningful trade exchanges between Mizoram and Bangladesh. The manner in which India pursues its relations with Myanmar (noted herein after) clearly attests to this. The political leadership in Mizoram sometimes spoke of proposals for setting up border trade posts along the border with Bangladesh. But such proposals do not figure in the notes of the Ministry responsible for the conduct of India's external relations.

As noted earlier, inland water transport and border trade posts, to begin with, can be easily arranged on the Karnafuli River and the Kaptai dam area in the south. What is missing appears to be close coordination by the State government with the central government. Small scale informal trade does exist in the area, with mainly bamboos and some agricultural products going into Bangladesh while fish and some merchandises come from there.

Except for a few underground Bru or Tuikuk volunteers, who are demanding a separate administrative arrangement for themselves in the northwestern area of Mizoram, the border area is largely free of insurgents. As the border with Bangladesh can be freely crossed in all seasons, however, migration from Bangladesh, particularly of the Chakmas, has long been a problem disturbing the Mizos. During the British rule and after Indian independence till 1954, the Standing Orders issued by the successive Superintendents of Lushai (Mizo) Hills District specified the Chakmas as foreigners and they were required to obtain permits to work in Mizoram. The Chakma tribe was also not listed among the minority tribes in the Indian Constitution at the time of its adoption. In the 1941 Census, there were

18 Chakmas in Mizoram and their number shot up to 15,297 in 1951. By 1971, when the Parliament passed the North Eastern Areas (Reorganisation) Act (NEAR Act), they became so numerous that the Government of India decided to set up the Chakma Autonomous District Council within Mizoram.

No public protest was orchestrated against the creation of Chakma District at the time. The then District Council formed by the Congress had not objected to the proposed NEAR Act; and on October 2, 1971 the General Assembly of the Mizo Union also accepted it. The PC party started the campaign against what it termed as the unjust creation of an administrative district for foreigners. Upon coming into power in 1979, the PC government headed by Brig. T. Sailo prepared plans to differentiate genuine Indian Chakmas, who entered Mizoram before January 26, 1952 from those Chakma foreigners who came after the adoption of Indian Constitution. It proposed to expel the latter, but could not execute its plans as the government was voted out in the 1984 election. In 1986, three MLAs from the PC party tabled a draft resolution in the State Assembly, proposing the dissolution of the Chakma Autonomous District Council. The MNF and the Congress combine voted against it and defeated it. (Proceedings of the 6th Session of the Fourth Legislative Assembly of Mizoram—pp. 161). Since then, the Chakma issue has been kept alive of and on mainly by the MZP. Political parties also often rake it up during election years. The population of Chakma District as per 2001 Census was 34,528.

Relations with Myanmar

Mizoram does not maintain direct political relationship with Myanmar, as the subject is the concern of the central government in Delhi. However, the Government of India conducts its relationship with the Myanmar regime, essentially with a view to promote and safeguard the interests of the North East States especially those bordering Myanmar. Without the active cooperation of the Myanmar authorities, India is clearly aware, the major problems of the North East, namely insurgency, underdevelopment, drugs and arms smuggling cannot be eliminated. A number of agreements that India has concluded as also its proposed projects with Myanmar clearly attest to this. Officials of the State government have invariably included in the Indian delegations when such delegations are mandated to discuss matters concerning the respective North East States. As a democracy, India is naturally bound to favour a democratic Myanmar, but its vital interests compel active cooperation with whatever regime that country has. A copy of a declassified Note on Indo-Myanmar Relations is at Appendix H.

The major project proposals that concerns Mizoram are India's offer to upgrade Rhi-Tiddim and Rhi-Falam roads linking Mizoram with Chin State, setting up of border trade post at Zokhawthar-Rhi and the Kolodyne or Kaladan Multimodal Project for a combination of inland water transport and highway linking southern Mizoram to Rakhine. These projects and other ideas of infrastructure links were already initiated during the time when the present writer was Indian Ambassador to Myanmar in the mid 1990s. It was however not possible to take them up quickly as the Myanmar authorities were at times frustratingly cautious and slow to respond. The bridge on the border river, Tiao, and a smaller one farther into Myanmar were constructed by India in that time, though. The same Mizo ethnic groups inhabit the entire regions adjoining Mizoram on the Myanmar side. And, perhaps, this is part of the reason that makes Myanmar cautious. The presence of some Chin pro-democracy activists in Mizoram and the fact that the Chin insurgents (the Chin National Army) have occasionally taken shelters inside Mizoram have not helped matters.

Though the border trade post is yet to be officially opened, the age-old traditional informal trade goes merrily on. Sources in the Customs authorities indicated that the goods "seized" during the last three years were :

2000-2001 : Rs. 13.2 million; 2002-2003 : Rs. 17.6 million; 2003-2004 : Rs. 38.6 million. These are supposed to be the costs of goods confiscated and sold in auction by the Customs. Except for narcotics and arms, real seizures are rare and so are real auctions. Except for trade in head loads of local produces within 30 kilometers on both sides of the border, the entire trade is illegal. And the Customs officials are supposed to seize all goods that come from Myanmar. However, this is not the case in reality. In the assessment of knowledgeable circles, the above figures should represent only 40 per cent of the trade or even less.

The main items of trade that come from Myanmar are : kitchen wares and gadgets; entertainment electronics like TVs, Hi-fi sets, radios; watches; electric goods; garments and other textile products; jewelleries including unworked gold and precious stones; furniture and carpentry tools; etc. Light goods and not so light goods like refrigerators and washing machines that a household needs are all available. Vendors often sell them from house to house. The products smuggled are mostly made in China, Japan, S. Korea, Thailand and Taiwan.

The goods that enter Myanmar have been estimated by the Customs to cost about the same as those that come from there. These are mainly Indian made products such as light building materials like kitchen and bathroom fittings and fixtures, bicycles and spare parts, sewing machines, all kinds of pharmaceutical products including proxyvon (which is abused), finished leather products, textiles (loin cloth pieces), plastics and linoleum products, etc. Much of the smuggled drugs and pharmaceuticals is said to reach southern China. Once legal border trade posts are established on both sides of the border and the roads across Mizoram are improved, the volume of trade exchanges is likely increase substantially. Then, there will have been an official channel that can be abused.

A large number of Myanmar "guest workers" (considering the size of Mizoram population) are in the State. Apart from a few handloom weavers from the plains of Myanmar, most of these workers are from the Chin Hills, who can become fluent in Mizo language in a matter of weeks as they belong to the same ethnic group. They are mainly engaged in menial jobs like housemaids, gardeners, drivers, farm workers and daily labours while a few are in trading and services. Before 2003, their number hovered around 40,000, about 5 per cent of the State population. In late 2003, an incident of rape of a minor girl committed by one of them triggered a widespread protest and a large number were forced to leave Mizoram, thereby attracting adverse comments even by the UN Human Rights Commission and the Amnesty International.

The State government has since started registering these workers and regulating the duration of their stay. Their number is said to have dwindled somewhat. However, the registration is done only at Zokhawthar-Rhi whereas the porous border can be crossed and is crossed at several points in the dry season. International agencies tend to regard these workers as victims of political oppression. They are more of 'economic migrants', some temporary, some not so, much like the Bangladeshis moving into India by various means elsewhere.

Regional Cooperation

Situated on the northeast end of the country, Mizoram is among the remotest of outposts in the North East. If the Partition put back the economy of the NER by a quarter-century, as reckoned by B. G. Verghese, (India's North East Resurgent, 1996), it must have put back the economy of Mizoram at least by half a century. The Partition completely cut off its main traditional market, now Bangladesh, and rendered its only inland waterways, the Karnafuli and the Daleshwari, useless. Its only fragile link to the rest of the world became by a mountainous fair weather road from Cachar to Aizawl, which was subjected to frequent blockages by landslides during the rains Though this road has been much improved and became a National Highway, it remains the main supply line for Mizoram. Fifty-seven years after independence, the isolation of Mizoram is still acute.

In order to break out of its isolation, it is an absolute must for Mizoram to have access not only to a network of transport systems but also to other infrastructure linkages in the NER and beyond. The proposed or existing Asian Highways (AH) and the Trans-Asian Railways (TAR) systems do not include Mizoram. It seems to remain a "forgotten patch" of geography. Without access to the regional or sub-regional transport systems, it will obviously not be able to benefit from the regional cooperation intended by such groups as the Bay of Bengal Initiatives on Multi-sector, Technical and Economic Cooperation, the South Asian Development Quadrangle and the Kunming Initiatives.

Following are a layman's suggestions to give additional connectivity to Bangladesh while providing Mizoram the much-needed integration to the regional network of transportation :

1. While the proposed diversion of AH from Sylhet—Karimganj (Assam)-Silchar—Jiribam—Imphal-Tamu (Myanmar) may still stand, the existing road link from Agartala—Aizawl—Champhai (Mizoram) Tiddim or Falam (Myanmar) can be extended to AH either in Bangladesh at Sylhet itself or in Cachar (Assam). This will also bring Tripura, Mizoram and Chin Hills, all underdeveloped States, into the AH network. The immediate

advantage is that there are no insurgent activities anywhere along this road whereas Jiribam—Imphal section of the other route is in the middle of insurgent area. The sections in Mizoram and Chin Hills in Myanmar pass through hilly terrains but can be upgraded without much difficulty, as they are essential supply lines constantly in use. Government of India has already offered to upgrade Rhi—Tiddim and Rhi Falam roads.

2. Linking Chittagong by Highway-cum-Inland Waterway via Kaptai dam and Demagiri (Mizoram) to the proposed Multi-Modal Highway-cum-IWT Project on the Kaladan through the existing road in Mizoram from Lunglei to Saiha is another possibility. Another road can also be constructed in south Mizoram to link with the proposed Chittagong-Yangon road, which is already in advanced stage of construction.
3. Once transit through Bangladesh by rail and road to Kolkata is possible, linking the existing network of roads in the middle section of Mizoram will not be difficult.
4. If Tripura is linked by rail across Akhaura in Bangladesh, the same can be extended to the proposed Hydel Project at Bairabi in Mizoram by road-cum-rail, thereby extending farther into Mizoram via IWT.
5. Linking Jiribam by rail or road or both to the proposed Hydel Project at Tipaimuk on the Barak River may also be feasible. This again will provide IWT links to the interior of both Manipur and Mizoram.

REFERENCES

Biakchhunga, former Army Chief and President, MNF, Nation Building (Hnam Kalsiam—Mizo), 1996, Mizoram Publication Board.

Centre for Monitoring Indian Economy. *Basic Statistics Relating to Indian Economy,* Bombay.

Centre for North East Studies and Policy Research 2004. *India's Northeast & Bangladesh, Problems & Opportunities.*

Comptroller and Auditor General of India. *Reports on Government of Mizoram,* Shillong.

Deputy Commissioner of Customs, Aizawl.

Government of Mizoram, Mid Term Appraisal for Tenth Five Year Plan (2002-2007).

————, Draft Tenth Five Year Plan (2002-2007).

————, Annual Report of Environment and Forests Department (2003).

————, Statistical Abstract of Department of Agriculture & Minor Irrigation.

————, 30 Years of Mizoram Assembly.

————, Unpublished Manuscript on Mizoram Economy and The Development of Mizoram in the Last 4 Years (2003) by the Directorate of Information & Public Relation.

————, 2003 Extracts from Draft Annual Plan of Horticulture Department for 2005 by courtesy of Samuel Rosanglura, Director of the Department, Statistical Handbook.

————, Extracts from the Records of Planning Cell of the Public Works Department (PWD)—courtesy of Mr. Sanghrima. Executive Engineer, etc.

Kyoko Inoue, Mayumi Murayama, M. Rahmatullah and Centre for Bhutan Studies. 2004. *Sub-Regional Relations in the Eastern South Asia : With Special Focus on Bangladesh and Bhutan.* Institute of Developing Economies, Tokyo.

Keivom. L. 1992, *Zoram Khawvel—I* (*The World of Zoram—Mizo*). Aizawl, M.C. Lalrinthanga.

Lalthanliana, Dr., Mizo History—Before 1900 (Mizo), 2000, Aizawl.

Lalthangliana. B., The History of Mizos In India., Burma & Bangladesh (Mizo), Remkungi. 2001, Aizawl.

Ministry of External Affairs, Government of India : Notes on Indo-Myanmar Relations and Indo-Bangladesh Relations. Personal interviews were conducted with Mrs. Neelam Deo, Joint Secretary (BSM), Mrs. Mitra Vashisht, Joint Secretary (SEA-I) and Mr. Lal Dingliana, Joint Secretary (FSI & Technical (Cooperation).

NKC. 1998, *Basic Statistics of Northeast Region,* Shillona.

Pudaite, L. T., Personal data bank based on materials collected in the process of extensive travel on both sides of the Indo-Myanmar border, experience and reports sent to Government of India as Indian Ambassador to Myanmar (1995-96) and later as a free-lance writer. The sources cannot now be listed as no record of references was made at the time.

Ray, Animesh, 1993, *Mizoram, India—Land and the People Series,* New Delhi; National Book Trust.

Sailo, Brig. T. 2001, *A Soldier's Story.* Calcutta : Cambridge Laser Print.

Sing Khaw Khai, 1995, *Zo People and Their Culture.* Lamka, Mainpur : Khampu Hatzaw.

Vanlalchhawna, Dr. 2004, *Zofate Economy* (*Economy of the Zos Mizo*), Aizawl : Zamzo Publishing House.

Yerghese, B.G., 1996, *India's Northeast—Resurgent,* Delhi : Konark Publishers (Pvt) Ltd.

Vumson, *Zo History,* Aizawl.

Zakhuma, Dr. K.M. 2001, *Political Development in Mizoram from 1946 to 1989,* Mizoram Publication Board.

APPENDIX A

Table 1. Rivers in Mizoram

No. Name of River	*Length in Kilometer (in Mizoram)*
Tlawng (Dhaleshwan)	185.15
Tiak	159.39
Chhimtuipui (Kolodyne)	130.46
Khawthlangtuipui (Karnaphuli)	128.08
Tuichang	120.75
Tuirial (Sonai)	117.53

Tuichawng	107.87
Mat	90.16
Tuipui (Khawchhak)	86.94
Tuivawl	72.45
Teirei	70.84
Tuirini	59.57
Serlui	56.35

Note : Tui in Mizo language means water.

Table 2. Hill Ranges and Peaks in Mizoram

Name of Range/Peak	*Height (in metre)*
Blue Mountain (Phawngpui)	2,157
Lengteng	2,141
Surtlang	1,967
Lurhtlang	1,935
Tantlang	1,929
Vapartlang	1,897
Chalfithlang	1,866
Hranturotlang	1,854
Zopuitlang	1,850
Tawitlang	1,837
Mawmrangtlang	1,812
Puruntlang	1,758
Hmuifangtlang	1,619
Saireptlang	1,555
Sakawrhmuituaitlang	1,535
Reiktlang	1,485
Thorantlang	1,387
Buia Hmuntlang (Aizawl)	1,383
Serkawn (Lunglei)	1,222
Laipuitlang (Aizawl)	1,188
South Hlmentlang (Aizawl)	1,179

Note : Tlang in Mizo Language mean hills.

APPENDIX B
GEOMORPHOLOGY, GEOLOGY, STRATIGRAPHY, MINERALS ETC. OF MIZORAM

Geomorphology

As the terrain in very immature in response to recent tectonism, topographical features show prominent reliefs. The major geomorphic elements observed in the area are both structural and topographic 'heights' 'depressions', 'flats' and 'slopes' sculptured on the topographic surface in a linear fashion. The physiography of the state shows north-south trending steep, mostly anticlinal., longitudinal (linear fashion) parallel to sub-parallel hill ranges and synclinal narrow valleys with series of parallel hammocks on topographic highs. In general, the western limbs of the anticlines are steeper than the eastern limbs. In many cases faulting has produce steep fault scarps.

Geology

T.H.D. La-Touche was the first geologist who explored the Mizo Hills. He took short traverses of the Mizo Hills falling within the then Assam-Arakan geological province. In his findings published in the records of the Geological Survey of India in 1891, the area was reported to consist of a great flysch facies of rocks comprising monotonous sequences of shale and sandstone which were thrown into north-south trending folds. He believed that the rocks were the southerly continuation of those of the Cachar Hills and were probably laid down in a delta or estuary of a large river during the late Tertiary period. Two main lithostratigraphic groups were established, *viz.*, the Barail and the Surma. Rocks of the Tipan group are also present. All these rocks are of Tertiary age. In 1964, M.M. Munshi mapped the rocks of the central part of northern Mizoram. He divided the rocks of the Surma series into Bhuban and Boka Bil stages. According to him the rocks were thrown into folds representing a series of longitudinal anticlinal effect.

Further studies in 1972 have led to subdivision of Bhuban and Boka Bil group into lower, middle and upper formations. Different structural patterns of Barails and Surmas were studied. The rocks belonging to Surma group have been laid down in relatively shallow water, near the shore basin under conditions as would have prevailed in lacustrine or deltaic environment.

Later studies indicate that the sedimentation took place in deep sea flysch environment by the action of turbidity current mechanism.

Stratgraphy

Of the two main lithostratigraphic groups found in Mizoram, the Barail group is of Oligocence age and has a total thickness of 4,500 m. It is further subdivided into three formations, Rengi (uppermost), Jenam and Laison (lowermost). The Surma group in of Miocene age and has a total thickness of 6,000 m. It is subdivided into two formations, the upper one being Boka Bil and the lower one being Bhuban. The Surma group overlies the Brazil group with a clearly defined unconformity.

Barail Group

This group of rocks which is in the east is different from those of the Bhuban formations lying to the weat. The Barails are predominantly shales and siltones with bands of weathered, medium grained yellowish sandstones. These are rather soft and micaceous. Some hard and dark grey compact quartzwacke bands are present. These rocks exhibit, on weathering, pink, violet, greenish grey and white colourations.

Surma Group

The lower Bhuban formation under this group contains fine grained, compact, bluish ash and grayish coloured massive sandstones. Silt stones and silty shales also occurs. The middle Bhuban comprises compact, medium to fine grained and grey to dull yellow coloured bedded sandstones. This occurs with well laminated, iron stained, green shales, silty shales and silt with shales and muds. The upper Bhuban comprise mostly hard, compacts, massive, bluish grey to grey coloured sandstones with siltstones and shale interlamination. The shales are olive green in colour. Sandstone bands sometimes contain large calcareous boulders of various shapes and size.

The rock samples near sairang have yielded some microfossils. These have been identified as Ostracoda : *Leguminocytheries* sp., *Foraminifera : Ammonia cf. beccan, Ammonia cf. pappaliloss, Globigerina* sp. 1, *Globigenna* sp. 2.

The rocks belonging to the Boka Bil formation occur conformably over the upper Bhuban. It is represented by soft, grey coloured and medium to fine grained feldspathic sandstones. Sandy shales with interlaminated siltstones and grey sandstones also occur. Brownish yellow ferruginous sandstones are occasionally present.

Geological Structure

The rocks of the state lie on highly compressed asymmetrical anticlinal ridges and narrow valleys with parallel to sub-parallel sub-vertical axial planes. The axes of the folds show convergence pattern in the directions of plunge. The limbs of the major folds are folded into small anticlines and synclines mostly in chevron style. The folds are long ones with axes running in nearly north-south direction, in continuation of the north Cachar Hills. The overall fold geometry maintains similarity throughout the state. The intensity of fold movements is greater in the sleepy, and are possibly overturned at places.

Primary sedimentary structures recorded in the area are of deep sea flysch type structures, viz., graded bedding, flute casts, load casts, ridge structures, chevron marks, parting lineations, groove marks, ripple drift cross laminations, ripple through convolutions and complete sequence of turbidite structures. The palace current directions shown by all primary features reveal a mean southerly transport direction indicating a southerly basinal plunge.

Geological History

The rocks of the Mizo Hills are the southern extension of those of the Surma valley. They fall within the part of Tripura-Mizoram miogeosynclinal basin which evolved after the regional uplift of the Barail group of sediments from the Indian Ocean. The deposition of later sediments took place after the uplift of the Barails in a tectonic trough having a 'bell-shaped' pattern.

The sediments was transported along the canyons and conyon-extension valleys to the lower slopes or continental rise, where the deposition took place from turbidity current. The thick bedded greywackes were deposited in the channel areas. The silt and shale interlaminations were deposited in the inter channel area. A shallow sea might have existed here during the late Boka Bil time as is evidenced by the presence of large scale planer cross-bedding, through cross-bedding and coarse grained sandstone with less clay in the top of the synclinal cores.

The Mizo Hills are southward continuation of the Patkai range. Geological evidence indicates that these areas formerly were a part of the estuary or delta of a large river issuing from the Himalayas in the Tertiary period. Primary evidences of such theory include marine fossils of the Tertiary age found in Mizoram. Some such fossils have been unearthen in Lunglei District. These were found embedded in grey sandstones and shales.

The beds of the Mizo Hills appear to have been laid down in a sea which was separated from the Burmese Sea during the Cretaceous times.

Mineral Resources

No major mineral deposits of economic importance have been reported so far in the state. All attempts by the Geological Survey of India were unsuccessful in locating any promising mineral occurrence of economic importance. Further exploratory operations are in progress with the objective of locating promising mineral deposits including oil and gas. Some Occurrences have been reported. An Occurrence of 3 m long and 10 cm thick grey pyrite bearing lignite streak in ferruginous brownish yellow soft Boka Bil sandstone has been found at a place south of Chubel village (92°25'55" : 24°03'30"). Rare disseminations of pyrite in siltstone has been found on the west bank of the Dhaleswari river between Baichhali bridge (92°39'45" 23°50'30") and Lengpui (92°38'45" : 23°49'45") along the road. Search in the nearby areas did not reveal more exposures of these minerals.

Building Material

The Massive and hard lower and upper Bhuban sandstones are being as road metal in different parts of Mizoram. This materials is very extensively available in the state. These can be conveniently used for construction of building.

Gas and Oil

In 1964 M.M Munshi reported indications of the occurrences of oil, saline springs and a few gas seepages in the central part of northern Mizoram. Oil and Natural Gas Commission (ONGC) is working in the area and has succeeded in locating several gas seepages.

Limestone

At a place north-west of Saitual village (92°39'00" : 23°41'15") in the Tamdil Lui nala section (92°51'30" : 23°44'30") sporadic occurrences of small quantities of limestone have been reported.

APPENDIX C-1
MANIFESTO TO THE INHABITANTS OF THE LUSHAI HILLS CONCERNING THE DECISION OF THE CHIEFS OF THE LUSHAI HILLS TO OFFER TOTAL RESISTANCE TO ANY INVADER

The decision of the Lushai Chiefs of the North on April 4th, and those of the South on April 16th, to offer total resistance to any invader places the Lushai Hills on the same basis of Total Defence as the peoples of England, Scotland and Wales. We are all from now on men and women, bound indissolubly together to respond to any call that may be made upon us.

Life for us from now on is no longer individual; it is communal. The failure of one village or another may bring death to many others.

We must not fail.

The road will be hard-not spectacular. We may lose life, limbs, or our loved ones. The enemy may not even come to the Lushai Hills, but we must assume he will and be prepared so we shall be strong.

It may be of interest to consider how this trial has been placed upon us. The Chiefs of the Lushai Hills had two courses open to them :

1. Not to oppose any invader, condoning his incursion, and falling to his promises, so broken elsewhere.
2. To oppose any invader.

How could the Chiefs follow course 1? The enemy come with no good intention. They have no peace to bring who have murdered the people of China for nearly five years. Any who have fallen to their promises are now paying the price and for the hope of physical security have now to behave as slaves, pay high taxes, and to suffer to make great the War Lords of Japan.

The Chiefs and people of Lushai could only follow

course 2. But if we are to face toil and tribulation, it behoves us well to ponder. It behaves us to weigh the results that hang upon our sacrifices.

You will remember that in 1935 the British peoples enacted and yet which had for its purpose the inauguration of Dominion Status for India. The British peoples could have included the destiny of Lushai straight away with that of the Indian peoples. But they made Lushai what is now known as an "Excluded Area" and they retained the right to protect Lushai from subjection to any other majority control.

Was that not an Act which gave proof that the British people's wish was to protect Lushai Land, and to ensure that the destiny of Lushai passes to no other hands without the consent of the Lushai peoples?

Forty-five years of close contact between the Lushai and the British people have served to disclose that there is no basic incompatibility between the British and the Lushai day to day outlook on life. The same harmony cannot be claimed in relation to any close contacts elsewhere.

If Lushai Land were handed over to India or Burma what chance would we, who are Lushais have of entering into the social and cultural framework of either power at this late stage, bearing in mind the fact that geographically or culturally we never have been a part of either.

So Lushai's destiny has really hung in the balance ever since 1935 when it became apparent that the desire of the British Government was to place the destiny of India in the hands of her own people.

If we can understand that, then how could the Chiefs and the peoples of the Lushai Hills on reflection choose any other course but to resist the invader? To remain passive at a time of trial for the peace-loving peoples of British, America, China, Russia, and all the Democracies would surely result in these great Nations ceasing, after the war, to evince any further interest in the peoples and the Land of Lushai, linking them up for ever elsewhere.

Not the Chiefs have made a wise decision. Let all of us be careful to see that we are worthy of the wisdom displayed by the Chiefs. Besides, the Lushai people have always been very loyal to His Majesty and it is natural that they should choose to stand by the Government in any hour of trial.

We penalty for any failure on our side may be cruelty and death at the hands of the enemy.

Some may feel we are not strong enough to resist. I we are too weak hearted to resist we must not expect to stand favourably in the eyes of the United Nations.

But we are strong. Let me give you some good reasons, apart from the fact that our General will do all he can to see we get what fighting help is possible.

In 1963 following upon the 1935 Government of India Act. Lushai's fate was clearly in the balance.

If we were to be deserving of the consideration of the great British peoples who have been Lushai's firmest friends for long we has to show we were a virile people, united, and keen to raise ourselves, to rise to national and united status.

The Superintendent, Lushai Hills, created certain avenues by which the Lushai peoples could prove themselves worthy. The Village Welfare Committee System was a great encouragement to a much needed unity. It brought Christians and non-Christians nearer, lessened the gap between Chiefs and people, the Chiefs and the Church, the men and the women. The 10-point code created a means for unity in out senses of what was expected to any good Lushai citizen. The Lushai Hills Cottage Industries created the means by which the skill of Lushai might spread far and wide and by which

Lushai might unite together in pride and satisfaction for the gifts of skill handed down from our forefathers. Lushais themselves write from Cairo and from Quetta and from elsewhere, proud to see Lushai products being used by the Army institutions and others, while even now Lushai articles have been specially sent by the Government of India to Johannesburg, the city of Gold, in Africa, as an example of our ancient and contemporary art.

Then in 1938, you, who keep in touch with world affairs, will remember the Munich agreement of 1938, by which Mr. Chamberlain managed to put off war with Germany for one more precious year. The Superintendent, Lushai Hills, them intensified the above avenues to create our national strength and unity and intensified Circle Conferences among Chiefs, culminating in October, 1941 in a full District Durbar of Circle Representative Chiefs from the North and the South Lushai Hills. Such a body is the initial personification of Lushai national life. It would be difficult to aspire to nationhood without such institutions as the above.

Thus from disunity we have progressed to unity. From suspicion and fear and petty disputes and rivalries we have come nearer and more unified in outlook, more alive to the importance of ourselves being worthy to beseech British never to abandon us to any other power except with our consent. This happy attainment has been due very greatly to our friends the Missionaries in our midst who have spent much and their energies that we shall prosper and rise.

So if we must suffer because a grabbing enemy is not far from our and we know we struggle for something worth while, *viz.*, the security of our whole future.

I appeal to each member of the Educational salaried cadre exert his influence among the people to obey and to help their Chiefs and village elders in their responsible tasks.

I make a personal appeal to each important member of the Lushai Church, North and South, to afford similar support to the endeavour of our unhappy peoples in meeting this threat of unprovoked aggression.

Together we can most certainly stand :

Disunited we must not only fall, but we shall bring death and destruction on ourselves far in excess of what which we may have to meet as a brave and united nation.

It is the wish of the Government that those non-Lushai who are not essential as part of the administrative war machine should leave the Lushai Hills for this short period of distress, which we hope may not be longer than one year at the most.

It is for this reason that those non-Lushais who are not directly concerned with the administration will be leaving the Hills temporarily.

The enemy is not here. The enemy may never dare to come. What we will be doing from time to time will be done so that if he comes, we shall not be taken by surprise and unprepared.

Let there be no panic. Panic is weakness, not a sign off bravery. It wastes energy, and hinders our security.

APPENDIX C-2
PROCEEDINGS OF MEETING OF THE ACCREDITED LEADERS LUSHAI HILLS HELD AT AIJAL ON 14TH AUGUST, 1947

(Chairman : Mr L.L. Peters, Superintendent, Lushai Hills (Elected)

Present :

1. Khawtinkhuma
2. R. Thanhlira, B.A.
3. Yanthuama
4. Pastor Chhuahkhama
5. Brig Kawlkhuma, (SA)
6. Khuma
7. Lal Buaia
8. Hrangaia
9. Muka
10. Rosiama

11. Vanchuanga	12. Chawnghnuaia
13. Phillipa	14. Capt Ngurliana (SA)
15. Pachhunga	16. Vanlawma
17. Vankhuma	18. Laihnuna
19. Chhunruma	20. Pastor Zairema, B.Sc., B.D.
21. Rina	22. Zawla
23. Sena	24. Rosema
25. Laupa	26. Lalhema
27. Saiaithanga	28. Pastor Liangkhaia
29. Lalbiakthanga	30. Lalropuia
31. Suaka	32. Hmingliana
33. Lalana	34. Lianhnuna
35. Pasena	36. Liansailova, Chief
37. Lalbuanga, Chief	38. Lianzuala, Chief
39. Lamhlira, Chief	40. Kamlova
41. Ch. Ngura	42. Zami (Mrs. Khawtinkhuma)
43. Kapthluah	44. Biakvekli (Mrs Buchhawna)
45. Lalrongenga	46. Thansela (Ex-sub)
47. R. Zuala (Ex-Jamadar)	48. Dahrawka, V.A.S.
49. Kapthianga	50. Saihlira. B.A.

1. Resolved that owing to the unexpected acceleration of the date of transfer of power by the British Government and as the Lushais have not as yet been definitely informed in the details as to what is to be the proposed future constitution and form of administration of the district and as section (7) sub-Section (2) of the Indian Independence Bill does not clarify the situation, it is accordingly thought that His Excellency the Governor of Assam should kindly inform them in writing as to what these are to be, also whether Lushais are at this stage allowed the option of joining any other dominion, *i.e.* Pakistan or Burma. Resolved further that

superintendent, Lushai Hills, should kindly communicate above request of the Lushai to the Adviser to His Excellency, the Government of Assam in order to clarify these points.

2. Resolved that if the Lushais are to enter Indian Union their main demands are :

(i) that the existing safeguards of their Customary Laws and land tenure, etc. should be remained.

(ii) that Chin Hills Regulation, 1896 and Bengal Eastern Frontier Regulation, 1873 should be retained until such time as the Lushais themselves through their District Council or other District authority declared that this can be abrogated.

(iii) that the Lushais will be allowed to opt out of the Indian Union, when they wish to do so subject to a minimum period of ten years.

Sd/-L.L. PETERS

14-8-1947

Superintendent,

Lushai Hills

No. 6927-76 G of 21-8-47

Copy forwarded to all the leaders who took part in the proceedings.

Sd/-L.L. PETERS

Superintendent.

Lushai Hills

APPENDIX C-3
MEMORANDUM SUBMITTED TO HIS MAJESTY'S GOVERNMENT, GOVERNMENT OF INDIA AND ITS CONSTITUENT ASSEMBLY THROUGH THE ADVISORY SUBCOMMITTEE BY THE MIZO UNION

Mizo Memorandum

Memorandum of the case of the Mizo people for the right of territorial unity and solidarity and self-determination within the province of Assam in free India submitted to His Majesty's Government and the Government of India and its constituent Assembly through the Advisory Sub-Committee for Assam and fully excluded areas and partially excluded areas.

Pursuant to the resolution passed by the General Assembly of the Mizo Union at Aijal in September 1946 subsequently supported by the Mizo Conference at Lakhipur (Cachar) in November 1946 this memorandum prepared by the Mizo Union and supported by the Mizos outside the Lushai Hills-Manipur State, Cachar, Tripura and the Chirragong Hill Tracts, etc.

The memorandum seeks to represent the case of Mizo people for territorial unity and integrity of the whole Mizo population and full self-determination within the province of Assam for the realization of which an appeal is made to His Majesty's Government, the Government of India and its constituent Assembly to make a special financial provision from year to year for a period of ten years or until such tome as the Mizos shall assert that they and maintain their self-determination without this financial provision.

The People and The Land

The Mizos are a numerous family of tribes, closely knitted together by common tradition, custom, culture, mode of living, language and rites. They are spread over a wider area extending far beyond Manipur State, Cachar, Tripura State, Chittagong Hill Tracts and Burma contiguous with the boundaries of the present Lushai Hills District which was carved out arbitrarily for administrative purposes.

The Mizo people have been known under different names. They were wrongly identified as Kudis during the time of Lord Warren Hastings when Administration of Chittagong sought help of the British against the Kuki raider and it continued to be applied to the whole group until 1871 when it was supplanted by the term Lushai as a result of the active and prominent part taken by the Lushai. Sub-tribe of Mizo race, against the British Expedition known as the First Lushai Expedition. The present Lushai Hills District was thus carved out of the Mizoram for administrative convenience and the Mizo people living within the District came to be known as Lushais while the other Mizos left out of the Lushai Hills District and annexed to the surrounding districts, continued to be known as Kuki without their consent. However, the solidarity of the Mizo people as a race and a distinct block is testified by the names of places, mountains and ranges on the Lushai Hills, Cachar, Manipur, Tripura, Chittagong Hill tracts, Burma, known and called after the name of them. Shakespeare, Stevenson, Liangkhaia, Shaw, Kingdonward and Kim of the Statesman are some of the authorities on this.

The Mizos have nothing in common with the plants nor with the Naga or Manipuri etc. They are a distinct block. The areas now under their occupation are mostly hilly except the eastern portion of Cachar district extending to the Barial range in the North Cachar Hills. Whenever they go and wherever they are, they carry with them primitive customes, culture and mode of living in its purest origin, always calling and identifying themselves as Mizo.

The nomenclature of the word 'KUKI' was and is ever

known to the Mizos; it was a name merely given to them by the neighbouring foreigners.

Again, it was wrong that the word Lushai should be used as covering all the Mizo tribes since it is misrendering of the Lusei, only sub-tribe of the Mizo race. Hence though, perhaps, not originally intended, it has created a division. Only the word 'Mizo' stands for the wholes group of them all : Ludei, Hmar, Ralte, Paite, Zo, Darlawng, Kawm, Pawi, Thado, Chiru, Aimoul, Khawl, Tarau, Anal, Puram Tikhup, Vaiphei, Lakher, Langrawng, Chawrai, Bawng, Baite, Mualthuam, Kaihpen, Pangkhua, Tlanglau, Hraangkhawl, Bawmzo, Mirta, Dawn, Kumi, Khiangte, Khiang, Pangte, Khawlhring, Chawngthu, Vanchiau, Chawhte, Ngente, Rnthlei, Hnamte, Tlau, Pautu, Pawite, Vangchhia, Zawngte Fanai etc. all closely related to one another culturally, socially, economically and physically thus forming a distinct ethnical units.

Traditional Origin

(a) The Mizo people in the Lushai Hills alone number 1,46,900 with an area of 8,143 square miles according to the census of 1941.

(b) The Mizo population of Manipur State contiguous to the Lushai Hills again comes to about 70,000 with and area of about 35,00 square miles.

(c) The Mizo in the Cachar District contiguous to the Lushai Hills number about 9,000 with an area of about 300 square miles.

(d) In Tripura State contiguous to the Lushai Hills, the Mizo again number approximately 7,000 with an area of about 250 square miles.

(e) In the Chittagong Hill Tracts, contiguous to the Lushai Hills, the Mizo population is generally approximated to be 15000 with an area of about 3000 square miles.

(f) In the Chin Hills (Burma) also contiguous to the Lushai Hills who are now commonly known and

termed as the Chins, number not less than 90,000 with an area of about 3800 square miles occupied by them.

The total Mizo population of the contiguous area alone thus conies roughly 3,38,400 and the areas about 18,9993 square miles.

It is a great injustice that the Mizos having one and the same culture, speaking one and the same language, professing one and the same religion, and knit together by common customs and traditions should have been called and known by different names sand thrown among different people with their homeland sliced out and given to others.

The whole contiguous area of the Mizo population as detailed above occupies the middle and the most important portion of India's Eastern Frontiers. It is, therefore, the more imperative that His Majesty's Government, the Government of India and its constituent Assembly should do the just and proper thing and grant the Mizos their just demand for TERRITORIAL UNITY AND SOLIDARITY.

Mizo History and British Connection

The Mizo people were independent, each village forming an independent unit, and their country was never subjugated by the Maharajas of Manipur, Tripura and Chittagong nor by the Kacharis. However, there had been frontier clashes between the Mizos and the neighbouring people which ultimately brought the British to the scene in 1871. The Mizo country was subsequently annexed to the British territory in 1890, when a little less than half the country was carved out for the Mizo people and name Lushai Hills while the rest have been parceled out to the adjoining districts. Since then Mizos have remained loyal, friendly and peaceful. At all time, whenever the British needed help as World War I.

Abhor Expedition, Houkip Rebellion, and World War

II, the willing services of the Mizo people were readily available.

The Mizos have an efficient systems of administration and discipline. Being a distinct block they retain to a considerable degree their ancient and traditional laws, and customs and organizations, beginning from village under the guidance of the Chief and the Elders, while young and old have their respective leaders in all walks of life.

Except the Cachar, the Mizo people are excluded from the Government of India's Act and the areas inhabited by them are kept as a special responsibility of the Governor of the province in his capacity as the Crown Representative and the Legislature have no influence whatsoever. In other words, the Mizos have never been under the Indian Government and never had any connection with the policies and politics of the various groups of Indian opinion.

Now that the British are quitting these Mizos who have never been under the Indian Government and whose ways are all different from others, cannot be thrown on a common platform with the rest of India. It is therefore, important to the highest degree that the Mizos be given self-determination in its fullest form.

The Present General Conditions of the Country

As stated in the foregoing paragraphs, the Mizo areas are mostly excluded. The political officer is supreme in every respect. The education is mostly carried on by the Christian Missionary groups. The general communication of the country is extremely poor. The land is extremely hilly without good roads; and the people poor and simple, primitive and divided into tribes and clans. The highest education is mostly derived from outside the district; but in mass literacy the Mizo people is highest in Assam. The people are mostly intelligent and as such given equal terms they always outshine their fellow-workers of other community in the fields and at home. They are born strategist. Their greatest shortcoming is lack of finance as a result of their trade and commerce and limited scope open for them. Their areas stretch from north to south parallel with the Burma border line for defence along the eastern border of India.

This being the background, it is all the more imperative that the Mizoram be given special financial provision by the Central from year to year while allowing them their territorial integrity as anything short of this will be detrimental to their upbringing. In other words, the Centre shall grant financial provision from year to year for the purpose of development of the country while the district shall join autonomous Assam through legislature with adequate representation and be also eligible to the provincial services with due reservations at the same time retaining their territorial integrity and self-determination : as otherwise thrown among forty crores of Indians the 3,38,400 Mizos with their unique systems of life will be wiped out of existence.

Our Case

In the light of the facts stated in the foregoing paragraphs and in view of geographical position and the strategical importance of the Mizoram for the defence of India and taking into consideration the unique characteristics of Mizo polity and compact block of Mizoram—this Memorandum is placed with the authority for—

1. Territorial unity and solidarity of the whole Mizo population to be known henceforth as Mizo and Mizoram for Lushai and Lushai Hills District, retaining the sole propriety fight over the land.

2. Full self-determination with the province of Assam :

(a) With the National Council having the supreme legislative authority and executive body and judiciary within the district the composition and function of which will be prescribe by rules.

(b) Any concurrent subjects in which the district may be connected with the autonomous province of Assam or India as a whole shall be by negotiation with the national councils which will be set up according to wishes of the general public, any legislation may be applied to the district only with sanction of the national council with any modification.

(c) Special financial provision by the Centre from year to year until such time as the Mizos shall assert that they are able to maintain their territorial and self-determination without this financial provision.

ALL ABOVE ITEMS SHALL BE SUBJECT TO REVISION ACCORDING TO THE FUTURE TREND OFF EVENTS TO THE EXTENT OF SECEDING AFTER TEN YEARS.

For this end it is to be understood that the democratic system of Government in its purest form shall at the very outset be introduced. Passed and approved by the Mizo Union representatives conferences at Ajjal, Lushai Hills, Assam on 22nd April, 1947.

Sd—KHAWTINKHUMA
President

26-4-1947

Sd-VANTHUAMA
General Secretary
The Mizo Union, Aijal
Lushai Hills Assam

APPENDIX D

MEMORANDUM SUBMITTED TO THE PRIME MINISTER OF INDIA BY THE MIZO NATIONAL FRONT GENERAL HEADQUARTERS, AIZAWL, MIZORAM ON THE 30TH OCTOBER 1965

This memorandum seeks to represent the case of the Mizo people for freedom and independence, for the right of territorial unity and solidarity; and for the realisation of which a fervent appeal is submitted to the Government on India.

The Mizos, from time immemorial lived in complete independence without foreign interference. Chiefs of different clans ruled over separate hills and valleys with supreme authority and their administration was much like that of the Greek City-State of the past. Their territory or any part thereof had never been conquered or subjugated by their neighbouring states. However, there had been border disputes and frontier clashes with their neighbouring people which ultimately brought the British Government to the scene in 1844. The Mizo country was subsequently brought under the British political control in February, 1890 when a little more than half of the country was arbitrarily carved out and named Lushai Hills (now Mizo District) and the rest of their land was parceled out of their hands to the adjoining people for the sole purpose of administrative convenience without obtaining their will or consent. Scattered as they are divided, the Mizo people inseparably knitted together by their strong bond of tradition, custom, culture, language, social life and religion wherever they are. The Mizo stood as a separated nation even before the advent of the British Government having a nationally distinct and separate from that of India. In a nutshell, they are a distinct nation, created, moulded and nurtured by God and Nature.

When British India was given a status by promulgation of Government of India Act of 1935, the British Government, having fully realized in the distinct and separate nationality of Mizo people, decided that they should exclude from the purview of the new constitution and they were accordingly classed as an EXCLUDED AREA in terms of the Government Order, 1936. Their land was then kept under the special responsibility of the Governor-General-in-Council in his capacity of the Crown Representative; and the legislature of the British India had no influence whatsoever.

In other words, the Mizos had never been under the Indian Government and never had any connection with politics of the various groups of Indian opinion. When India was in the threshold of Independence, the relation of the Mizos with the British Government and also with the British India were fully realised by the Indian National Congress leaders. Their top leader and spokesman Pandit Jawaharlal Nehru released a press statement on the 19th August 1946 and stated : 'the tribal areas are defined as being those along the frontier of India which are neither part of India, nor of Burma, nor of any Indian State, nor of any foreign power.' He further stated : ' The areas are subsidized and the Governor-General's relation with the inhabitants are regulated by sanads, custom or usage. In the matter of internal administration, the areas are largely left to themselves.' Expressing the view of the Indian National Congress, he continued, 'Although the tribal areas are technically under the sovereignty of His Majesty's Government, their status, when a new Constitution comes into force in India, will be different from that of Aden over which the Governor-General no longer has executive authority. Owing to their inaccessibility and their importance to India in its defence strategy, their retention as British possession is most unlikely. One view is that with the end of sovereignty in India, the new Government of India (*i.e.* Independent Government of India) will enter into the same relations with the tribal areas as the Governor-General maintains now, unless the people of these areas choose to seek integration with India.'

From the foregoing statement made by Pandit Jawaharlal Nehru and the Government of India Act of 1935, it is quite clear that the British Government left the Mizo Nation free and Independent with the right to decide their future political destiny.

Due solely to their political immaturity, ignorance

and lack of consciousness of their fate, representatives of the Mizo Union, the largest political organization at that time and Fifty accredited Mizo leaders representing all political organizations including representatives of religious denominations and social organizations that were in existence submitted their demand and choose integration with free India imposing condition, inter alia. 'THAT THE LUSHAIS WILL BE ALLOWED TO OPT OUT OF INDIAN UNION WHEN THEY WISE TO DO SO SUBJECT TO A MINIMUM PERIOD OF TEN YEARS."

The political immaturity and ignorance which lead the Mizo people to the misguided choice of integration with India was a direct result of the banning by the British Government of any kind of political organization till April 1946 within Mizoland which was declared 'a political area.'

During the fifteen years of close contact and association with India, the Mizo people had not been able to feel that their joys and sorrows have really ever been shared by India. They do not, therefore, feel Indian. Being created a separate nation they cannot go against the nature to cross the barriers of nationality. They refused to occupy a place within India as they consider it to be unworthy of their prosperity. Nationalism and patriotism inspired by the political consciousness has now reached its maturity and the cry for political self-determination is the only wish and inspiration of the people, ne plus ultra, the only final and perfect embodiment of social living for them. The only aspiration and political cry is the creation of MIZORAM, a free and sovereign state to govern herself, to work out her own destiny and to formulate her own foreign policy.

To them Independence is not even a problem or subject of controversy : there cannot be dispute over the subject nor could there be any different of opinion in the matter. It is only a recognition of human rights and to let others live in the dignity of human person.

While the present world is strongly committed to

freedom and self-determination of all nations, large or small, and to promotion of Fundamental Human Rights, and while the Indian leaders are strongly wedded to that principle—taking initiative for and championing the cause of Afro-Asian countries, even before the World body, particularly deploring domination and colonization of the weaker nations by the stronger, old and new, and advocating peaceful co-existence, settlement of international disputes of kind through the medium of non-violence and in condemning weapons mankind, the Mizo people firmly believed that the Government of India and their leaders will remain true to their policy and that they shall take into practice what they advocate, blessing the Mizo people with their aspiration for freedom and independence per principle that no one is good enough to govern another man without that man's consent.

Though known as head-hunters and a martial race, the Mizos commit themselves to a policy of non-violence in their struggle and have no intention of employing any other means to achieve their political demand. If, on the other hand, the Government of India brings exploitative and suppressive measures into operation, employing military might against the Mizo people as id done in the case of Nagas, which God forbid, it would be equally erroneous and futile for both the parties for a soul cannot be destroyed by weapons.

For this end, it is in goodwill and understanding that the Mizo Nation voices her rightful and legitimate claim of full self-determination through this memorandum. The Government of India, in their turn and in conformity with the unchangeable truth expressed and resolved among the text of HUMAN RIGHTS by the United Nations in its august assembly that in order to maintain peace and tranquility among mankind every nation, large or small, may of right be free to work out her own destiny, to formulate her own internal and external policies and shall accept and recognize her political independence. Would it not be a selfish motive and design of India, and would it not amount to an act of offence against humanity if the Government of India claim Mizoram as part their territory and try to retain her as their possession against the national will of the Mizo people simple because their land is important for India's defence strategy?

Wheather the Mizo Nation should shed her tears in joy to establish firm and lasting friendship with India in war in peace or sorrow and anger, is upto the Government of India to decide.

Sd/- S. LIANZUALA

Sd/- LALDENGA

General Secretary,

President

Mizo National Front, Mizoram

DATED AIZAWL THE 30TH OCTOBER 1965

16 Gross State Domestic Product of Mizoram

Gross State Domestic Product at Current Prices

(Rupee in Crores)

Year	*GSDP (Current Prices)*	*% Growth over previous year*
1999-2000	1550	—
2000-2001	1737	12.06
2001-2002	1947	12.09
2002-2003	2166	11.25
2003-2004	2325	7.34
2004-2005	2455	5.59
2005-2006	2721	10.84
2006-2007	2996	10.11
2007-2008	3305	10.31
2008-2009	3663	10.83

Source : Central Statistical Organisation (As on 12-04-2010).

Gross State Domestic Product at Constant (1999-2000) Prices

(Rupee in Crores)

Year	*GSDP (Constant Prices)*	*% Growth over previous year*
1	*2*	*3*
1999-2000	1550	—

(Contd.)

(Contd.)

1	*2*	*3*
2000-2001	1627	4.97
2001-2002	1733	6.52
2002-2003	1913	10.39
2003-2004	1974	3.19
2004-2005	2056	4.15
2005-2006	2105	2.38
2006-2007	2221	5.51
2007-2008	2344	5.54
2008-2009	2495	6.44

Source : Central Statistical Organisation (As on 12-04-2010).

Sectoral Contribution

Gross State Domestic Product (GSDP) at Factor Cost by Industry of Origin in Mizoram (At Current Prices)

(Rs. in Lakh)

Sector	*1999-00*	*2000-01*	*2001-02*	*2002-03*	*2003-04*	*2004-05*	*2005-06*	*2006-07*	*2007-08*	*2008-09*	*2009-10*
1	*2*	*3*	*4*	*5*	*6*	*7*	*8*	*9*	*10*	*11*	*12*
Agriculture	31792	31589	37113	37954	39264	39603	41196	42337	43414	44893	50301
Forestry & Logging	1491	1666	1771	2198	2033	2272	2402	2474	2641	2777	2365
Fishing	1627	1782	2585	2665	3027	3020	3036	3171	3221	3291	2087
Agriculture and Allied	**34910**	**35037**	**41469**	**42817**	**44324**	**44895**	**46634**	**47982**	**49276**	**50961**	**54753**
Mining & Quarrying	776	244	477	234	927	804	634	681	731	785	2965
Manufacturing	**2447**	**2617**	**2667**	**2745**	**3073**	**3491**	**4012**	**4717**	**5546**	**6520**	—
Manu-Registered	536	597	688	695	702	745	819	963	1132	1331	899
Manu-Unregistered	1911	2020	1979	2050	2371	2746	3193	3754	4414	5189	7280
Construction	15205	15945	19731	22635	26940	25970	36567	42308	48950	56636	53337
Electricity, Gas and Water supply	6567	8400	7463	9738	8110	9071	10015	10745	11528	12368	15021
Industry	**24995**	**27206**	**30338**	**35352**	**39050**	**39336**	**51228**	**58451**	**66755**	**76309**	—

(Contd.)

(Contd.)

1	2	3	4	5	6	7	8	9	10	11	12
Transport, Storage & Communication	**3147**	**3532**	**3977**	**4437**	**4915**	**5617**	**6409**	**7466**	**8564**	**9874**	—
Railways	16	15	17	30	33	37	29	34	37	41	56
Transport by Other Means	2093	2526	2861	3036	3625	4196	4640	5494	6378	7441	9140
Storage	56	59	61	57	59	75	81	86	92	97	118
Communication	982	932	1038	1314	1198	1309	1659	1852	2057	2295	1930
Trade, Hotels and Restaurants	15020	14431	16852	16855	18263	17311	18200	19759	20939	22214	27816
Banking & Insurance	3873	4524	4530	7237	8086	8379	9414	10916	12657	14675	13068
Real Estate, Ownership of Dwellings and Business	22768	28204	31762	35835	42154	49832	58430	67844	79945	94306	109994
Services											
Public Administration	27469	35433	39948	48598	48623	50701	51470	54816	58379	62173	87113
Other Services	22824	25375	25777	25448	27083	29386	30301	32332	33994	35751	43183
Services	**95101**	**111499**	**122846**	**138410**	**149124**	**161226**	**174224**	**193133**	**214478**	**238993**	—
State Domestic Product (Rs. Lakh)	155006	173742	194653	216579	232498	245457	272086	299566	330509	366263	426673

Source : Central Statistical Organisation (CSO) (As on 29.01.2010).

Gross State Domestic Product (GSDP) at Factor Cost by Industry of Origin in Mizoram (At 1999-2000 Prices)

(Rs. in Lakh)

Sector	*1999-00*	*2000-01*	*2001-02*	*2002-03*	*2003-04*	*2004-05*	*2005-06*	*2006-07*	*2007-08*	*2008-09*	*2009-10*
1	*2*	*3*	*4*	*5*	*6*	*7*	*8*	*9*	*10*	*11*	*12*
Agriculture	31792	29069	29095	30056	29558	30791	31542	32053	32931	33677	37058
Forestry & Logging	1491	1666	1735	2035	1832	2059	2181	2232	2384	2503	1829
Fishing	1627	1633	1777	1832	2080	2077	2113	2216	2263	2329	1351
Agriculture and Allied	**34910**	**32368**	**32607**	**33923**	**33470**	**34927**	**35836**	**36501**	**37578**	**38509**	**40238**
Mining & Quarrying	776	237	467	179	685	651	435	491	554	626	2066
Manufacturing	**2447**	**2560**	**2632**	**2635**	**2902**	**2874**	**3921**	**4213**	**4527**	**4864**	—
Manu-Registered	536	578	654	644	616	614	720	774	832	894	585
Manu-Unregistered	1911	1982	1978	1991	2286	2260	3201	3439	3695	3970	7525
Construction	15205	15769	19590	22146	25222	23362	29030	31771	34312	39005	35325
Electricity, Gas and Water supply	6567	8318	7348	9485	7629	8226	7987	8251	8525	8808	8955
Industry	**24995**	**26884**	**30037**	**34445**	**36438**	**35113**	**41373**	**44726**	**47918**	**53303**	**54456**

(Contd.)

(Contd.)

1	2	3	4	5	6	7	8	9	10	11	12
Transport, Storage & Communication	**3147**	**3485**	**3882**	**4291**	**4562**	**5656**	**6500**	**7386**	**8439**	**9673**	—
Railways	16	15	17	28	30	32	27	29	31	33	42
Transport by Other Means	2093	2489	2783	2928	3351	3788	3767	4172	4658	5224	5209
Storage	56	58	60	55	55	68	65	67	68	70	77
Communication	982	923	1022	1280	1126	1768	2641	3118	3682	4346	5759
Trade, Hotels and Restaurants	15020	13429	13929	13818	14476	14719	14846	15431	15786	16166	24096
Banking & Insurance	3873	4432	4096	6290	6469	7152	8338	9159	10061	11053	12487
Real Estate, Ownership of Dwellings and Business Services	22768	24830	27076	29529	32234	35308	37739	41369	45377	49819	54633
Public Administration	27469	32162	36260	44112	44135	46021	41209	42548	43931	45359	56211
Other Services	22824	25128	25441	24855	25645	26732	24672	24937	25280	25634	27683
Services	**95101**	**103466**	**110684**	**122895**	**127521**	**135588**	**133304**	**140830**	**148874**	**157704**	—
State Domestic Product (Rs. Lakh)	155006	162718	173328	191253	197429	205628	210513	222057	234370	249516	280891

Source : Central Statistical Organisation (CSO) (As on 29.01.2010).

Net State Domestic Product of Mizoram

Net State Domestic Product at Current Prices

(Rupee in Crores)

Year	*NSDP (Current Prices)*	*Growth over previous year*
1999-2000	1410	—
2000-2001	1567	11.13
2001-2002	1752	11.81
2002-2003	1933	10.33
2003-2004	2083	7.76
2004-2005	2181	4.70
2005-2006	2398	9.95
2006-2007	2629	9.63
2007-2008	2887	9.81
2008-2009	3184	10.29

Source : Central Statistical Organisation (As on 12-04-2010).

Net State Domestic Product at Constant (1999-2000) Prices

(Rupee in Crores)

Year	*NSDP (Constant Prices)*	*% Growth over previous year*
1999-2000	1410	—
2000-2001	1463	3.76
2001-2002	1555	6.29
2002-2003	1705	9.65
2003-2004	1760	3.23
2004-2005	1839	4.49
2005-2006	1858	1.03
2006-2007	1967	5.87
2007-2008	2073	5.39
2008-2009	2205	6.37

Source : Central Statistical Organisation (As on 12-04-2010).

Sectoral Contribution

Net State Domestic Product (NSDP) at Factor Cost by Industry of Origin in Mizoram (At Current Prices) (1999-2000 to 2009-2010)

(Rs. in Lakh)

Sector	*1999-00*	*2000-01*	*2001-02*	*2002-03*	*2003-04*	*2004-05*	*2005-06*	*2006-07*	*2007-08*	*2008-09*	*2009-10*
1	*2*	*3*	*4*	*5*	*6*	*7*	*8*	*9*	*10*	*11*	*12*
Agriculture	30697	30394	35739	36290	37540	37693	38424	39163	39719	40473	46916
Forestry & Logging	1396	1562	1651	2041	1865	2071	2190	2242	2384	2499	2089
Fishing	1464	1589	2256	2302	2572	2485	2405	2440	2398	2370	1542
Agriculture and Allied	**33557**	**33545**	**39646**	**40633**	**41977**	**42249**	**43019**	**43845**	**44501**	**45342**	**50547**
Mining & Quarrying	615	195	380	196	774	796	625	671	721	774	2939
Manufacturing	**1463**	**1502**	**1438**	**1390**	**1495**	**1571**	**1683**	**1979**	**2326**	**2735**	—
Manu-Registered	536	597	688	695	702	745	819	963	1132	1331	899
Manu-Unregistered	927	905	750	695	793	826	864	1016	1194	1404	2890
Construction	14805	15502	19133	21928	26136	25141	35554	41136	47594	55067	52100
Electricity, Gas and Water Supply	3674	4601	3754	5314	4276	4285	4441	4765	5112	5484	5394
Industry	**20557**	**21800**	**24705**	**28828**	**32681**	**31793**	**42303**	**48551**	**55753**	**64060**	**245603**
Transport, Storage & Communication	**2516**	**2809**	**3088**	**3290**	**3925**	**4522**	**3957**	**4589**	**5246**	**6029**	—

(Contd.)

(Contd.)

1	2	3	4	5	6	7	8	9	10	11	12
Railways	8	7	9	16	17	17	18	21	23	26	41
Transport by Other Means	1701	2007	2198	2212	2914	3433	2586	3062	3555	4147	5822
Storage	52	55	56	51	52	68	70	74	77	81	102
Communication	755	740	825	1011	942	1004	1283	1432	1591	1775	938
Trade, Hotels and Restaurants	14649	14059	16466	16466	17808	16759	17463	18959	20091	21315	26011
Banking & Insurance	3761	4375	4388	7030	7855	8120	9124	9754	10427	11146	12558
Real Estate, Ownership of Dwellings and Business Services	20940	26070	29112	32756	38564	45493	53320	61911	72953	86059	98474
Public Administration	22908	29629	33132	40133	40062	41789	42423	45181	48118	51245	62324
Other Services	22063	24441	24662	24132	25465	27391	28178	30067	31612	33246	39333
Services	**86837**	**101383**	**110848**	**123807**	**133679**	**144074**	**154465**	**170461**	**188447**	**209040**	—
State Domestic Product (Rs. Lakh)	140951	156728	175199	193268	208337	218116	239787	262857	288701	318442	360372
Population	857200	879200	901700	924900	948600	973000	997900	1023500	1049800	1076700	11043
State Per Capita Income (Rs. Lakh)	16443	17826	19430	20896	21963	22417	24029	25682	27501	27506	32634

Source : Central Statistical Organisation (CSO) (As on 12.04.2010).

Net State Domestic Product (NSDP) at Factor Cost by Industry of Origin in Mizoram (At 1999-2000 Prices) (1999-2000 to 2009-2010)

(Rs. in Lakh)

Sector	*1999-00*	*2000-01*	*2001-02*	*2002-03*	*2003-04*	*2004-05*	*2005-06*	*2006-07*	*2007-08*	*2008-09*	*2009-10*
1	*2*	*3*	*4*	*5*	*6*	*7*	*8*	*9*	*10*	*11*	*12*
Agriculture	30697	27893	27802	28533	28039	29230	29342	29617	30162	30479	35029
Forestry & Logging	1396	1564	1622	1891	1683	1894	2016	2059	2202	2315	1651
Fishing	1464	1448	1479	1503	1679	1636	1603	1681	1716	1767	906
Agriculture and Allied	**33557**	**30905**	**30903**	**31927**	**31401**	**32760**	**32961**	**33357**	**34080**	**34561**	**37586**
Mining & Quarrying	615	190	378	145	553	644	428	483	545	616	2049
Manufacturing	**1463**	**1494**	**1523**	**1444**	**1592**	**1420**	**2263**	**3311**	**3456**	**3608**	—
Manu-Registered	536	578	654	644	616	614	720	774	832	894	585
Manu-Unregistered	927	916	869	800	976	806	1543	2537	2624	2714	5286
Construction	14805	15349	19047	21511	24514	22678	28231	30909	33392	37991	34391
Electricity, Gas and Water Supply	3674	4645	3959	5550	4330	4415	3794	3919	4050	4184	6817
Industry	**20557**	**21678**	**24907**	**28650**	**30989**	**29157**	**34716**	**38622**	**41443**	**46399**	**49128**
Transport, Storage & Communication	**2516**	**2795**	**3065**	**3253**	**3080**	**4741**	**4514**	**5166**	**5941**	**6849**	—

(Contd.)

(Contd.)

1	2	3	4	5	6	7	8	9	10	11	12
Railways	8	7	9	15	17	19	20	21	23	24	34
Transport by Other Means	1701	1998	2174	2177	2108	3134	2074	2297	2565	2876	3693
Storage	52	54	55	50	49	62	57	58	59	60	69
Communication	755	736	827	1011	906	1526	2363	2790	3294	3889	5050
Trade, Hotels and Restaurants	14649	13076	13579	13470	14085	14278	14283	14846	15187	15553	22156
Banking & Insurance	3761	4291	3967	6105	6270	6944	8116	8919	9803	10773	12219
Real Estate, Ownership of Dwellings and Business Services	20940	22777	24709	26860	29249	32059	34119	37401	41024	45040	50387
Public Administration	22908	26501	29944	36504	36670	38826	33966	35060	36199	37376	42248
Other Services	22063	24233	24425	23682	24271	25174	23093	23341	23662	23993	25912
Services	**86837**	**93673**	**99689**	**109874**	**113625**	**122022**	**118091**	**124733**	**131816**	**139584**	–
State Domestic Product (Rs. Lakh)	140951	146256	155499	170451	176015	183939	185768	196712	207339	220544	248482
Population	857200	879200	901700	924900	948600	973000	997900	1023500	1049800	1076700	11043
State Per Capita Income (Rs.)	16443	16635	17245	18429	18555	18904	18616	19220	19750	20483	22501

Source : Central Statistical Organisation (CSO) (As on 12.04.2010).

Per Capita NSDP

Per Capita Net State Domestic Product at Current Prices

(Rupees)

Year	*Per Capita NSDP (Current Prices)*	*% Growth over previous year*
1999-2000	16443	—
2000-2001	17826	8.41
2001-2002	19430	9.00
2002-2003	20896	7.55
2003-2004	2196	5.11
2004-2005	22417	2.07
2005-2006	24029	7.19
2006-2007	25682	6.88
2007-2008	27501	7.08
2008-2009	29576	7.55

Source : Central Statistical Organisation (As on 12-04-2010).

Per Capita Net State Domestic Product at Constant (1999-2000) Prices

(Rupees)

Year	*Per Capita NSDP (Constant Prices)*	*% Growth over previous year*
1999-2000	16443	—
2000-2001	16635	1.17
2001-2002	17245	3.67
2002-2003	18429	6.87
2003-2004	18555	0.68
2004-2005	18904	1.88
2005-2006	18616	1.52
2006-2007	19220	3.24
2007-2008	19750	2.76
2008-2009	20483	3.71

Source : Central Statistical Organisation (As on 12-04-2010).

17 New Industrial Policy of Mizoram 2002

POLICY FRAMEWORK

Background

The Industrial Policy of Mizoram State was first notified on 15.3.89 with a view to give direction to the strategies for industrial development of the State. While announcing the said policy statement, the Govt. of Mizoram took full cognizance of the Industrial Policy Resolutions of the Govt. of India announced during 1948-1956 and the amendments made thereof during 1973, 1977 and 1983. Policy resolutions were taken on 1989 with a sense of commitment to the people of Mizoram to improve the economy of the State and thereby bring about higher quality of life and happiness to the people of Mizoram.

While making the policy resolutions in 1989, the Govt. was fully aware of the objectives of the Central Govt. in regards to upgradation of technology, export promotion, balanced growth, broad-basing entrepreneurial skill and to improvement of technical skill for rapid growth of industries under a fast changing industrial scenario of the country.

The Industrial Policy of Mizoram 1989 laid stress on reducing shifting cultivation by encouraging a shift from primary to secondary sectors by way of developing rural industries like handloom and handicraft and village and cottage industries. Priority was assigned to agro-and forest-based industries, handloom and handicraft industries, sericulture industries and electronics industries. The policy, interlia, laid emphasis on even development of all sectors, large and medium, small scale, tiny, village and cottage industries. For rapid development of all these sectors, various kinds of supports like institutional, organizational and marketing supports, and schemes for infrastructure development and manpower development apart from initiating several state-level incentive schemes to attract prospective entrepreneurs were announced by the Government.

Industrial Policy of 1989, considering the nascent stage of development in the State laid accent on protection of the local small scale entrepreneurs in order to safeguard the socio-cultural and ethnic identity of the indigenous enterprise of Mizoram. Therefore, setting up of industries in the small scale sector by outsider was not allowed. However, investment from outside was allowed in medium and large scale industries in joint and assisted sectors.

Approach to industrial development in the State since then was based on the following resolutions of Industrial Policy of 1989.

Setting up of viable industrial projects in large and medium sectors through State-owned corporation.

Setting up of modern small scale industries at the level of private entrepreneurs by providing all necessary promotional supports with the help of incentive schemes.

Development and promotion of artisan-oriented industries like handloom and handicraft, village and tiny industries in rural areas by providing necessary supports like grant in-aid, subsidies, raw-materials, shed, marketing and training facilities etc.

Development of infrastructure.

Manpower development.

Development of electronics Industry.

Strengthening of organizational set up.

Exploration and development of mineral resources.

The intention of the government of Mizoram while announcing its first Industrial policy was not industrial growth per se but was rather directed towards all round development in the interest of the indigenous people of Mizoram and towards giving them gainful employment and self-employment opportunities in the industrial and allied sectors.

As a result of a policy direction given during the 8th plan period, significant growth in small scale industries, increase in production, awareness amongst the local entrepreneurs to set up modern small scale industries, availability of technical manpower and improvement in basic infrastructure and agro based industries are now noticeable in the State. It has been observed that, though there is no lack of enthusiasm amongst the local entrepreneurs to go for hi-tech investment, lack of finance and lack of locally available resources are the main bottle-necks. Further, resources at the level of the government is also very limited to fund big projects through the public sectors undertaking.

In view of the continuing backwardness of the North Eastern Region, the Government of India vide its notification No.EA/1/2/96-IDP Dt. 24th Dec. 1997 announced New Industrial Policy for the North Eastern Region. This Policy aimed at encouraging investment in the industrial sector by announcing fiscal and other incentives for the purpose of overall economic growth of this region.

In view of the National Industrial Policy and the New Industrial Policy for the North Eastern region, the Government of Mizoram felt it necessary to announce a New Industrial Policy in the new millennium, 2000 for accelerated industrial and economic development of the State.

Aims and Objectives

The main aim of this New Industrial Policy of Mizoram,

2000 will be to engineer rapid growth in the State by industrialization of the State to a sustainable extent for the fulfillment of the following objectives :

Enrichment of industrial growth potential lying in the sectors like agriculture, horticulture, forest and establishment of proper linkage amongst the industries based on resources available in these sectors.

Formation of suitable mechanism for attracting and growth of capital formation in Mizoram by taking full advantage of the policy changes initiated by the Central Government in respect of industry, trade and commerce from time to time.

Identifying and develop entrepreneurial and managerial skills by providing suitable training programmes at District, Sub-Division and Block levels and to create facilities for training of industrial labour on sustained basis.

Ensuring balanced sectoral and regional growth by promoting industries under all sectors.

Promotion and modernization of textile industry including traditional Sericulture and Handloom and Handicraft sectors by induction of improved design, quality and technology so as to make textile industry a potential export-oriented sector.

Encouraging joint ventures between local entrepreneurs and industrialists from outside the State on selective basis.

Encouraging joint venture from outside the State with State's own public sector undertakings and with resourceful local entrepreneurs.

Encouraging self-employment especially among technically qualified unemployed persons of the State for generating additional employment opportunities in the State.

Allowing convergence of activities of all government

agencies so as to make a concerted approach towards industrial growth.

Identifying sick industries and take measures for the revival of such units which have the potential to turn around.

Making Mizoram a major center for the growth of fruit and food based industries by encouraging plantation and growth of different kind of livestocks in the State.

Making major entry in bamboo-based industries by optimum utilization of bamboo resources of Mizoram.

Developing Mizoram as an attractive region for tourism industries.

Encouraging quality control, standardization and competitiveness of the local products.

Envisaging industrial development in Mizoram by encouraging private entrepreneurship and confining the role of government to that of promotional and catalytic agent for the growth of industry, trade & commerce in the State.

Ensuring minimization of pollution and encouraging eco-friendly units.

Encouraging industry based on medicinal plants.

Approaches

The Government, therefore, shall adopt the following approaches to achieve the desired objectives :

Identification of thrust areas and promotion of specific industries.

Announcement of a package of fiscal and other incentives.

Catalyze development of industrial infrastructure.

Provide special promotional packages for rural and traditional industries and for industries based on sericulture.

Re-structuring of public sector undertaking to make them more efficient for achieving commercial viability.

Evolving rehabilitation package for sick industries.

Development of market support system including encouragement of export market.

Development of appropriate training facilities.

Adoption of new administrative measures to back up the system.

Adoption of broad policy on Foreign Direct Investment (FDI) and Joint venture (JV) proposals keeping in view the necessity of safeguarding the interest of the tribal entrepreneurs and tribal population of Mizoram.

Development of a mechanism for protection of environment and affluent reduction and phasing out use of chemical dyes and to prevent pollution in industrial sector.

Thrust areas and encouraging growth of specific industries in these areas

Identified thrust area for concentrated industrial development will enjoy additional incentives as follows. Major thrust, however, will be on small scale sector and local resources based industries.

Electronics and Information Technology : Electronics & Information Technology is going to be the industry of the new millennium. The pollution free atmosphere in the State is congenial for development of this sector. The State government will attach top priority to these sectors and will announce a separate policy on Information Technology.

Bamboo-based and timber-base products : The vast Bamboo resources of Mizoram will be optimally exploited for setting up of industry for manufacturing various bamboo-based products such as fibre-board, bamboo mat-ply, different kind of house-hold products and high quality toothpick, chop-stick and joss-stick. This sector, therefore, will attract special attention of the Government. Plantation of high value timber and bamboo will be encouraged to sustain timber-based industries. Timber-based and bamboo-based industries will be encouraged to the limit sustainable by the Mizoram ecology and environment.

Food and Fruit processing Industries : The climatic condition of Mizoram is favourable for cultivation and growth of various kinds of fruits. The condition is also very favourable for poultry and animal husbandry and mushroom cultivation. Government shall therefore, encourage development of these sectors so that raw-materials base for food and fruit processing Industry, mainly at the level of private entrepreneurship, is well developed. Further, the State government will assist in establishing appropriate linkages between the growers and processors.

Textile, Handloom and Handicraft Industry : Handloom and Handicrafts, which is a traditional industry in Mizoram, will continue to receive prime attention from the government. Modernization of this sector by induction of improved design and technology to make it an export oriented sector will be encouraged and promoted. Export oriented textiles and readymade garments industries will receive special attention of the government. Induction of power-looms will be encouraged selectively while safeguarding the interests of traditional weavers of Mizoram.

Plantation Fibre and Hill Brooms : Industry based on plantation fibre and Hill Brooms will be encouraged keeping in view the sustained extraction of such items from the forest of Mizoram.

Tung Oil and Non-edible oil extraction : With the encouragement and assistance of the State government, vast area of land has been planted with Tung trees at the village level. The indigenous demand of Tung oil is in laminates, paints and ink industries, which, at present, is being met in India by import only. Extraction of oil from Tung seeds will be considered by the government as priority industry and will be encouraged. Extraction of Citronella oil, having ready market in pharmaceutical and health-care industries will be encouraged. In addition, plantation of edible oil seeds and extraction of oil thereof will be encouraged.

Tea, Rubber and Coffee Industry : Entire Mizoram has been declared as non-traditional area for Tea development which qualifies to receive incentives unlike traditional areas. Tea plantation is not new in Mizoram. However, scientific and commercial Tea Plantation will be encouraged as family oriented scheme, with encouragement for setting up of processing plants in the private sector. Coffee and Rubber based industries will receive due attention from the government for their cultivation and processing. Interest of indigenous labourers will be protected while promoting tea industry.

Industry based on Mines and Minerals : As the whole of the State is far-behind in development of mines and minerals, all proposals for setting up units based on mines and mineral resources of Mizoram will receive attention and will be promoted. Units based on indigenous and imported gems and gemstone will receive special attention of the government.

Tourism Industry : Mizoram with its soothing climate and exquisite natural beauty resting on the undulating hills and greenery, offers good scope for developing tourism Industry. Government will encourage and promote this industry.

KVI Sector Units : Industries on KVI patronized by KVIC will also continue to receive patron age from the State Government as units in this sector generates a large number of employment and items of common-use.

Fiscal and Other Incentives

To encourage flow of capital into industrial sector, the State Government announces an attractive package of fiscal and other incentives to the entrepreneurs in addition to the various types of incentives already offered by the Government of India. Further, special incentives are offered by the State to industries set up in thrust areas. Details of this scheme can be seen under Part-III.

Development of Infrastructure

Infrastructure is pre-requisite for Industrial development. The government will take integrated approach towards improvement of general infrastructure in the State like road, power, communication and water supply.

Industries department will take the responsibility of providing inbuilt infrastructure facilities to the suitable types of Industries by establishing Growth Centers, Industrial Estates, Export Promotion Industrial Park, Information Technology Park Integrated Infrastructure Development Centre, Special Economic Zone and Industrial Areas.

Special Promotional Package for Rural and Traditional Industries

To make the rural economy self-sustained and to check the migration of rural population into urban area, it will be necessary to strengthen the non-farm sector in the rural area by encouraging establishment of village, cottage and tiny industries. Special promotional measures will be undertaken by the government to strengthen this sector.

Re-structuring of State Public Sector Undertaking

The public sector undertaking set up by the government of Mizoram to serve specific purpose could not perform up to the expectation. Most of them are running with accumulated loss inspite of their contribution to the social sector. The role of public sector undertaking will be reviewed by the government and re-structuring and rehabilitation, will be undertaken leading them to commercial viability.

Rehabilitation Package for Sick Industries

Sick Industries will be identified and their cause of sickness will be studied. A model rehabilitation package will be evolved for those sick units which merit revival.

Training Facilities

The State government recognizes that the basic problem in the process of industrialization in the State is lack of technical, managerial and entrepreneurial skill among the people. The State government will continue its efforts to improve training infrastructure in the State and open more training centers in various disciplines to ensure supply of technical manpower to meet the requirement of local industries. The Department of Industries will organize chain of EDPs in collaboration with IDBI, SIDBI, NEDFI State PSUs and other agencies.

Research and Development Facilities

In order to achieve TQM, it is necessary to encourage and facilitate setting-up of R/D cells/Division in as many units as possible. Government will consider formulating a separate set of Rules for providing 100% Grant for setting-up R & D cell/division in industrial units.

Administrative Support

The government will take all possible administrative measures to oversee implementation of the resolution taken in the present policy frame work. The details of such measures are elaborated at Part II of this Policy.

Policy on Foreign Direct Investment (FDI) Including Investment from Outside the State

Mizoram is economically backward state inhabited by a distinct ethnic group of people having their own socio-cultural and religious identity. The State government nevertheless, will encourage foreign direct investment and from outside the State with caution and restraint so as to safeguard the socio-cultural identity of the indigenous people of Mizoram. The State government fully appreciate the policy of liberalization and globalization and the benefit being derived thereof due to in flow of capital in the industrial sector in our country, and therefore, does not like to lag behind other States to attract investment from outside but will adopt a cautious approach keeping in view the interest of the tribal population of Mizoram. FDI in fruit and Bamboo processing sector will be given higher preference.

The Government reserves the cottage, village & tiny industries for development at the level of local entrepreneurs only. However, in case of small scale industries, investment in plant and machineries anything above Rs. 50.00 lakhs will be open for investment from outside for joint venture with local entrepreneurs only in the thrust areas. Any such investment proposal should be submitted to the government in detail for consideration and clearance.

FDI and investment from outside the State in the large and medium sectors only in the thrust areas will be encouraged in joint sector with State PSUs or/and with resourceful local entrepreneurs as this can induce ancilarization and establishment of down stream industries in the State in small scale sectors, and generate employment opportunities to the local people.

Any such investment proposal has to be submitted in detail to the government for consideration and clearance. For an attractive proposal which will contribute to the economy of Mizoram, the government will make the land available to the promoters of such proposal on long-term lease basis.

In the JV sector, non-supervisory and non-technical employments will be reviewed to the local people whereas preference will be given to local talents in technical employment.

Environment and Pollution Control

All new units, excepting those under IT sectors, will necessarily obtain clearance from State Pollution Control Board.

All Existing units shall also endeavours to make their units compatible to Rules and Regulation under State Pollution Control Board within 3 years from the date of issue of this Policy.

Prior clearance of Department of Environment & Forest, Government of Mizoram shall be obtained before setting up new units in areas other than Industrial Estates, Growth Centre, EPIP, IT Parks, IIDC and declared industrial area.

ADMINISTRATIVE SUPPORT SYSTEM

With a view to take an integrated approach toward industrialization of the State, the following administrative measures will be adopted :

Cabinet Committee for Investment Promotion (CCIP)

There will be a Cabinet Committee for Investment Promotion (CCIP), of which the Chief Minister will be the Chairman. This Committee will be the final authority to give clearance to any proposal for Joint Venture and for investment coming from outside the State including foreign direct investment (FDI). This Committee will also give direction to various Department for proper implementation of the policy on such investments and Joint Venture proposals.

Mizoram Investment Promotion Committee (MIPC)

A Mizoram Investment Promotion Committee will be constituted with the Chief Secretary of the State as its Chairman and the Secretary Planning, Secretary Finance, Secretary Industries and Director Industries as Members. This Committee will sit at least once in six months to over-see implementation of the policy resolutions on investment and Joint Venture proposals and will issue direction down-stream and advice up-stream on such matters. Proposal cleared by MIPC will be placed to the CCIP for final decision. The Chairman of the Committee will have the discretion to co-opt members of Industries Association into the Committee.

Market Support System

The State government will provide a strong and effective marketing support to the local industries by taking various measures including effective implementation of the State government Store Purchase Programme. The State government will consider formation of Market Promotion Council under the New Industrial Policy of Mizoram, 2000 which will function in an advisory capacity. This Council will co-ordinate and interact with the marketing agencies elsewhere to promote sales of local products inside and outside the country. One of the major area of operation of this Council will be export promotion of locally identified exportable products like garments, processed foods, handicrafts and handloom product as well as products from agro-forest based industries.

Single-window Clearance

A prospective investor should get all his requirement and information relating to setting up of a Industry cleared through a single authority. The Department of Industries will offer this single window facility through a Green Channel Committee of officials of all other concerned Departments and the Committee will be headed by the Secretary, Industries.

Rehabilitation Cell for Sick Units

A Rehabilitation Cell in the Department of Industries will be set up and will be headed by the Director of

Industries. This Cell will work in co-ordination with Zoram Industrial Development Corporation (ZIDCO) and will jointly participate in analyzing the viability of the sick industries of the State and suggest measures for their rehabilitation. A separate mechanism for Rehabilitation of Sick Units will be evolved by the Industries Department.

Public Enterprise Cell

A Public Enterprise Cell will be constituted in the Department of Finance to over-see functioning of the public sector units and formulate guidelines for revamping their management and for organizational and structural adjustment. This Cell will be headed by the Secretary, Finance Department with members from Planning and concerned Departments under which the PSUs are created. The Secretary Industries and Director, Industries shall also be the Members.

Task Force for Fast Track Implementation of Industrial Projects

A standing Task Force will be constituted in the Industrial Department to identify specific Industrial Projects that can be implemented by placing them on Fast Tract. Depending on the techno-economic viability of such projects, project profiles will be prepared for distribution to the interested entrepreneurs. Reputed consultants may be co-opted to the Task Force who can tender advice on technological aspects of a Project including marketing of products.

INCENTIVES

Incentive Scheme, 2000

From the date the New Industrial Policy of Mizoram, 2000 will come into force, a new package of incentives (herein after referred to as Incentive Scheme of 2000) shall come into force and shall remain in operation till such time the State Govt., gives due notice towards discontinuance of its operation or till amendments are made to the Scheme. The commitments already made under this Scheme shall not be adversely affected by any such discontinuation or amendment.

Eligibility

All new industrial units in the private, State public Sector and in Joint Sector set up on or after 24.12.1997 will be eligible under Incentives Scheme of 2000.

Existing industrial units undertaking expansion, modernization or diversification made after 24.12.1997 shall be eligible for the incentive for the expanded portion only under this Scheme.

To be eligible for this incentives, the Industrial units should be located and have their registered Offices in the State of Mizoram.

Those existing industrial units which have already availed incentives similar in nature under the Incentives Scheme of 1989 and thereafter shall not be eligible under Incentives Scheme of 2000.

Special preference shall be given in the matter of incentives available from State and Centre to those units located in Growth Centre, EPIP Industrial Estates and such other areas identified and declared as such by the State Government.

New Units

An industrial units which has undertaken one or more 'effective steps' on or after 01.04.2000 would be considered as a new unit for the purpose of Incentive Scheme of 2000.

Explanation

Effective Steps : Effective steps means one or more of the following steps :

60 p.c. or more of the capital issued for the industrial unit has paid up. Substantial part of the factory building

has been constructed. A firm order has been placed for substantial part of the plant and machinery required for the industrial unit.

Existing Units

Any industrial unit which is/was in commercial production at any time prior to 24.1.1997 would be considered as an existing unit for the purpose of incentive scheme of 2000.

Continuance of Existing Incentives

The existing incentives offered under the New Industrial Policy of Mizoram, 2000 shall not be applicable to units which were sanctioned incentives under the rules of incentives/subsidies under the Industrial Policy of Mizoram State, 1989. All such units will continue to be governed by the provisions of sanctions already issued under the relevant rules of the Industrial Policy of 1989. However, the units which were set up prior to the commencement of this Scheme, but have not so far availed any of the benefits under aforementioned rules may chose to exercise one-time option in favour of either of the Schemes.

The incentives offered under the Rules for the grant of incentives/subsidies under the Industrial Policy of Mizoram State 1989 are as follows and all new units set up on or after 24.12.1997 shall be eligible to these incentives :

Subsidies on the cost of Project Report (Appendix-A)

Land subsidy (Appendix-B)

Factory rent subsidy (Appendix-C)

Manpower development subsidy (Appendix-D)

Interest subsidy (Appendix-E)

Power subsidy (Appendix-F)

Subsidy on Power Line (Appendix-G)

Subsidy on Power Generating set (Appendix-H)

State Transport subsidy on Plant and Machinery.

Existing State Rules for grant of incentives/subsidies also will be reviewed by the Government to incorporate suitable amendments conforming with the New Industrial Policy of Mizoram, 2000.

New Incentives

In addition to the existing incentives, the government of Mizoram offers further incentives under the New Industrial Policy of Mizoram 2000 as follows :

State Capital Investment Subsidy : An investment subsidy on the total investment made in plant and machinery shall be provided on a graded scale to the new industrial units. It will be available to both new units as well as to existing units carrying out expansion, diversification and modernisation activities.

The graded subsidy will be as under :

Types of Industry	*Subsidy eligible in general*	*Subsidy eligible to unit set up in the thrust area*
(i) Artisan and tiny scale units	15% of total capital investment in plant and machinery	20% of total investment in plant and machinery
(ii) Small scale capital units	10% of total capital investment in plant & machinery subject to a maximum of Rs. 5.00 lakhs	15% of total investment in plant & machinery subject to a maximum of Rs. 7.00 lakhs
(iii) Medium scale units	5% on total capital investment in plant & machinery subject to a maximum of Rs. 10.00 lakhs	10% of total capital in plant & Machinery subject to a maximum of Rs. 15.00 lakhs.

Concession on State and Central Sales Tax

State Sales Taxes shall be exempted for a period of 7 year from the date of commencement of actual commercial production. However, for the units set up in the thrust area, the exemption period will be 10 years.

Exemption of Central Sales Taxes and Excise duties will be governed by various Notifications/Orders issued by Government of India in this regards.

Price Preference

Price preference well be given for the products of local units as per the provision of Mizoram Preferential Stores Purchase Rules 1994. Broadening and depending of the coverage of the Rules will be carried out.

International Standard Organization/Bureau of Indian Standard Certification

The State government shall encourage the small Industries to obtain Bureau of Indian Standard (BIS))/ International Standard Organization (ISO) Certificate for their product to enable them to compete at the State and National levels. For this purpose, the State Government shall re-imburse 100% of the expenditure incurred on registration fee, testing fee etc., and purchase of testing equipment subject to actuals up to the maximum limit of Rs. 50,000/-.

This limit shall be Rs. 1,00,000/- for units set up in the thrust areas.

Subsidy on Registration Fee of Promotion Council, Commodity Board and Chamber of Commerce

The amount spent by an industrial unit in obtaining a registration with recognised promotion council, commodity board, chamber of commerce etc., shall be re-imbursement to the unit subject to a limit of Rs. 20,000/- or the actual registration fee which ever is less.

Incentives for Export Oriented Units

For 100% Export Oriented Units (EOU) : An additional

5% capital investment subsidy for investment on plant and machinery subject to a maximum of Rs. 5.00 lakhs will be made available to 100% EOUs.

Other Units with an Export Commitment of Less than 100% of the Total Turn Over : An additional 2% of capital investment subsidy for investment of plant and machinery subject to a maximum of Rs. 2.00 lakhs will be make available to units of less than 100% export commitment.

State-level Review Committee

This Policy statement shall be reviewed and recommendations made annually for adjustments and for providing additional policy support to the industry by a State-level Review Committee to be headed by Secretary, Industries Department, Government of Mizoram with Members drawn from various Departments involved in Industrial development of Mizoram. The State Pollution Control Board, Environment and Forest Department, Geology and Mining Wing of Industries Department and Mizoram Industries Association will also be represented in the Committee.

APPENDIX-A
SUBSIDY ON COST OF PROJECT REPORT

A. Eligibility Condition

(i) An Industrial unit is eligible to claim subsidy only for the amount of cost of Project Report already paid to the concerned consultant/agency as approved/recognized by the Government of India/Director of industries.

(ii) An Industrial unit is eligible to claim the subsidy only after taking effective steps.

B. Limit of Subsidy

Subsidy on cost of Project Report to an Industrial unit shall be :

(i) 90 per cent in case of tiny unit subject to a ceiling of Rs. 5.000/- per unit.

(ii) 75 per cent in case of small scale and ancillary units and small scale service establishments subject to a ceiling of Rs. 25,000/- per unit.

(iii) 50 per cent in case of medium and large scale units subject to a ceiling of Rs. 50,000/- per unit.

C. Application for Claim

Application for grant of subsidy on cost of Project Report shall be submitted in duplicate to the concerned District Office in the prescribed form under Appendix 'A'.

D. Selection Committee

Composition of the State Level Committee shall be :

(1)	Secretary, Industries Department	*Chairman*
(2)	Secretary, Finance Department or his not below the rank of Deputy secretary	*Member*
(3)	Branch Manager Industrial Development-Bank of India, Mizoram Branch	*Member*
(4)	Representative from North Eastern Industrial Consultants Ltd.	*Member*
(5)	General Managers, District Industries Centres	*Members*
(6)	Director of Industries	*Member Secretary*

[Detailed procedure incorporated in the rules for the Grant of Incentives/Subsidies under the Industrial Policy of Mizoram to 1989]

APPENDIX-B
LAND SUBSIDY

A. Eligibility Condition

An Industrial Unit is eligible to claim subsidy on the amount of lease charge/fee on developed land allotted to the unit on the amount spent for development of the allotted undeveloped land within the Industrial Estate, Industrial Growth centre or Industrial Area declared by the Industries Department.

B. Limit of Subsidy

(i) 25% of the lease charge/fee of allotted developed/undeveloped land will be subsidized for a period of 5 years.

(ii) 25% of the amount spent by the unit on development of undeveloped land allotted to the unit wilt be subsidised.

C. Application for Claim

Application for grant of land subsidy shall be submitted in duplicate to the concerned District office in the prescribed form under Appendix 'B'

D. Selection Committee

Composition of the State level Committee shall be :

(1)	Secretary, Industries Department	*Chairman*
(2)	Secretary, Finance department or his Nominee not below the rank of Deputy Secretary	*Member*
(3)	General Managers, District Industries Centres	*Members*
(4)	Director of Industries	*Member Secretary*

[Detailed procedure incorporated in the rules for the Grant of Incentives/Subsidies under the Industrial Policy of Mizoram State, 1989]

APPENDIX-C
FACTORY RENT SUBSIDY

A. Eligibility Condition

(i) The Subsidy can be claimed by new tiny and small scale unit occupying the built up factory sheds within the declared Industrial Estates/ Industrial Growth Centre 1 Industrial Area on monthly rent basis.

(ii) The Subsidy can also be claimed by the existing tiny and small scale units on rents of built up factory sheds occupied for the expanded portion only.

(iii) The Subsidy can be claimed by the aforementioned units for a period of 5 years from the date of commercial production.

B. Limit of Subsidy

Subsidy on factory Rent to an Industrial unit shall be 50 per cent of the duly assessed rent of factory Shed subject to a ceiling of Rs. 30,000/- per unit per year.

C. Application for Claim

Application for grant of Subsidy on Factory Rent shall be submitted in duplicate to the concerned District Office in the prescribed form under Appendix "C".

D. Selection Committee

Composition of the State level Committee shall be :

(1) Secretary, Industries Department	*Chairman*
(2) Secretary, Finance department or his Nominee not below the rank of Deputy Secretary	*Member*
(3) General Managers, District Industries Centres	*Members*
(4) Director of Industries	*Member Secretary*

[Detailed procedure incorporated in the rules for the Grant of Incentives/Subsidies under the Industrial Policy of Mizoram State, 1989]

APPENDIX-D
MAN POWER DEVELOPMENT SUBSIDY

A. Eligibility Condition

(i) New and existing Industrial units which have already gone into production which send their workers to Institutions or registered/licensed Industrial units outside Mizoram duly approved by the Director of Industries for training for upgradation of their skill are eligible to claim the subsidy.

(ii) An Industrial unit is eligible to claim subsidy on expenditure for managerial and technical training of its workers.

(iii) An Industrial unit to claim the subsidy should give an undertaking that the trained workers will continue to be employed by it after training atleasts for a period of 3 years.

(iv) An industrial unit to claim the subsidy should take prior approval of the Director of industries before sending of its workers for training.

B. Limit of Subsidy

Subsidy shall be limited to 50 per cent of the actual expenditure for training subject to a ceiling of Rs. 3000/- per trainee and Rs. 25,000/- per unit per year.

C. Application for Claim

Application for grant of Subsidy on Manpower development shall be submitted in duplicate to the concerned District Office in the prescribed form under Appendix 'D'.

D. Selection Committee

Composition of the State level Committee shall be :

(1) Secretary, Industries Department *Chairman*

(2) Secretary, Finance department or

his Nominee not below the rank of Deputy Secretary — *Member*

(3) General Managers, District Industries Centres — *Members*

(4) Director of Industries — *Member Secretary*

[Detailed procedure incorporated in the rules for the Grant of Incentives/Subsidies under the Industrial Policy of Mizoram State, 1989]

APPENDIX-E
INTEREST SUBSIDY

A. Eligibility Condition

(i) An Industrial unit is eligible to claim subsidy only on the amount of interest on term loan and working capital loan already paid to the concerned Banks/Financial Institutions/ Agencies.

(ii) An Industrial unit is eligible to claim subsidy only for the amount of interest where the repayment is made in time. No subsidy can be claimed for overdue repayment.

(iii) An Industrial unit is eligible to claim subsidy on interest on term loan and working capital loan for 5 years from the date of commissioning of the unit.

B. Limit of Subsidy

(i) The interest on loan paid by an industrial unit in excess of 8 Y2 per cent shall be subsidized up to a maximum of 4 per cent.

(ii) Subsidy shall be limited to a claim on a total amount not exceeding Rs. 3,60,000/- paid by an industrial unit towards interest on term loan in a full year. However, for working capital loan, the total amount paid towards interest on which

subsidy can be claimed shall be limited to Rs. 1,20,000/- in a full year.

C. Application for Claim

Application for grant of interest subsidy shall be submitted in duplicate to the concerned district Office in the prescribed form under Appendix 'E'.

D. Selection Committee

Composition of the State level Committee shall be :

(1)	Secretary, Industries Department	*Chairman*
(2)	Secretary, Finance department or his Nominee not below the rank of Deputy Secretary	*Member*
(3)	Managing Director, Zoram Industrial Development Corporation	*Member*
(4)	Branch Manager, State Bank of India Aizawl Main Branch	*Member*
(5)	General Managers, District Industries Centres	*Members*
(6)	Director of Industries	*Member Secretary*

[Detailed procedure incorporated in the rules for the Grant of Incentives/Subsidies under the Industrial Policy of Mizoram State, 1989]

APPENDIX-F
POWER SUBSIDY

A. Eligible Condition

(i) Subsidy is eligible for charges on power consumed for Industrial production. A separate energy meter should be installed for the industrial purpose.

(ii) The industrial unit should have power supply connection from authorized Department/ Agency.

(iii) No subsidy is eligible for power consumed for domestic lighting and other purposes.

(iv) The subsidy can be claimed by an industrial unit for 5 years from the date of commissioning of the unit.

B. Limit of Subsidy

(i) 60 per cent of total expenditure on power consumption in case of tiny, small scale and ancillary units.

(ii) 50 per cent of the total expenditure on power consumption in case of medium scale unit.

(iii) 30 per cent of the total expenditure on power consumption in case of large scale unit.

C. Application for Claim

Application for grant of Power Subsidy shall be submitted in duplicate to the concerned District Office in the prescribed form under Appendix 'F'.

D. Selection Committee

Composition of the State level Committee shall be :

(1) Secretary, Industries Department	*Chairman*
(2) Secretary, Finance department or his Nominee not below the rank of Deputy Secretary	*Member*
(3) Chief Engineer, Power & Electricity Dept. Mizoram or his nominee not below the rank of Executive Engineer	*Member*
(4) General Managers, District Industries Centres	*Members*
(5) Director of Industries	*Member Secretary*

[Detailed procedure incorporated in the rules for the Grant of Incentives/Subsidies under the Industrial Policy of Mizoram State, 1989]

APPENDIX-G
SUBSIDY ON POWER LINE

A. Eligible Condition

An Industrial unit is eligible to claim subsidy on cost of drawal of power line from the main power lines to the site of the Industrial unit/factory shed which is executed by the approved Department/agency.

B. Limit of Subsidy

Subsidy on costs of drawal of powerlines to an Industrial unit shall be limited to 50 per cent of the actual expenditure to a ceiling of Rs. 50,000/- per unit.

C. Application for Claim

Application for grant of subsidy on costs of drawal of powerlines shall be submitted in duplicate to the concerned District Office in the prescribed form under Appendix 'G'.

D. Selection Committee

Composition of the State level Committee shall be :

(1)	Secretary, Industries Department	*Chairman*
(2)	Secretary, Finance department or his Nominee not below the rank of Deputy Secretary	*Member*
(3)	Chief Engineer, Power & Electricity Dept. Mizoram or his nominee not below the rank of Executive Engineer	*Member*
(4)	General Managers, District Industries Centres	*Members*
(5)	Director of Industries	*Member Secretary*

[Detailed procedure incorporated in the rules for the Grant of Incentives/Subsidies under the Industrial Policy of Mizoram State, 1989]

APPENDIX-H
SUBSIDY ON POWER GENERATING SET

A. Eligible Condition

(i) An Industrial unit is eligible to claim subsidy on the cost of captive generating set and installation charge thereof actually used for industrial purpose.

(ii) The captive generating set for which subsidy claimed should be brand new and purchased directly from the manufacturers or its regional/local agent.

(iii) In the case of second hand generating set, the cost of the generating set shall be calculated on the basis of the life of the generating set and the exact depreciated value.

(iv) The installation of the generating set, on whose charge the subsidy to be claimed should be executed by the supplier of the generating set or its regional/local agent or other approval agency.

B. Limit of Subsidy

Subsidy on cost and installation charge of captive generating set to an industrial unit shall be limited to 50 per cent of the cost of generating, set and installation charge thereof subject to a ceiling of Rs. 3,00,000/- per unit.

C. Application for Claim

Application for grant of subsidy on costs of generating shall be submitted in duplicate to the concerned District Office in tie prescribed form under Appendix 'H'.

D. Selection Committee

Composition of the State level Committee shall be :

(1) Secretary, Industries Department *Chairman*

(2)	Secretary, Finance department or his Nominee not below the rank of Deputy Secretary	*Member*
(3)	Chief Engineer, Power & Electricity Dept. Mizoram or his nominee not below the rank of Executive Engineer	*Member*
(4)	General Managers, District Industries Centres	*Members*
(5)	Director of Industries	*Member Secretary*

[Detailed procedure incorporated in the rules for the Grant of Incentives/Subsidies under the Industrial Policy of Mizoram State, 1989]

APPENDIX-I
STATE TRANSPORT SUBSIDY ON PLANT & MACHINERIES

A. Eligible Condition

(i) A new industrial unit is eligible to claim the subsidy on actual cost of transportation of plants and machineries from place of purchase to location of the unit.

(ii) An existing industrial unit is eligible to claim subsidy on actual cost of transportation of plants and machineries for the expanded portion only from place of purchase to location of the unit.

(iii) For movement of plants and machineries from outside the state actual costs of transportation by railway or on road or both from place of purchase to location of the industrial unit is eligible for the subsidy.

(iv) For movement of plants and machineries within the state, actual costs of transportation on road

from the godown of the approved supplier/local agent of the manufacturer of the plants and machineries to location of the industrial unit is eligible for subsidy.

(*v*) For the cost of transportation on road, the cost of transportation charged by the road transport agency approved by the Director of Industries or the rate of transportation approved by the Director of Industries will be eligible.

B. Limit of Subsidy

Subsidy on cost of transportation of plants and machineries shall be 50 per cent of the actual cost of transportation by railway or on road or both.

C. Application for Claim

Application for grant of State Transport Subsidy on plant and machineries shall be submitted in duplicate to the concerned District Office in the prescribed form under Appendix 'I'.

D. Selection Committee

Composition of the State level Committee shall be :

(1)	Secretary, Industries Department	*Chairman*
(2)	Secretary, Finance department or his Nominee not below the rank of Deputy Secretary	*Member*
(3)	Director of Transport, Mizoram	*Member*
(4)	Superintendent, railway out Agency	*Member*
(5)	General Managers, District Industries Centres	*Members*
(6)	Director of Industries	*Member Secretary*

[Detailed procedure incorporated in the rules for the Grant of Incentives/Subsidies under the Industrial Policy of Mizoram State, 1989]

ARJUN